World of Art

Colin Rhodes is an artist, writer, curator and educator. He is author of *Primitivism and Modern Art*, *Outsider Art* and *The World According to Roger Ballen* (all published by Thames & Hudson), a regular contributor to *The Burlington Magazine*, and a contributing editor of *Raw Vision*. He is a specialist in modern and contemporary Western art, and has written and lectured widely on Expressionism, including book chapters and specialist parts of a Dutch Open University course. He studied Art and Art History at Goldsmiths, University of London, before completing a PhD at the University of Essex with Professor Peter Vergo. He led the art schools at Loughborough University, the University of Sydney, and Kingston University, and is currently Distinguished Professor, Xiaoxiang Scholar and Yangtze River Scholar in the Fine Arts Academy, Hunan Normal University, China.

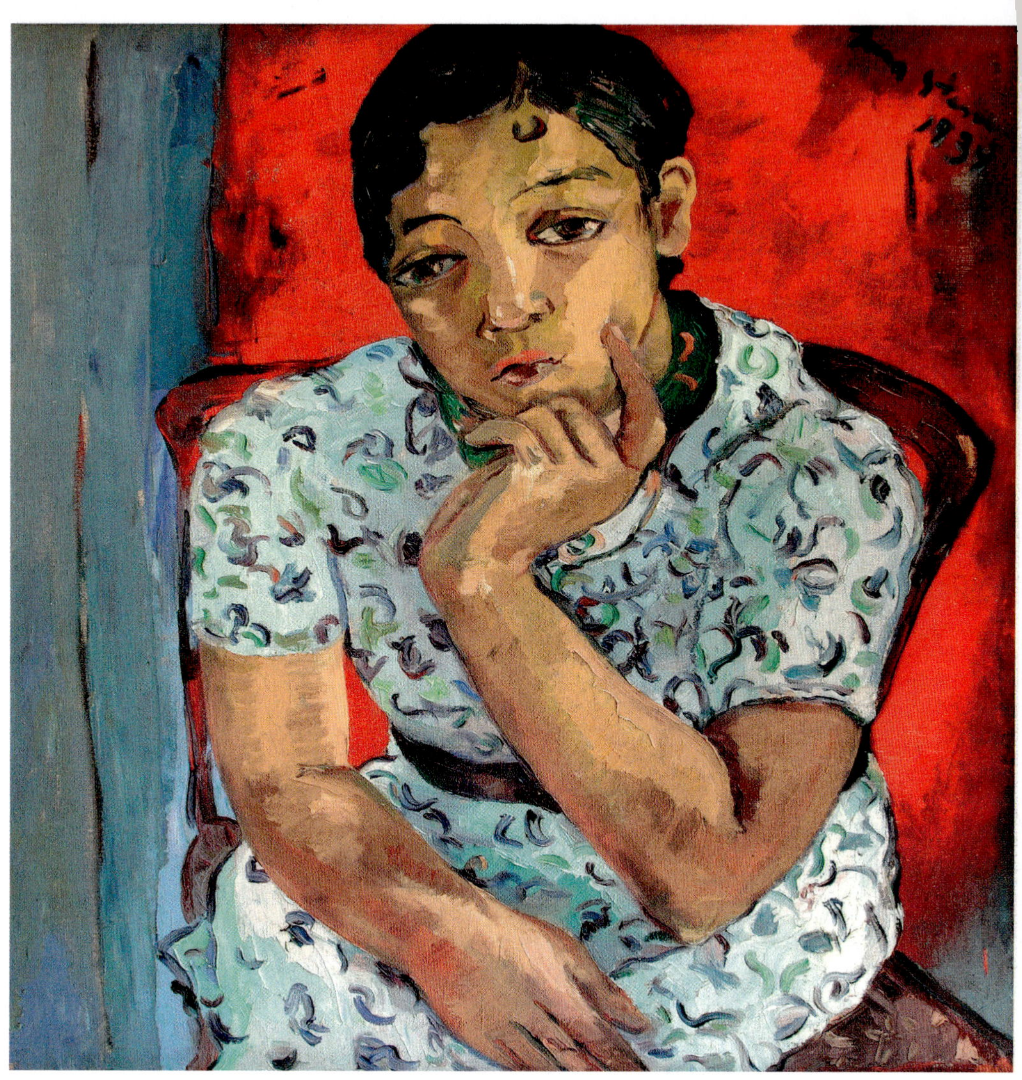

1 Irma Stern, *Girl in a Print Dress*, 1939

World of Art

Expressionism

Colin Rhodes

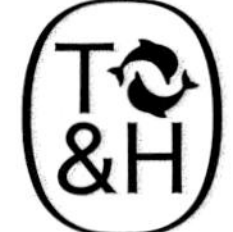

For my Dad

First published in the United Kingdom in 2025
by Thames & Hudson Ltd, 181A High Holborn,
London WC1V 7QX

www.thamesandhudson.com

First published in the United States
of America in 2025 by Thames & Hudson Inc.,
500 Fifth Avenue, New York, New York 10110

www.thamesandhudsonusa.com

Art direction and series design: Kummer and Herrman
Layout: Adam Hay Studio

British Library Cataloguing-in-Publication Data
A catalogue record for this book is available from
the British Library

Library of Congress Control Number 2024948449

ISBN 978-0-500-29775-9

Impression 01

Printed and bound in China through Asia Pacific Offset Ltd

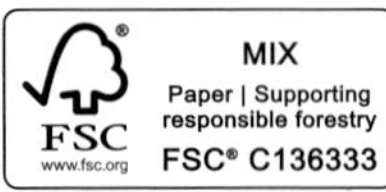

Contents

Introduction

Expressionism in art is based on a belief that materials and objects manipulated by artists can themselves possess a fundamental ability to communicate directly with viewers. While the agency enacted by artistic practice is crucial to the formation of the work, in this view of the world the completed art object can speak, as it were, for itself. In different times and places this has been viewed both metaphorically and literally by artists and critics. Where most other art before the last century functioned as representation of some other thing or group of things in the world, there is an assumption that an Expressionist work of art is always to some extent a thing-in-itself. The Expressionist art object, it is argued, takes its place alongside other autonomous things in the world, rather than as mere representation of some other thing (although it can simultaneously be that as well). Expressionism is always phenomenological, stemming from the profoundly individual experience of the creator of the work, and relying for its reception on a similarly direct, and relatively unmediated psychological-emotional experience on the part of viewers.

It is perhaps unsurprising that Expressionist art is sometimes underpinned by a mystic sensibility. Artists have often worked from a belief that they are in some way connecting directly with a dynamic, living cosmos and creating out of the very sources of universal energies, beginning with painters like Emil Nolde (1867–1956), Wassily Kandinsky (1866–1944) and Hilma af Klint (1862–1944), and reappearing in various times and places throughout the twentieth century and beyond. In this model, the artist acts as an active conduit for the communication of profound truths. Viewers, on their part, are presumed to be attuned to attending to art with intuitive immediacy, without the need for explanation or exegesis. There are clear connections here with nineteenth century Romantic ideas of the world as organism, with every object, whether organic or inorganic, containing life force, interconnected and interdependent. In Romantic art, especially in Germany and Britain, through figures such as Philipp Otto Runge (1777–1810), Caspar David Friedrich (1774–1840), William Blake (1757–1827) and Samuel Palmer (1805–1881), this sensibility is commonly communicated through symbolist devices and metaphor. In Expressionism, the tendency is to attempt to make that communication direct, without the need for a symbolic lexicon.

If Expressionism has its roots in romanticism in the early nineteenth century, its emergence as a self-conscious idea belongs to the beginning of the next one, most clearly in France. It is bound up with the history of Modernism, a loosely connected set of ideas that emerged in the second half of the nineteenth century as a reaction to massive social changes in the West. In the face of unprecedented rapid industrialization, population displacement, and technological development, modernists sought to break with the past and to introduce new ways of thinking about and engaging with contemporary life. A new spirit of experimentalism arose in the arts, accompanied by the idea that artists were the harbingers not only of a new way of representing the world and ideas, but also somehow of a new age. An idea of an artistic avant-garde developed, with succeeding waves of artists claiming ascendancy in the search for an authentic expression of the times. Specifically Expressionist ideas about the world emerged out of late nineteenth-century Symbolism, in the work of painters such as Paul Gauguin (1848–1903), Paul Sérusier (1864–1927) and Émile Bernard (1868–1941), and took hold most strongly in the work of Henri Matisse (1869–1954) and his circle in the first decade of the twentieth century.

Ironically, the development of Modernism is unthinkable without the technological developments it often questioned and resisted, including the advent of steam power and the railways, which facilitated quick, mass travel on a scale unheard of a century before. Advances in chemistry increased artists' understanding of the science of colour and facilitated the development of new pigments and mediums for colour mixing. Perhaps most revolutionary was the development of the paint tube, which allowed paint to be produced in bulk and stored for long periods. This meant that artists did not have to produce their colours from scratch and that paints were portable, enabling painters easily to work in oils outside the studio environment, whether that be outdoors, public interiors, such as theatres or cafés, and even private, domestic spaces. Impressionism was the first modernist movement to make full use of these developments, with artists such as Claude Monet

(1940–1926) and Camille Pissarro (1830–1903) famously painting major works entirely *en plein air*. Both engaged directly with the visual reception of modern life, painting the contemporary boulevards of Paris. They are perhaps most popularly known for their landscape paintings, including agrarian scenes, which are almost always, whether intentionally or inadvertently, tinged with evidence of the incursion of modern industrial change into the countryside, whether it be steam trains darting past newly built garden suburbs or distant views of factory chimneys. Even views of country leisure activities were no mere reflection of ageless pastimes, but evidence of a newly mobilized urban middle class with both the time and the money to briefly escape the city.

Expressionism is one of the key tendencies in modernist painting produced in the last century or so. As 'German Expressionism', it came to be most closely associated with the dominant strand in German Modernism from shortly before the First World War until around the mid-1920s, exemplified in the work of artists such as Ernst Ludwig Kirchner (1880–1938), Franz
2 Marc (1880–1916), and Gabriele Münter (1877–1962). But its origins lie in France at the end of the nineteenth century, and it was from there, especially through Matisse, that its influence spread, not only to Germany, but also throughout much of the world, from Russia and as far afield as South America, South Africa and China. In Northern Europe Expressionism was arguably the dominant modernist strain throughout the 1920s, when post-Cubist and Constructivist movements were uppermost in Paris and much of Western Europe. It also remained so in the following decade in work by artists such as Ernst Wilhelm Nay (1902–1968), Carl-Henning Pedersen (1913–2007) and Asger Jorn (1914–1973), and when Surrealism had assumed the place of the dominant modernist movement elsewhere.

There was a resurgence of Expressionist practices and ideas in Paris and New York in the years immediately following the end of the Second World War. Characterized as 'Informal Art' in the former city and 'American Abstract Expressionism' in the latter, it was now tinged with Surrealist ideas, evident in artists
3 such as Wols (1913–1951) and Mark Rothko (1903–1970), but it also clearly demonstrated a continuation of a generally embedded Expressionist tendency in progressive art, rather than something newly reinvented after a period of dormancy and rupture. Similarly, Expressionism can be detected in important art made throughout the 1960s and 1970s, in the work of artists
4 such as Gillian Ayres (1930–2018), Maria Lassnig (1919–2014) and Arnulf Rainer (b. 1929), when dominant art history would suggest that Pop and Conceptual art constituted the paradigm.

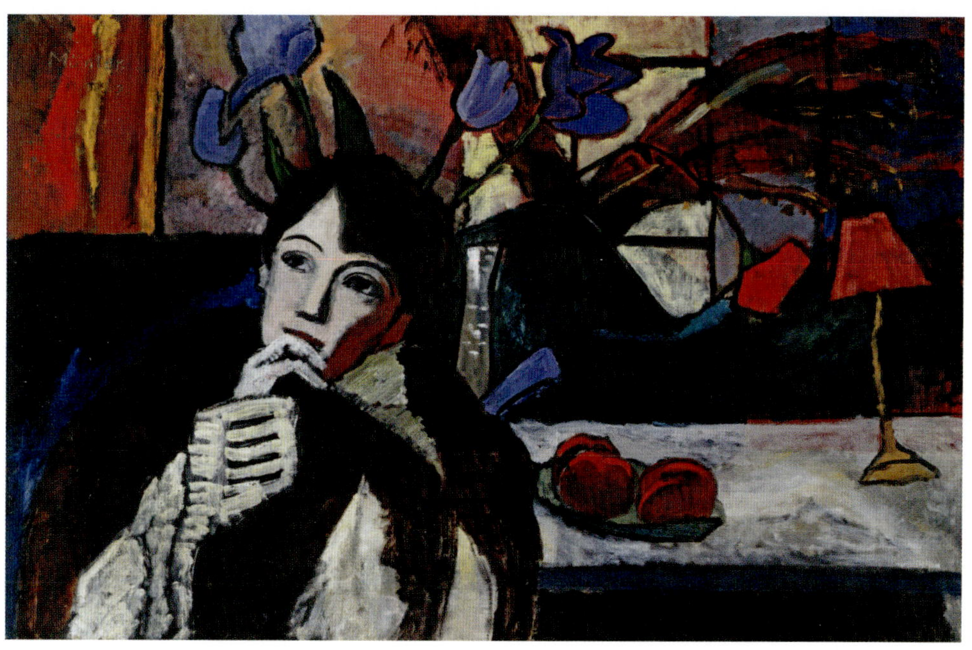

2 Gabriele Münter, *Sinnende (Sensitive)*, 1917

It emerged once again into the forefront of international art narratives around 1980, as 'Neo-Expressionism', exemplified in the work of artists such as Jean-Michel Basquiat (1960–1988), Elvira Bach (b. 1951) and Markus Oehlen (b. 1956). By that time modernist narratives of art history as a progressive development towards some putative goal had dissipated, and the global art world had become distinctly heterogenous, characterized by a mixture of styles, ideas and media, which had knowingly been taken from, often in combination, pre-existing and hitherto competing models. Initially described as 'postmodernist', prominent new art is nowadays known by the catch-all title of 'contemporary art'. There is clear evidence even in the most recent generations of practitioners, though, of much art that demonstrates distinct Expressionist characteristics, as in the work of artists such as Iris Kensmil (b. 1970), Eddie Martinez (b. 1977) and Jadé Fadojutimi (b. 1993).

This book looks at Expressionism as a broad, recognizable tendency present throughout the art of the twentieth century and since. While its scope is international, Expressionism was, at heart, a Western construct, born out of European philosophies and world views that in themselves also spoke to colonial narratives and political imperialism. Its most visible

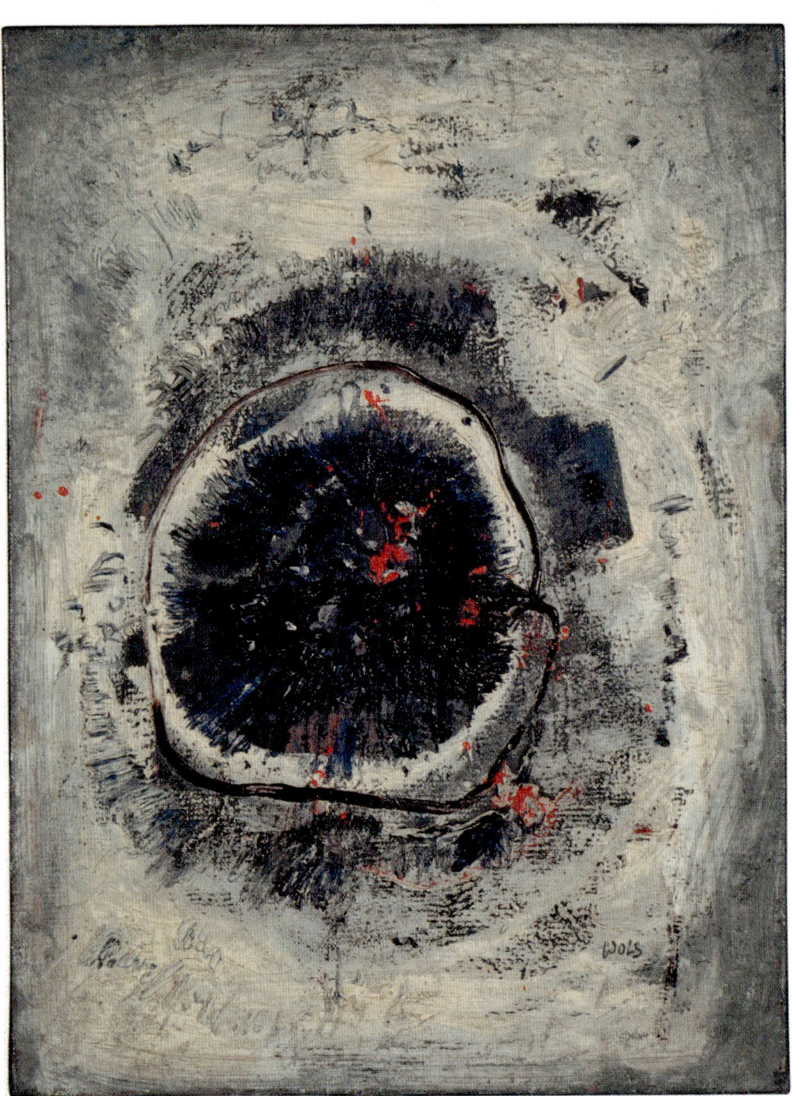

3 ABOVE Wols, *Grenade bleue* (The Blue Grenade), 1946
4 OPPOSITE Gillian Ayres, *Sun Up*, 1960

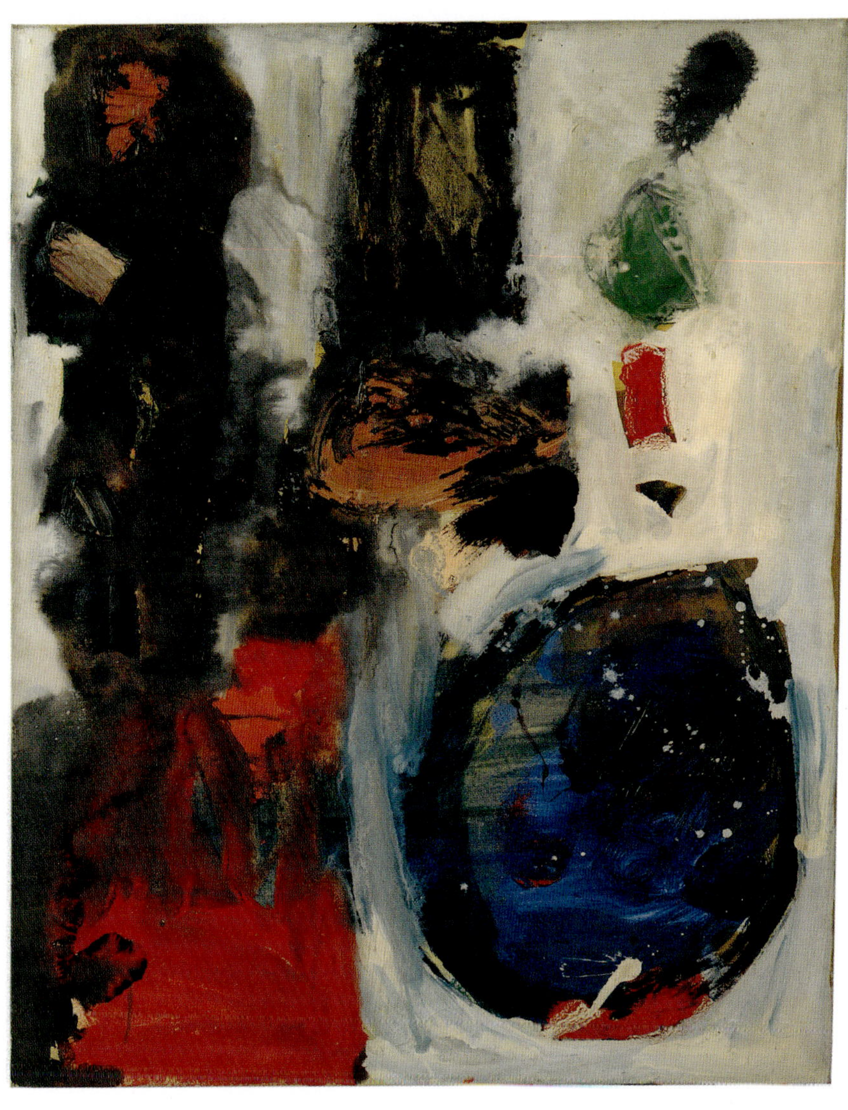

manifestations, therefore, have been staged in Europe and the United States, which were not only primary geopolitical centres, but also the dominant locations of global art markets and, consequently discourses concerning art. It is in such centres that art histories are first written, and during the period of Modernism especially, this meant the description of a heady stream of competing movements that echoed the speed of technological and social change in the industrialized west, with each one seeking to supplant its predecessor. In this view of recent history, therefore, forms of 'Expressionism' appear periodically, first in Germany around 1910, again in New York in the mid-1940s, and once more in Europe and the United States at the end of the 1970s. The reality is that Expressionism was much more pervasive. Some other modernist movements that were distinctly Expressionist were named differently, either for political reasons, as in the case of Fauvism (at a time when Franco-German relations were at a nadir), or to distinguish a group of artists from immediate precedents, as in the cases of CoBrA and Informal Art, whilst some other manifestations of Expressionist tendencies were resolutely discussed in different contexts, as with the work of Francis Bacon (1909–1992), for example.

Similarly, continuations of individual practices or movements away from the spotlight of the putative centres, are commonly overlooked in dominant narratives that are keen to move on to the 'next big thing'. This also produces a skewed view of artistic activity and the market more generally. Artists have their moment, so to speak, before being supplanted in critical attention by others. Their practices and careers do not end, though, and their influence generally continues – through collectors, admirers, and often through their teaching. Moreover, until relatively recently, art markets were much more regionalized and dispersed. The absolute dominance of, first Paris, and subsequently New York as centres of the global art world narrative notwithstanding, most artists in the twentieth century made their careers and found fame in their countries of domicile, with national modern art museum collections generally reflecting local production. In this way, Expressionism could be dominant in Copenhagen, for example, long after the Parisian narrative had turned its attention elsewhere. This is a long way from the situation today, where contemporary art museums throughout Europe, North America and many other locations tend to present a generally similar core range of global art market stars.

When adjustments are made for the narrow focus and obsession with tracing difference that dominates modernist

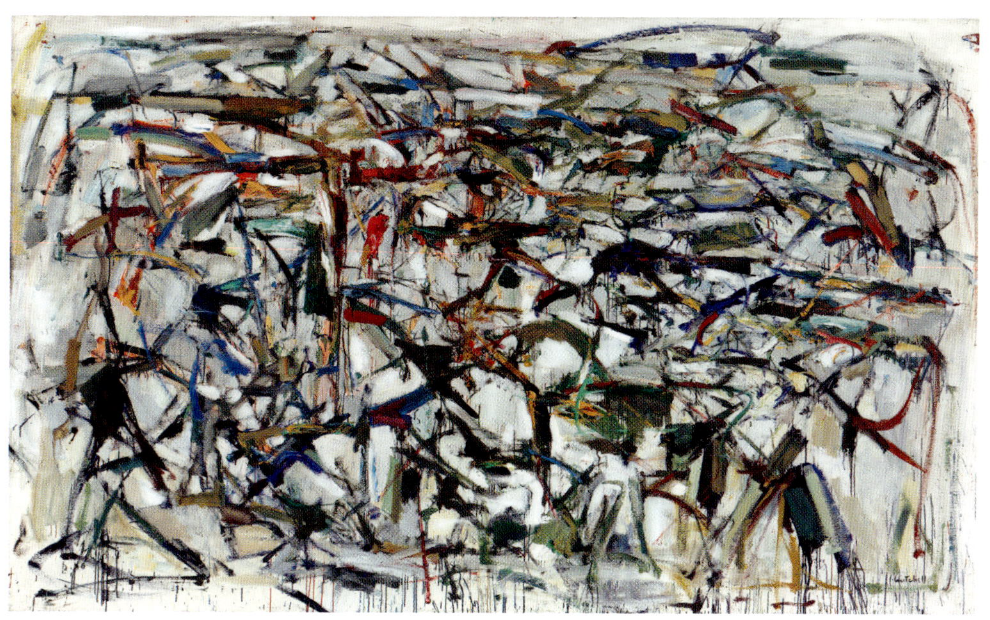

5 Joan Mitchell, *Piano mécanique*, 1957

histories of art, not only does Expressionism's position as a dominant strand of modern and contemporary art become clear, but also some of the confusions arising from definitions that seek to separate art practices are erased. Another feature of received histories of art in general, and Expressionism in particular, has been a bias towards male heteronormative narratives. Writers have commonly focused on received notions of an entrenched brutalist, hetero-masculinist ideology at the heart of Expressionism. But, while such rhetoric characterized the dominant contemporary American critical response to Abstract Expressionism, it masks more complex histories and approaches, and flies in the face of the historical evidence. Much has been done in more recent years by scholars to show that women were at the centre of Expressionism from the start, as artists, dealers and collectors. This book addresses that imbalance head on, with first generation Expressionists such as Münter and Marianne Werefkin (1860–1938) and American Abstract Expressionists such as Lee Krasner (1908–1984) and
5 Joan Mitchell (1925–1992), for example, featuring prominently
in hitherto male-dominated narratives. Moreover, as the book will show, a great deal of Expressionist art engages with issues of gender and sexuality at much more sophisticated levels than was hitherto accepted, from coded works by artists such as

Kirchner and Marsden Hartley (1877–1943) to much more direct representations by artists such as Francis Bacon.

Expressionism emerged in Europe at the height of the colonial enterprise, so it is unsurprising that its ideas and themes often reflected an interest in non-European others that was informed by the science – most often in its populist forms – of the day. Expressionism's tendency towards universalizing and embracing metaphysical theories of creativity, together with a common discontentment with contemporary Western society, led it to embrace primitivist ideas. Too often understood in simplistic terms, this book analyses the complex and shifting nexus of ideas contained in modernist primitivism, both positive and negative. It does not shy from examination of racist and social-evolutionist assumptions that lay at the base of many of the manifestations of some modernist cultural appropriations, whilst also presenting a sensitive and nuanced critique of Expressionist primitivism. In terms of the postcolonial moment, that primitivizing rhetoric has often been taken by artists of colour and repurposed as a powerful symbol of identity and weapon of social and political critique.

There are clear signs of an intensification of Expressionist ideas and practices in contemporary art, notable especially in a rise in interest in painting as a practice, not only as a vehicle for conveying meaning, but also as engagement with the very materiality of the medium in and for itself. Expressionism has had clear manifestations in all of the arts, from theatre, dance and cinema to literature and architecture. Whilst there are compelling arguments to address this broader history of Expressionism, it would be impossible to do so effectively in a study of this length. Because of this, and since Expressionism has both its roots and, arguably, its clearest expression in painting, this book focuses primarily on Expressionism in that medium.

Chapter 1
Modern Art as Expressionism

Significant Form – Fauvism, Post-Impressionism, Expressionism

By the time that Henri Matisse and André Derain (1880–1954) came to spend the summer of 1905 in the French coastal port of Collioure they had devised a painterly method that totally undermined the self-important, 'scientific' theories of nineteenth-century Neo-Impressionism, even as they made a knowing nod in its direction. Its nineteenth-century instigator Georges Seurat (1859–1891), together with followers like Paul Signac (1863–1935) and Henri-Edmond Cross (1856–1910), had looked to a particular technique to produce real approximations to ordinary visual perception in their paintings, which consisted of building up images in thousands of tiny dots of complementary colour and which they called 'Divisionism', but which not surprisingly came to be known as *pointillisme* (or dotting). Matisse and Derain, though, seemed to revel in using the technique for expressive ends. Both were sensitive to, and knowledgeable about, the way colour works, but they used their know-how to produce daring juxtapositions of high key, unnaturalistic pigment. The 'dots' became larger and more obviously part of the visual aesthetic, as in Matisse's *Luxe, Calme et Volupté* from the year before (although at the time Signac had hailed Matisse as a new disciple of the *pointilliste* style).

In pictures like *Woman with a Hat* (1905), an image of Mme Matisse, or *Open Window* (1905), painted from the inside of Matisse's lodgings at Collioure, the artist was enjoying colour almost for its own sake. As he later said, sending a clear message to the disciples of pointillism, 'My choice of colours does not rest on any scientific theory; it is based on observation, on sensitivity, on felt experiences.' By means of the open window composition, which allows inside and outside, nature and artifice to interact

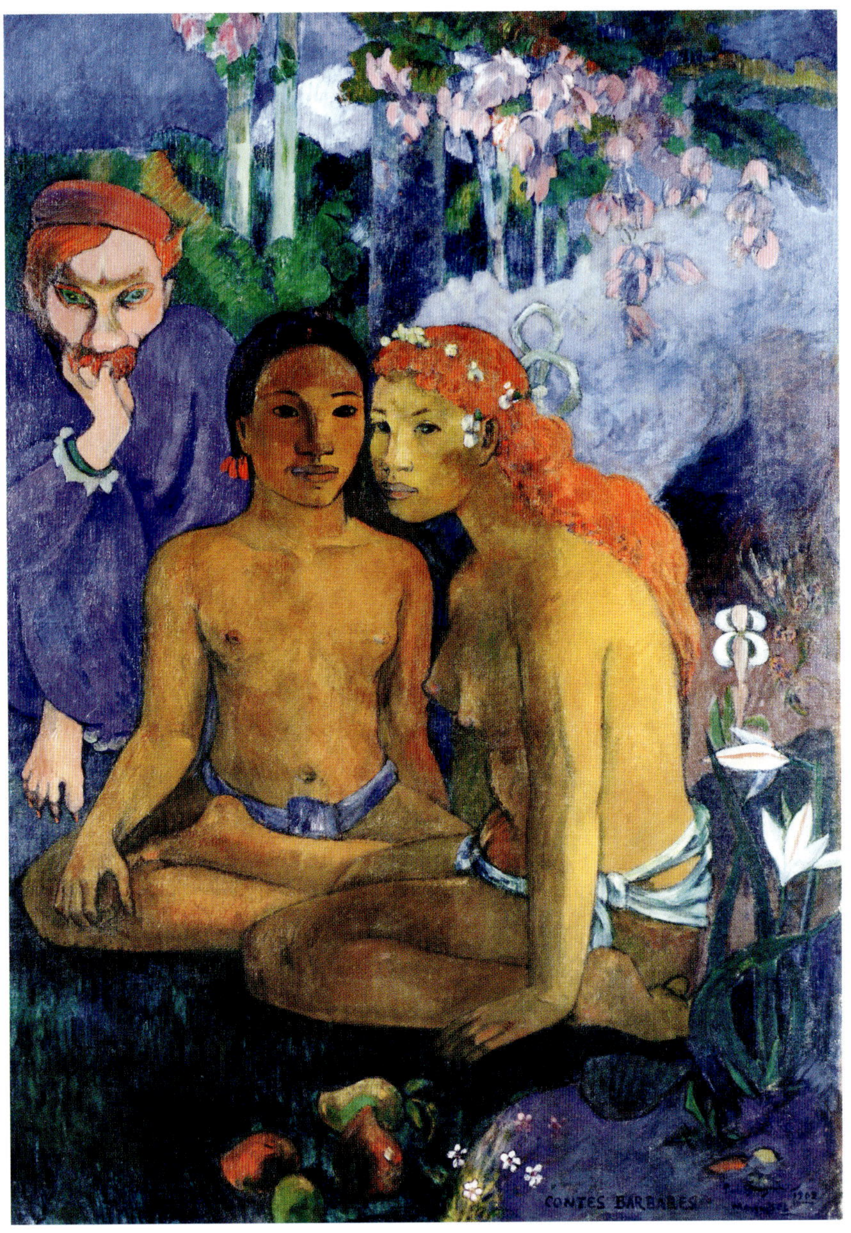

6 ABOVE Paul Gauguin, *Contes barbares* (Barbarian Tales), 1902
7 OPPOSITE Vincent van Gogh, *Le parc de l'hôpital, à Saint-Rémy*
(A Corner of the Asylum and the Garden with a Heavy, Sawed-Off Tree), 1889

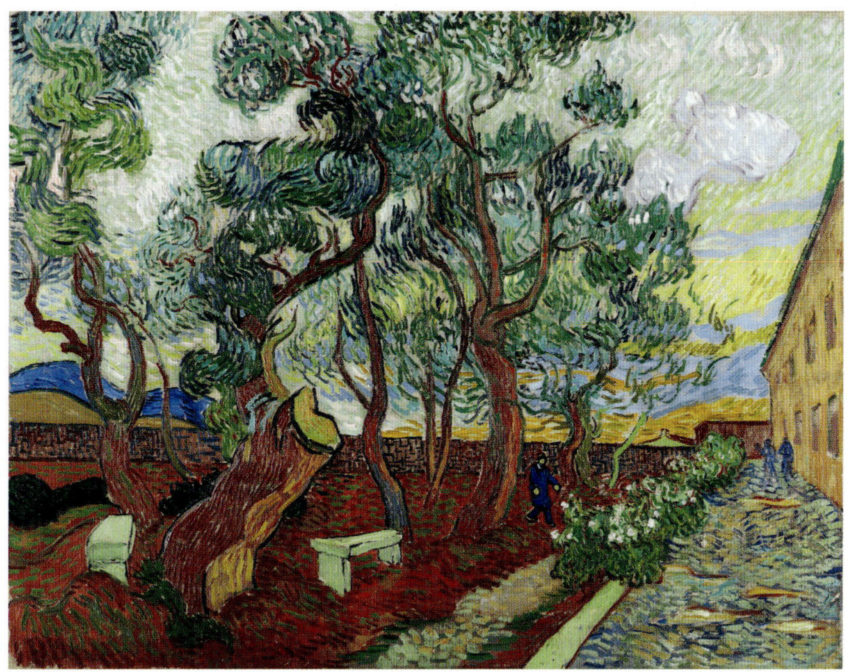

visually, and which Matisse used repeatedly throughout his
long career, the artist turned the sketchy naturalism of the
Impressionists into an essay in sensitive evocation of mood.
Derain, like his friend Maurice de Vlaminck (1876–1958),
was more brash. Taking their lead more from the fiery later
7 canvases of Vincent van Gogh (1853–1890), they used great slabs
of intense, high-key colour, which seemed almost to vibrate
against the areas of white, primed canvas that still showed
8 through, as in Vlaminck's *Les Coteaux de Rueil* (1906) and
Derain's *View of Collioure* (1905).

Fauvism

In autumn 1905 the fruits of Derain's and Matisse's labours in the south of France contributed to one of the first sensations of twentieth century art, when their work was hung alongside that of Vlaminck, Henri Manguin (1874–1949), Albert Marquet (1875–1947), and Charles Camoin (1879–1965) in the now infamous Room VII of that year's annual Salon d'Automne in Paris. Matisse had been advised by friends not to show new paintings like *Open Window* and *Woman with a Hat*, and there is plenty of evidence that the jury was not keen to accept his work that year. The press attacked these novel paintings in a way that has now become very familiar. The conservative magazine, *L'Illustration*, for example, chose irony as its weapon, devoting a whole issue to the Salon in which positive statements about the artists were hung up for ridicule against reproductions of the works jumbled together untidily on the page. From the very start modern art has been consistently associated with untidiness and disorderliness in negative criticism.

The press reaction to the Salon also provided the formulation that would eventually result in the naming of the group of artists associated with Matisse as '*les fauves*' (wild animals), coming from a passing remark by a generally sympathetic critic, Louis Vauxcelles, contrasting two classicizing portrait busts by the sculptor Albert Marque (1872–1939) with the intense, non-naturalistic canvases of the painters in Room VII. Although the word '*fauve*' began to be used in the French press from around 1907–08, reference to *fauvism* first appeared only around 1912, and the artists themselves preferred to define themselves less controversially as proponents of *la nouvelle peinture* (the New Painting); an appellation that would soon also include Cubists and Futurists. In any case, the rhetorical model of the 'wild animal' was less to do with ferocity or actual violence and much more to do with the idea that here was evidence of a primitivizing return to untutored, intuitive expression.

Although 'Fauvism' came to be a dominant designation in histories of modern art after the First World War, it has always proved problematic and sometimes confusing for commentators. This is partly because it never described a formal grouping or school, in the way that Impressionism or Symbolism had, for example, and it refers to a very narrow window of time, from around 1904 to 1910, which seemingly severs those artists associated with its inception, notably Matisse, Derain and Vlaminck from the work they made subsequently. The years around 1905 to 1906 can be seen as an important breakthrough moment in painterly modernist avant-gardism, which changed attitudes to picture-making and the principles of representation radically. And since Paris was generally regarded at that time as the epicentre of the contemporary art world, both the forms and, more importantly, the underlying ideas, of the new art were soon widely evident in art throughout Northern and Central Europe.

The challenge of the New Painting was really based in a kind of breaking down of conventional expectations of what the medium should be, and how an artistic career should unfold. In Paris, artists like Matisse, Derain, Vlaminck, Othon Friesz (1879–1949), Georges Rouault (1871–1958), Georges Braque (1882–1963),

Émilie Charmy (1878–1974) and Kees van Dongen (1877–1968) became dissatisfied with what they saw as the constraints of the Academy and were drawn to a way of painting that emphasized intuition and personal expression. Quite maddeningly for many critics and fellow artists, they were constantly experimenting, so that their art was seemingly always in flux. Just as the audience thought it could see a logical developmental path, each of these artist's painterly research took a new turn. As Matisse later said, 'I do not repudiate any of my paintings but there is not one of them that I would not redo differently, if I had it to redo.' Because of this, there was never really a Fauve style, as such. Each painter's character revealed itself in different individual mannerisms – if there are times when works by Derain and Matisse, for example, are similar, their divergences are also quite apparent, and there is a gulf between the gentleness of touch of Matisse and the no-nonsense directness of Vlaminck. But there are also stylistic differences within the body of each artist's work, sometimes in paintings made very close together in time. The expressive slabs of colour in Derain's pictures from 1905 were replaced soon after by a kind of colour-saturated version of late Impressionist form-building that owes a lot to Paul Cézanne,
46 and which became increasingly architectonic, as in *Forest at Martigues*. Similarly, Matisse moved between approaches that privileged flatness and the decorative at one extreme, as in
10 *Le Luxe I*, to a sense of heavy, sculptural relief at the other, as with *Blue Nude* (1907). This is because the inherent problem of painting was their major concern. In other words, their subject, in a way, was painting itself. By extension, it might be argued that they were painting primarily for – and out of – themselves.

Almost from the start Matisse was considered to be the leading artist of the New Painting. This was due in part to his being slightly older than the others, and to his successes at earlier Salons. The work that helped to establish his cutting-edge credentials was *Luxe, calme et volupté* (1904). The title, a line taken from Charles Baudelaire's poem *L'Invitation au voyage* (1857), would have led viewers to expect the kind of Arcadian theme favoured by nineteenth-century academic painters, and Symbolists like Pierre Puvis de Chavannes (1824–1898). But the subject is modern. These are not classical nudes but emphatically a group of contemporary women bathers on a beach at St. Tropez in southern France. In spite of the fact that Fauvism's reputation rests on landscape paintings like
11 Derain's *The Mountains, Collioure* (1905), or Charmy's *L'Éstaque*, the human figure was the central theme in Matisse's work, and he always represented the modern person, even when he developed a 'timeless' theme, as in *Music* (1907, 1910) and *Dance*

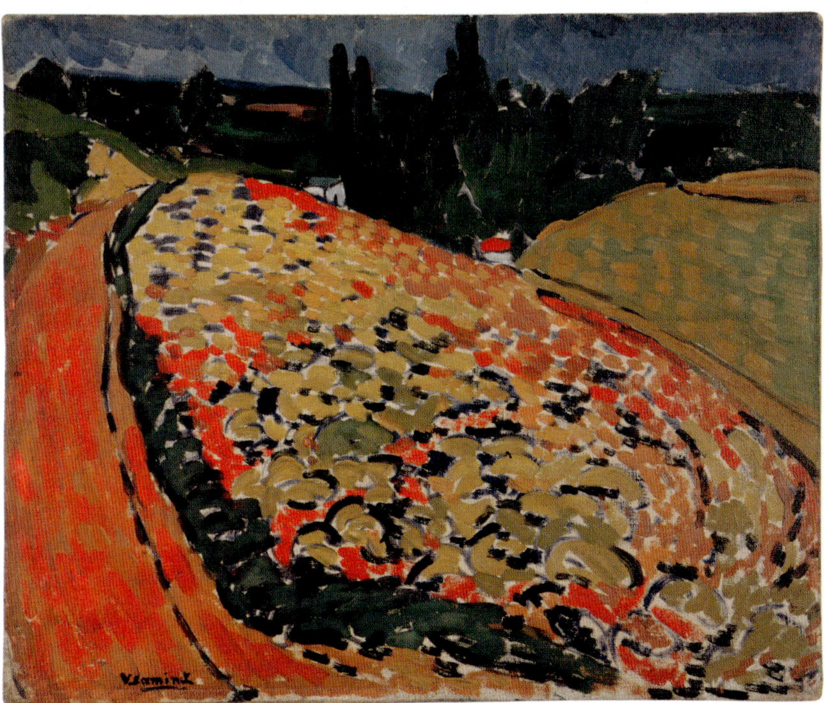

8 Maurice de Vlaminck, *Les Coteaux de Rueil* (The Slopes of Rueil), 1906

(1910). The human body, much more than landscape, lent itself to an intuitive, empathic response to visual stimuli. At its best, in
9 pictures like Matisse's *Femme au chapeau* or Derain's *Portrait of Maurice Vlaminck*, both from 1905, this resulted in striking studies of the sitter; at its worst, in a painting like Vlaminck's *Reclining Nude* (1906), where empathy gives way to ugly misogynistic stereotyping of the sitter.

If the individuality of the Fauve painters accounts for the lack of a Fauvist school, this is deepened by their fundamentally Expressionist point of view. When Matisse tried to sum up his attitude to art in his short essay, 'Notes of a Painter' (1908) he emphasized both the special quality of his psychology of expression and the essentially organic nature of the resulting art object. 'I am unable to distinguish,' he said, 'between the feeling I have about life and my way of translating it.' Furthermore, he implied that any art worthy of the name somehow embodies the sum of the experience of the artist and conducts itself in a kind of living way at the end of the shared process of making: 'A work of art must carry within itself its complete significance and impose that upon the beholder even before he (*sic.*)

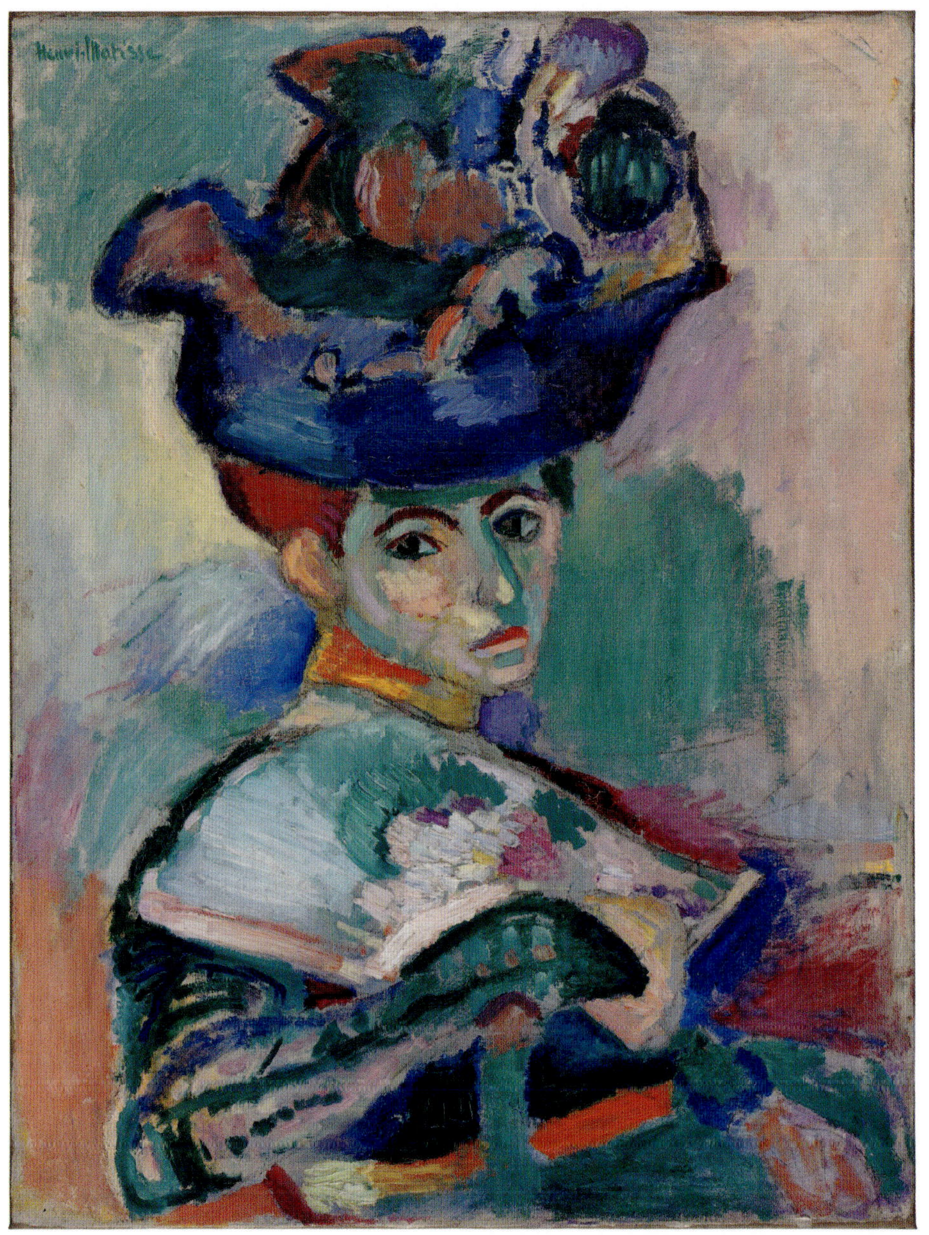

9 Henri Matisse, *Femme au chapeau* (Woman with a Hat), 1905

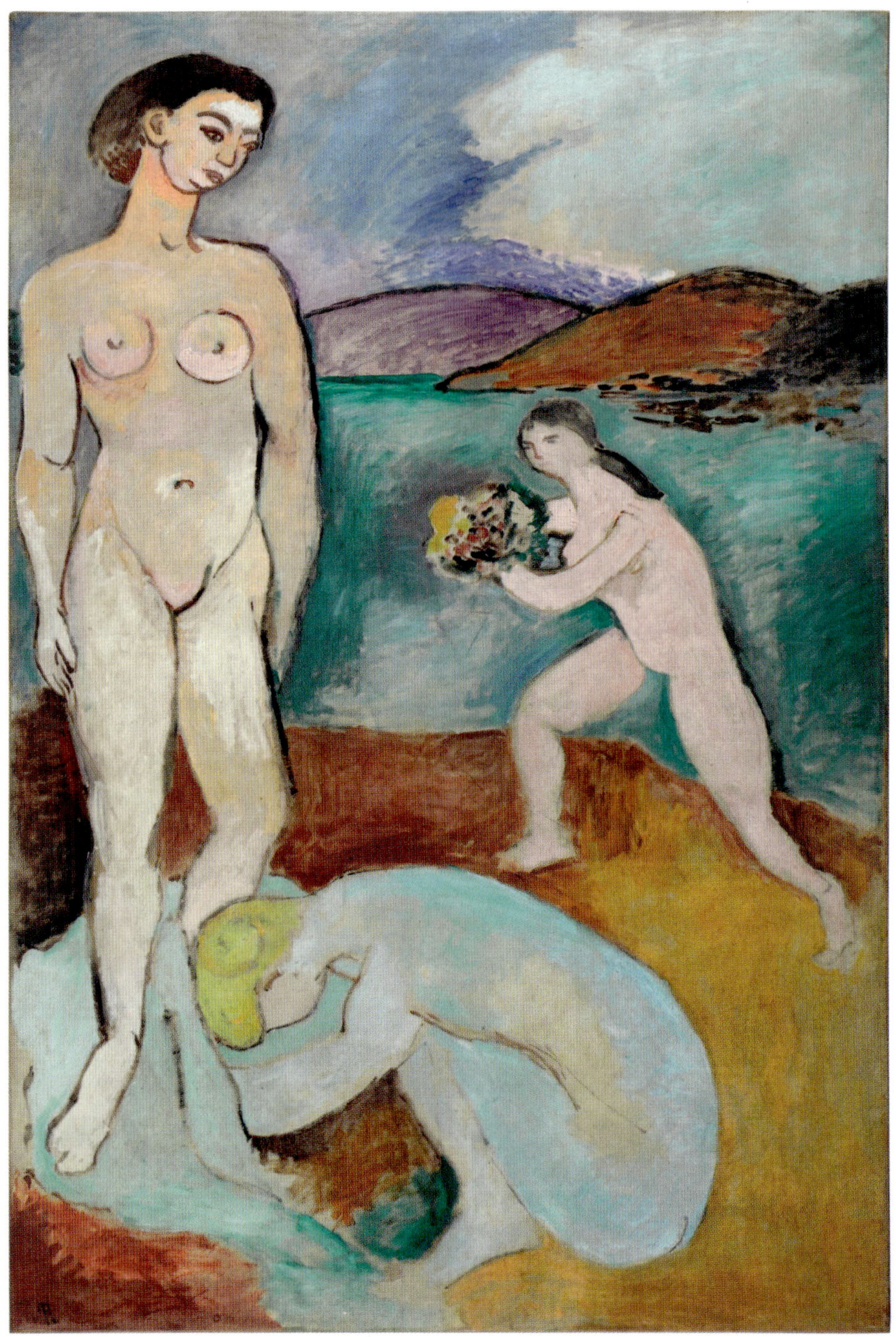

10 Henri Matisse, *Le Luxe I*, 1907

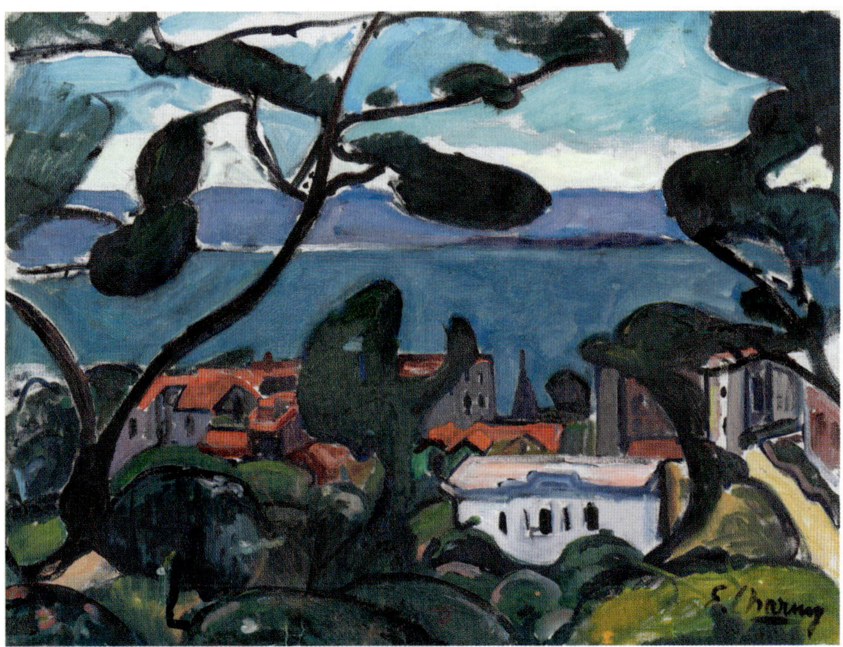

11 Émilie Charmy, *L'Éstaque*, c. 1910

recognizes the subject matter.' In this theory the art object itself becomes a communicating vessel, demanding, through intrinsically painterly qualities – form, line and colour – rather than narrative ones – subject matter – that viewers engage openly and directly with it. In this formulation, symbolism, narrative and literary allusion lose the importance they have in academic art as providers of content and are replaced by something altogether more emotive and evasive of verbal definition. In the new art, it would seem viewers are not being asked to 'read' content, but to use instead their intuition, to 'feel' it. This is a significant point that runs through so much of twentieth-century art, where there is a characteristically Expressionist blurring of the separation between art and life. Matisse's 'Notes of a Painter', epitomized in his statement, 'What I am after, above all, is expression,' became a rallying call for a generation of critics and Expressionist artists alike throughout Europe and beyond.

Together with his impressive sense of the decorative Matisse's interest in the 'feel' of the evolving picture also accounts for the distortion of form and flattening of the picture space in much of his work: 'I cannot copy nature in a servile way; I am forced to interpret nature and submit it to the spirit of the picture.'

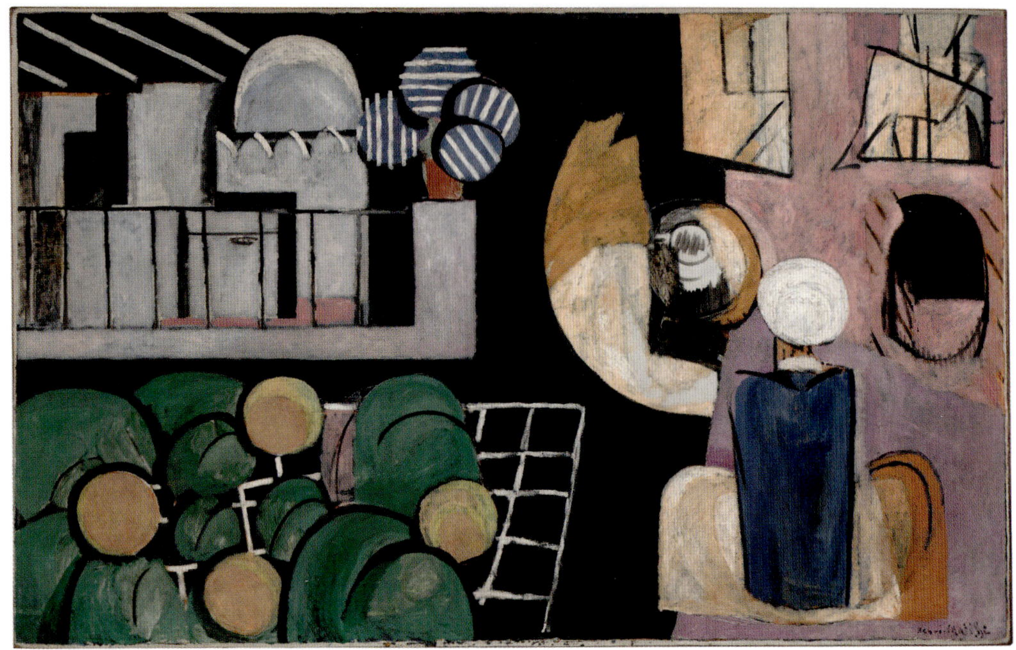

12 Henri Matisse, *The Moroccans*, 1916–17

He reasserted the importance of looking at nature while investing his work with the sum of his experience. In this he allied himself with Paul Cézanne rather than Impressionists like Claude Monet or Alfred Sisley, saying he wanted 'to reach that condensation of sensations that makes a painting. I might be satisfied with a work done at one sitting, but I would soon tire of it; therefore, I prefer to rework it so that later I may recognize it as representative of my state of mind.' Time and again Matisse would work over paintings that others might consider finished, often entirely obliterating the original image. For example, although the main representational elements of a dinner table and female figure remain more or less constant in the *Harmony in Red* (1908–09), the painting had previously had very different decorative schemes, as 'harmonies' in blue and green. Traces of earlier parts of the process can often be clearly seen under the top layer of paint. The process of over-painting and distillation of the image was later, at times taken
12 to the verge of abstraction in works such as *The Moroccans*. Yet, interestingly these were no longer regarded as unwelcome evidence of the painter's corrections of mistakes or indecision, as they would have been in paintings from previous periods in art history, but seen, rather, as signs of the organic growth of the image.

Organizing and Communicating

Matisse's 'Notes of a Painter' was widely circulated throughout Europe and quickly translated into other languages. The text was very influential in itself, but it also reflected a new European artistic attitude that came to epitomize the art of the first two decades of the century. This was a period of intense activity and rapid change in Western art. For many it seemed to conclude and sum up a movement away from naturalism in the arts that had begun in earnest less than a century earlier. Predictably the art establishments of Europe strongly resisted the change, but they could not stop a host of self-proclaimed new 'movements' emerging. Each one was driven by artists and writers who believed they represented the vanguard of the new art, ready to replace all previous pretenders. It is not farfetched to talk about a pan-European network of cutting-edge artists and modernist critics during this time. In spite of political tensions across Europe that would erupt into wars and bloody revolutions, contact between countries was good and movement relatively easy. Artists from North America, Asia and the rest of Europe travelled to Paris to experience the new art, many studying in the Académie Matisse, which operated during the crucial period between 1907 and 1911.

Advances in communication technologies also added to the increased speed of spreading ideas and – tremendously important for artists – images. By the beginning of the twentieth century there were a number of art magazines that boasted high quality photo reproductions of paintings in black and white and colour, where previously viewers had to rely on engraved copies. In this way, for the first time in history, it seemed possible to artists that they might be able to keep up with the latest developments in the cultural capitals of Europe without necessarily having to be there in person. So, if Paris was still generally regarded as the global centre for visual art, it was becoming increasingly possible for artists to operate elsewhere, and moreover, for the lines of communication to be working in both directions, so that they were up to date with what was going on at the centre and it was possible to get their work seen there.

In the first decade of the twentieth century most of the new generation of art magazines and critics were publishing on three late nineteenth-century artists in particular, Paul Cézanne, Paul Gauguin and Vincent van Gogh. All were seen as progenitors of the new art, with their work embodying something essentially modern, largely through their struggles to make something lasting out of Impressionism. Roger Fry (1866–1934), the influential British critic and later Director of the Metropolitan Museum of Art, New York, named these three, along with artists like Seurat, 'Post-Impressionists' when he introduced their work to the London art scene in 1910 and 1912. But these shows also included Derain, Matisse, Picasso and others from the younger generation. The name stuck for the nineteenth-century painters – we still tend to think of them as the post-Impressionists today – but not the twentieth-century ones, who have come down to us as representatives of apparently separate groupings, Fauvists, Cubists, Futurists, Expressionists, and so on. Yet, at the time they were all regarded as generally part of a more or less recognizable and single avant-garde scene. This was how they were exhibited at the large and important 1912 'Cologne Sonderbund Exhibition' in Germany, for example, and how they arrived in America, en masse at the '1913 International Exhibition of Modern Art in New York' – the now famous 'Armory Show'.

At the turn of the century new artists' groups and collectives and art 'movements' sprang up all over Europe. There were Secession groups throughout Germany and Austria, consisting of artists who had broken with the official academic exhibition outlets. Soon after, there came artists who saw even the Secessions as too conservative and formed their own new exhibiting groups which made a further break, as in the 'New Secession' in Berlin, or the 'Phalanx' and NKVM (New Artists' Association) in Munich, as well as progressive artist-led exhibition groups elsewhere, such as *Bubnovy Valet* (Jack of Diamonds) in Moscow. Smaller collectives of independent-minded artists joined together, such as the Nabis in France, the Brücke (Bridge) in Dresden, and the neo-primitivists in Russia. In Italy, a group of post-Impressionist painters and Symbolist poets gathered around the banner of 'Futurism', a movement driven by manifestos and declarations about its own leading status as against the art of the older generation, which it described as *passéist*. Futurism's claim for being absolutely contemporary and forward-leading meant that it quickly gained many international adherents who were eager to be included as part of a new world-historical wave. Notably, there were 'Futurists' in Russia and Germany, 'Orphists' in France, and 'Vorticists' in England. In retrospect, however, all these groups, jostling for position as pioneers of the New Age, probably shared more in common than the differences they claimed for themselves.

Naming Expressionism

One of the common threads that ran through claims about the thinking of these various artists at the time was a belief in the expressive potential of artworks over and above illusionistic concerns; that is, the ways in which paintings or sculpture might be able to communicate directly to the viewer emotionally, irrespective of any representational content, and without much care for high levels of realism. If Fry had eventually fixed on the rather neutral term 'Post-Impressionists' as a title for the group of nineteenth- and twentieth-century painters in his London exhibition, another English critic, Arthur Clutton-Brock suggested in a 1911 article that they should be called 'Expressionists', because, as he said (paraphrasing Matisse), 'their only end is expression.' He suggested that they were connected by a desire to rid their work of all 'irrelevant feats of representation' and pare it down to essentials. In that way they might be able to replace 'the interest of curiosity' (Impressionism) with 'the deeper and more lasting emotional interest' (Expressionism). In this view of the creative process, it is about knowing your subject intimately and empathetically, rather than being merely acquainted.

The word 'expressionism' was clearly being bandied about in artistic circles throughout Europe around this time. The French painter Julien-Auguste Hervé (1854–1932), exhibited his own paintings at the annual Salon des Indépendants, Paris under the heading '*Expressionisme*' between 1901 and 1914. After the publication of Matisse's 'Notes of a Painter' in 1908 and its subsequent translation into English, German and various Scandinavian languages, it quickly began to be widely taken up as a descriptor for the 'New Art'. In Germany especially, until 1914, it was consistently used in exhibitions and print media to describe contemporary French art. In the 1911 Berlin Secession exhibition, a group of Parisian painters including Derain, Vlaminck, Marquet and Kees van Dongen were described as '*Expressionisten*' – a clear derivation from the French. In the international Sonderbund exhibition, Cologne the following year, the organizers used the term '*Expressionismus*' to describe the new trend in painting throughout Europe, which not only showcased Parisian artists such as Van Gogh and Gauguin, but also Germans such as Kirchner and Max Pechstein (1881–1955), and the Norwegian painter, Edvard Munch (1863–1944). That both of these now epochal exhibitions derived conceptually from Fry's 'Manet and the Post-Impressionists' further emphasizes a general pan-European agreement on what the new art looked like at that time, and, moreover, suggests that the word expressionism, in its French and English language forms, was already in use among artists and critics. This is further implied by the fact that there is no etymological root for the word in German; it is a straight appropriation, in much the same way that the term '*Impressionismus*' had already been 'imported' into German from the French.

One American critic, Christian Brinton used the term 'Expressionism' in 1913 in his article on the New York Armory Show, which was modelled on the Sonderbund exhibition, and it continued to have some currency in the United States. In his book about modern art from 1934, the American writer Sheldon Cheney went so far as to include all avant-garde art produced from around 1880 to the time of publication as 'expressionist', reasoning that in every case modernist artists 'were tracing art as expression of the artist's feelings or imaging, instead of art as illusion or transcription.' Similarly, he points to a general leaning towards subjectivism: 'Possibly a purely subjective art would be wholly abstract, without observable relationship to concrete reality. But only a very small part of Modern art is of that sort; though obviously the typical Modernist tends *towards* abstraction, as compared with the Realist confining himself (*sic.*) to the surface look of nature.' He even refers to the anonymous writer of the entry on 'Post-Impressionism' in the 1929 edition of the *Encyclopædia Britannica* as suggesting that 'Expressionism' is the 'more apt' term, 'but unfortunately of German origin!' Therein lies one of the issues with the broader use of the term outside northern and eastern Europe after the First World War, namely that it had become identified with Germany as a politically hostile nation to the American-British-French axis. In the twenty-first century it should be possible to see past such political posturing to define more clearly the spread of early twentieth-century Expressionism. Cheney's pan-modernist designation, though, is perhaps too broad. Where Matisse and other 'post-Impressionists' can reasonably be called 'expressionists', it is difficult to see how the term can be applied to the Cubism of Picasso and Braque, or to Surrealism, both of which seem to have been underpinned by different theoretical premises.

Expressive Art Theories

If painterly Expressionism arose in France, it is true to say that it received its most considered theoretical definition in Germany between 1912 and 1920. When the German art historian Paul Fechter (1880–1958) published his important monograph *Expressionismus* in 1914 he used current pan-European art terms to situate contemporary German art: Expressionism, Cubism, and Futurism, where 'Expressionism' referred broadly to 'Post-Impressionism'. He does not use the word 'Fauvism' but refers to the work of Matisse and the Fauves as 'Expressionism of the heart'. Cubism is described as 'Expressionism of the head' (perhaps prefiguring Cheney's embrace of Cubism in his book). Gauguin, Signac, Matisse and Picasso all loom large.

The timing of Fechter's book, however, coincided with a nadir in German relations with France, Britain and the United States. Some British critics, such as Herbert Read (1893–1968) and T. E. Hulme (1883–1917) were enthusiastic followers of many of the ideas enshrined in German Expressionist criticism, with Read later, in 1927, translating a book by one of its founding thinkers, Wilhelm Worringer (1881–1965): *Formprobleme der Gotik* (1912). However, although Read remained committed to much of the rhetoric and sentiment of Expressionist theory in his writings, he tended to use the term only in respect of its German forms. In 1911, Fry had already seemingly rejected the term 'expressionism' for the title of what became his 'Post-Impressionists' exhibitions on the grounds of anti-German sentiment in a London already generally hostile to modernist art, and by the summer of 1914, Britain and France were at war with Germany. This, more than anything skewed art criticism in all three countries towards nationalistic posturing, and after the war ended, resulted crucially in an Anglo-French narrative of modernist art being dominant. The word 'expressionism' had not only lost its more general meaning and come to be associated almost exclusively in French and English language criticism with German art, but as 'German Expressionism', it came to be seen as somewhat derivative and second tier.

Expressive theories of art were the common stuff of the early twentieth century, however. And these were usually bound up with a 'formalist' aesthetics; that is, a theory about the way art works that concentrates primarily on the operation of qualities specific to the medium – shapes, colour, brush marks, materials – rather than those that refer to other objects in the world. The two major theorists and supporters of this kind of aesthetics at the time were probably Fry and another British writer, Clive Bell (1881–1964), both of whom knew the European and particularly Parisian scenes well. In 'The Aesthetic Hypothesis' (1914) Bell introduced the reader to the idea of 'significant form', which he judged to be the only quality common *and* peculiar to all works of art. The aesthetic response, he argued, is dictated by the ability of an artwork to move the viewer emotionally without falling back on description or allusion. This opens up the possibility of being able to understand work from any time or culture, for in Bell's terms, 'To appreciate a work of art we need bring with us nothing but a sense of form and colour and a knowledge of three-dimensional space.' The organization of the formal elements of a work themselves act as the carriers of aesthetic emotion. In a way, this theory operates on the belief that something of the artist's personality is transferred into an artwork so that the object carries within it the potential to communicate directly with the 'sensitive' viewer. At its extreme this appears as the Expressionist claim that the work itself exists as a kind of organism, with its own communicative power.

Bell did not reject representational works as such: 'Let no one imagine that representation is bad in itself; a realistic form may be as significant, in its place as part of the design, as an abstract. But if a representative form has value, it is as form, not as representation.' In keeping with all apologists for Modernism, however, he was quick to reject the naturalism of academic art, precisely because of the pre-eminence of subject matter and narrative content in this kind of work: 'We are all familiar with pictures that interest and excite our admiration, but do not move us as works of art. To this class belongs what I call "descriptive painting" – that is, painting in which forms are used not as objects of emotion, but as means of suggesting emotion or conveying information.'

Fry's formalism relied less on the abstract communicative power of form and colour and more on the ability of images to arouse aesthetic reactions in the viewer that are different *in kind* from the ways in which we react to real, physical events. In 'An Essay in Aesthetics' (1909), he chose not painting, but the up-to-date example of the movie, which he said, 'resembles actual life in almost every aspect', in order to demonstrate what he meant (notwithstanding the fact that movies were silent and in black and white when he wrote this): 'If, in a cinematograph, we see a runaway horse and cart, we do not have to think either of getting out of the way or heroically interposing ourselves. The result is that in the first place we *see* the event much more clearly; see a number of quite interesting but irrelevant things, which in real life could not struggle into our consciousness, bent, as it would be, entirely upon the problem of our appropriate reaction.' The key was that art is specifically, 'the expression of imaginative life' and therefore subject to 'disinterested intensity of contemplation.' All that Fry asked of the work is that it possessed the qualities of order, variety, unity and evidence of 'consciousness of purpose,' so that viewers might become aware of emotions and an intensity that would connect them to the investment made by the artist.

Art functions best, Fry argued, when viewers feel that the artist 'has expressed something which was latent in us all the time, but which we never realized.' There is no moral order here, only the rule that the artist arouses emotions 'in a way that satisfies fully the needs of the imaginative life.' Thus, the way is left open for 'ugly' art and any forms that challenge the dominance of the academic (naturalistic) tradition. Such is the case that, for example, we find Fry in 'The French

Post-Impressionists' (1912) openly using his general ideas about aesthetics to praise Matisse and his colleagues specifically, in language that echoes that used by Matisse himself in his 'Notes of a Painter'. According to Fry, artists like Matisse, Derain, Gauguin and Cézanne 'do not seek to imitate form, but to create form; not to imitate life, but to find an equivalent for life. By that I mean that they wish to make images which by the clearness of their logical structure, and by their closely knit unity of texture, shall appeal to our disinterested and contemplative imagination with something of the same vividness as the things of actual life appeal to our practical activities.'

Empathy and Abstraction

Matisse's 'Notes of a Painter' was both widely read *and* reflected many common ideas that were current in the popular mind across Europe at the time, such as the philosophy of Henri Bergson (1859–1941) and, to a lesser extent, that of Friedrich Nietzsche (1844–1900). In fact, it was another German, the art historian Wilhelm Worringer who seemed to encapsulate the general mood among modern artists and forward-looking critics and curators in Europe and the United States in his book, *Abstraktion und Einfühlung* (Abstraction and Empathy, 1908). Subtitled, 'A Contribution to the Psychology of Style', it was a book not about modern art, but about Europe's past. However, it tapped into a common current of dissatisfaction with the stranglehold of the classical tradition, dating back to Ancient Greece and Rome, in academic art practice and conservative art history. Traditional aesthetics had tended to marginalize or even ignore great swathes of artistic production both in Europe and elsewhere that lay outside the classical tradition. Worringer introduced a way of thinking about the spectrum of historical production that argued they differed only by psychological approach rather than necessarily by qualitative difference.

From the second half of the nineteenth century in Europe there had been increasing interest in the visual arts of the Far East, particularly those of China and Japan, in addition to its decorative arts, which had long been admired and copied in the West. European art magazines in the first couple of decades of the twentieth century were as likely to carry serious articles on Oriental art (and not just decorative arts) as they were on that of Europe. At the same time admiration for the art of periods in European history previously regarded as low points or aberrations in comparison with the classical tradition began to be taken seriously on their own terms.

By the beginning of the twentieth century, the list included not only fifteenth-century Italian painting and sculpture (generally seen as marking the first primitive stirrings of the European Renaissance – literally 'rebirth' of the classical tradition), but also the art of Byzantium, ancient Spanish sculpture and the creative production of the Romanesque and Gothic periods, not to mention Coptic art from Egypt. Unsurprisingly Clive Bell was a supporter of this 'primitive' art, claiming that in it 'you will find no accurate representation; you will find only significant form.' The case was similar with Fry and many others.

As a young doctoral student visiting Paris around 1904, Worringer picked up on all this and, starting from the ideas of the great nineteenth-century Austrian art historian Alois Riegl (1858–1905), produced a theory which assigned value back to this marginalized art by shifting readings of past art from the perspective of the development of ever-increasing technical ability to a history of changes in the exercise of artistic will, which he defined as, 'that latent inner demand which exists *per se*, entirely independent of the object and of the mode of creation, and behaves as will to form.' Art, in Worringer's schema, was a product of its times and of culture – which is not to say merely of 'fashion', but of shared beliefs and ways of understanding and reacting to the world – and its values shifted accordingly. But this was not an open door for cultural relativism; judgments about individual artworks could still be made, but in line with the specific social and psychological contexts of their production.

Most importantly, Worringer set up a dialectic that described two poles of absolute artistic will, represented at one end by the naturalistic 'urge' – exemplified by the classical tradition – and at the other by the urge toward flat patternmaking, or abstraction. Following the German philosopher, Theodor Lipps (1851–1914), he argued that naturalistic art is marked by a desire for empathy in the viewer; that is, a need to feel your way into an art object, so to speak, as you would in a physical space and to feel comfortable with this sense of intimate participation. Worringer's original contribution to the field was to formulate an explanation of how non-naturalistic art operates in an equal but opposite relationship with nature.

By conflating a consideration of the forms and construction of aesthetic objects and ideas about the relative social evolutionary state of the makers of such objects, which drew on the racist science of his time, Worringer was able to argue that Byzantine art, medieval art and the traditional art of Sub-Saharan Africa all stand characteristically at the *beginning* of artistic development because of the relatively intuitive and therefore essentially primitive worldview of their creators. As a result, in this kind of art 'the urge to abstraction' is the dominant tendency. What is most important from the perspective of how early twentieth-century art movements defined themselves, is the fact that Worringer also saw abstraction as the main tendency in art of China and Japan, which he described as highly cultured, but 'above cognition' – that is, transcending Western models of reason – rather than 'before' it – that is, at the beginning of a developmental cycle toward attaining reason. So, 'abstraction', or more precisely a movement of forms away from lifelikeness and towards the imposition of a more schematized, tightly structured order could be justified by Worringer's artist contemporaries who wanted to be seen both as 'primitives' of a new art *and* as sophisticated modern citizens; both at the beginning of and above the 'normal' (that is, Western) pattern of periodicity in the development of art traditions.

Crucial to the acceptance of Worringer's theory were what he called the 'psychic presuppositions' of the two urges: 'Whereas the precondition for the urge to empathy is a happy pantheistic relationship of confidence between man and the phenomena of the external world, the urge to abstraction is the outcome of great inner unrest inspired in man by the phenomena of the outside world,' which shows itself in 'an immense spiritual dread of space.' For those artists who saw themselves as pioneers of a radical new aesthetics this kind of justification for the art of the past was easily adopted to serve their project because it seemed to do two major things: it said that different kinds of artist will exist, and that only art that arises necessarily from the creative context of its own time is authentic.

Furthermore, Worringer also seemed to confirm that academic artists and critics from the old order simply wouldn't get it, precisely because they were working out of a different (and outmoded) view of the world. Thus, his claim that, 'What appears from our standpoint the greatest distortion must have been at the time, for its creator, the highest beauty and the fulfilment of his artistic will,' can be turned around and reformulated in the Expressionist context: what appears to the old order as the greatest distortion is actually the highest beauty and the fulfilment of the artistic will of the moderns. Indeed, Kandinsky said as much in 1912 in his highly influential book, *Über das geistige in der Kunst* (On the Spiritual in Art): 'Every work of art is a child of its time...Any attempt to give new life to the artistic principles of the past can at best result in a work of art...that remains soulless for all time.'

Moreover, Kandinsky argued that, 'Literature, music, and art are the first and most sensitive realms where...spiritual change becomes noticeable in real form. These spheres immediately reflect the murky present; they provide an intimation of the greatness which first becomes noticeable only to a few, as just a tiny point, and which for the masses does not exist at all.' Characteristically, he cites the example of Cézanne in art as precursor, describing him as 'the seeker after new laws of form [who] knows how to create a living being out of a teacup – or rather how to recognize such a being within this cup.' But, he says, 'It is not a man nor an apple, nor a tree that is represented; they are all used by Cézanne to create an object with an internal, painterly quality: a picture.'

The Bridge

If the birth of Expressionism and the hub from which it spiralled across the world can be seen as a French event, the origins of the movement that came to be known as German Expressionism can probably be pinpointed to the city of Dresden, in Saxony, which is famous more for its baroque splendour and its role in the eighteenth-century Western Enlightenment, than as a hotbed for revolutionary modern art. Yet it was there, on 7 June 1905 that four young architecture students, Fritz Bleyl (1880–1966), Erich Heckel (1883–1970), Ernst Ludwig Kirchner and Karl Schmidt-Rottluff (1884–1976), formed an artists' group which they named *Die Brücke* (The Bridge).

Dresden is well known for its fine bridges across the Elbe River, which divides the city, but the group's choice of name almost certainly came instead from Nietzsche's description of humankind as being the metaphorical bridge between animal and 'superman' in his *Thus Spoke Zarathustra* (1883–85), a book that was much read in Germany at the turn of the century by college students. *Zarathustra* is memorable partly for its excessive tone and messianic content; for its championing of individuality and free will against unthinking sociability and anonymity among the crowd. Most of all, the book's eponymous hero/anti-hero is convinced by the correctness of his beliefs in spite of their radical and disruptive nature, and he is unmoved by rejection by the social majority. In any case, Zarathustra regards that rejection as a sign of weakness in the innately conservative crowd of people (the 'vulgar herd', as he calls them), rather than any fault in him. In many ways Zarathustra is the prototype for the (anti-)heroic social outsider or rebel, who became a staple figure of twentieth-century Western culture. All of this seems an appropriate credo for a group like Brücke, which announced its revolutionary intention from the start in language that echoes Nietzsche. Its 'programme', hand-printed shortly after its formation, as a woodcut by Kirchner, emphasized the importance of youth as the way to the future and the necessity of unceremoniously sweeping away the past:

With faith in progress and a new generation of creators and viewers we call together all youth. As youth we carry together the future and want to create for ourselves freedom of life against the long-established older forces. Everyone who reproduces with directness and authenticity that which drives him to creation belongs to us.

The Brücke artists saw themselves as that bridge between what they regarded as the inferior, derivative art of the previous generation in Germany and a new art whose hallmarks were vitality and originality. Like Zarathustra they would ignore the followers of the current artistic orthodoxy – artists and audience alike – and seek out instead, as Nietzsche would have it, 'fellow-creators, those who inscribe new values on new tables.'

They sought new members in whom they saw common ground, including the German painters Max Pechstein and Emil Nolde in 1906, and the Silesian painter Otto Müller (1874–1930) in 1910. They also invited other already-established artists who seemingly embraced the new Expressionist art, and who came from 'northern', rather than 'Latin' traditions in their view, such as the Swiss painter Cuno Amiet (1868–1961), the Norwegian painter Edvard Munch, the Finnish artist Akseli Gallen-Kallela (1865–1931), and the Paris-based Dutch painter Kees van Dongen. In a remarkably business-like act, they also sought out so-called 'passive members', supporters of the new art who would pay an annual subscription and receive in return a report and original artworks.

Despite their fine words it was to be some time before the Brücke artists broke away from the French Symbolist and German *Jugendstil* (the German version of Art Nouveau) models they initially looked to for artistic direction in their work. The major earliest 'expressionist' influences on their development between 1906 and 1907 were not Matisse and his circle, but Van Gogh and Gauguin. Both artists were enthusiastically collected early on in Germany, notably by at the influential private Folkwang Museum in Hagen, established by the collector and patron Karl Ernst Osthaus (1874–1921). Van Gogh's *Le parc de*
6 *l'hôpital, à Saint-Rémy* (1889) and Gauguin's *Contes barbares*
(1902) were both in the museum collection, and their influence
13 can be seen in works such as Heckel's *Brickworks* (1907) and
14 Nolde's *Dance Around the Golden Calf* (1910), for example. Amiet's

invitation to join the Brücke in 1906 was in large part driven by him being a one-time resident of the artist colony at Pont-Aven, France where Gauguin and others had also lived and worked.

Van Dongen was a Fauvist and neighbour of Picasso in Montmartre who Pechstein had met in 1908 on a trip to Paris. His subsequent invitation to join Brücke reflected the new importance of the example of Matisese and the Parisian Expressionist group to them, which really only became apparent in their work the following year, as in Kirchner's *Japanese Theatre* (1909) and Pechstein's *Two Girls* (1909). Interestingly, one of the prototypical expressionists, Munch rejected the group's advances on more than one occasion. Unlike Matisse's circle in France, in Brücke we have an example of a group of artists consciously forming an identity and attempting to position themselves at the centre of the contemporary art debate; something that would, of course, occur time and again as the century progressed. There is no evidence, though, of any of them referring to themselves specifically as 'expressionists' by name before the Cologne Sonderbund exhibition in 1912, when Kirchner and Pechstein were included, along with some of the contemporary Parisian painters, and with Van Gogh and Munch foregrounded. The term was certainly in use in the German capital, Berlin a year earlier, though, by which time the core Brücke members had relocated to the city. The concept, referring initially to pan-European Modernism, was used in the hugely influential *Sturm* (Storm) project, overseen by the writer and publisher, Herwarth Walden (1878–1941).

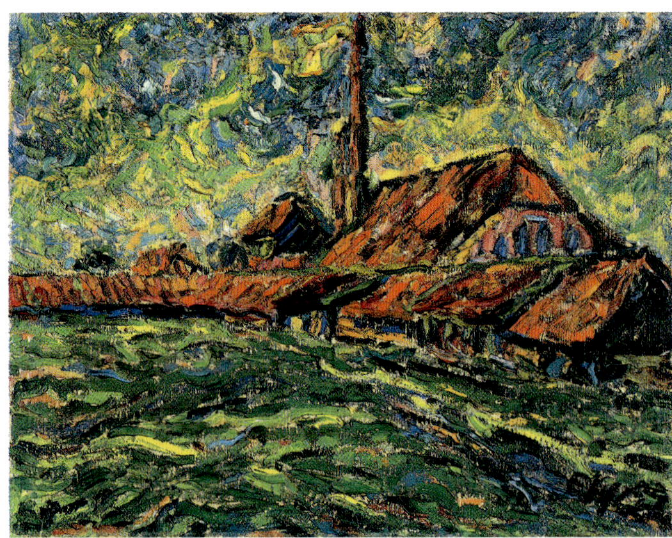

13 Erich Heckel, *Ziegelei* (Brickworks), 1907

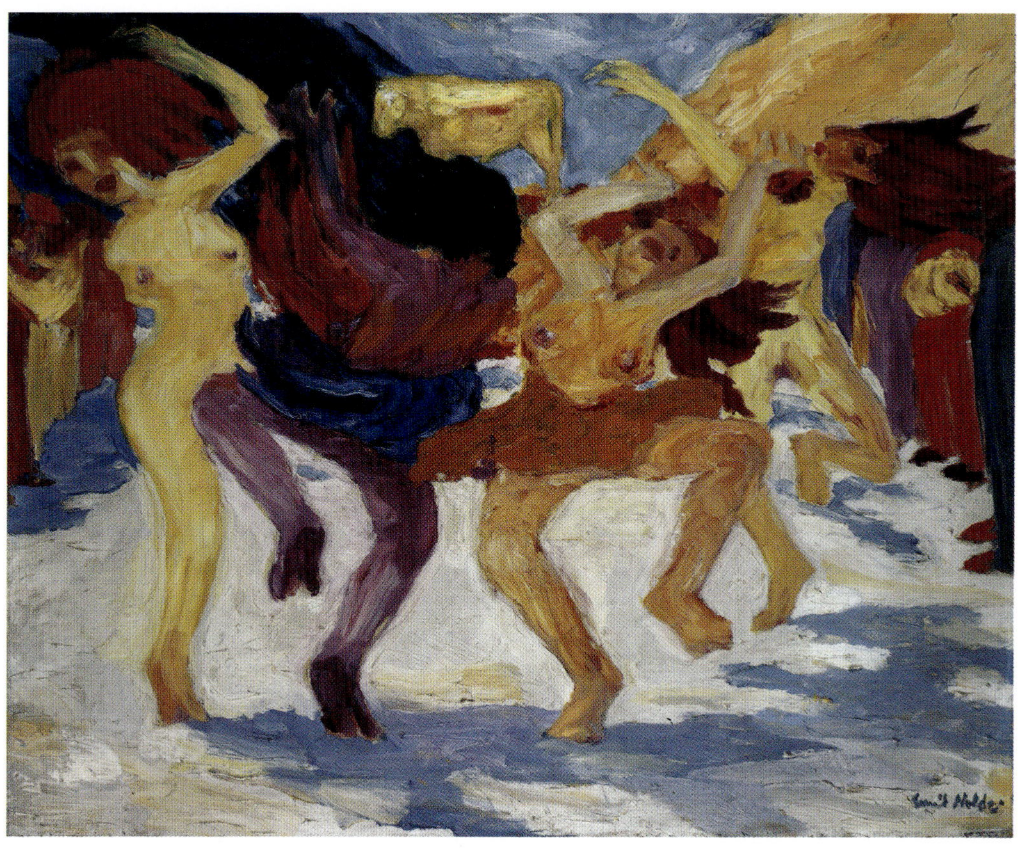

14 Emil Nolde, *Dance Around the Golden Calf*, 1910

Der Sturm consisted of a gallery and journal of the same name, founded in 1910, which foregrounded significant modernists, including members of Brücke, Kandinsky, Marc, Oskar Kokoschka (1886–1980), Marc Chagall (1887–1985) and Ludwig Meidner (1884–1966). Walden also premiered new writing in the pages of *Der Sturm*, including work by his first wife, Else Lasker-Schüler (1869–1945), one of the leading representatives of expressionist poetry. Walden's second wife, the Swedish artist, writer and gallerist Nell Walden (née Roslund) (1887–1975), was a key figure in the activities of Der Sturm, as well as writing on the German cultural scene in the Swedish media, thereby contributing to the spread of Expressionism in Scandinavia.

From the point of view of sheer physicality of handling of materials, the Expressionism of Brücke and many other German artists had much more in common with the likes

45 Vlaminck, Chaïm Soutine (1893–1943) and Georges Rouault in France, than with Matisse, Marquet or Charmy. There was also a characteristic intensity in their images which tended to contrast with the latter's more temperate picture-making. Early
13 Brücke landscape paintings, such as Heckel's *Brickworks* (1907), Schmidt-Rottluff's *Um die Mittagszeit* (1907), and Pechstein's *Flußlandschaft* (1907) are storms of colour blocks which threaten to destroy any figuration even as they suggest it. This is painting as struggle, rather than the gentle repose of Derain and Matisse's images of the South of France from a couple of years earlier. Nolde is probably one of the most extreme examples of this. Paintings like *Wildly Dancing Children* (1909) deliver pointillism into an instinctual storm of licks of thick paint, which helps the viewer to sense the closeness of the uninhibited swirling of the children to nature, and which is, coincidentally, close in feel and handling of paint to the last works of the impressionist, Claude Monet.

Art, Life, Freedom

At Expressionism's core was a belief in the necessity of breaking down the boundaries between art and life, which grew out of a Jugendstil idea that art exists throughout the whole of human production; that it is essential to, and synonymous with life. This extends the ideas of people like Bell, Fry, and even Worringer, about the way in which art operates by implying not so much that artworks are somehow emotionally charged, as that they are pathways to universal experiences. Here the artist is almost a kind of seer, who taps into the essence of things and produces objects – works of art – that communicate directly with the sensitive viewer at a visceral level; that is, at the level of feeling rather than thinking. As Kirchner put it, 'The great mystery which lies behind all events and objects of the environment sometimes becomes schematically visible or sensible when we talk with a person, stand in a landscape, or when flowers or objects suddenly speak to us.' In this worldview artists should respond to visual sensations and make art out of instinct and emotion rather than thinking and following rules. Collapsing art and life together enabled artists, in theory, to immerse themselves in the 'spirit' of that which was to be represented. In this view
15 of the world, images like Heckel's *Badende am Waldteich* (1909) and Pechstein's *Zwei Frauenakte im Zimmer* (1909) embody a threefold encounter: the artists' active participation in the scene to be represented; the artists' creative encounter with the materials; and the active imaginative-psychological participation of the viewer with the image.

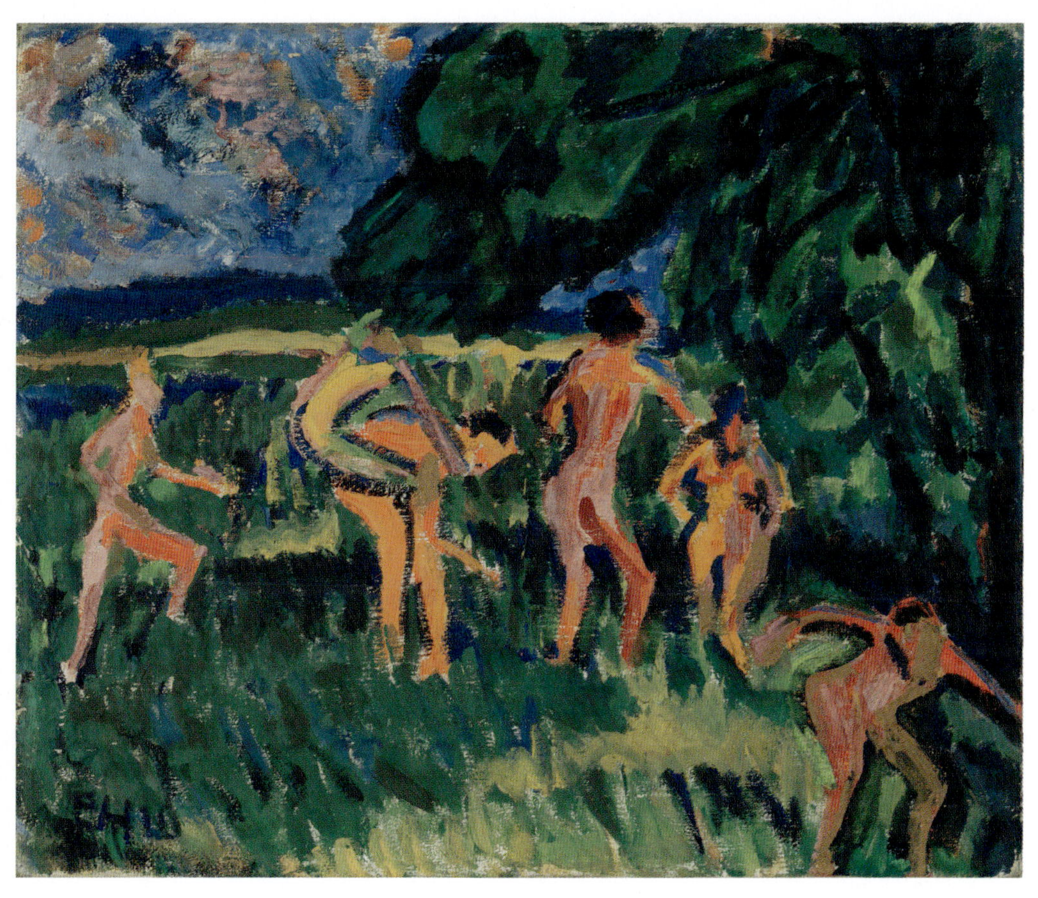

15 Erich Heckel, *Badende am Waldteich* (Bathers at the Forest Pond), 1909

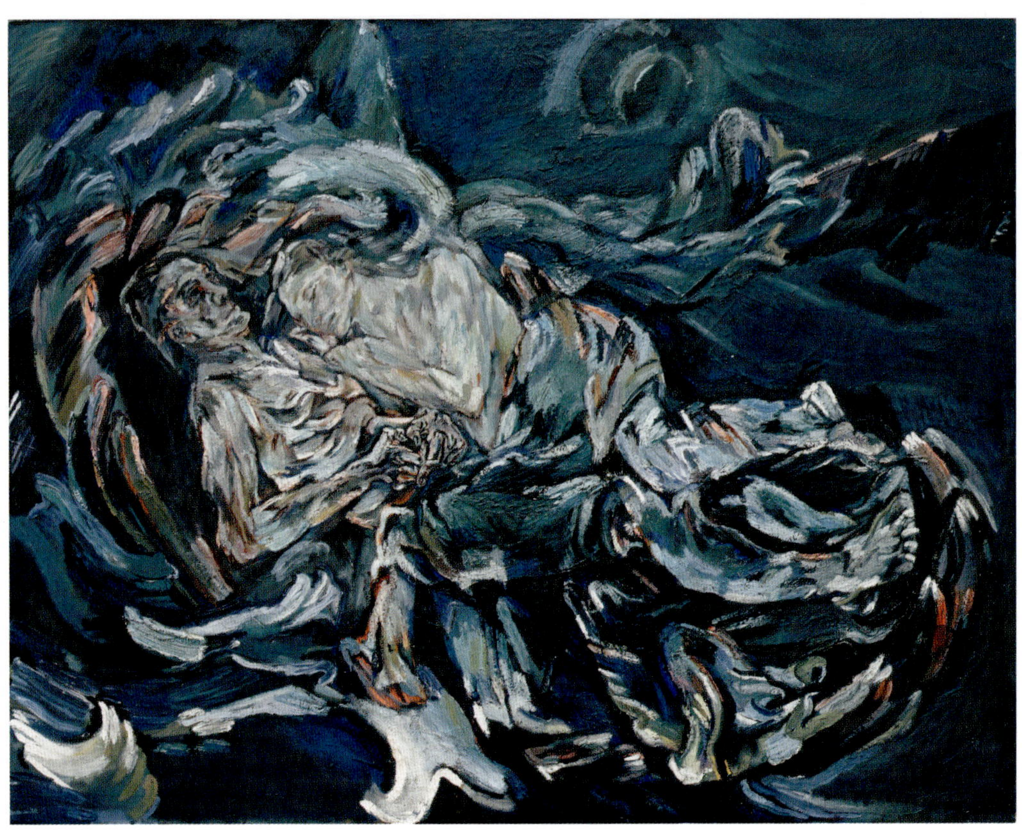

16 Oskar Kokoschka, *The Bride of the Wind*, 1914

If Bell and Fry had argued that subject matter should be merely a pretext for form-making, in Brücke art it regains its importance because it is part of that synthesis of art and life, of experience and its direct translation. Since the experience of being human is the one that people know inside out, and since empathy is easiest to achieve with another person, it is perhaps not surprising that the human figure is the dominant subject in German Expressionist art. Hence,
16 Kokoschka's masterpiece, *The Bride of the Wind* is at once a paean to the artist's intense, doomed relationship with the Austrian writer and composer Alma Mahler (1879–1964) and an image of cosmic transfiguration, in which the lovers assume their place in a universal nature. The Brücke painters were at their strongest when the human figure was not in isolation, but in a meaningful, emotional relationship with its surroundings, whether that was primordial 'nature', as
38 in Heckel's *Badende an der Förde* or Schmidt-Rottluff's *Three*
17 *Nudes*, religious scenes, as in Nolde's *Dance Around the Golden*
18 *Calf*, or the contemporary metropolis, as in Kirchner's *Women on Potsdamer Platz*.

The young Brücke artists and their companions played out a fantasy of living in complete freedom from the rules and conventions of 'civilized' life on summer drawing and painting trips to Moritzburg near Dresden and later further afield. Dresden was a centre of the Hygiene Movement (Nolde's first connection with the city had been through his wife, Ada's recuperative visits to sanatoria there) and, like so many others at the time, the Brücke artists embraced nudism and the cult of 'fresh air'. However, their participation went much deeper than the simple, restorative health activities enjoyed by most people, and was conceived as part of a more focused attempt to critique the social status quo, and to free themselves from what they regarded as the constraints and over-sophistication of 'culture' in both their lives and work. Besides Nietzsche's *Zarathustra*, their strongest guides were Gauguin's *Noa Noa* (1901), an autobiographical account of his first trip to Tahiti which fed their yearnings for a life of simple abundance, and the American poet Walt Whitman's (1819–1892) *Leaves of Grass* (1855), whose hymns to sexual and social freedom spoke to them powerfully.

In their artistic styles, too, the Brücke artists looked for inspiration to a melange of artistic sources from cultures they believed somehow embodied similar values to theirs, including sixteenth-century Buddhist cave paintings from Ajanta, India (which they knew from high quality book reproductions), carvings from Palau, Micronesia

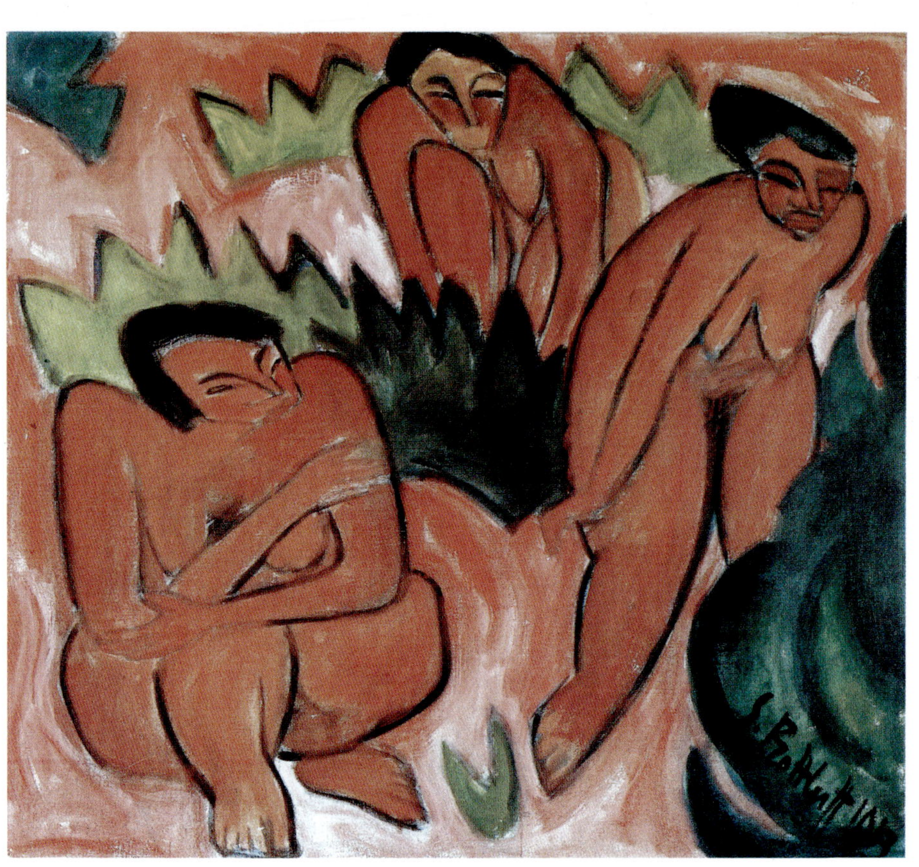

17 ABOVE Karl Schmidt-Rottluff, *Three Nudes (Dune Painting from Nidden)*, 1913
18 OPPOSITE Ernst Ludwig Kirchner, *Women on Potsdamer Platz*, 1914

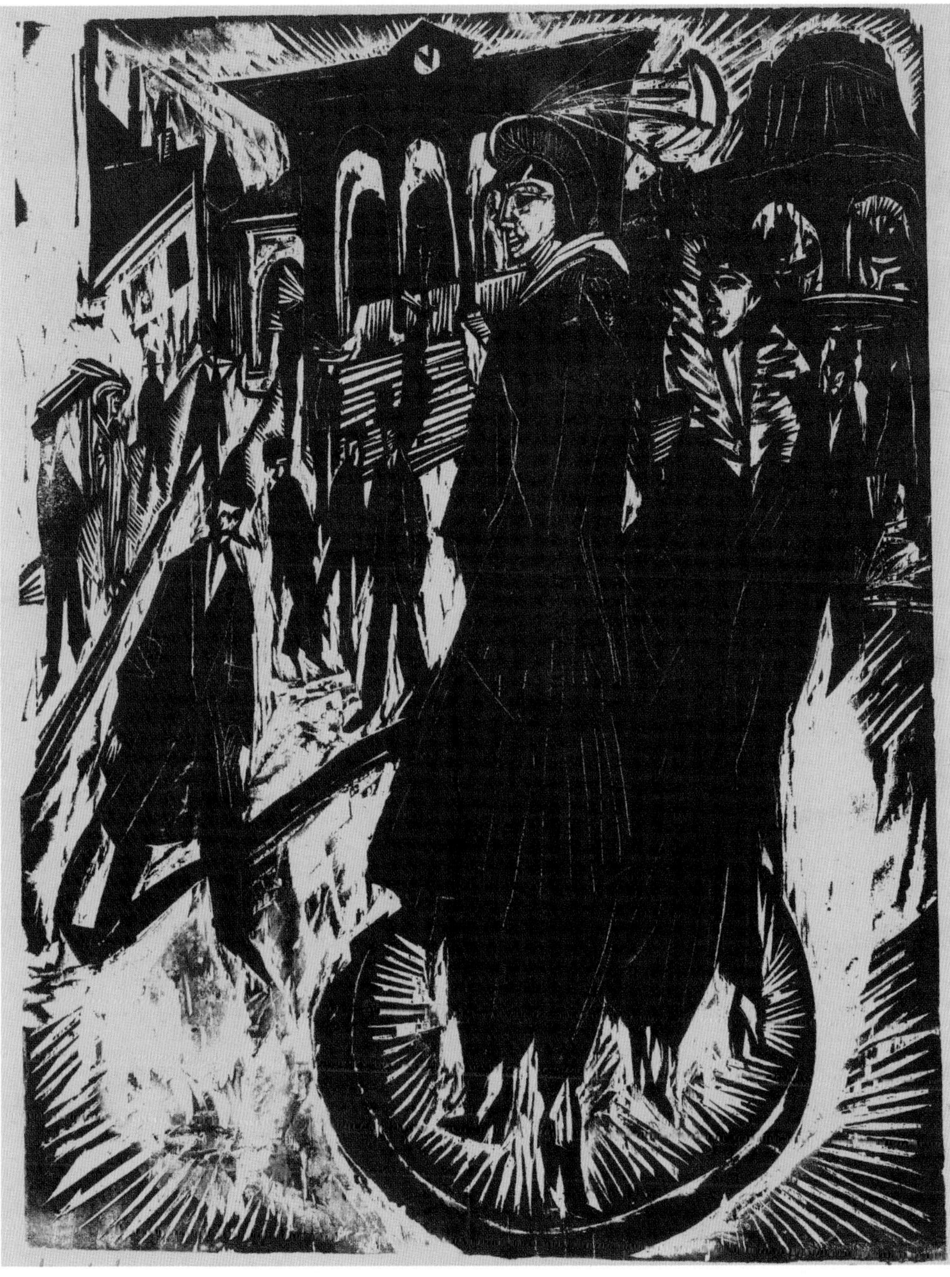

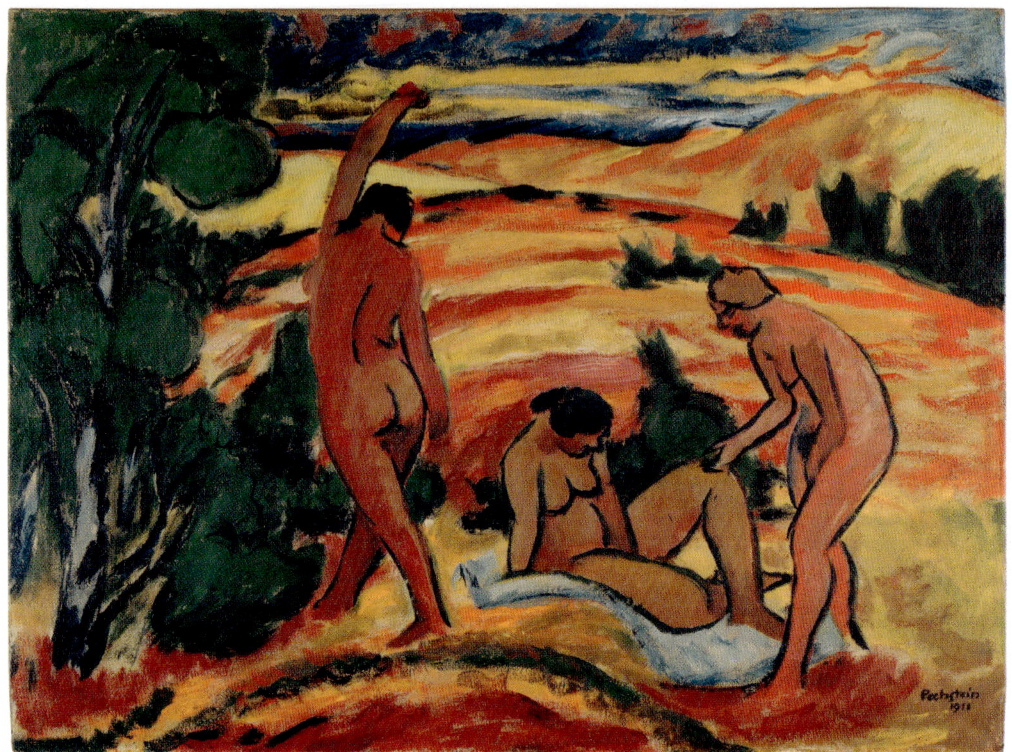

19 Max Pechstein, *In den Dünen* (In the Dunes), 1911

(which they saw in the Dresden ethnographic museum) and Gothic painting and sculpture. The artistic result was, in part, a group of 'natural' images of men and women unselfconsciously enjoying themselves in the landscape, as
15, 19 in Heckel's *Badende am Waldteich* (1909) or Pechstein's *In den Dünen* (1911), that were unparalleled in European art at the time. Indeed, from around 1914, Kirchner's work included powerful and sometimes poignant images of men, often together in their nakedness, that spoke to a queering of conventional images of women in art at that time. In these, the importance of Whitman's verse becomes even clearer. The charges of 'obscenity' laid against him in German culture at the time referred not only to his frank talk of the sexual act, but also of the homoeroticism that runs through *Leaves of Grass*.

One of the most compelling and intriguing aspects of the core Brücke members was their decision around the end of 1909 to convert their living spaces-cum-studios into exotic environments, decorated and furnished with a heady mix of non-European objects and elements made by the artists themselves after Japanese, African, Oceanic and Indian sources. These included curtains that were hand-painted by them with patterns derived from low-relief carvings from Palau they had seen in the ethnographic museum, to anthropomorphic wooden chairs and bowls carved after Cameroon models. Although some of the objects still exist, the studios are long since destroyed, and were recorded in only a few tantalizing photographs by Kirchner. They appear, though, in countless Brücke drawings, prints and paintings. Although it was fairly common at that time in Europe for artists to furnish their studios with 'exotic' props for use in paintings, and for photographers to build sets to suggest ethnographic 'authenticity' in exoticized images of women, the Brücke studios represented something quite different. If Whitman's poetry charted experiences from extensive travels across the United States, the studios were Whitmanesque microcosms that provided a kind of sanctuary from the social conventions and physical chaos of the urban environment that existed literally on the other side of the front door. They functioned as neutral spaces – socially, sexually, creatively – in the very heart of the city. Human figures could perform and be reassigned for a time to the realm of the 'natural'. For most of the Brücke artists, it was as close as they would ever get to Gauguin's experience of the South Seas – only Nolde and Pechstein would travel to Palau, in separate touristic journeys, that revealed their participation in racist colonial stereotypes, rather than confirmation of any mythical fellowship with the 'exotic' other.

Arguably the tension between the highly unconventional studio life in Dresden and subsequently Berlin, and the proximity of the teeming life of a modern big city contributed to the power of the images they produced. Despite the apparently subversive nature of their lifestyle, Kirchner later insisted that they were people 'whose lifestyle, rooms and work, though appearing strange to the normal person, was not a conscious "Épater les bourgeois" but a totally naïve and clear necessity to bring art and life into harmony.' As with the bathers, the study of the nude from life formed a crucial aspect of the development of their studio pictures. The Brücke artists rarely employed models in the conventional sense – the figures in their pictures were friends, acquaintances, the artists themselves. In this way their images often subvert any sense of the voyeuristic gaze and allow the viewer to share in
20 the frank intimacy of works like Pechstein's *Zwei Frauenakte im Zimmer* (1909).

In Ernst Ludwig Kirchner's drawing, *A Visitor in the Studio with Dodo and Marzella* (1910), three people – two clothed and one naked – a wooden sculpture and two large painted figures on the studio wall are raised by the artist to something like the same level of reality and interaction. Another painting by
21 Kirchner, *Frauenbildnis* (Portrait of a Woman) (1911) depicts a Black visitor in contemporary fashionable dress seated in front of a mural depicting bathers at Moritzburg. Kirchner's style at this time owed much more to Matisse and Ajanta cave painting than any Melanesian or African precedent, and in a remarkable inversion of conventional primitivizing images of Black bodies in early Expressionism, the visitor (commonly identified as Milli or Milly although her exact identity is unknown) is rendered as cultural, while the white body on the mural can be read as being of nature. Kirchner did make a few images of naked Black bodies at this time which are notable, not because they are rendered as exotic others, but because they conform physiognomically to the other European bodies represented in Kirchner's paintings and drawings, which was itself an aspect of the complex primitivism at work in the artist's practice (see Chapter 2).

20 BELOW Max Pechstein, *Zwei Frauenakte im Zimmer* (Two Female Nudes in a Room), 1909
21 OPPOSITE Ernst Ludwig Kirchner, *Frauenbildnis* (Portrait of a Woman), 1911

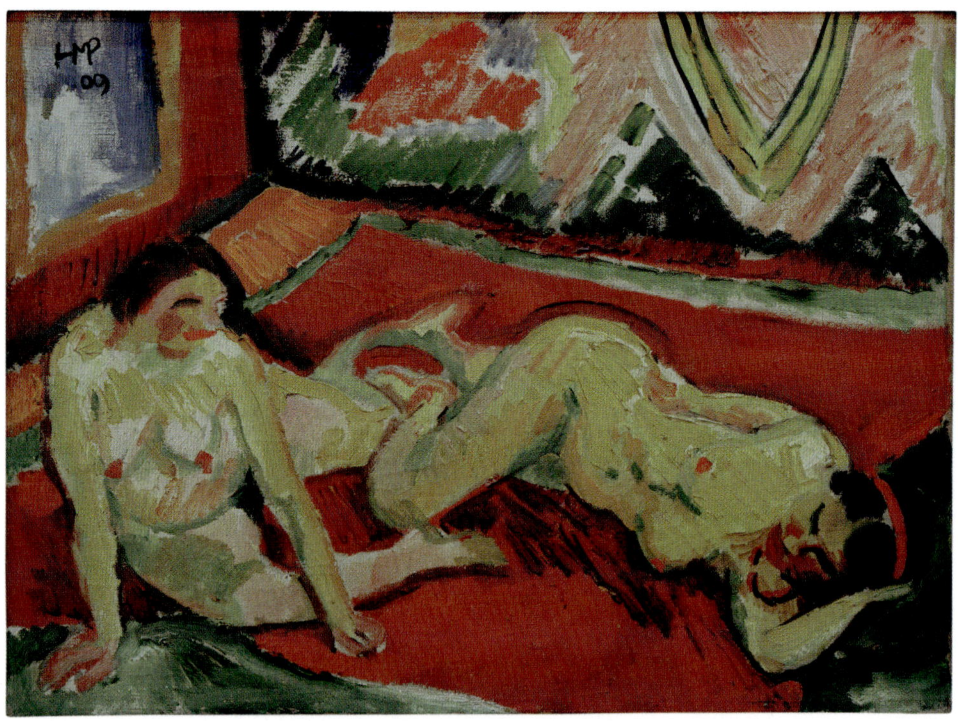

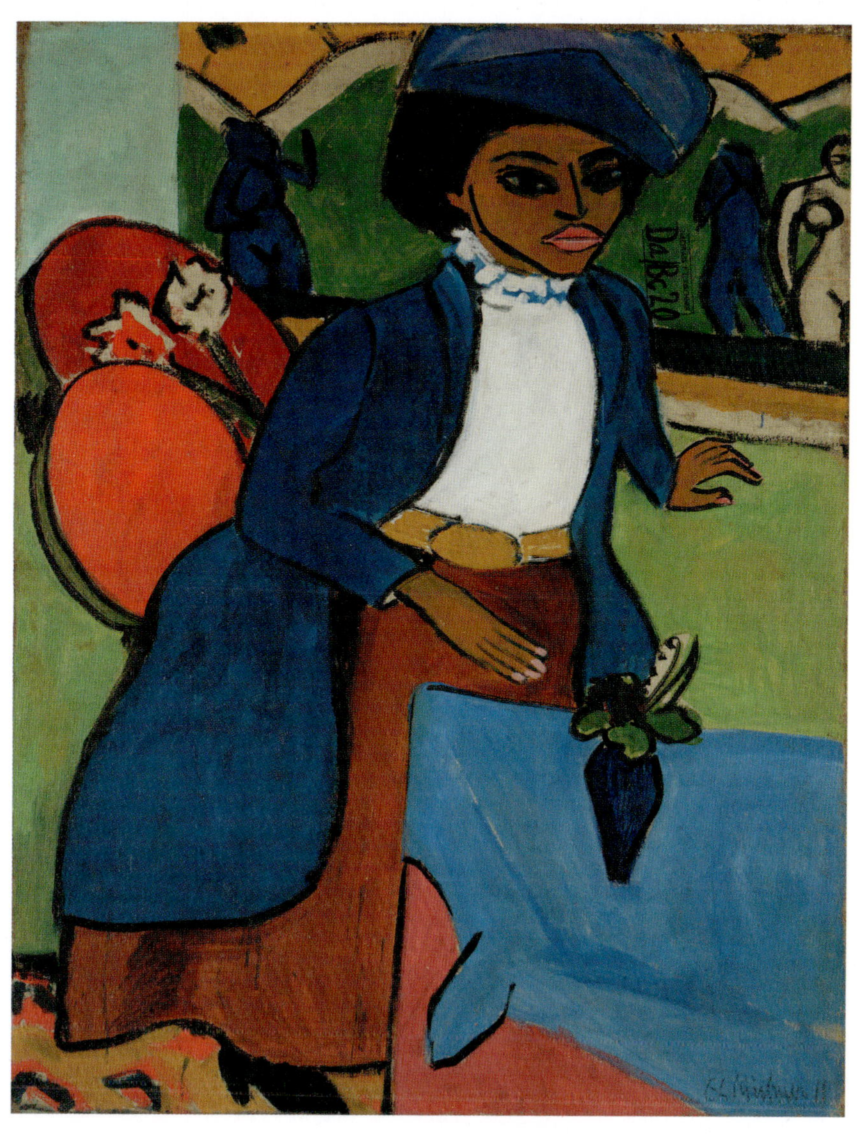

In keeping with their Nietzschean ideals the Brücke artists saw themselves as primary creators rather than merely as artisans. As a result, they took control of all the processes they employed. There is no question of a workshop environment with them, as in traditional studio set-ups of masters and assistants, and neither would they employ specialist printmakers, for example, to produce their graphic work. As a result, there is rarely anything like a convention edition, and sometimes there is only a series of unique prints. The centrality of the person of the artist as a kind of performer of the work became an important general characteristic of Expressionism, as part of the claims for 'uniqueness' and 'authenticity' that would be repeated consistently throughout the rest of the twentieth century. Such qualities came to be seen as important differentiators between fine and decorative, or industrial arts, in an age that saw the growth of mass production and consumer culture.

Similarly, by keeping performance at the heart of art making, the idea that artworks communicate directly (without the need for explanation, or previous learning) the intuitive artistic experience could be preserved. It follows that the adoption of techniques that seemingly preserved or were at least sensitive to the natural qualities of the materials being employed was a key factor in Expressionism. The idea that the stuff that the work was made of might be in some way contribute actively to its meaning deepens the sense of the idea of the artist working directly with the creative forces of nature and, since these processes are residual in the completed art object, suggests the possibility of the 'autonomy' of the artwork.

The application of paint in much Expressionist work is
usually rough, or apparently ham-fisted, from Matisse's *Femme*
8 *au chapeau* (1905) and Vlaminck's *Les Coteaux de Rueil* (1906),
22 to Schmidt-Rottluff's *Gutshof in Dangast* (1910) and Munch's
Dance of Life (1899–1900), which suggests spontaneity in the making process, and reminds viewers that they are looking at paint laid on a flat surface, as well as seeing a representation of something else in the world. When the Expressionists in Germany turned to printmaking the woodcut was most often the medium of choice. This was partly because they saw it as representative of the Gothic tradition, which they regarded as archetypally 'Germanic' – the angular, Gothic 'feel' of Kirchner's *Women on Potsdamer Platz* is no coincidence. Because of the relatively unsophisticated nature of woodblock printing, woodcuts had long since been overtaken by etching and then lithography as the way of producing multiple copies of images. Yet, it was precisely the technical difficulties it presented which attracted the Expressionists.

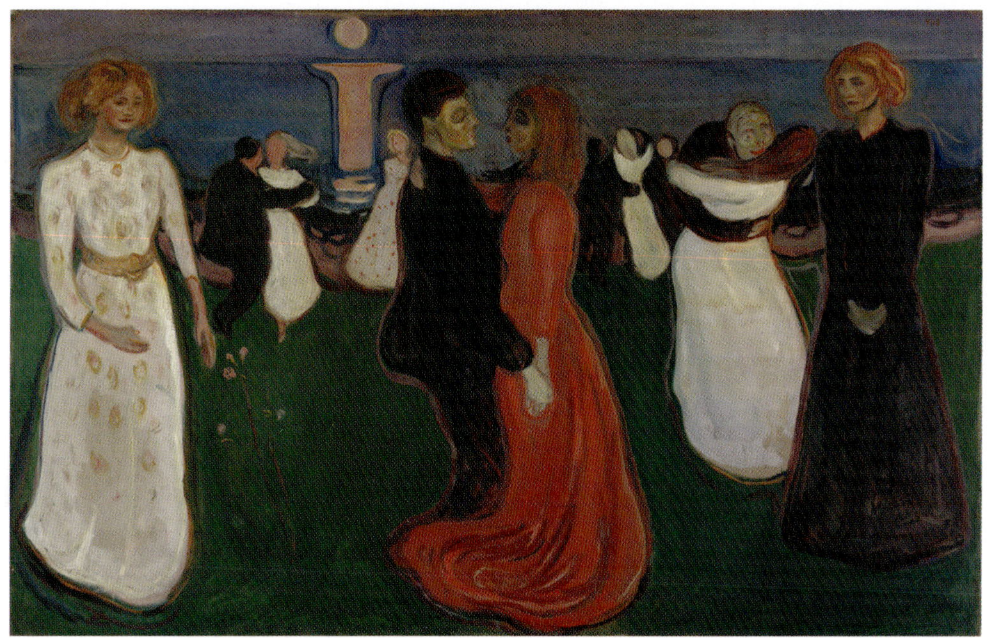

22 Edvard Munch, *Dance of Life*, 1899–1900

The Brücke artists deliberately broke the rules of the master printmaker. They chose woodblocks with uneven surfaces and carved directly into them without any preparatory designs, as
23 in Nolde's *Prophet* (1912), Schmidt-Rottluff's *Mourners on the Beach* (1914), or Heckel's *Liegende* (1909) and *Zwei Frauen* (1910). This meant that the imprints of the pattern of the grain of the block, together with evidence of any splintering and gauging were also transferred onto the sheet of paper. Little care was taken to achieve an even spread of ink on the block and the prints were made as often as not by hand rather than being put through a press. The results were highly individual pieces which laid bare the full physicality of the medium and the process of making.

Sculpture also underwent an Expressionist transformation. Direct carving became the favoured technique. By working straight into the material, without the aid of preliminary maquettes or measurements, sculptors like Constantin Brâncusi (1876–1957), Henri Gaudier-Brzeska (1891–1915), Jacob Epstein (1880–1959), and Henry Moore (1898–1986), for example, were able to respond to the built-in peculiarities of the wood or stone – grain, flaws, and so on – and work with rather than against them. The resulting forms were often distorted.

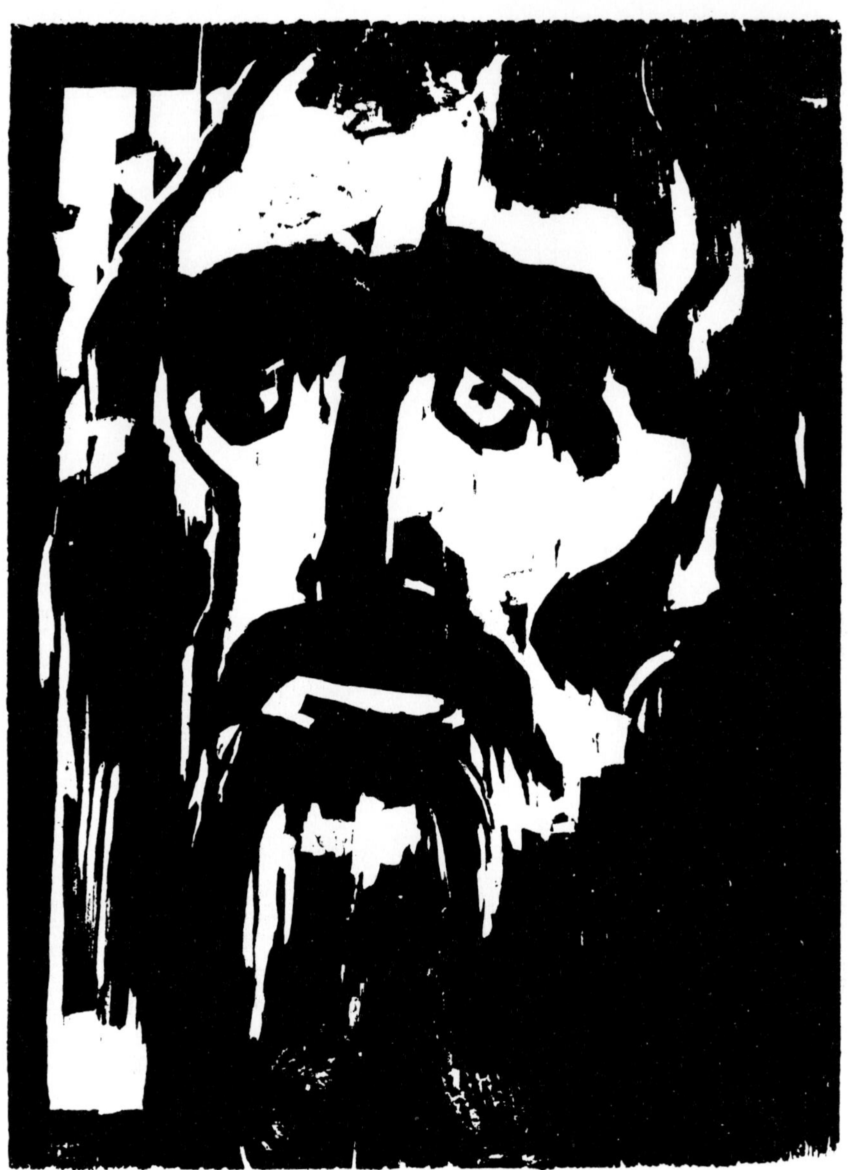

23 Emil Nolde, *Prophet*, 1912

This might result from the particular qualities of the stone – some might suggest, because of the necessity of being true to its 'stoniness', as in Brancusi's *The Kiss* (1907–08) and Epstein's *Maternity* (1910). At other times distortion of the proportions of figures was a direct result of artists following the peculiarities of an oddly shaped piece of wood, as in the case of Kirchner's *Dancer with Necklace* (1910).

The high level of idealism contained in Expressionist ideas about making art is in stark contrast to the arguments and accusations that led to Brücke's break up in 1913. In common with many other individuals and groups in the century, the bohemian lifestyles and outsider rhetoric of the core members, Heckel, Kirchner, Pechstein and Schmidt-Rottluff went hand in hand with a paradoxical desire to establish reputations in the conventional art world and achieve material success. By 1912 Pechstein had begun to attract significant attention, and the German contemporary art world generally attributed leadership of Brücke to him – a mantle which Kirchner jealously guarded. Pechstein's facility and more easily digestible style, as well as no doubt his more agreeable personality, led many in Germany to regard him as the best painter of the young generation and originator of the new Expressionist style; a claim that was intolerable to the indignant Kirchner. It led to the ending of their previously close friendship and Pechstein's expulsion from Brücke that year. Further internal squabbling – mostly about who did what first – led to the rest splitting a year later.

What is most interesting about this split is the fact that, besides issues of straightforward professional jealousy, the arguments were played out in basically Nietzschean terms, which also chime with all the other apologists for modern art: if the Brücke were trailblazers, or 'primitives' of a new art, then the very fact that Pechstein's work was more universally acceptable automatically made it suspect. The 'established older forces' were *not supposed to* understand. That was the point. As Kirchner later said, the artist can either be mainly 'an interpreter of ideas for the general public' or be 'the artist per se, the seeker, advancing into the unknown, possessed and consumed by art, like Heckel, Schmidt-Rottluff, Kirchner.' It made no difference at the time. Pechstein was undoubtedly the most successful of them before the 1930s, but his posthumous reputation has been much less than those of the others, with art historians' explanations echoing Kirchner's position and usually citing Pechstein's 'facility' or 'derivativeness' against the 'difficulty' and 'originality' of the others' work.

The Blue Rider

There were pockets of Expressionist activity in other parts of Germany at the time, including a loosely affiliated group in the Rhineland. Given the name 'Rhenish Expressionism' by August Macke (1887–1914) in 1913 for a group exhibition that year in Bonn, his intention was to establish the area of Western Germany along the axis of cities such as Bonn, Cologne and Düsseldorf as a recognizable centre for the new art alongside Berlin and Munich. Besides Macke, it included painters such as Heinrich Nauen (1880–1940), Marie von Malachowski-Nauen (1880–1943), Heinrich Campendonck (1889–1957), Olga Oppenheimer (1886–1941) and the young Max Ernst (1891–1976), some of whom went on to form the largely Expressionist Junge Rheinland group in 1919 after the initial impetus was cut short by the war and Macke's death on the Western Front. Other artists not affiliated with any of the major Expressionist groups included Hermann Stenner (1891–1914) in Bielefeld, Christian Rohlfs (1849–1938) in Hagen, and Paula Modersohn-Becker (1876–1907), in Worpswede, near Bremen.

The most prominent, and historically most important, Expressionist group in Germany besides Brücke, was a group of mainly Russian and German artists active mostly in Munich, which came to be known as *Der Blaue Reiter* (The Blue Rider). Most notable among them were Wassily Kandinsky, Franz Marc, Gabriele Münter, Marianne Werefkin, Alexei Jawlensky (1864–1941), August Macke, and Heinrich Campendonck. Other artists were involved in the specific Blue Rider project in a more peripheral way, notably Erma Bossi (1875–1952), Elisabeth Ivanowna Epstein (1879–1956), Paul Klee (1879–1940), Lyonel Feininger (1871–1956) and Jean Arp (1886–1966) – although Kandinsky, Klee, Feininger and Jawlensky later formed another group, the Blue Four (1924–1934), initiated largely as a marketing ploy by the German-American painter, dealer and collector Galka Scheyer (1889–1945).

The work of the Blue Rider artists had grown out of much the same sources as Brücke, although in addition to recent European influences such as Jugendstil and Symbolism, where the Dresden group had been especially interested in traditional art from India, Sub-Saharan Africa and Micronesia, the Munich painters turned to Russian and German folk art and children's drawings for added inspiration. From around 1908, Kandinsky and Münter collected Bavarian *Hinterglasmalerei* (behind glass paintings), a technique used traditionally in the region primarily to produce popular Roman Catholic Christian votive imagery. Beginning with Münter, some of the Blue Rider artists experimented with the technique themselves, believing that by doing so they might somehow regain something of the untutored, primitive spirituality they believed to be emblematic of the practice. Sometimes this amounted to no more than free copies of folk art originals, as in Kandinsky's *Santa Francisca* (1911) and Münter's *Votivbild* (Votive Picture, *c.* 1908–09), but mostly the imagery and style reflected Expressionist concerns, as in Macke's *Drei Mädchen in einer Barke* (Three Girls in a Boat, 1912), Münter's *Bayerische Landschaft mit Einödhof* (Bavarian Landscape with Farm, 1910), or Kandinsky's *The Last Judgment* (1912).

From 1908 until 1914 Münter and Kandinsky also amassed a collection of more than two hundred and fifty pieces of art by children, many by Münter's niece Elfriede Schröter and Annemarie Münter. During that time in Munich both artists used motifs from their collection in their own art, in Münter's case sometimes transposing both motif and composition into paintings that nevertheless imposed a painterly Expressionist handling of paint.

Munich had been an important artistic centre since the mid-nineteenth century, and because of its location was attractive as an alternative to Paris for artists travelling from Eastern Europe and Russia. Thus, it was that the Russians Kandinsky, Jawlensky and Werefkin, and the Ukrainian Epstein found themselves in the city. At the turn of the century Munich was the centre of the Jugendstil and between 1908–1910 there were exhibitions of work by Cézanne, Gauguin, Van Gogh and Matisse. It was therefore a fertile ground for contemporary art developments. The work shown by Münich's first Expressionist group, the *Neue Künstlervereinigung München*, or NKVM (New Artists' Society of Munich), initiated by Werefkin, Jawlensky, the painter Adolf Erbslöh (1881–1947) and sound artist Oscar Wittenstein (1880–1918), was redolent of French post-Impressionism, especially Gauguin and the Symbolists. Other members included Alexander Kanoldt (1881–1939), Alfred Kubin (1877–1959), Erma Bossi and Kandinsky (who became its first chairperson). The NKVM credo was distinctly Expressionist, reflecting Matisse's words in 'Notes of a Painter', and prefiguring Kandinsky's subsequent published writings:

We start from the idea that the artist, in addition to the impressions he (sic.) receives from the outer world, nature, continually collects experiences in an inner world; and the search for artistic forms that are intended to express the mutual interpenetration of all these experiences – for forms that must be freed from everything extraneous in order to express strongly only what is necessary – in short, the striving for artistic synthesis, this seems to us to be a slogan that is currently uniting more and more artists spiritually.

The sense of a clear translation of external visual perception and its transformation through the artist's psychological and emotional response is clear in works such as Werefkin's *Wäsherinnen* (Washerwomen, 1909), or Jawlensky's *Woman in a Grey Apron* (*c.* 1909) and *Murnau Landscape* (1909). In
24 *Wäscherinnen*, Werefkin chose a subject that depicts the mundane activities of peasants in the mountains around Munich, an area seen by the NKVM artists as closer to nature – not only because of the lack of urban development, but also because they supposed its population was somehow more connected to the rhythms and processes of the natural cycle of life. This echoed Gauguin and his circle's perception of the putatively primitive in Pont-Aven and Le Pouldu in France. The forms in Werefkin's painting are large and simple, and realized crudely, in a drawing style reminiscent of children's art or European folk carvings. Crucially, her colour is saturated and intense, significantly accentuating that of ordinary visual

24 Marianne Werefkin, *Wäscherinnen* (Washerwomen), c. 1909

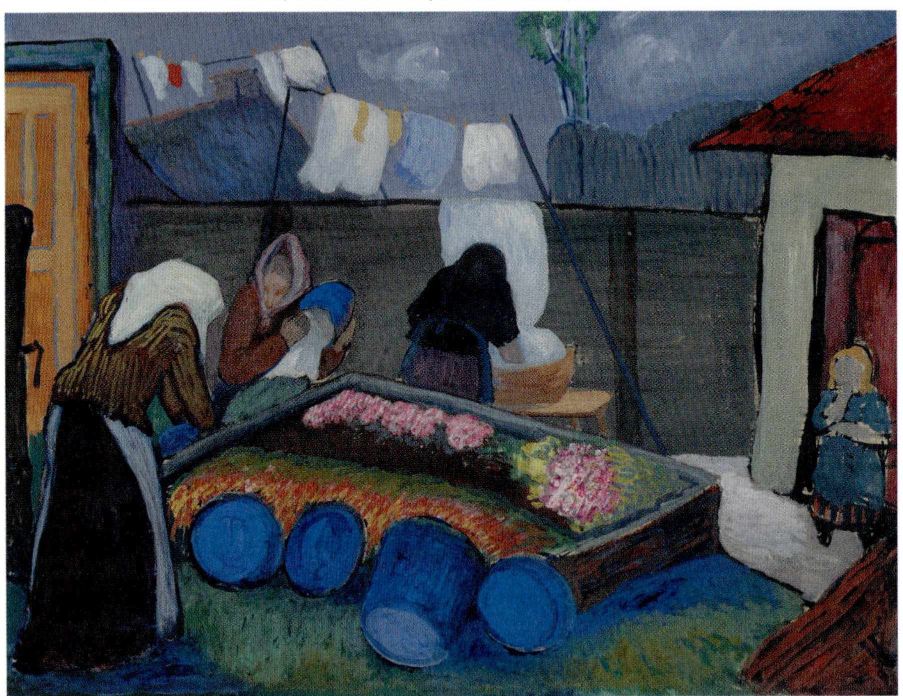

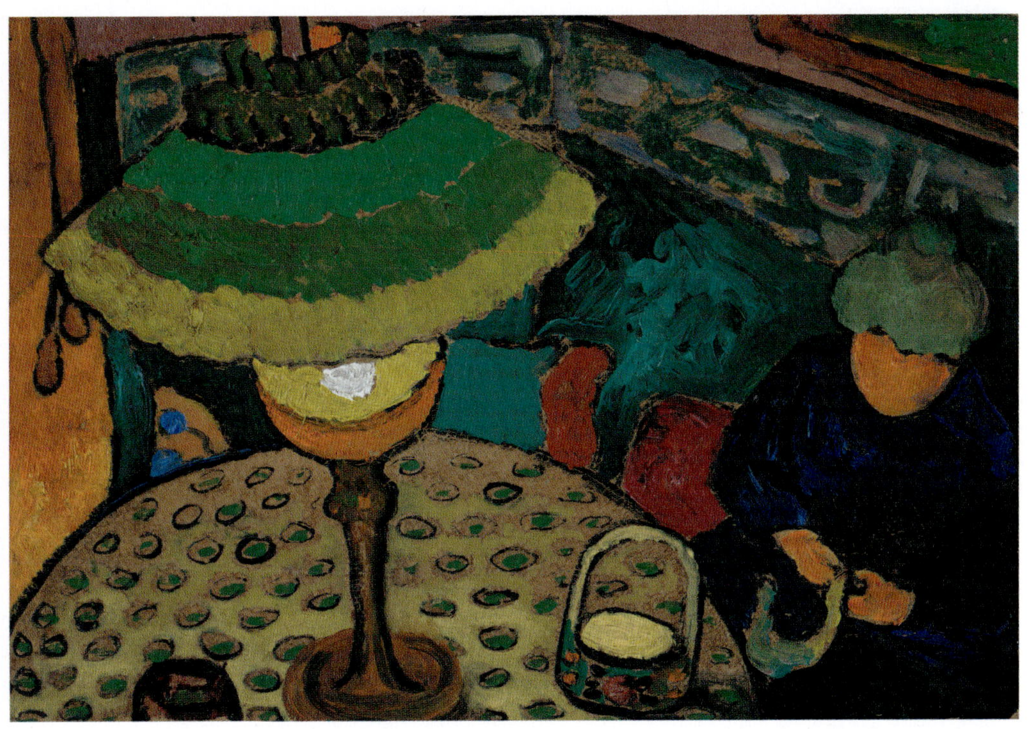

25 Erma Bossi, *Interior with Lamp*, 1909

perception, and differentiating the work emphatically from
the drab colour of contemporary German realist painting.
25 Similarly, Erma Bossi's *Interior with Lamp* also utilizes a
heightened, saturated colour palette. The composition is
dynamic and angular, with the perspective tipped on end,
giving the sense of an extremely shallow and claustrophobic
picture space. The use of these techniques raises the rather
ordinary domestic subject matter into something intense
and visually exciting.

The Blue Rider Almanac

Kandinsky resigned from the NKVM in 1911 to pursue a new, radical project. If the general sense of the NKVM was of a Parisian-inspired, figurative Expressionism, what was to follow would see both a deepening of idealist and metaphysical responses to the world and a move towards abstraction in painting. Kandinsky and Marc began to work on exhibitions and the publication of a book intended to showcase the most radical of the new art, and to signal the philosophical, social

and aesthetic contexts of its production and, perhaps most importantly, the desired direction of its travel. Though never a self-conscious group, the artists most closely associated with the project are usually referred to as *Der Blaue Reiter* (Blue Rider). The name comes from a 1912 book edited by Marc and Kandinsky, *The Blue Rider Almanac*, and two associated exhibitions curated by them in 1911 and 1912, the first of which later travelled successfully all over Germany, and besides Kandinsky and Marc, included artists such as Klee, Kubin,
26 Picasso, Heckel and the Russian artist Natalia Goncharova (1881–1962), whose work at that time was also heavily indebted to folk art, as well as being decidedly avant-garde.

The *Almanac* was unashamedly cosmopolitan in outlook and conceived as a melting pot for the new art. Its guiding idea was the demonstration of a new 'spiritual' quality in art, after an era of materialism and rationalism, emblematized in art that was based primarily in optical reproduction, such as Impressionism, and narrative figuration, such as Realism. Along with Kandinsky's book, *Concerning the Spiritual in Art* (1911), the Almanac served as a signal for the emergence of abstraction or non-figuration as a major issue and presence in modern art, and it is no coincidence that both books were produced by the same publisher as Worringer's *Abstraction and Empathy*. The essays in the Almanac were not written by critics, but artists, and the text was supported by a large body of high-quality photographic reproductions of art. The work of contemporary artists, such as Matisse, Picasso, Robert Delaunay (1885–1941), Goncharova, Mikhail Larionov (1881–1964), Kirchner, Heckel and, of course, Kandinsky, Marc and Münter, was juxtaposed with examples of putatively 'savage' and oriental art, medieval sculpture, Russian folk prints, Bavarian behind-glass paintings, and children's drawings. By using a comparative method borrowed from the Swiss art historian Heinrich Wölfflin (1864–1945), they hoped to reveal what Marc described as modern art's 'subtle connections with Gothic and primitive art, with Africa and the vast Orient, with the highly expressive, spontaneous folk and children's art,' based on the kinds of psychological affinities claimed in the writings of Bell, Fry and Worringer. Readers were invited to test the awkwardness of Heinrich Campendonck's *Jumping Horse* (1911) against a nineteenth-century Bavarian folk mirror painting; a Cubist still life by Picasso is placed without irony beside two drawings by children; and the modern master Henri Rousseau (1844–1910) and the recently rediscovered Baroque painter El Greco (1541–1614) are treated as companions on the same spiritual journey.

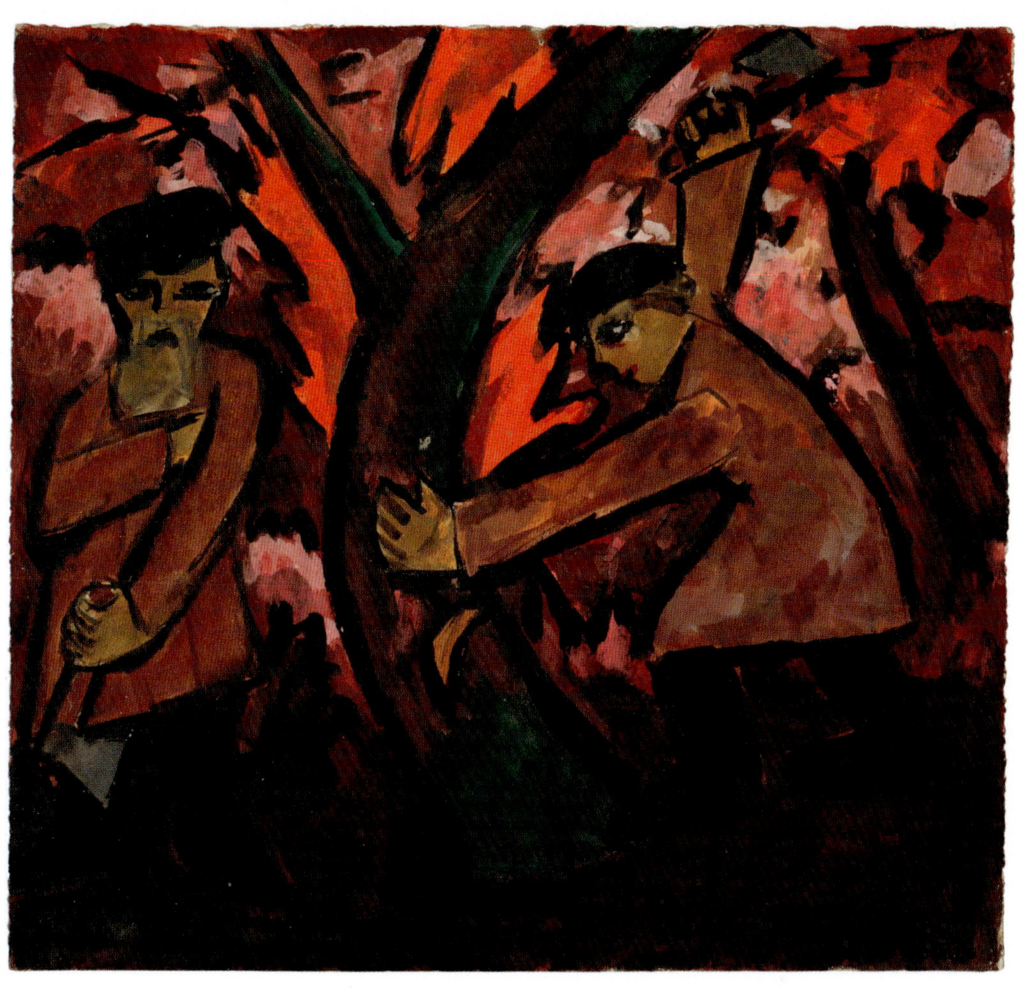

26 Natalia Goncharova, *Bûcherons* (Lumberjacks), 1911

Once again, the sense that the young century could effect a tabula rasa and bring with it a new and more spiritually enlightened age was very strong. Marc wrote at one point, 'We must be brave and turn our backs upon everything that until now good Europeans like ourselves have thought precious and indispensable. Our ideas and ideals must be clothed in hair shirts, they must be fed on locusts and wild honey, not on history, if we are ever to escape from the exhaustion of our European bad taste.' In a move that reflected an increasing interest among white Europeans in the indigenous peoples of the lands they colonized – viewing them in racist social evolutionary terms as wild and unsocialized, and therefore at the 'beginnings' of culture – the *Blue Rider* referred to the pioneers of the new art as 'savages'.

Germany was late to the colonial-imperialist enterprise. Parts of Sub-Saharan Africa and Micronesia were relatively recent subjects of invasion and subjugation by Germany, and rendered visible there via popular media and displays of actual people in zoos and colonial exhibitions. The difference between artists such as Marc and Macke and the general culture was the distinctly positive spin they placed on such essentialist descriptions, claiming at least an aspirational kinship with the 'exotic' other. In a consciously contrarian act, they identified with the 'savages' depicted in the immensely popular adventure stories of authors like the American James Fenimore Cooper (1789–1851) and the German Karl May (1842–1912), and early movies set in the American 'Wild West' and Africa. Although images of particular groups of indigenous peoples are largely absent in Blue Rider art, Native American people are imaginatively depicted in Macke's *Indians on Horseback* (1911), although he places them in a nostalgic setting that looks suspiciously like Munich's pastoral hinterland. Marc emphasized the Blue Rider position by using the same kind of overblown language employed by Nietzsche, describing contemporary artists' battle 'against the old, established power,' which, though 'unequal' would be decided not by physical power or force of numbers, but 'by the power of ideas.'

Art and Abstraction

Kandinsky argued for abstraction in principle before his own work became non-objective. He was a formalist in the sense that he believed that meaning lay in the expressive potential of forms and colours rather than any representational content. But there is also an important mystical side to his ideas. He didn't talk about 'significant form' but about the 'spiritual content' of artworks. He talked about the 'inner life of forms', and the possibility of the artist's connection with physical objects at a cosmic level, through the undifferentiated, primal part of consciousness (the 'spirit'). The secret, he said, was for artists to be 'natural', or in other words, free, uninhibited and open in their vision. In this way they might discover what he called, echoing the language of Theosophy, the 'inner sound' of things, and then create form out of 'inner necessity'. In line with much Expressionist thought, he saw works of art as organic creations, with 'life and being'. And if the artist's job was to breathe life into inert materials, form – drawing, the use of colour – could only be judged on its capability of bringing out 'corresponding vibrations in the soul' of the viewer, and not on its resemblance to other physical objects.

In *Concerning the Spiritual in Art*, Kandinsky extended to fine art, the German philosopher Arthur Schopenhauer's (1788–1860) belief that only music is representative of the drives and impulses – the Will – that characterizes the essence of the world, as opposed to the mediated representation of things. Where Schopenhauer regarded art as fundamentally content-laden and representational, Kandinsky used similar arguments to make a claim for abstract or 'non-material' painting, which, he said, devotes itself 'not to the reproduction of natural phenomena, but rather to the expression of the artist's soul in musical sound.' Of colour he said, 'Generally speaking, colour is a power which directly influences the soul. Colour is the keyboard, the eyes are the hammers, the soul is the piano with many strings. The artist is the hand which plays, touching one key or another, to cause vibrations in the soul.' He attempted to make art as though composing music, suggesting different types of pictures allied to, and using the same descriptive language as, symphonic composition: 'Impressions', which are 'a direct impression of outward nature', as in *Impression III (Concert)* (1911); 'Improvisations', which are 'a largely unconscious, spontaneous expression of inner character',
27 as in *Improvisation 26 (Rudern)* (1911); and 'Compositions', which are 'an expression of a slowly formed inner feeling, which come to utterance only after long maturing', as in
28 *Composition VII* (1913), which even exists as preparatory drafts – see *Draft 2 for Composition VII* (1913). Continuing the musical metaphor, a 1914 painting was titled *Fugue*.

Kandinsky wrote widely on art throughout his career, but rarely about the meanings of individual pictures or his working methods. In 1913, however, at the height of an astonishingly rich period of creativity, he described how three key abstract paintings came about, including the large composition,

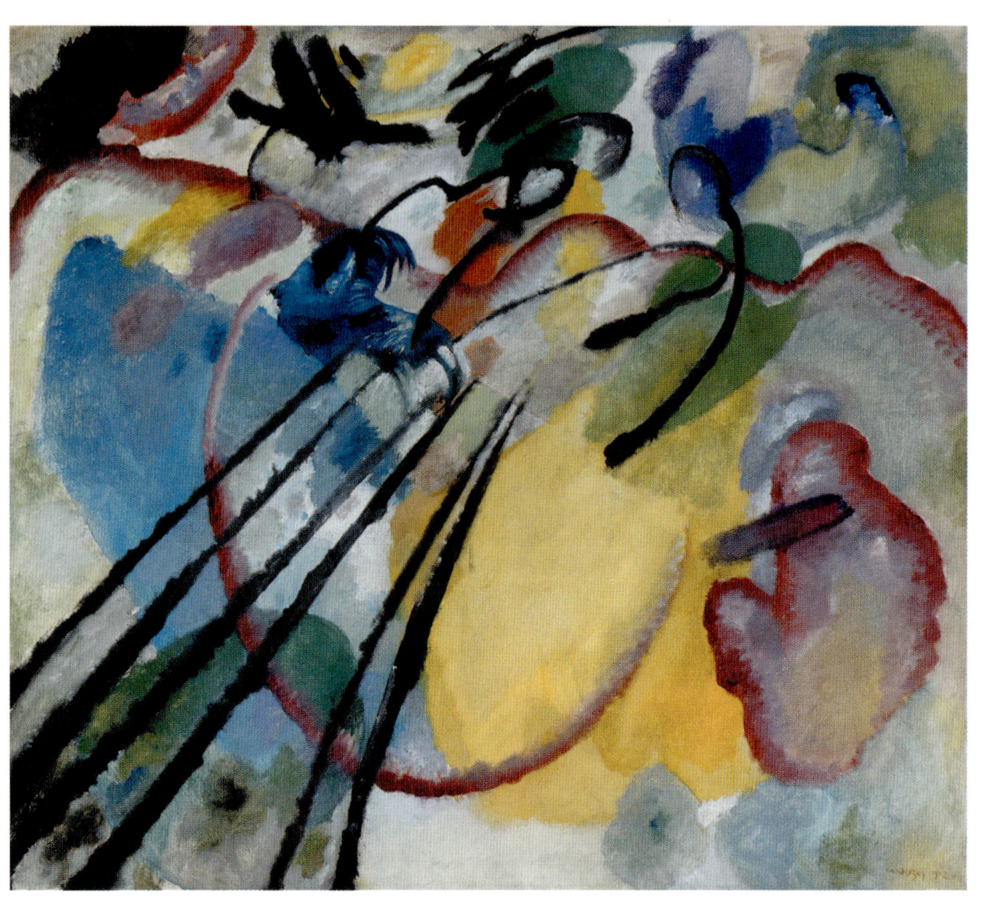

27 ABOVE Wassily Kandinsky, *Improvisation 26 (Rudern)*, 1911
28 OPPOSITE Wassily Kandinsky, *Fragment 2 for Composition VII*, 1913

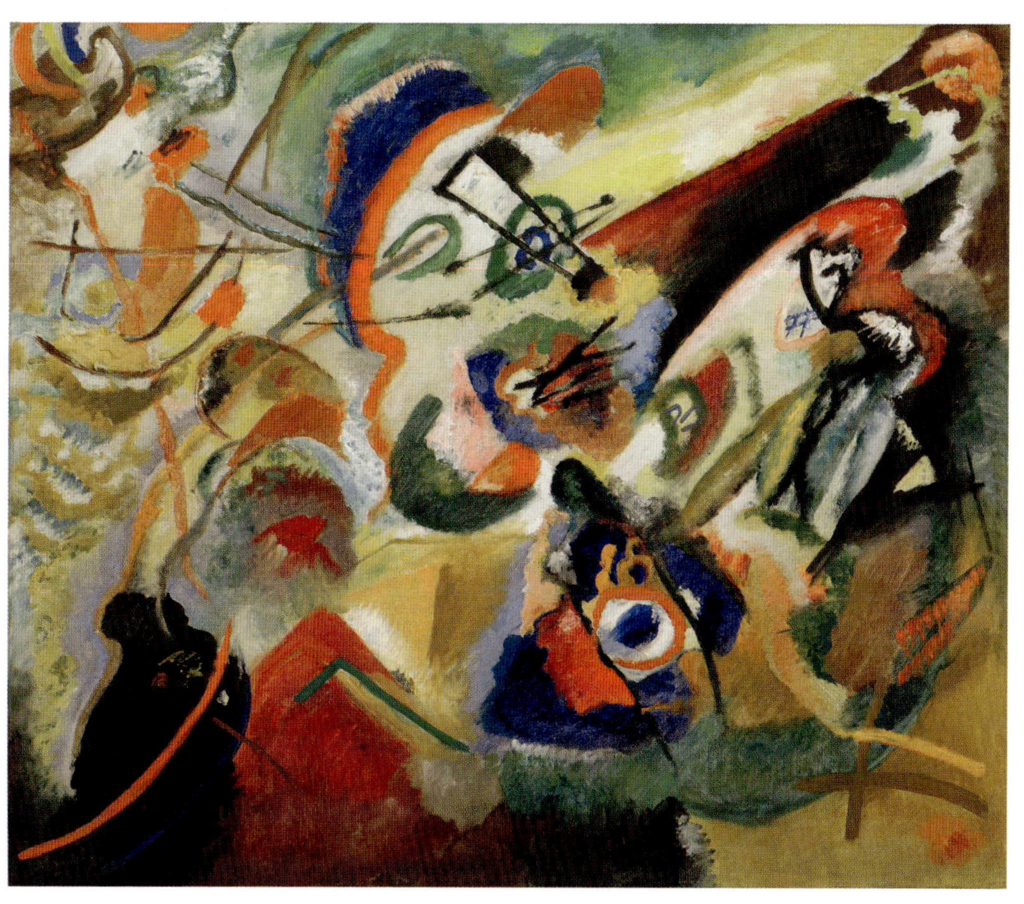

Painting with a White Border. It was characteristically long in the making, needing a large number of preparatory sketches and drawings – a long way, then, from the direct, spontaneous Expressionism of the Parisian Expressionists or Brücke. A lot of the picture, he said, was resolved early on, but 'I made slow progress with the white edge. My sketches did little to help, that is, the individual forms became clear within me – and yet I could still not bring myself to paint the picture. It tormented me. After several weeks, I would bring out the sketches again, and still I felt unprepared.' After living with the problem for five months he intuitively recognized that what he had been missing was that the picture demanded a white border: 'I treated this white border in the same capricious way it had treated me: in the lower left a chasm out of which rises a white wave that slowly subsides, only to flow around the right-hand side of the picture in lazy coils...' Not surprisingly the artist didn't discuss the content of the picture – it is up to the 'sensitive' viewer to discover meaning. He also failed to describe the picture's figurative elements. Yet, almost without exception, Kandinsky's abstract paintings contain veiled representations of objects, which act as a kind of formal armature; in this case, these include a rider with lance in the centre, a many-headed dragon on the left, and the Bavarian mountains ranged across the top third of the picture. Such elements are much clearer in slightly earlier work, like *Bowman* (1909), but remarkably they are also still present in highly schematized form in much later, apparently totally non-objective pieces, as with the rider with lance in *Intimate Communication (Oval no.1)* (1925), who is now reduced to only a circle, horizontal line and icicle-like triangle.

By 1919, the sculptor Oswald Herzog (1881–1939), writing in *Der Sturm*, proclaimed that 'Abstract Expressionism is Expressionism perfected. It is the purest form of creation. It gives bodily form to spiritual objects.' And in words that echo Kandinsky's evocation of Schopenhauer, 'Abstract Expressionism is giving form to events – life in itself.... The artist's intuition takes no account of objects. Life demands only creation. He (*sic.*) conjures up forms which are and must be vehicles of his experience. Nothing is random, everything is will, will is art.' Of the other core Blue Rider artists, only Marc, Klee and Jawlensky came consistently close to abstraction, although Münter produced some remarkable abstract studies,
29 including *Studie mit weißen Flecken Program* (Study with White Spots) (1912). Along with Bossi and Werefkin, though, she maintained a figurative Expressionism, while Macke (who died young on active service in France in 1914) used restrained Cubist

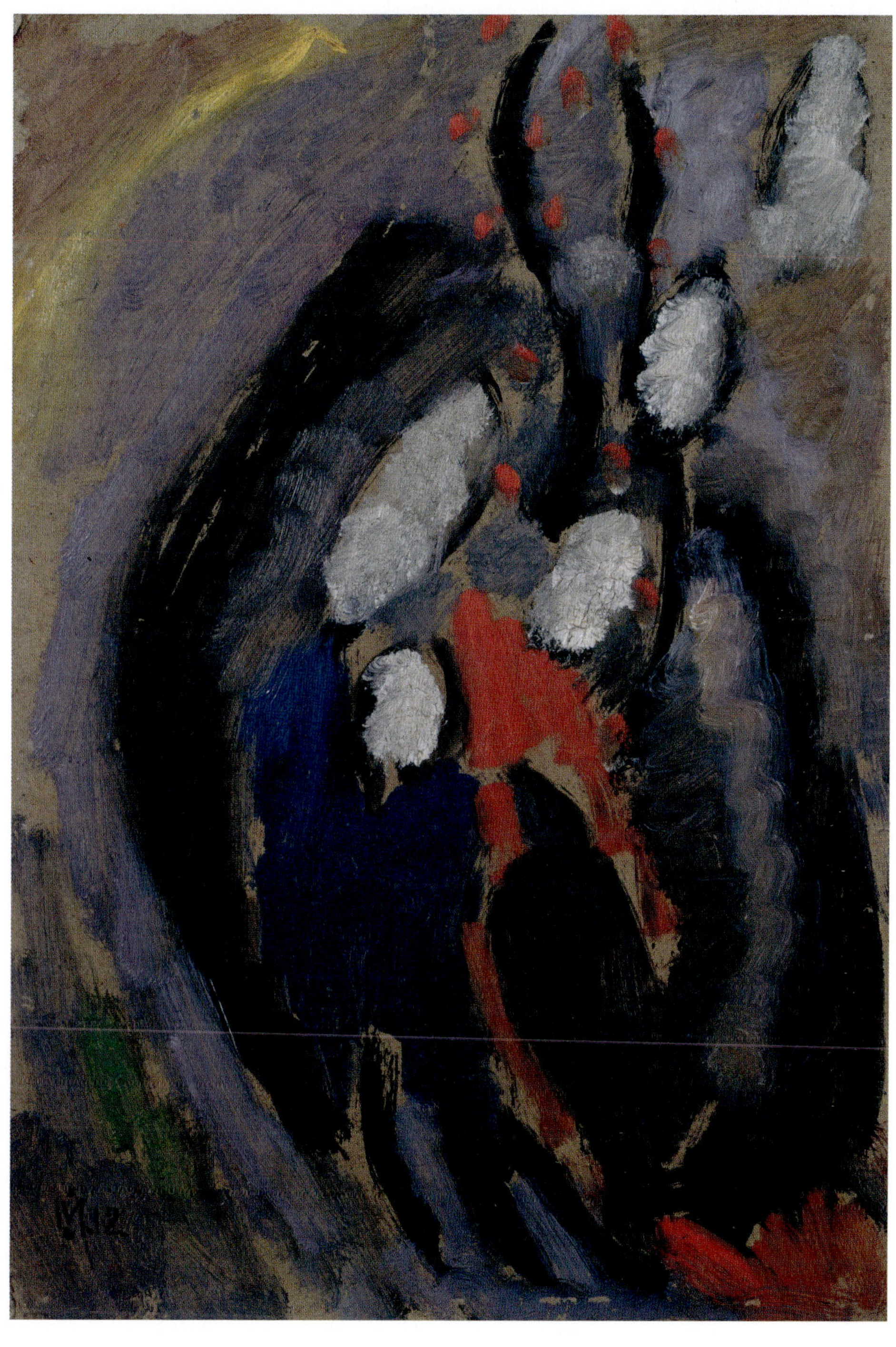

29 Gabriele Münter, *Studie mit weißen Flecken Program* (Study with White Spots), 1912

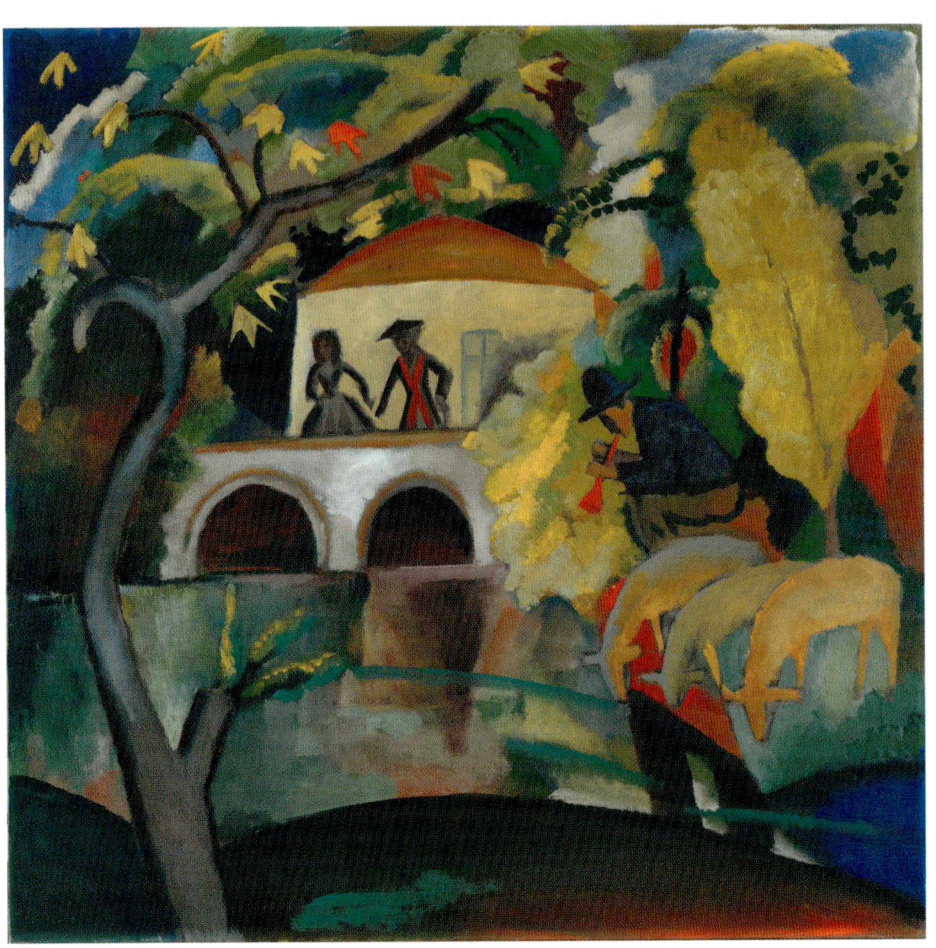

30 ABOVE August Macke, *Rokoko*, 1912
31 OPPOSITE Franz Marc, *Kühe, rot, grün, gelb* (Cows, Red, Green, Yellow), 1911

faceting to produce lyrical versions of traditional bourgeois
30 subjects, such as *Rokoko* (1912) and *Promenade à trois* (1914).

Like Kandinsky, Marc's path to near-abstraction came from a mystical angle; in his case the search for a means of translating into art a purer and more profound perception of the world. Believing that even the vision of children, or the idealized 'noble savage' was already clouded by materialism, he turned away from the human 'spirit' and instead attempted to see the world through the eyes of animals. As early as 1908 he had talked about the possibility of an 'animalization' of art and wrote, 'I am trying to enhance my sensitiveness for the organic rhythm that I feel in all things, and I am trying to feel pantheistically the rapture of the flow of "blood" in nature, in the trees, in the animals, in
31 the air.' *Kühe, rot, grün, gelb* (Cows, Red, Green, Yellow) (1911) is a vision of creatures moving with easy dignity and in complete harmony not only with nature, but also the cosmos.

Yet it is a paradox of this extreme emotional rejection of the human spirit that the means he used to create his visions of the cosmos in its pristine clarity were reliant not only on his interest in folk art, but more so in the most fashionable

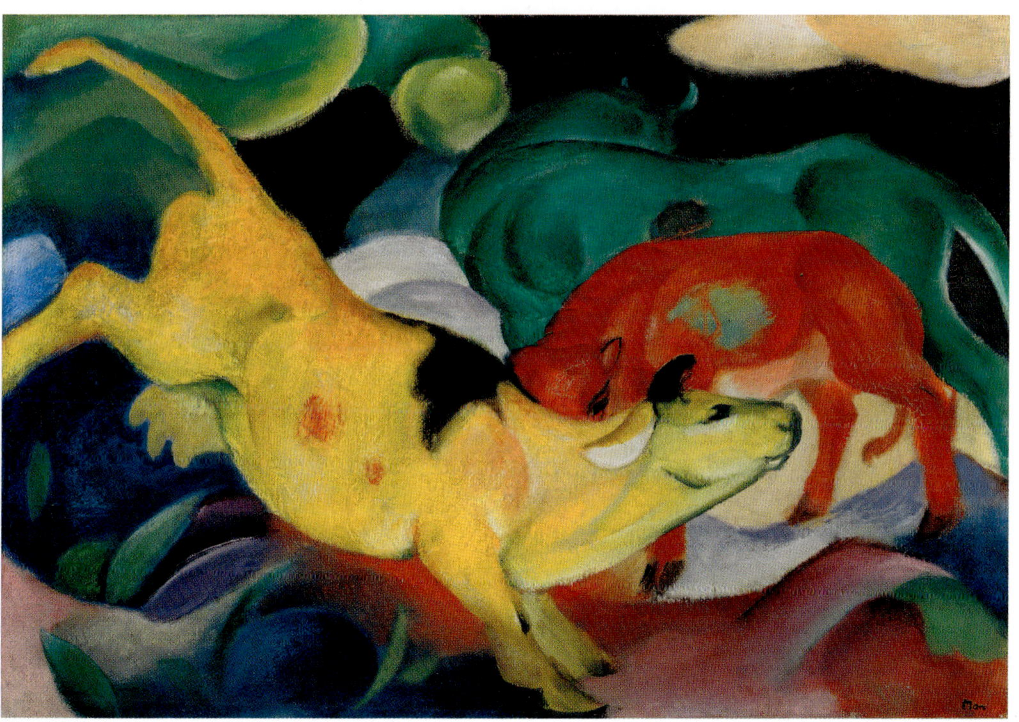

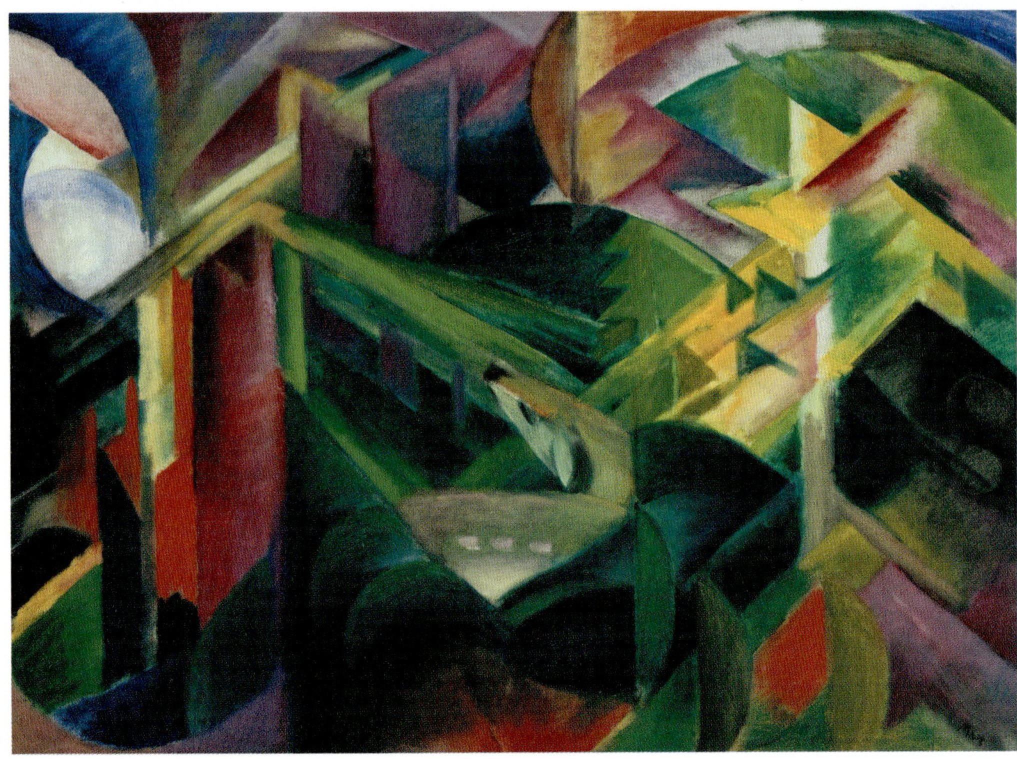

32 Franz Marc, *Reh im Klostergarten* (Deer in a Monastery Garden), 1912

modernist styles available to him, including Cubism and
32 Futurism. The creature in *Deer in a Monastery Garden* (1912), for example, is rendered in the same cubo-Futurist forms as the rest of the image. The picture space is extremely shallow, suggesting that all the elements are in something like the same order of existence, and the dynamic x-shaped composition points to tangible, organic Earth on the right of the canvas, and the infinity of the universe on the left. It is a model of a highly sophisticated attempt to render profound simplicity; making something of a synthesis in that monastery garden of the contrasting perspectives of innocence and experience described in William Blake's poem, *The Garden of Love* (1794).

Expressionist Synthesis of the Arts

The *Blue Rider Almanac* doesn't simply cover visual art; music and theatre also figure strongly. It contains an essay, for example, by the inventor of atonal music and friend of

Kandinsky, the Austrian composer, Arnold Schönberg (1874–1951) – his self-taught, visionary self-portraits are also illustrated. Another essay, by the Russian musicologist, critic and composer Leonid Sabaneyev (1881–1968) addresses *Prometheus: the Poem of Fire* (1910), by his countryman Alexander Scriabin (1872–1915). This tone poem is redolent with many of the mystical and Symbolist ideas embraced by Kandinsky. The Ukrainian composer Thomas de Hartmann (1884–1956) contributed an essay, 'On Anarchy in Music', and Kandinsky himself wrote a text, 'On Stage Composition' and the script for a piece of stage art in which he attempted a 'synthesis' of the arts, titled 'The Yellow Sound'. This picks up the nineteenth-century romantic theme of producing a *Gesamtkunstwerk* (Total Work of Art), in which all the senses might be used in experiencing a single piece. Kandinsky argued consistently that the various arts are only different 'externally', that is in their material form, whilst 'in their innermost core' they are identical. It follows, he said, that if artists 'must watch only the trend of the inner need', then they must be given absolute freedom in their choice of materials. This does not necessarily refer only to the traditional range of materials available to visual artists, which is an important point, since it brings to light a rupture that was beginning to appear at the turn of the century in the definitions of the shape that visual art could legitimately take.

By 1900 the boundaries defining the individual arts – fine and decorative art, music, theatre, and so on – and within each, the specificity of media proper to those arts, were set. Visual artists were supposed to be specialists – painters, sculptors, printmakers, illustrators. Kandinsky was among those who were now seriously questioning the legitimacy and durability of those borders. This peculiarly twentieth-century attitude was made possible as much as anything by the great emphasis that modernists were giving to individual expression over any questions of method and technique in the making and judging of art. If the expressive effect was foremost, then the need to master a particular medium – to follow technical rules – would, it was argued, actually get in the way of clear and direct communication. Freed of the need for long technical apprenticeships, the way began to open for artists to choose a medium each time they began a new work according only to its fitness for the specific expressive purpose. One of the negative aspects of this view of creativity were the accusations of artistic ineptitude and shoddy workmanship consistently levelled at modern art by its enemies.

In the first couple of decades of the century the possibilities open to visual artists who wanted to explore their ideas outside traditional media boundaries were limited. Kandinsky's 'Yellow Sound' was experimental, but nevertheless took the form of theatre. The same is true of other Expressionist artists, such as Ernst Barlach (1870–1938), who is known primarily as a sculptor, but was also a writer and dramatist, and Oskar Kokoschka, whose plays *Murderer, Hope of Women* and *Sphinx and Strawman*, both from 1907, caused outrage among contemporary audiences because they broke the rules of structure, realism and taste in theatre. Art events became popular in which performance, poetry reading and talks would be collaged together into an experience that was not quite variety, not quite theatre, and not particularly logically structured. These would reach their first important flowering as unique manifestations in 1916 with the first 'Dada' soirées in Zurich, Switzerland. It is worth recalling, though, that many of the participants had been active in Expressionist circles in Munich and Berlin before the war, and one of Dada's driving forces, the poet Hugo Ball (1886–1927) had worked closely with Kandinsky in the theatre. Zurich Dada was really an extension of pre-war Expressionism in Germany and Eastern Europe, including a young Romanian Expressionist, Marcel Janco (1895–1984). It was only after the war, most notably in its Parisian form, that Dada began to take on the theoretical imprimatur that would develop into Surrealism, which in its 'pure' state was distinctly un-Expressionist.

Kandinsky and Kokoschka continued to use the medium of oil paint primarily throughout their careers, and Barlach was always a sculptor. Because there was no actual *rejection* of painting, sculpture, and printmaking at this moment in time – only a recognition of wider possibilities – the multiplication of visual art media is often regarded as something that belongs to later in the century. But its beginnings are there, at the century's dawn. The other thing to bear in mind is that in the early years of the twentieth century the means of recording events photomechanically were primitive. There are no films or videos of Kokoschka's plays or Expressionist events, and only a couple of grainy, black and white photographs survive that even suggest the spontaneous performances that took place in the Brücke studios, often with all concerned naked. So, time-based aspects of an artist's practice were at that point inevitably part of the ephemera of their careers, often passing unheard of and unknown among the audiences for their other work.

The Second Generation in Germany

By the end of the First World War, Expressionism in Germany had come to be regarded as not only the dominant tendency in the new art in that country, but also as the official form of German Modernism. This had been achieved through the use of generally nationalist and racial-mythologizing rhetoric by its most prominent early chroniclers. In *Expressionismus*, Paul Fechter emphasized the emotionalist aspects of the movement and what he saw as its specifically German character, embodied in a continuation of the Gothic tradition. His approach, though heavily indebted in many respects to Blue Rider anti-materialist and spiritual claims, unintentionally served to allow the demonization of one of the key figures in his book, the Russian Kandinsky, as an unwelcome 'foreign', and therefore 'un-German' influence. It also paved the way, especially in light of Marc's untimely death at Verdun in 1916, for Pechstein's, and thereby figurative Expressionism's, ascendancy. This was explicitly confirmed in books such as Eckart von Sydow's *Die deutsche expressionistische Kultur und Malerei* (German Expressionist Culture and Painting, 1919), which also claimed that in Expressionism, 'the German spirit again has connection to the soul of the world, as it was during the Middle Ages.'

Such institutionalization flew in the face of the bohemian stances of Expressionism's first wave, and the irony was not lost on Kirchner, for example, who by that time was in Switzerland recovering from the effects of a severe mental health crisis precipitated by the war. Nevertheless, a new generation of self-proclaimed Expressionists arose in Germany, with Pechstein as elder statesman and active participant in the 'movement', and periodicals like *Der Sturm* and *Die Aktion* as their mouthpieces. Expressionist groups sprang up across the country, notably in Darmstadt, Dresden, Düsseldorf, Hamburg, Kiel, Magdeburg, and of course, Berlin.

Many Expressionists volunteered for military service at the war's outset, believing that it might be the apocalyptic event that would clear the tables of the old culture and usher in a new anti-materialist, spiritual age. The reality was rather different. Many were killed, including Macke, Marc, and Stenner, and others suffered significant trauma, which subsequently fed into their art, such as Otto Dix (1891–1969), George Grosz (1893–1959), and Max Beckmann (1884–1950). Both Dix and Grosz employed aggressive Expressionist styles as young artists during the war, as in Dix's brutalist *Self-Portrait as a Soldier* (1914) and *Dying Warrior* (1915), or Grosz's *The Street* (1915) and *The Lovesick* (1914). The sense of a world that has become insane is strong in all these works, not only in the trenches but also in the experience of the city itself. Grosz consistently depicts humanity in its worst guises, reducing ordinary people to fully pathologized, primitive

types, lacking culture or morals. This reaches a kind of climax
33 in the painting *The Funeral (Dedicated to Oskar Panizza)* (1918), which is as much a contemporary update of Breughel and Bosch as it is Futurist-Expressionism. Oskar Panizza (1853–1921) was a German psychiatrist and writer, who spent the last sixteen years of his life in an asylum because of deteriorating mental health caused by the repressive censorship imposed on him during the reign of Wilhelm II. Grosz's painting is a visual manifestation not of Panizza's presumed state of mind, but of the contemporary collective consciousness of the world. As he said of the work: 'In a sinister street at night a hellish procession of dehumanized figures rolls on, faces, representing Alcohol, Syphilis, Pestilence. One figure blows the trumpet, and one shouts "hurrah!" parrot fashion. Over this crowd rides Death on a black coffin – direct as a symbol, the boneman....Against Mankind gone mad, I painted this protest.'

In the period at the end of the war, many of the new artist groups were politically activist in nature, with members espousing left-wing and Marxist positions, as with the Berlin *Arbeitsrat für Kunst* (Workers' Council for Art) and the *Novembergruppe* (November Group), named for the German November Revolution (1918–19), which saw the fall of the Wilhelmine Empire and establishment of the Weimar Republic. If pre-war Expressionism in Germany had been marked by a certain imperiousness in relation to the publics for art, the new generation claimed a universal inclusiveness. The first publication of the *Arbeitsrat für Kunst* declared that, 'Art and the people must form a unity. The arts shall no longer be the enjoyment of the few but the happiness and life of the masses.'

The art of the second generation was primarily figurative, perhaps because it was mostly content-laden and desired to convey it messages clearly and unambiguously, including artists such as Conrad Felixmüller (1897–1977), Hans Siebert von Heister (1888–1967), Walter Jacob (1893–1964), and Georg Tappert (1880–1957). There was also a tendency to depict the demimonde of Germany's rapidly industrializing cities, including works
34 like *Boîte de nuit* (Nightclub) by a new generation of independent women like Lou Albert-Lasard (1885–1969). Nevertheless, abstractionists did exist, characteristically incorporating Cubist and Futurist elements into their styles, including the Germans Max Dungert (1896–1945), Otto Möller (1883–1964), Johannes Molzahn (1892–1965) and Karl Völker (1889–1962), and the Romanian Arthur Segal (1875–1944).

Since artistic political activism carried with it a need for mass communication and democratic means, it is no surprise that print culture was an important aspect of second-

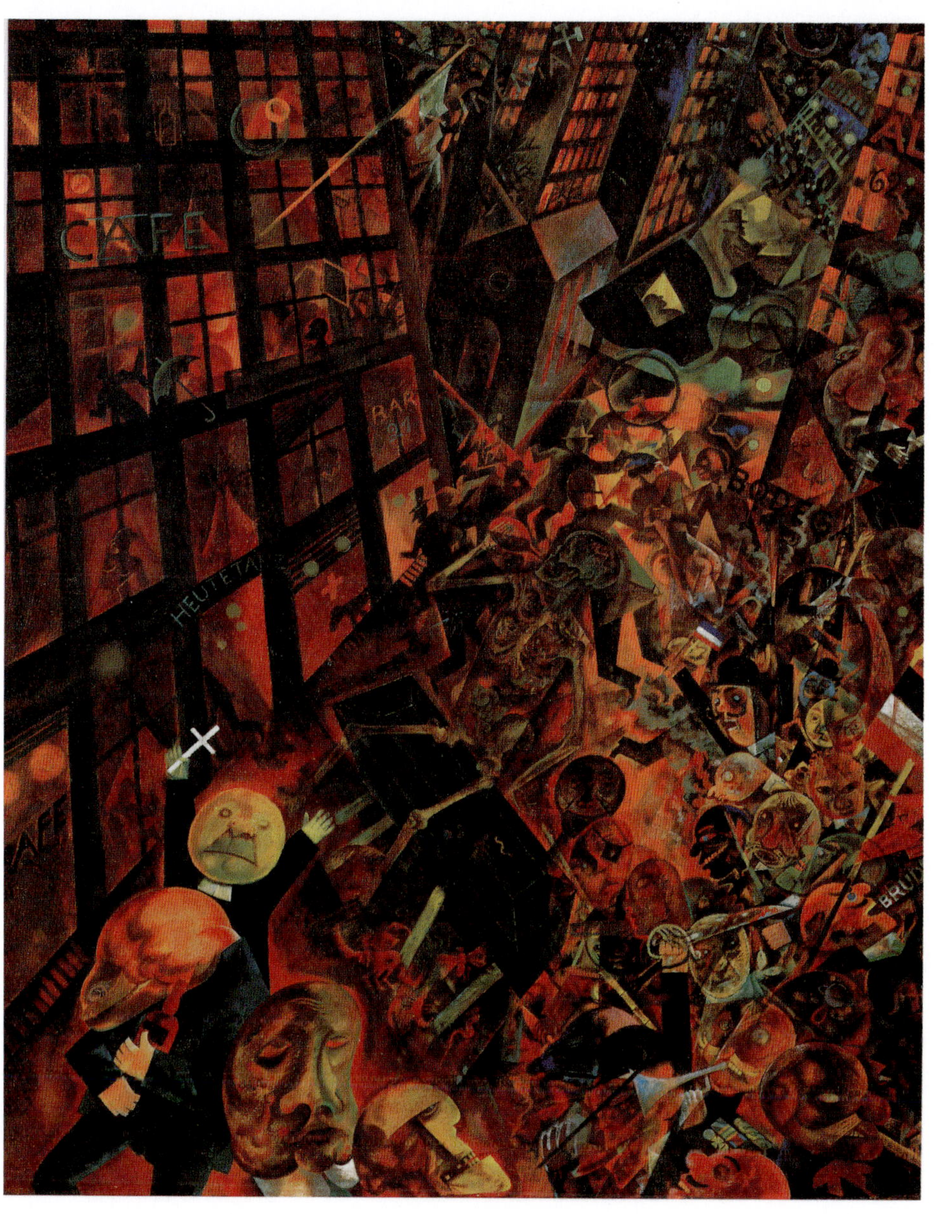

33 George Grosz, *The Funeral (Dedicated to Oskar Panizza)*, 1918

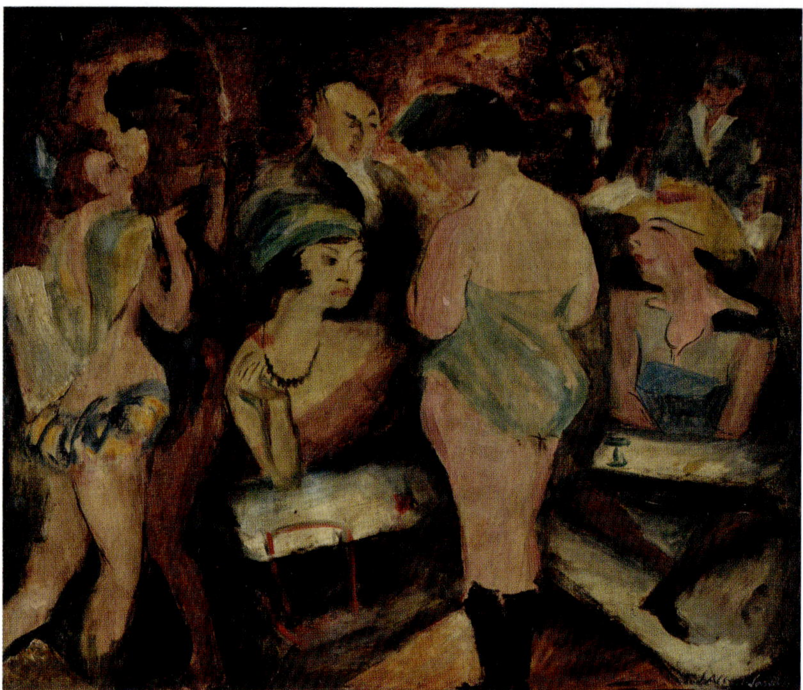

34 Lou Albert-Lasard, *Boîte de nuit* (Nightclub), date unknown

generation Expressionism. It was also a moment when an artist from an older generation, Käthe Kollwitz (1867–1945) came to the fore. Her powerful graphic works had long spoken to the struggles of ordinary people, especially the urban proletariat in Germany's rapidly industrializing cities. At the end of the war, she turned her scrutiny on the political establishment that had, as she saw it, sent so many Germans – including her son – to early deaths, and which now threatened to kill many more from the privations and disease that came in the aftermath of military defeat. Kollwitz's favoured mediums had
35 previously been etching and lithography, but in *In Memoriam Karl Liebknecht (Gedenkblatt fur Karl Liebknecht)* (1920), she utilized the archetypally Expressionist medium of the woodcut, which allowed her to achieve a feeling of rough immediacy and monumental simplicity. The subject is the workers' lament over the body of the Spartacist leader Karl Liebknecht (1871–1919) who, along with the group's co-founder Rosa Luxemburg (1871–1919), was brutally murdered by soldiers returning from the Western Front to prevent a Communist putsch. The murders caused widespread revulsion at the time.

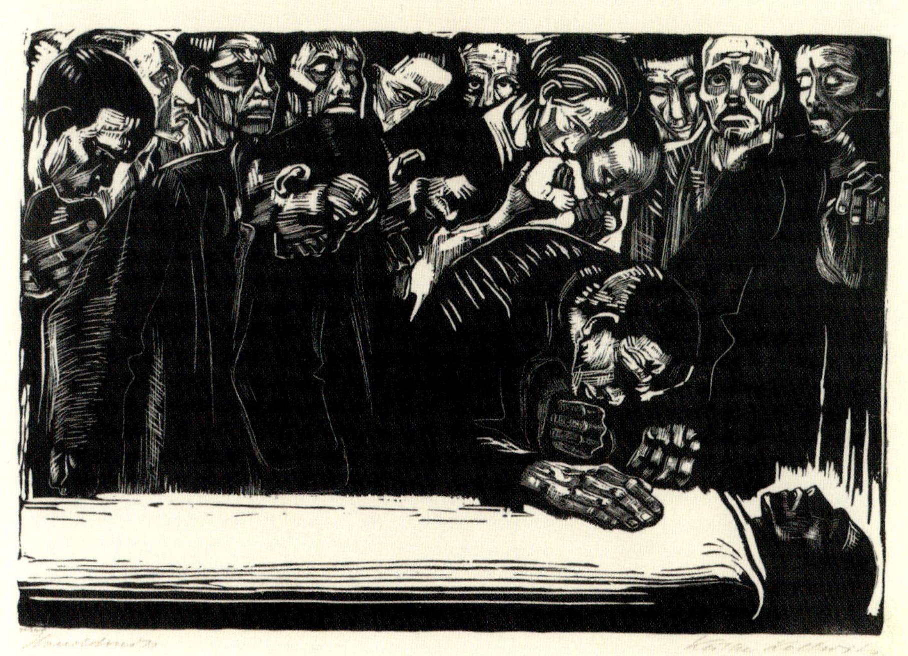

35 Käthe Kollwitz, *In Memoriam Karl Liebknecht (Gedenkblatt fur Karl Liebknecht)*, 1920

Kollwitz's composition is reminiscent of Christian images of the lamentation over the dead Christ, reinforcing Liebknecht's status as a martyr for the socialist cause. Felixmüller's contemporary lithograph *Menschen über der Welt* (People Across the World, 1919) depicts idealized figures of Luxemburg and Liebknecht rising in a seeming apotheosis. The two figures look straight at the viewer, in a way that suggests both accusation and a demand to those still left to continue the struggle. This was the image used on the cover of the memorial issue of *Die Aktion* in July 1919.

Felixmüller's commitment to socialism led him to produce
many images of workers in a characteristic Expressionist style
that merged simplified, often folkish drawing with cubo-
Futurist facets and acid colour, as in paintings such as *The
Ruhr District* (1920) and *Workers on the Way Home* (1921). He
was also concerned with psychological subjects, producing
36 in 1918 a series of lithographs depicting soldiers locked away
in a 'madhouse'. On one level, these images can be read as
the effects on individuals of the brutal experience and
trauma of war. On another, they can be read as a metaphor

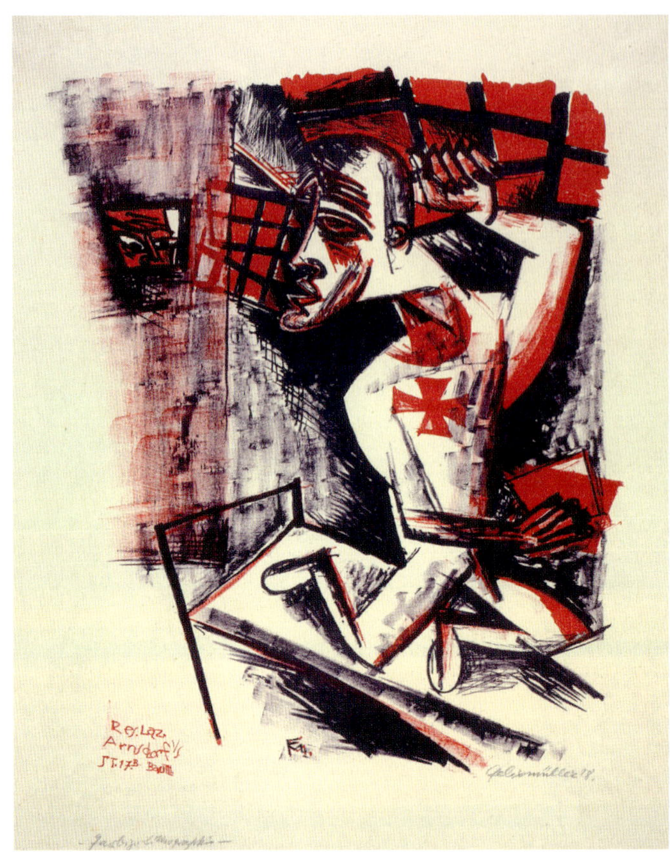

36 LEFT Conrad Felixmüller, *Soldier in a Madhouse*, 1918
37 OPPOSITE Conrad Felixmüller, *Death of the Poet Walter Rheiner*, 1925

for the alienation and hopelessness caused by the modern military-industrial machine. Felixmüller also produced a profoundly psychological image that can be read in retrospect as symbolic of the end of Expressionism as the dominant force in German art before 1945.

37 Felixmüller's *Death of the Poet Walter Rheiner* uses a similar composition to that employed in the earlier *Menschen über der Welt* to suggest not so much an apotheosis as an ironic merging with the metropolis that is at once physical and psychological. Rheiner was a friend of Felixmüller who had cultivated a cocaine habit to avoid conscription at the beginning of the war. He died from an overdose in 1925. In this image viewers are seemingly invited to experience with Rheiner from the perspective of his own drug-fuelled perception that moment of final rapture, as if floating above all mundane things, before plummeting into the abyss.

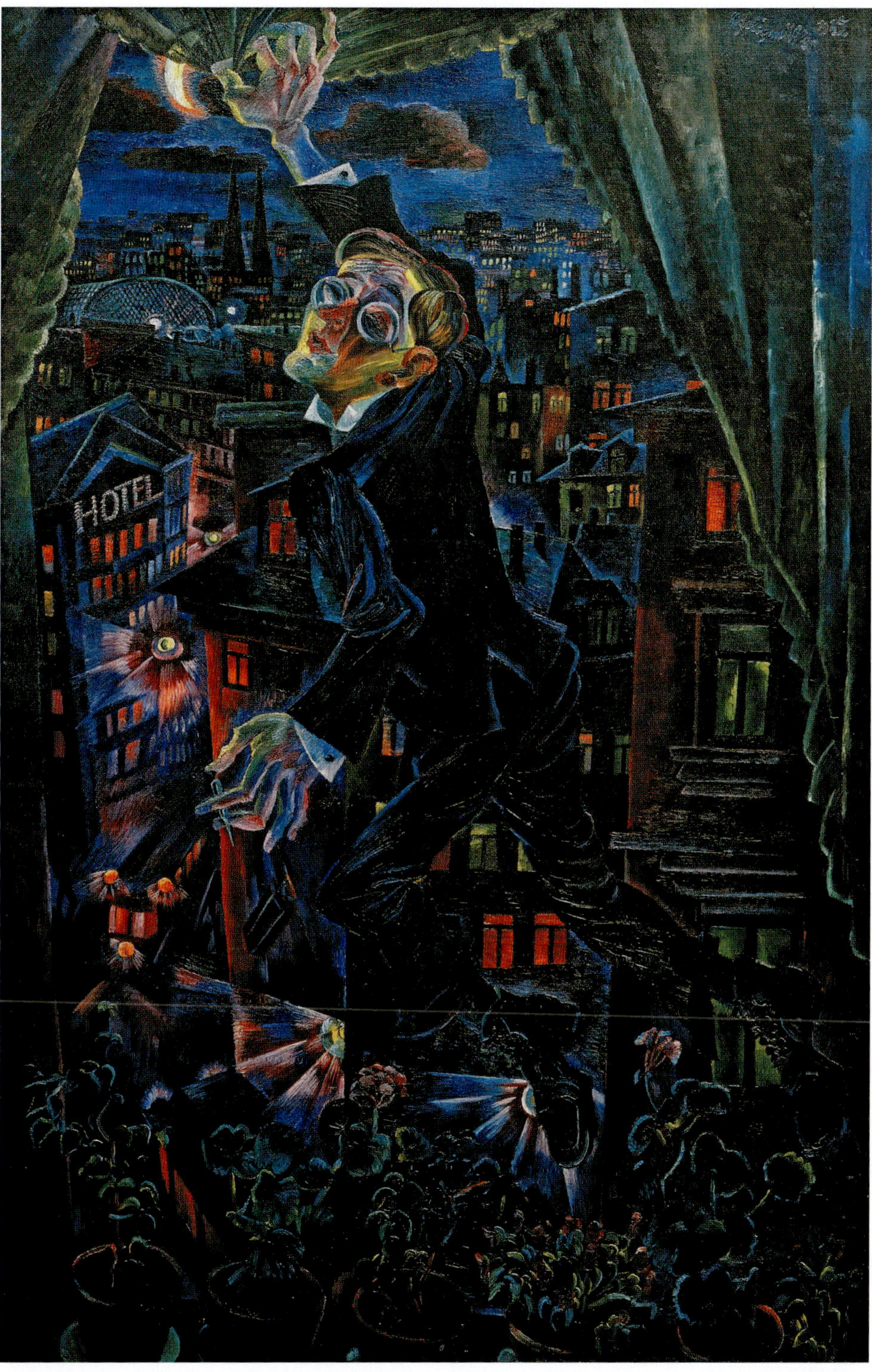
HOTEL

Chapter 2
Primitivism

Expressionism in art and the primitivizing impulse almost always go hand in hand. Expressionist primitivism was born of a sense of alienation in the face of a rapid industrialization and urbanization in much of Europe that brought with it ever-increasing specialization in work functions and regulation in social ones. A 1922 editorial in *The Burlington Magazine* summed up well the source of modernist cultural alienation, and where those overwhelmed by it looked to for relief: 'Our complex culture is demanding for its sustenance a more and more intimate experience of the simplest and remotest manifestations of man's emotional and intellectual life.' Primal psychological functions were equated with primitive ones, and at times places and people at a geographical distance from Europe were equated with metaphoric 'inner' distance.

There is, then, at the heart of much Expressionist primitivism an element of rejection of the dominant culture and a kind of social self-loathing. The Expressionist project almost invariably contains cultural (and sometimes political) resistance, which takes the form of dismantling systems that are regarded as over-complicated and over-regulated. It is a search for a kind of freedom that privileges the intuitive and the emotional over controlling rationality. The act of painting, then, is primarily visceral rather than intellectual; a free-flowing relationship between the body of the artist and the body of their materials. This was something that the French author associated with the school of naturalism, and friend of Cézanne, Émile Zola (1840–1902) intuited in the late nineteenth century: 'Like everything else, art is a human product, a human secretion; it is our body that sweats out the beauty of our works.' The resulting artwork, therefore, is not simply – or even primarily – a representation of a 'subject', but 'a personality, an individual' in its own right.

The positive valuing of, and yearning for, the notionally 'primitive' is at the root of the phenomenon of primitivism, which has existed since at least Classical Antiquity as an intellectual tendency. The usefulness of the term, 'primitivism' has been challenged in many quarters, partly because of the negative cultural overtones that its root, the 'primitive' has acquired, and particularly in light of a tendency to privilege its function as a noun rather than an adjective. This is problematic in cases where its signification has been reduced to describing groups from the indigenous populations of Sub-Saharan Africa, the Americas and Oceania, thereby situating its meaning unequivocally within discourses of Western colonial imperialism. Adoption of this narrowly specific definition of what constitutes the 'primitive' consequently implies that the range of meaning of the term 'primitivism' is also rather narrow, both in terms of its referents (subject indigenous peoples) and its cultural and historical sweep (more or less consonant with the most intensive period of European colonialism, spanning around two hundred years until the mid-twentieth century). In this way, primitivist discourse is seen specifically as an aspect of modern Western racist constructions of otherness. The questioning of primitivism is also in part a result of a common tendency, even among academics, to conflate the words 'primitive' and 'primitivism', where both are used as descriptive nouns alluding to 'primitive' states or to simple technologies. This conflation is unfortunate because it not only turns idea into subject through fusion, but thereby also empties the term 'primitivism' of its agency.

Contrary to this, I want to argue that primitivism is a useful idea that can be effectively applied to art history, and whose articulation can, crucially, be detected in both stylistic and psychological terms. Whilst not shying away from the implications of the Western colonialist context, it is important to recognize the complexity of primitivist discourse as an agent of interculturalization. Primitivism is an idea whose currency cuts across a much broader timescale and spread of referents. It is transhistorical and transcultural, and the identity of the notionally primitive subject shifts according to time and cultural specificity, so that non-urban, indigenous cultures from Africa, the Americas and Oceania are not the *only* focus of primitivist ideas, nor, at times, necessarily part of the primitivizing project at all.

In adopting this view of primitivism as a more generally pervasive discourse I am also broadly accepting the specific intellectual construction of primitivism introduced by the great proponent of the History of Ideas at the Johns Hopkins

University, Arthur Lovejoy (1873–1962) in the 1920s, and later developed with his colleague George Boas (1891–1980) in *Primitivism and Related Ideas in Antiquity* (1935). For them the 'primitive' is most often used as a rhetorical device or metaphor in opposition to 'civilization'. As a generally recurring 'unit-idea' primitivism, therefore, is always an event that is concerned with cultural *self-criticism*; or, as Lovejoy and Boas put it, it is 'the discontent of the civilized with civilization, or with some conspicuous and characteristic feature of it. It is the belief of men (*sic.*) living in a highly evolved and complex cultural condition that a life far simpler and less sophisticated in some or in all respects is a more desirable life.'

The perception of existing in a state of social, cultural and technological complexity, and discontent with that state, are, therefore, the base conditions for primitivism to arise. Intrinsic to this is a sense of *loss* in the attainment of sophistication. Nostalgia for a simpler and (usually) spiritually healthier cultural past lies at the heart of primitivism; a real or hypothesized primordium, a time or condition of perfect beginnings. Lovejoy and Boas proposed two meta-categories of primitivism that they called 'chronological' and 'cultural', defined respectively as longing for times other than the present and by dissatisfaction with one's own society. Crucially, they suggest that subdivisions of cultural primitivism are organized around the 'identification of the good with that which is "natural" or "according to nature"'. The appeal to nature is, as they point out, one of the 'most potent and most persistent factors in Western thought,' yet one that contains a 'multiplicity of meanings...in its normative uses.' When nature refers to the way of life of the humans existing in a natural state they further identify two tendencies, which they call 'hard' and 'soft' primitivism. The first is based on the belief that the peoples in question 'wanted less, and therefore knew how to be content with little.' The second imagines a people free to do as they please, and 'of infinite leisure.' In both cases we are dealing with two aspects of the same idea: that of the 'noble savage'.

Nature not Naturalism

Rejection of the exactitudes of modern, urban life was (and remains to this day) full of contradictions. This is perhaps best shown in the example of several utopian artists' colonies that had sprung up by the beginning of the last century in relatively remote rural places like in Pont-Aven in Brittany, France, Worpswede in Germany, Monte Verità in Italy, St. Ives in Britain and Provincetown in the United States. All provided supposedly unspoilt, natural environments far from the city,

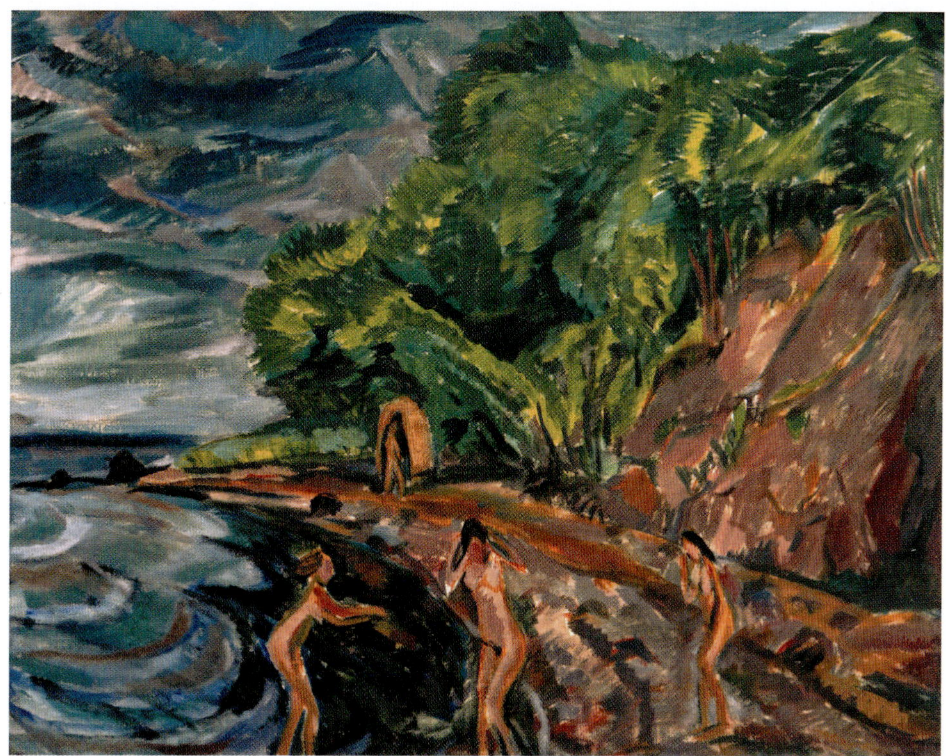

38 Erich Heckel, *Badende an der Förde* (Bathers at the Fjord), 1913

complete with an indigenous population refreshingly naive and free of cynicism associated with city life. At the same time, their founding and continuation was made possible by rapid improvements in travel networks for moving people and goods (including art materials and finished products), the low cost of living compared with the city (which often allowed relatively poor artists to maintain studios in both environments), and the demand of urban markets for their work.

Quitting the urban environment for 'nature', as represented by rural and emerging economies, wasn't always a wholly reactionary move. The idea of removing oneself temporarily from 'civilization' often stemmed from a primitivist belief that cultural revitalization could only come out of a period of regression to simpler modes of existence. The Worpswede sculptor Bernhard Hoetger (1874–1949) and painters Georg Tappert and Paula Modersohn-Becker all merged ruralist ideas
39 with self-consciously modernist styles. In a work like *Kneeling Mother with Child at her Breast*, Modersohn-Becker celebrated

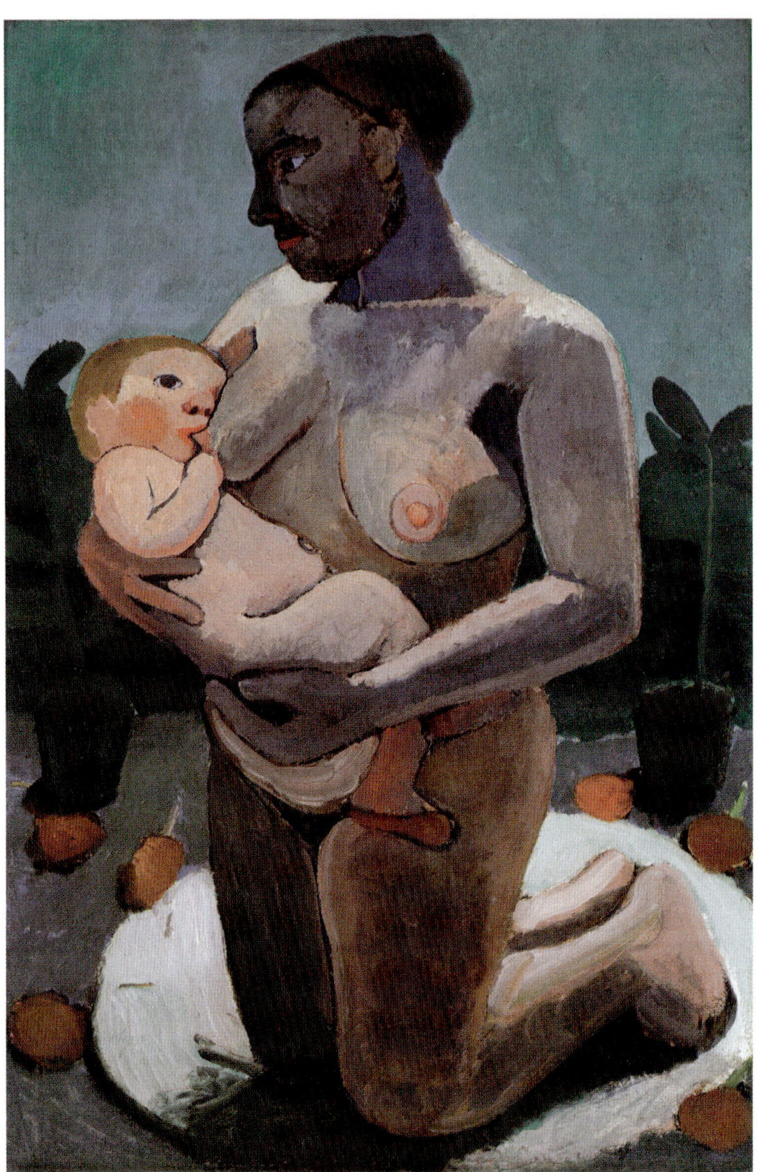

39 ABOVE Paula Modersohn-Becker, *Kneeling Mother with Child at her Breast*, 1907
40 OPPOSITE David Bomberg, *The Gorge, Ronda, Spain*, 1935

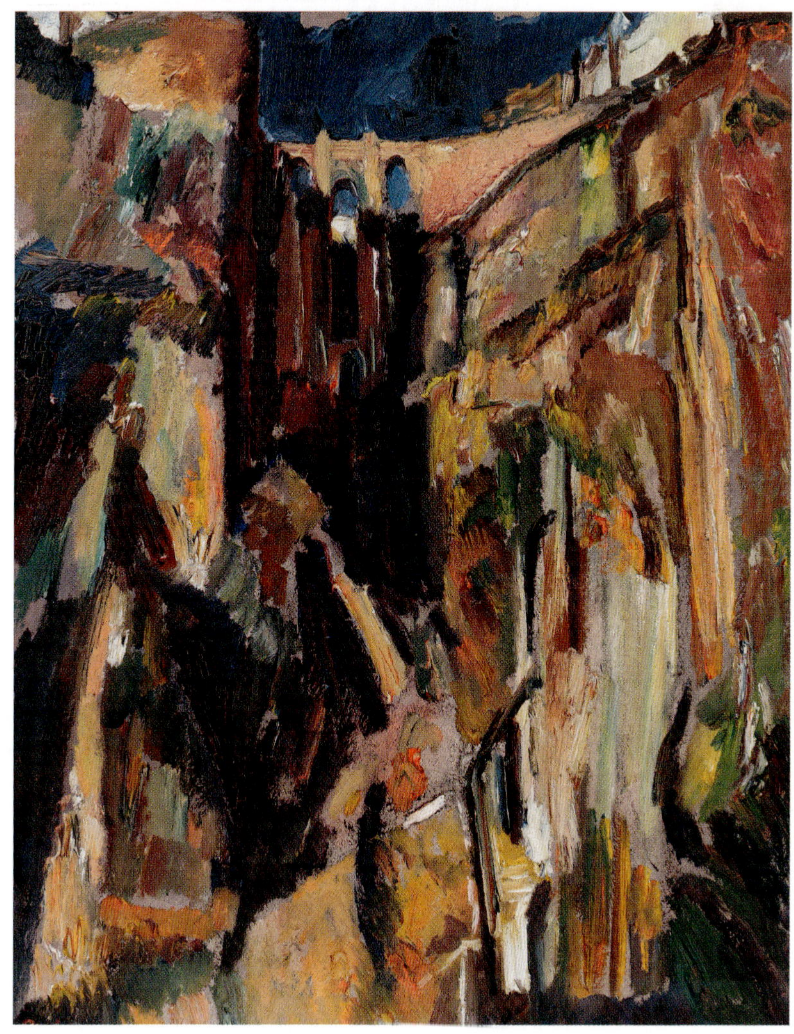

both the 'earthiness' of the peasant and the primal bond between mother and infant in a style developed through her experience of contemporary Parisian trends which emphasize simplicity and pictorial flatness. Most of her work relies on the viewer's tacit supposition of connections between the 'primitive' and the feminine – part of the stream of dialectics current in popular thought until well after mid-century that had on one side woman, nature, tradition, continuation, intuition and on the other man, civilization, innovation, reason. In this way even 'sophisticated' contemporaries, such as Hoetger's wife, in *Lee Hoetger in Front of a Floral Background* (1906), are pictured as being of nature through association between physical weightiness and implied co-extensiveness of her simple floral-patterned dress and the large flowers surrounding her.

Images of place as well as people had already long been a tremendously important marker of identity. Against the new subject of the transnational modern urban landscape in Expressionism a picturing of the characteristics of local geography persisted, providing images of connectedness for metropolitan audiences. This is evident in Brücke images of the German landscapes of Moritzburg, Fehmarn and Nidden, and Kirchner's images of the Swiss landscape. It is arguably strongest in the case of Nolde who came close to achieving that rapturous merging with elemental forces dreamt of by the Romantics, in brooding, sumptuous paintings of the inhospitable coast and marshlands of his native Schleswig-Holstein. Interestingly, however, his attempts to represent the people and landscapes he regarded as primal when he accompanied a German government sponsored trip to German New Guinea in 1913 struggle to transcend the essentialist racist views he had formed much earlier.

There were times when the landscape was an adopted one, the result of empathic responses to other places by displaced people and travellers. The English painter David Bomberg's
40 (1890–1957) sublime images of the Ronda Valley in Spain, where he spent as much time as his teaching commitments would allow, are a case in point. Also interesting are Kokoschka's restless wanderings throughout a long life, from Germany to North Africa and England. Each image was infused with its own pulsating life, inviting the viewer to participate in the artist's own emotional reaction, which is particularly strong in works made during times of world crisis, as in paintings of the English coastline from the Second World War or Berlin at the time of the construction in the mid-1960's of the wall which divided the city for thirty years.

Primitive and Modern Art

Wild landscapes were important symbols of the primitive forces underlying the fragile order that humanity had placed on the universe. However, overall, artists looked not to nature but to other art for inspiration and confirmation of their ideas. *Primitivism and Related Ideas in Antiquity* is concerned specifically with Graeco-Roman literature, but its premises are meant to be broadly applicable to other periods and cultural products, and it has clear potential applications to the cultural mores of the modernist period. Undoubtedly one of the major reasons that primitivism came to be widely regarded as a peculiarly modernist discourse in the visual arts is the singularity and deep impact in scholarship and the curatorial world of the first book on primitivism and visual art to follow the publication of Lovejoy and Boas's book, *Primitivism in Modern Painting* (1938), by the American art historian Robert Goldwater (1907–1973). He was well versed in the history of modernism and acquainted with figures in the contemporary New York and European art worlds, which in the Surrealist milieu of the 1920s and 1930s had taken a decidedly ethnographic turn. An increasingly self-reflexive attitude toward otherness was therefore evident in much of the art closest to him, enabling more clear-sighted analysis of artistic primitivism's mythologizing tendencies; knowledge about peoples and the world could be more objectively balanced against primitivizing assumptions.

The intellectual underpinnings of his thesis spring from fin-de-siècle questioning of mimesis and decoration, as exemplified in the writings of critics like Adolf Loos (1870–1933) in Austria and Worringer in Germany, and especially artists like Kandinsky, versions of whose personal credo were, in many ways, institutionalized in the New York art world of the 1930s. Thus, for Goldwater, as an *idea* primitivism was defined by: 'the assumption that externals, whether those of a social or cultural group, of individual psychology, or of the physical world, are intricate and complicated and *as such not desirable*. It is the assumption that any reaching under the surface, if only it is carried far enough and proceeds according to the proper method, will reveal something "simple" and basic which, because of its very fundamentality and simplicity, will be more emotionally compelling than the superficial variations of the surface; and finally that the qualities of simplicity and basicness are things to be valued in and for themselves.' In this view the primitive is therefore that which somehow represents or at least indicates the possibility of a kind of quintessence from which new (Western) art styles might be forged. The process of apprehension and artistic creation (and significantly the two are interlinked in Goldwater's conception) might be 'intellectual' – approaching the Kantian *Ding an sich*, as in the case of the Cubists or De Stijl – or irrational – approached either viscerally through raw emotion, as in Expressionism, or psychologically through accessing more primal modes of consciousness, as in Surrealism.

By the close of the nineteenth century a strong, fundamentally Expressionist, artistic current had come to prominence that privileged precisely those elements of decoration and conceptual content that the academies largely marginalized. In essence, the academic dogma of objectivity, based on the Renaissance mimetic visual paradigm, was replaced by a new belief in individual subjectivity underpinned by emotionalism. Accordingly, technical virtuosity – which is associated with complexity and specialization – came to be regarded by modernists as at best anterior to that which is proper to art, and untutored expression was privileged. As Fry put it in 1917, 'We have to recognize that our admiration of an artist's skill is not aesthetic.... We have to get rid of the idea that our favourable aesthetic judgement of a work of art is a kind of prize conferred on the artist for meritorious effort.' In this model artistic training is viewed as a damaging rather than meritorious commodity.

In 1920 Roger Fry reflected that it was the 'collectible' qualities of artefacts produced outside a perceived Greco-Roman tradition rather than aesthetics that initially allowed them to enter European culture. Collectors, he argued, felt no need to establish the claims of things like Byzantine enamels, Coptic textiles and Islamic and Far Eastern material culture as high art because 'they were curiosities and they were of precious quality and workmanship.' Antiquarian interest was at the forefront in their accumulation in European and North American private and, increasingly, public collections. As Europe's own Christian 'primitive' art – especially Gothic and Romanesque production, and Early Renaissance painting and sculpture from Northern Europe and Italy – was re-evaluated by art historians at the beginning of the last century, so comparisons began to be drawn between its visual language and that of these other cultural forms. What connected them all, and what was supposedly primitive about them was their creators' lack of technical means to produce convincing naturalistic reflections of the world. But as we have already seen Expressionist qualities were read into them and affinities claimed with an emerging modern art that prized intuition over rationality. Kirchner, for example, claimed that the Brücke artists 'went back beyond the tenth century and started from there'. There is evidence of the artists adapting Gothic stylistic elements in their art, especially in the woodcut medium, but this was part of a mixture of notionally 'primitive' sources that included Javanese puppets, Indian Buddhist painting and African sculpture. There is also an interesting inversion of this in Russia, where the European primitives were treated as 'exotic' sources and Asian arts seen as representing the 'national' character.

The 'primitive' works to which artists wishing to subvert the academic tradition turned from the 1870s on were, then, precisely those which appeared to privilege directness and intuition over planning and the employment of practised representational models. In many ways the 'primitive' art to which European artists turned from the end of the nineteenth century until the 1920s was a kind of *Orbis pictus*; a mélange of cultural and historical forms. Crucially for the received history of modernist primitivism, Goldwater wrote his book at a moment when the term 'primitive art' lost its previous primary connection to pre- and early-Renaissance European art in the United States and became the generally used category designation for 'tribal' and prehistoric artefacts, largely owing to the popularization of the ideas of the German-American anthropologist Franz Boas (1858–1942) and his followers. As a result, Goldwater considered 'tribal' art to be the paradigmatic 'primitive' art, although most of the modernist artists he discussed used the term in its older sense, and when they referred specifically to the indigenous cultures of Sub-Saharan Africa, Oceania and North America, they used variations on the word 'savage'. In overlooking this Goldwater effectively closed off a significant aspect of modernist primitivism which was not concerned primarily, if at all with 'savage' culture, and remarkably he set a trend in art history that has been a feature of almost all treatments of primitivism in modern art since.

The history of primitivism in the visual arts is analogous with that of primitivism in general precisely because wherever primitivizing cultural discontentedness arises it finds voice across a broad spectrum of activity, from the arts to politics. Primitivism presupposes primitiveness, but it does not necessarily presuppose the wholly primitive character of the creative subject or culture; it is perfectly possible to be technologically primitive and psychologically highly sophisticated. Therefore, at different times and in different places, the 'primitive' object of the primitivizing impulse can be partial, residing in some aspect of culture. This has particular resonance in art, where the forms of objects and the cultural information they convey is inextricably linked.

Affinity-ism was essential not only to the rehabilitation of a diverse range of previously undervalued cultural products, but also in establishing a cultural system of values in contemporary Europe that privileged expression over technical mastery and classical canons of beauty. We have seen how this was presented visually by Kandinsky and Marc in the *Blue Rider Almanac* through a heady mix of art from different cultures and times. Among non-European peoples, the qualities of simplicity and freedom to which the critics of culture aspired were first read into the arts of China and Japan at the end of the nineteenth century, although they were still very much current at the beginning of the next one. In 1910 *The Burlington Magazine* could still declare that in Europe, 'we are more disillusioned, more tired with our own tradition' than ever before and suggested that, 'To us the art of the East presents the hope of discovering a more spiritual, more expressive idea of design.' The key was supposedly the triumph of sensitivity and suggestiveness in art from the Far East over European realism, which left nothing to the imagination. 'One might almost describe the difference between the art of the East and the art of the West,' said the writer and curator Charles Holmes in 1905, 'by saying that while Europeans are concerned with the aspect of things, Orientals are concerned with their vitality.'

Acting like Children

Far Eastern art was a relatively safe role model because although European critics considered its forms 'primitive', they regarded the cultures which produced them to be highly civilized. But the art of the Far East could also be seen as representing a finely honed endgame rather than a beginning. In European art where the need to somehow demonstrate 'originality' and 'invention' were strong this could actually be seen as a problem. So artists looked for other, more comprehensively primitive sources for inspiration. The obvious group is children who are by definition less developed than the adults they will eventually become. The child is the 'primitive' par excellence. The freshness of children's vision and their closeness to 'nature' had been common ideas since the philosopher Jean-Jacques Rousseau revolutionized European views of childhood in the eighteenth century, and in 1897 Gauguin had urged that, 'moments of playfulness, and infantile things, far from being injurious to serious work, endow it with grace, gaiety and naivety.' But it was Matisse and his circle who first thought that not just childlike feelings but also children's *art* might itself be worthy of emulation. The influence can be seen in Vlaminck's *The Bar* (1900) as well as many of his landscape paintings, and also in works like Derain's *Portrait of*
41 *Henri Matisse* (1905) and *Dance* (1905–06), or Matisse's *Marguerite au chat noire* (1910).

It is also strong in the work of their contemporaries elsewhere, such as Münter and Jawlensky in Germany, and Russian 'neo-primitivists' like Larionov, Goncharova and Kazimir Malevich (1878–1935). Significantly, they looked at first to images by older children, whose formal qualities have much in common with folk and naive art by untutored adults. This allowed the creation of a chain of connection and affinity that ultimately confirmed the validity of the modern art through

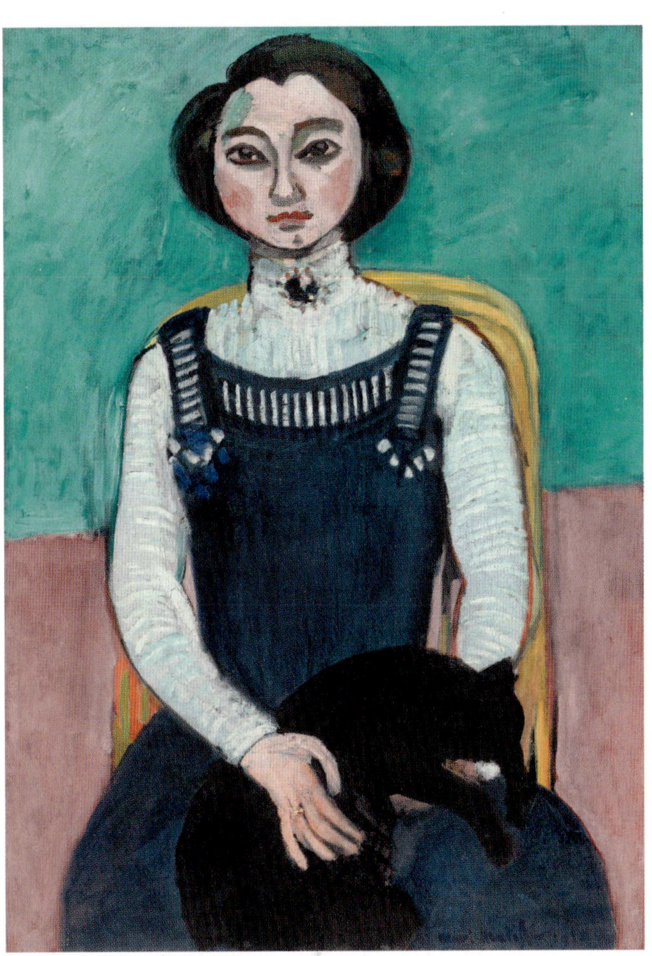

41 Henri Matisse, *Marguerite au chat noire*, 1910

the implied dynamic between modern sensibility, childlike freshness of vision and people living simply, in harmony with the rhythms of 'nature'. The Russians, for example, were people with cosmopolitan lifestyles and tastes who also at times professed a dislike for the urban environment. The apparent paradox of their modernist stance and their interest in 'low' subject matter, such as peasant life and off-duty soldiers and use of a 'primitive' style can be explained politically to some extent. Malevich explained, 'Goncharova and I worked more on a peasant level. Every work of ours had a content which, although expressed in primitive form, revealed a social concern.'

If the drawings of older children seemed to provide connections with culture, those of younger children approached a more

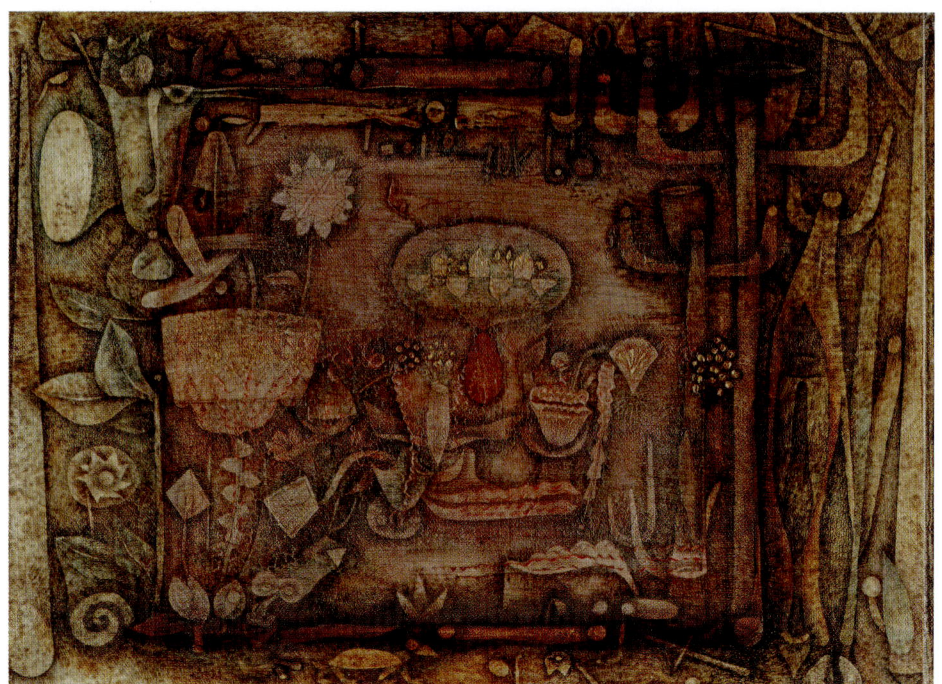

42 Paul Klee, *Botanical Theatre*, 1934

primal and undifferentiated level, more in keeping with explorations of the force of individual vision. For example, much of the veiled imagery in Kandinsky's organic abstract paintings from around 1911 to 1920 derives from drawings he and Münter had collected by very young children, whose ability to picture the world objectively is severely restricted through lack of manual skill and accumulated knowledge. Klee, too, saw immense value in the art of very young children, which for him was part of a lifelong personal search to 'penetrate to the region of that secret place where primeval power nurtures all evolution.' Klee digested his experience of child art so that it was revealed in extraordinary subtle ways in works such as
42 *The Twittering Machine* (1922) and *Botanical Theatre* (1934).
In some respects, the scratchy, linear drawing, schematic representation and flooded watercolour overlay is very similar to children's work, but the sophisticated decision-making and incredible sensitivity to the way form and colour can be manipulated are very much adult qualities. As Klee himself famously said, 'If my works sometimes produce a primitive impression, this "primitiveness" is explained by my discipline,

which consists of reducing everything to a few steps. It is no more than economy; that is the ultimate professional awareness, which is to say the opposite of real primitiveness.'

Later in the century (see Chapter 4) a number of artists seized on the energetic aspects of children's drawings. In the 1940s, for example, Jean Dubuffet (1901–1985), Asger Jorn, Karel Appel (1921–2006) and Constant (1920–2005) produced intensely physical paintings and sculptures that were not only intentionally ham-fisted and unsubtle technically, but also adopted the formal language of children's art more directly. Dubuffet's *Ménage de cyclists aux vaches* (Group of Cyclists with Cows, 1943), for example, is remarkably similar to one of the pieces of child art in his own collection. Ultimately, though, it was the immediacy, conceptual nature and what they saw as the 'freedom' of children's image-making that were to have a lasting effect on their production. The artistic ground came to function as an arena in which anything was thinkable, and the sense of being unrestrained was only intensified with the addition of an adult experience and sensibility. These works impacted in several ways. In large oil paintings like Appel's *Hip, Hip, Hoorah!* (1949) and Jorn's *Letter to my Son* (1956–57), a scale and medium normally aimed directly at gallery display rather than domestic spaces combine with 'infantile' technique in a gesture that mocks what the artists regarded as the self-regarding pomposity of cultural consumption. Similarly with Dubuffet's portraits, which summarily destroy through brutalist technique and caricature the sense of purpose of a genre designed to show subjects in their best light for posterity. Others, like Arnulf Rainer explored less overtly socially polemical, but nonetheless fundamental themes of the baseline of creativity, by using scribbled marks as the base unit of their process. Scribbling stands at the beginning not only of picture-making, but also of writing. It represents that liminal point where mute, primal experience begins to find form.

The 'Tribal' and the Modern

In Europe before 1914 the idea of the 'savage' was not only *not* the central notionally primitive grouping, but it was largely absent in the discourse. Art periodicals that, largely because of improvements in print technologies and particularly photographic reproduction, proliferated at the turn of the century tended to focus on areas other than 'savage' art, even when they espoused an interest in primitivizing ideas. In *The Burlington Magazine*, for example, founded in 1903, there was broad coverage of non-European art and decorative objects from the start. Yet, in spite (or perhaps because) of some of its most influential figures being important players in the European avant-garde, most notably Fry, it is the arts of China and Japan rather than Africa that are central to its primitivism. By the end of the nineteenth century much of this work was being reclaimed by the European art world precisely on aesthetic terms; although this was a new aesthetics that was antithetical to what had come to be seen by many as a restrictive post-Renaissance tradition.

A comprehensive exhibition of early Islamic art in Munich in 1910 was, by the very fact of its staging and its impact, a symptom of changes in aesthetic attitudes. It also awoke a primitivizing interest in Islamic art in many Expressionist artists, not so much because of its exoticism, as because it seemed analogous with another European 'primitive' source much in vogue at the time, Gothic art. The exhibition attracted enthusiastic visitors from many parts of Europe, including Matisse.

Artistic interest in tribal art only really began to gain ground around 1905, in Paris, and then among a relatively closed social group, including Picasso, Derain, Vlaminck and Matisse. In 1910 André Derain told an American journalist: 'These Africans, being primitive, uncomplex, uncultured, can express their thought by a direct appeal to the instinct.' But, characteristically, directness and reliance on instinct were also qualities Derain read into Japanese and Egyptian art. Racist popular thought in Europe and the United States regarded so-called 'tribal' peoples from Sub-Saharan Africa, Oceania and North America as essentially intuitive and psychologically immature. This view was reinforced by an instrumentalist politics of control in both colonial and so-called settler nation contexts, which treated indigenous (and enslaved) populations as children unable to manage their own affairs. This is how even those dealers and artists who were enthusiastic promoters of African and Oceanic art portrayed the contexts of the production of the work. In the book accompanying the landmark exhibition of '*sculpture nègres*' in his gallery in 1917 Paul Guillaume, for example, described Oceanic art as fundamentally other to his normative European, and based entirely on childlike superstition: 'Everything for them is a subject for anxiety, and they are entirely preoccupied with driving away evil spirits.' This explains, he said, the 'monstrousness' of their forms: 'The more hideous they are, the more powerful they are supposed to be.' There is nothing in the history of European art before 1907 to compare with the look of, for example, Fang reliquary figures from Gabon, Senufo rhythm pounders from the Ivory Coast, or tikis from the Marquesas Islands. Tribal sculpture, as opposed to weapons and tools, only began to make its way into Europe in significant numbers in the last third of the nineteenth century, a time which coincides with a period of concerted colonial expansion, especially by France, Germany and Britain. So, here were radically different, non-naturalistic forms produced by contemporaries or near-contemporaries of European modernists. Tribal art's 'modernity' was claimed from the start, but racist assumptions about its primitive cultural underpinning were an essential part of the argument for, as well as against its aesthetic importance.

Unlike other notionally primitive art forms, traditional carvings from West Africa, Oceania and North America could not be recuperated by appealing to their status as historical relic. Rather, they were viewed as the products of cultures that were simultaneously presentist (or ahistorical) *and* in a state of 'barbarism' *preceding* civilization. In the scientific racist models of evolution that were still current in the first part of the twentieth century, they were said to occupy a place at the wellsprings of cultural development. In this way they were typed as both physically contemporary and psychologically and socially 'ancient' (in the argument that intuitive and magical worldviews arise *earlier* in the development of the individual than the rational cognitive faculty). Without a history that could be mapped against European-style art historical family trees of artistic development they were seen inevitably as being outside art history. So, the reappraisal, and admittance of tribal objects into European art history was only made possible by shifts in the language of intentionality and terms of criticism of contemporary European modernist art itself. In the absence of a sense of history, tribal art *had* to accord in the first place with the present. So, if modern art was, ultimately to provide validation for tribal art, it was itself validated at least partly through comparison with other non-European and putatively 'primitive' art. The paradox inherent in early twentieth-century views of tribal art is that although they allow for an argument that European and African artists stood at the same point of a new beginning, only the European will move forward, while the other is fated to remain in an unchanging cultural present.

Tribal art came to be seen by later historians as the chief model underlying European primitivism, but this is not really the case. The criteria for artistic primitivism were well established before its 'discovery', and ideas about the 'savage' mind, for example, mixed with long-held views about the evolution of European thought and culture. However, its importance is not in doubt as a strong confirmatory argument for the legitimacy of Expressionism and other early modernist tropes. Tribal art, and in particular African sculpture, was generally regarded as 'modern' until well into the 1920s – one of the first exhibitions staged with this intent was 'African Negro Art' at the Photo-Secession Gallery, New York in 1914. Tribal art regularly rubbed shoulders in France and elsewhere with cutting-edge European painting, before going out of fashion somewhat with the modernists.

The 'Primitive' Body

The reception of 'tribal' sculpture is complicated by European attitudes to non-European, and especially, African bodies. The 'Africanizing' of the European female body is a common feature in early twentieth-century art, not only through formal appropriations from tribal sculpture, as in pieces such as
43 Picasso's *Trois figures sous un arbre* (1908) and Brancusi's *Little French Girl* (1914–18), but also as transpositions of physical stereotypes of blackness, as in Matisse's *Blue Nude* (1907) and Kirchner's *Nude in Bathtub* (1911). This rendering 'strange' is energized through European beliefs about the relationship between women and primitiveness, anchored in the colonial context of the late nineteenth century and first part of the twentieth century. The gendering of the primitive as feminine

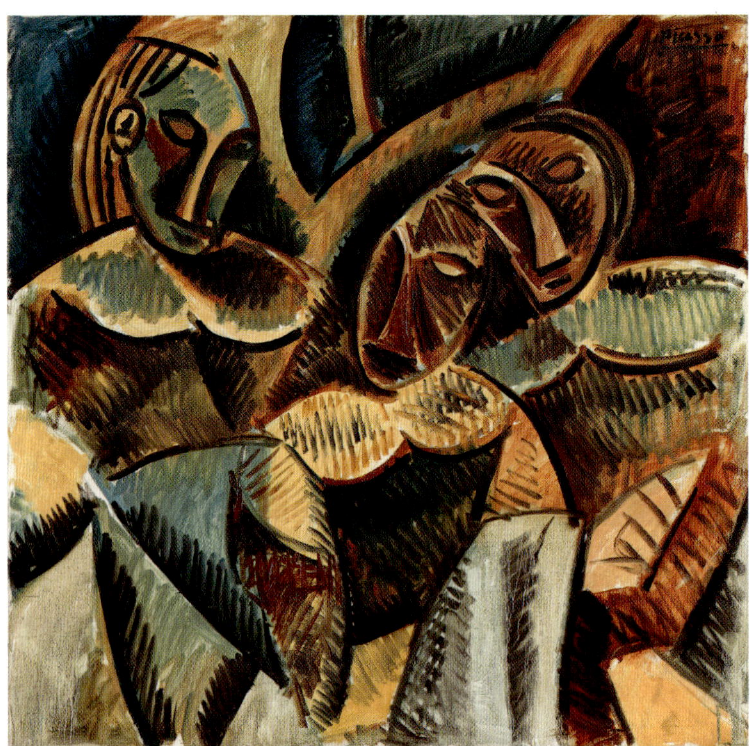

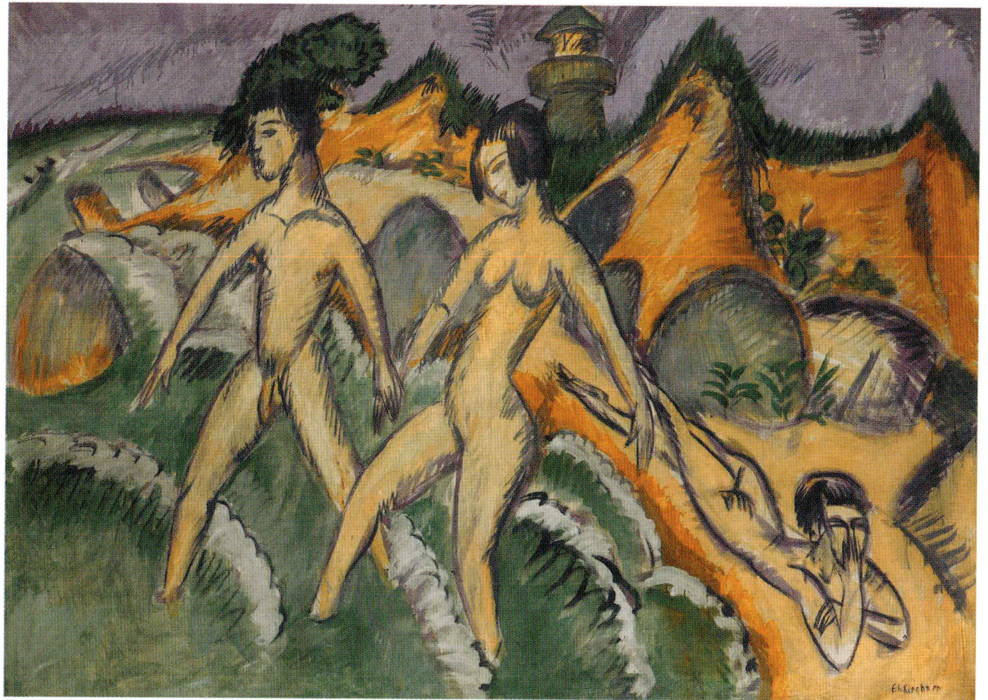

43 OPPOSITE Pablo Picasso, *Trois figures sous un arbre* (Three Figures Under a Tree), 1908
44 ABOVE Ernst Ludwig Kirchner, *Ins Meer Schreitende* (Striding into the Sea), 1912

corresponds to now outdated misanthropic ideas that place women closer to 'nature', as more intuitive and passive, as against supposedly masculine qualities of culture, reason and activity. In fact, at times such stereotypes could function as modes of cultural resistance, as in Brücke depictions of mixed groups of naked bathers or studio nudes in which both male and female participants were 'feminized' in a shared
44 primitivity, as in Kirchner's *Ins Meer Schreitende* (Striding into the Sea) (1912).

Furthermore, early anthropology measured non-European bodies against a supposedly absolute canon of beauty that found them lacking not only through physical difference to European bodies, but also as more primitive and therefore displeasing to 'civilized' sensibility. As a result, when artists depicted 'Africanized' figures they subverted conventional ideas of physical beauty and decorum as much as stylistic appropriations from primitive art challenged conventional aesthetic canons. The clearest example of this is probably the emphasis on protruding buttocks in certain works by artists like Matisse and Kirchner, which refers to steatopygia, a physiological condition that is reasonably common in peoples of southern Africa and which had come to be seen as a specific sign for the primitive sexuality of African women in general. There is more than mere rejection of Matisse's modernist style when contemporary critics described the body of the woman in *Blue Nude* (1907) as 'ugly', for even as it disrupted conventional European stereotypes of feminine beauty, viewers also recognized in her *shape* her active sexuality.

Apocalypse

Primitivist attitudes to western culture and art revealed themselves in apocalyptic terms at certain times. The Italian Futurists' glorification of war as 'the world's only hygiene' was based on a belief that the New Age could only really begin after the physical destruction of all that had gone before. Only then could they really be primitive revitalisers of culture. This was the reason that when war came to much of the rest of Europe in August 1914 they enthusiastically welcomed it and they were at the forefront of those agitating for Italy to join in. In Germany many Expressionists volunteered to fight precisely because they imagined the war would bring forward the end of the materialist civilization they loathed and usher in a new age of the spiritual. Many, as we have seen, did not return. There had been a distinctly apocalyptic leaning in modern art since at least 1910 that not only reflected the metaphysical leanings of Expressionism at the beginning of the end of the Christian second millennium, but also an increasingly tense political situation, including a war in the Balkans in 1910. Kirchner painted street scenes in Berlin that have an air of ominous brooding, and Ludwig Meidner (1884–1966) painted a series of pre-war apocalyptic landscapes in which towns were demolished and bodies shattered. Kandinsky's abstractions from around 1912 took on the air of full-blown biblical deluges, and Marc's once Edenic animal paintings turned into nightmares from the Book of Revelation, most forcefully in the great canvas *Animal Destinies* (1913). Metaphysics and primitivizing rhetoric aside, arguably one of the most potent metaphors for the continued fragility of humankind's control of the world in this emerging technological age is Max Beckmann's huge modern history painting, *The Sinking of the Titanic* (1913).

The experience of war at first hand introduced a note of chaotic aggressivism into cubo-Expressionist styles. The young Otto Dix, likely suffering already from undiagnosed PTSD, seemed to revel in the sickening possibilities of driving home the horror of the battlefield in spiky, fragmented images like *Signal Flare* (1917). And the full force of his transformation into dehumanized amoral fighting machine is celebrated in the *Self-Portrait as Mars* (1915). For others, such as George Grosz, the collapse of society in the cities, as Germany sank deeper into despair and anarchism toward the end of the war, provided a similarly awful backdrop for stingingly powerful apocalyptic imagery, as in *Funeral (Dedicated to Oskar Panizza)* (1918).

After Primitivism?

Primitivism remained a feature of Expressionism throughout the twentieth century. However, definitions of the notionally 'primitive' remained fluid, and the putative sources of primitive manifestations changed significantly with the advent of increasingly globalized understandings of culture fuelled as much by the international reach of capitalism as by decolonization and political reorientation. The idea of the very possibility of a 'primitive' subject came to be seen as outdated and fundamentally racist. But primitivizing obsessions with technological and social simplicity, and primitive psychological and cognitive operations persists. This partly answers the question as to whether primitivism is – or can be – a feature of progressive art practice in the postcolonial West, or the global art world. More problematical is whether primitivism can ever be an aspect of the ways in which artists might negotiate sensitively the complex relationships between the diverse material cultures of the contemporary world. There is a large body of art produced since 1945 that owes much to children's art and psychotic art, for example, but are Expressionists like Arnulf Rainer, A. R. Penck (1939–2017), Eddie Martinez, or Jean Michel Basquiat (1960–1988) acting upon the same ideas about primitivity as earlier artists? In each case the answer is almost certainly in the negative, insofar as none subscribe to essentialist ideas about human difference or cultural evolutionism. However, here are three artists whose cultural discontentedness has found voice and form through some kind of primitivism, whether through a preference for less codified or more chaotic visual cultures, such as graffiti and handmade commercial art, or emotionalism and forms of unreason – both of which are still widely regarded as more primitive aspects of human psychology.

Chapter 3
Expressionism Between the Wars

Expressionism spread quickly throughout Europe and beyond, especially after the publication and translation into several languages of Matisse's 'Notes of a Painter'. This chapter will consider some of the key elements of that geographical diaspora, and the possibility of considering a 'long expressionism' that existed as a dominant modernist trope throughout the 1920s and '30s in places remote from Paris, which continued to be the putative centre of avant-garde artistic activity and development. Expressionism's diaspora has been largely invisible in dominant English and French language histories of modern art, which typically privilege the trail of developments out of Paris, and which focus on the succession of avant-garde movements that characterized a modernist, evolutionist view of art history. Berlin and Munich were, to be sure, on the map in these narratives before 1914, as centres for Brücke Expressionism and Blue Rider Abstraction, but Expressionism in Germany was otherwise absent from dominant histories of modernism until the late twentieth century. It is instructive, for example, that the Ukrainian-born art historian and collector, Rosa Schapire (1874–1954), who was close to, and an important early supporter of Brücke, was met with rebuffs from museum directors in London, most notably Sir John Rothenstein at the Tate Gallery, when she tried to donate her significant collection of Expressionist art to the nation after she moved to England, fleeing Nazi persecution, in 1939, largely on the grounds of the relatively marginal position Expressionism supposedly held in the public perception of modern art. Similarly, most of the Expressionist art produced outside France and Germany in the period 1920–1940 is represented only in the collections of museums in the countries of its production.

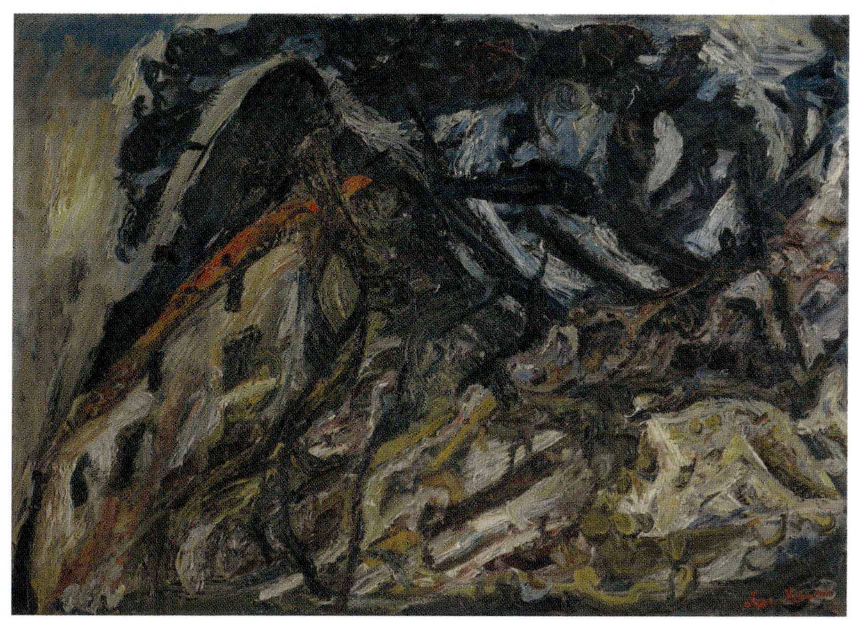

45 Chaïm Soutine, *Landscape at Céret*, c. 1920–21

The Legacy of Cubism

It is, though, impossible to talk about Expressionism's spread without saying something about Cubism, another significant modernist movement arising in Paris. Although generally regarded as sharing little in common with Expressionism – and especially that of Matisse and his circle, or the Brücke artists – the development of Expressionist art after around 1912 is unthinkable without acknowledging the part played by artistic responses to Cubism.

In France, at the same time that Matisse revealed the basic ideas behind Expressionism in 'Notes of a Painter', two artists with little or no interest in either mystical affect or a Romantic synthesis of the arts began an artistic partnership that was to produce probably the major revolution in twentieth-century art. Cubism grew essentially out of the friendly competition between an erstwhile Fauvist, Georges Braque (1882–1963) and an expressive Symbolist, Pablo Picasso (1881–1973), whose closeness, mutual trust and sense of adventure led them to being compared to two mountaineers roped together as they explored the possibilities of painting. Along with the Expressionists
46 Derain and Raoul Dufy (1877–1953), in 1908 they began to restrict the range of their palette and look closely again at the work of Cézanne, who had died two years earlier. But despite early signs

of Derain and Dufy taking Cézanne in a radical new direction, in works like Dufy's *Boats at Martigues* (1907), or Derain's *Forest at Martigues* (1908), it was left to Picasso and Braque to be the real creators of the new style.

Cubism was to prove central to the history of twentieth-century art, not only because many other artists eagerly took up its banner, but also because of the ways in which its innovations in both painting and sculpture were adopted and transformed in movements as otherwise distinct as Futurism, constructivism, surrealism, Abstract Expressionism and Pop Art. Yet of all the avant-garde modern art movements of the last century, Braque and Picasso's cubism was a deliberately private affair. The artists' primary audience consisted only of their bohemian friends and acquaintances, at first mainly writers, such as Guillaume Apollinaire (1880–1918), Max Jacob (1876–1944), Gertrude Stein (1874–1946) and André Salmon (1881–1969). After 1910 neither Braque nor Picasso exhibited publicly, and most of their work was sold through a single dealer, Daniel-Henry Kahnweiler (1884–1979), which created a great air of mystique around the pair. Nevertheless, Cubism spread rapidly and widely throughout Europe, although in its diasporic guise, it was inevitably mixed with the dominant tendency in the new art, namely Expressionism. Its stylistic influence – as much through Cubist-derived Italian Futurism – is clear in works by Kirchner, Klee, Marc, Macke, Felixmüller, Grosz,
47 Larionov and others, who used it for expressive ends without much evidence of digesting its methodological underpinning, that were rooted in exploring possibilities of finding new ways of translating the visual perception of three-dimensional forms and space into a new kind of two-dimensional pictorial space.

In a century marked by manifestos and artist's statements, Cubism is perhaps remarkable for the public silence of its two main participants. This is not to say that Braque and Picasso did not speak about art, they were involved in lively discussions with each other and with other artists and writers, some of whom were the public face of Cubism. The premium placed on Picasso and Braque as mysterious outsiders is entirely in keeping with early twentieth century cultural valorizations of the individual hero, battling away unacknowledged, but at the same time breaking new ground and arriving at new truths.

The artists generally regarded as the leaders of the Cubist *movement* at the time were those that continued to use the traditional exhibition and market systems, *and* who were prepared to represent themselves as the Cubist avant-garde; people like Jean Metzinger (1883–1956), Albert Gleizes (1881–1953), Le Fauconnier (1881–1946) and Robert Delaunay. The latter two were also associated with the Blue Rider, and work by them was illustrated

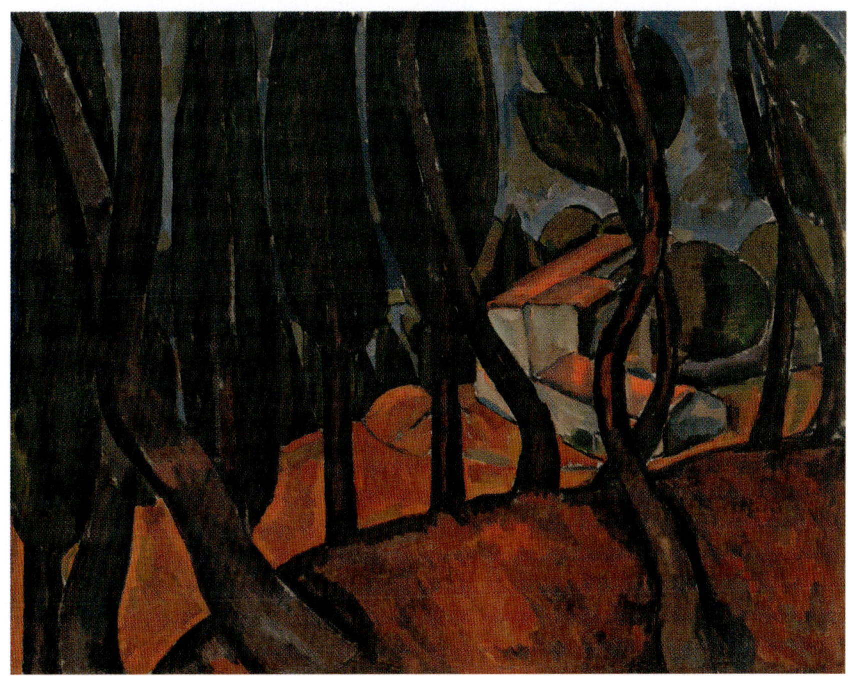

46 André Derain, *Forest at Martigues*, 1908

in the Almanac. In his contribution to the Almanac, 'Signs of Renewal in Painting', the French critic and poet Roger Allard (1885–1961) distinguishes their work from that of Matisse and his circle, emphasizing their commitment to a conscious methodological approach, in contrast to the intuitive one of the Expressionists. This is clearest in his statement that, 'Cubism is no new fantasy of "savages", no scalp dance around the altars of the "officials", but an honest search for a new discipline.' This, of course, is in opposition to Marc's essay, 'The "Savages" of Germany', and the Ukrainian artist and poet David Burliuk's (1882–1967), 'The "Savages" of Russia', both of which were published in the Almananc.

Generally contemporary claims about the importance of Cubism rested on its fundamental rejection of Impressionism and reflected those made for Expressionism. However, it was argued that Cubist pictures were more 'truthful', and that their vision was more incisive, so that they somehow represented Kantian ideal objects – the elusive 'thing-in-itself' – rather than merely that which appears to our senses. Compare this to Expressionist appeals to Schopenhauer's 'Will'. The poet and critic Olivier Hourcade, an early supporter

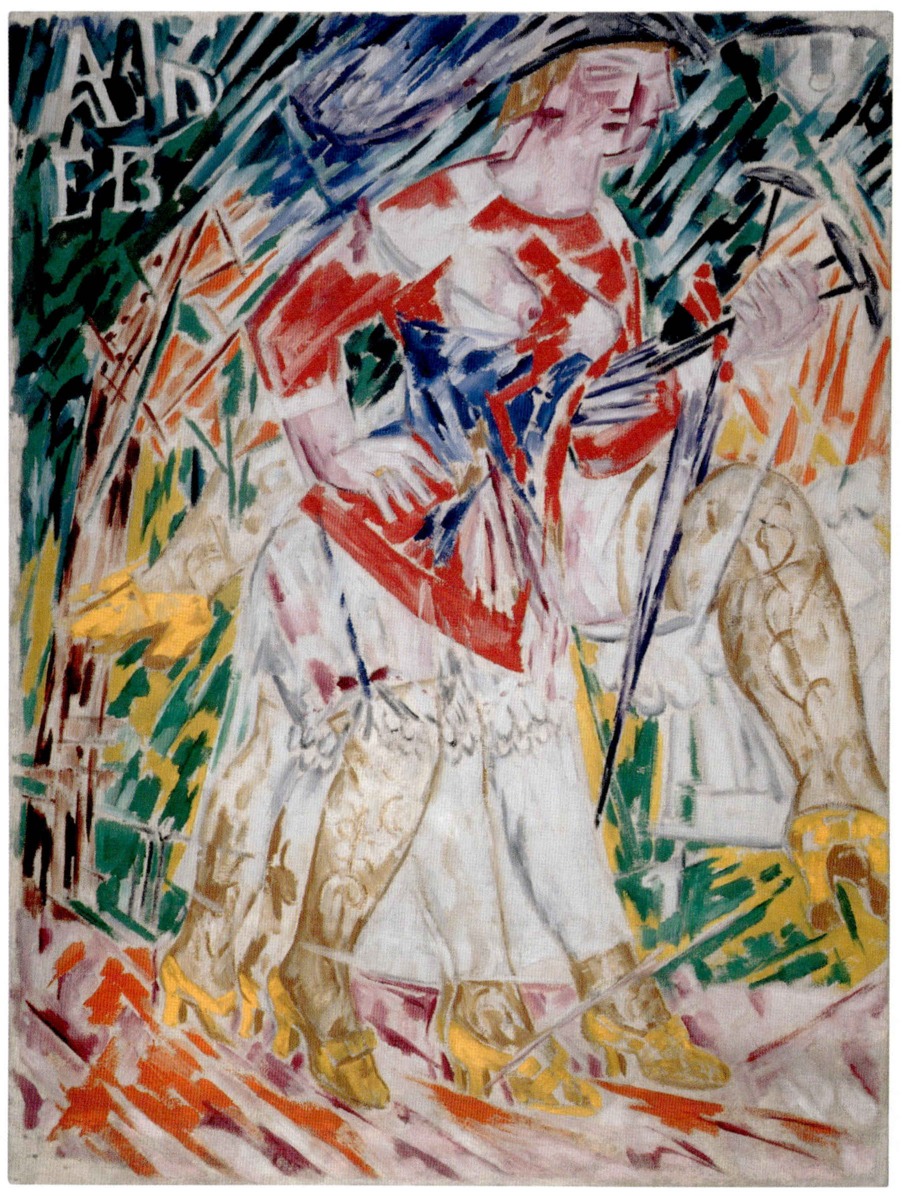

47 Mikhail Larionov, *Promenade. Vénus de boulevard*, 1912–13

of the Cubists, wrote: 'The external appearance of things is transitory, fugitive and relative. One must seek the truth and stop making sacrifices to the banal illusions of optics.' This was the application of philosophical idealism stripped of its mystical guise. Yet, Cubist theory nevertheless engaged with the metaphysics of the philosopher Henri Bergson, who was immensely popular in the years before the First World War. His anti-positivistic ideas about time, matter and consciousness struck a chord among those who wanted a new philosophy for the new century and were as relevant for the Expressionists in France as for the self-styled Cubist movement, and in Germany the prominent writer and art theorist Carl Einstein (1885–1940) had invoked Bergson as early as 1914 in an article in the Expressionist periodical, *Die Aktion*.

Bergson believed that the universe is in a constant state of flux; that in nature nothing, including inert matter is ever actually still. He also argued that rational thinking only allows a person to gain relative knowledge about things in the world and that *intuition* is the way of gaining absolute knowledge of it – something very reminiscent of Expressionist theory. Intuition, for him, was a quality of empathizing into an object in order to touch what is unique and inexpressible in it. Moreover, he argued that life is separate to matter and its organizing force, delaying the chain of vibrations and giving opportunities for free acts. Since intuition is a creative and non-rational faculty, Bergson also held up artists, rather than scientists as the people most likely to be able to communicate this kind of knowledge about the world. The Salon Cubists certainly discussed Bergson and his ideas resonate in their published statements. Gleizes and Metzinger wrote in *On 'Cubism'* (1912), for example, that contemporary painting allowed the expression of the idea of 'real time' – an effect of Bergsonian flux – as well as more traditional qualities, so that the artist might 'present within a limited space governed by a complex rhythm, a true fusion of objects.' They seized on the importance Bergson placed on freedom and creativity and insisted on the absolute right of artists to constantly remake the world. This was mixed with an equally enthusiastic reading of Nietzsche, enabling them to make the apparently democratic statement that, 'the ultimate aim of painting is to reach the masses,' while at the same time insisting that it was their Cubist vision that would be enforced from above. Cubist 'realism', they insisted, existed 'in order to move, to dominate, to direct, and not in order to be understood.'

Northern Expressionism

The development of an art in which the distortion of natural form and the use of heightened, intense colour appeared often to be the driving forces was probably most consistently pursued in northern and central Europe. In addition to Germany, in the years immediately before the First World War, Expressionism took hold as the major tendency in many countries. By the early 1920s, it was also established as an important style in the United States, Canada, and several other countries outside Europe. Expressionism remained central to histories of modern art in many of these areas until at least the end of the 1930s, so that later claims in English-language histories of modern art about 'Expressionist revivals' (notably in the late 1940s and early 1980s) are more often than not signs of a general refocusing of critical attention on a particular place, rather than some renaissance or reinvention of an earlier forgotten practice.

In Norway the figure of Edvard Munch, whose influence was pan-European, looms large, while in Denmark Oluf Høst (1884–1966), Erik Hoppe (1896–1968) and Astrid Noack (1888–1954) were important figures. In Prague Expressionism was strong among German-speaking Czechs with contacts both to Paris and the group around *Der Sturm*, notably Emil Filla (1882–1953) and Bohumil Kubišta (1884–1918). In the Netherlands Expressionism's most influential manifestation was under the umbrella of the group *De Ploeg* (The Plough), based in the northern city of Groningen, whose members included Jan Wiegers (1893–1959), Johann Dijkstra (1896–1978) and Jan Altink (1885–1971), and there was a dominant strand of Flemish Expressionism. In German-speaking Switzerland there were artists like Johannes Itten (1888–1967) and members of the *Rot-Blau* (Red-Blue) group, founded in 1924, and based on the Brücke, which included the sculptors Albert Müller (1897–1926) and Hermann Scherer (1893–1927), and Austria
48 produced artists like Kokoschka, Egon Schiele (1890–1918) and Max Oppenheimer (1885–1954).

It is important to note that these artists and groups self-consciously identified with Expressionism and called themselves Expressionists. In Scandinavia this took place as early as 1911 and was explicitly related to Matisse and his erstwhile Swedish and Norwegian pupils. In her scrupulously researched book, *The Concept of Expressionism: Origin and Metamorphosis* (1984) the Norwegian art historian Marit Werenskiold (b. 1942) showed that the term 'Expressionism' began to be used in Scandinavia in connection with Clutton-Brock's article on Fry's 'Post-Impressionists' exhibition;

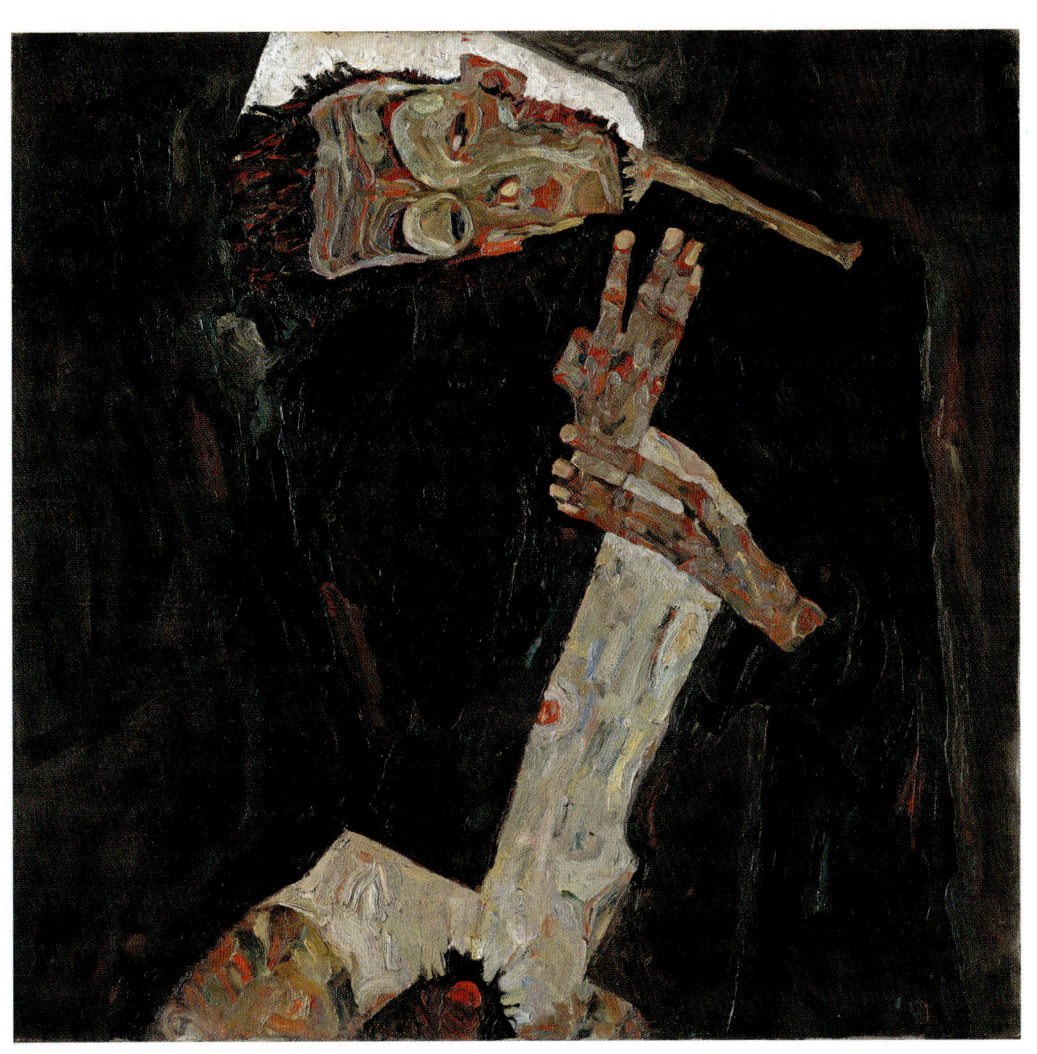

48 Egon Schiele, *Lyricist*, 1911

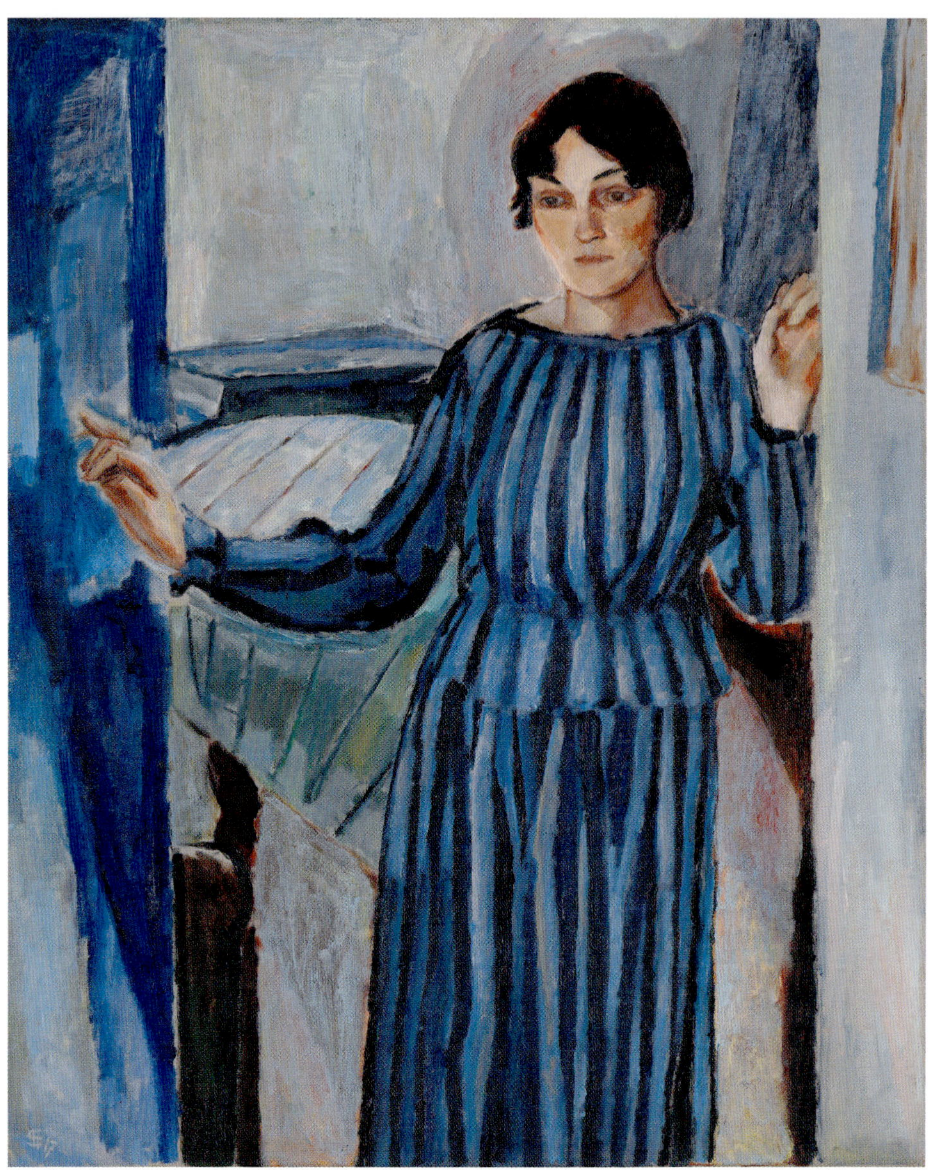

49 Henrik Sørensen, *Gudrun at the Door*, 1917

in Sweden by Carl David Moselius in an article, '*Impressionism och Expressionism*' (March 1911), which was a reaction to exhibitions in Stockholm by Matisse's Norwegian pupil Henrik
49 Sørensen (1882–1962) and the Swedish group *De unga* (The Young Ones); and in Norway, in a piece by another pupil of Matisse's, the journalist Walther Halvorsen, for the summer 1911 issue of *Kunst og Kultur*. Expressionism – and the English-language form was used by him – was, then, as Werenskiold says, 'associated with Matisse's concept of "expression", which was already known in Sweden and Norway through pupils who had returned home from Matisse's school of painting in Paris.' Sørensen was highly active in both Norway and Sweden during the war years and was described as 'Expressionism's young leader' in 1917 in the Norwegian press.

Expressionism in Sweden was initiated by members of the artists group, *De unga* and other contemporaries, including Tor Bjurström (1888–1966), Birger Simonsson (1883–1938) and Isaac Grünewald (1889–1946), all of whom had been pupils of Matisse in Paris. Another significant figure was the painter Sigrid Hjertén (1885–1948), who was married to Grünewald, but excluded from membership of *De unga* because of her gender. Crucially, besides their Parisian connections, she and Grünewald knew the German scene, notably the group around *Der Sturm*, through friendships with Nell and Herwarth Walden, and members of the Blue Rider group.

Grünewald and Hjertén are widely credited with introducing avant-garde modernism to Sweden. The pair had staged a large Expressionist exhibition in Stockholm in May 1918, together with Leander Engström (1886–1927), and in an accompanying manifesto, 'The New Renaissance in Art', Grünewald proclaimed, 'The different trends in modern art are by and large striving for the same goal, and one can collect them under a common name, Expressionism.' Hjertén's work was at first heavily influenced by Parisian Expressionism, but she developed a more linear, Cubist-inspired style that dealt directly with contemporary issues of identity and conventional
50 gender-assigned roles. In *The Red Blind* (1916) she subjects the familiar male theme of a reclining female nude to a woman's gaze. She utilizes a characteristically Expressionist shallow picture space, with the effect that everything is tipped vertiginously towards the viewer. The image of the woman has been emptied of the salacious sexuality or misanthropy often accompanying the subject historically, and instead viewers are presented with a strong, self-contained individual, seemingly deep in thought. An electric lamp, showering jagged, futurist light confirms the modernity of the painter and her subject.

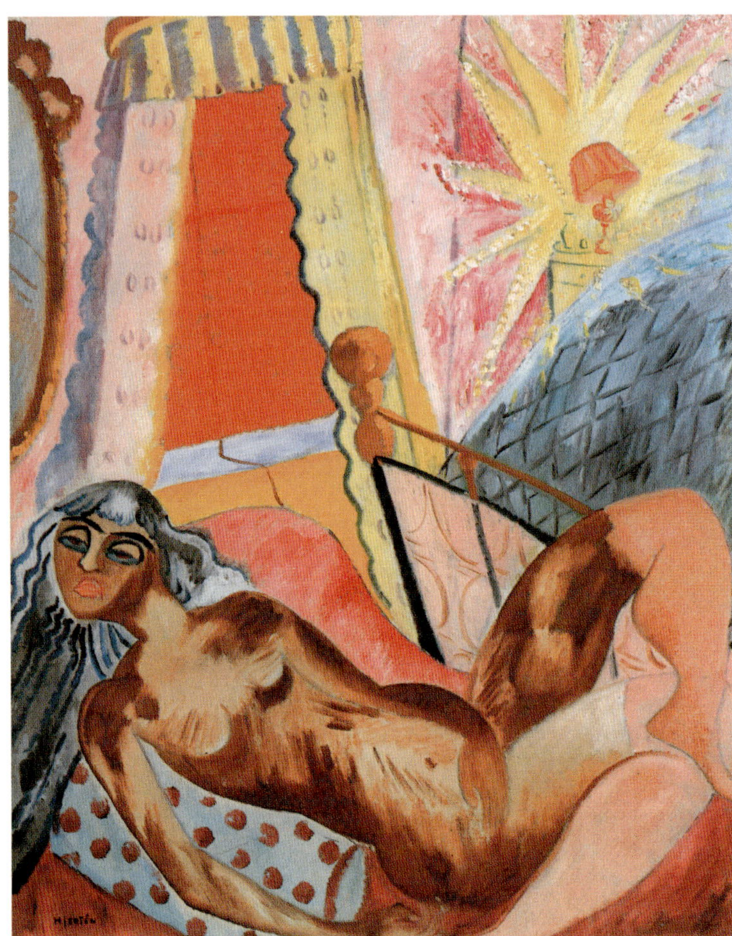

50 LEFT Sigrid Hjertén, *The Red Blind,* 1916
51 OPPOSITE Siri Derkert, *Self-Portrait,* 1915

Women artists were at the forefront of much of the spread of Expressionism. In Sweden, Siri Derkert (1888–1973) encountered Expressionism and Cubism during her studies in Paris before the outbreak of the First World War, incorporating their examples into her own paintings, as
51 in her *Self-Portrait* (1915). Derkert worked for a long period primarily as a fashion illustrator, with her designs in the 1910s and early 1920s reflecting a cubo-Expressionist aesthetic. In 1917, she collaborated with the artist Anna Petrus (1886–1949) and others to create an avant-garde dance show, in the spirit of the kind of Expressionist *Gesamtkunstwerk* envisaged by Kandinsky or Hugo Ball. Derkert was fiercely independent, and self-consciously projected the image of the 'New Woman',

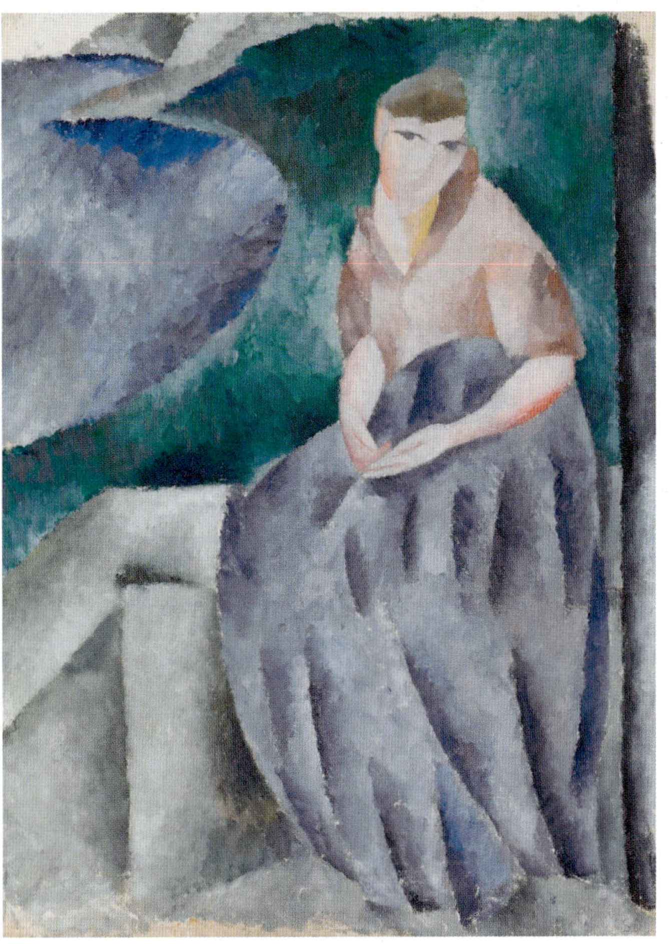

resisting social stereotypes, especially in the domestic sphere. Although she had three children, she never lived with their fathers, and she adopted a bohemian clothing style common among proto-feminist women of the late nineteenth and early twentieth century, appropriating traditionally male-gendered attire, especially trousers.

Munch's presence was strong in the development of Scandinavian expression, though perhaps less directly so than in Germany. Where the self-proclaimed Expressionists looked to Matisse, the French art which had most influenced Munch, who was a generation older, was that of the Symbolists and post-Impressionists, and particularly the work of Gauguin, whose use of closed forms in his paintings and insistence

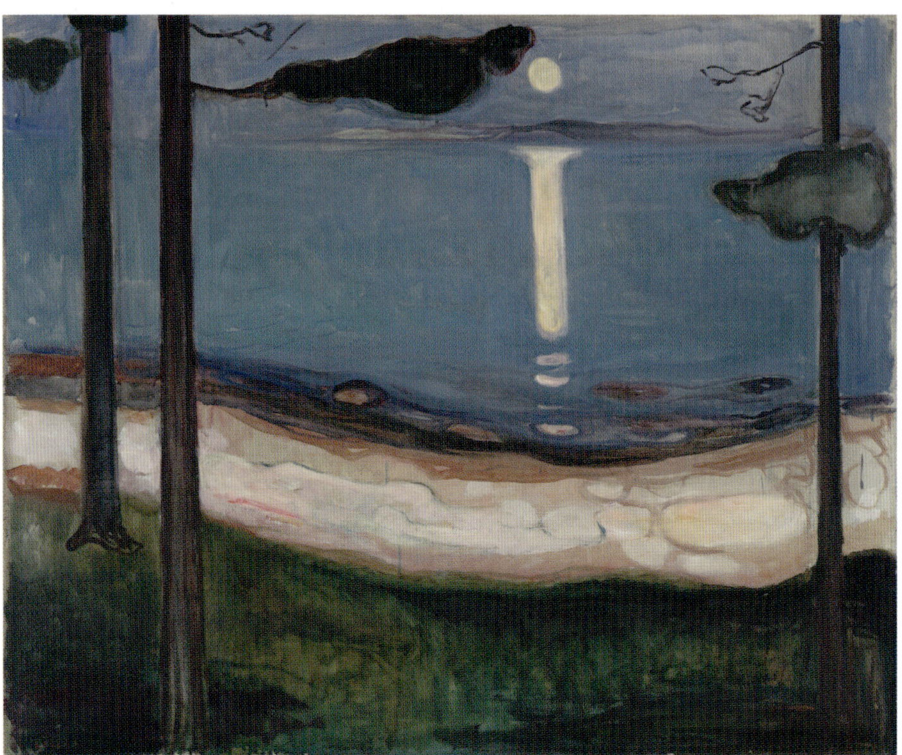

52 Edvard Munch, *Moonlight*, 1895

that the purpose of art was to express one's inner vision resonated strongly with him, evident in landscapes such as
52 *Moonlight* (1895). Munch was an Expressionist *avant la lettre*, and despite his living presence, was often seen as a progenitor of the new art in much the same way as Gauguin and Van Gogh in Germany before 1914; indeed, the three were represented prominently at the 'Cologne Sonderbund Exhibition' in 1912.

Most of Munch's immediate family died when he was quite young, and he lived for a while with a bohemian group of artists and writers in Oslo. There he was exposed to progressive attitudes to the prevailing social order, and a direct and open approach to sexuality. He shared an interest in attempting to represent emotional states with many Scandinavian realist painters from the nineteenth century, but he differed from them in the apparently direct and empathic way he was able to translate psychological conditions into image. Arguably one of the most powerful early examples is the painting,
53 *Puberty* (1894), which depicts a naked girl, covering her crotch

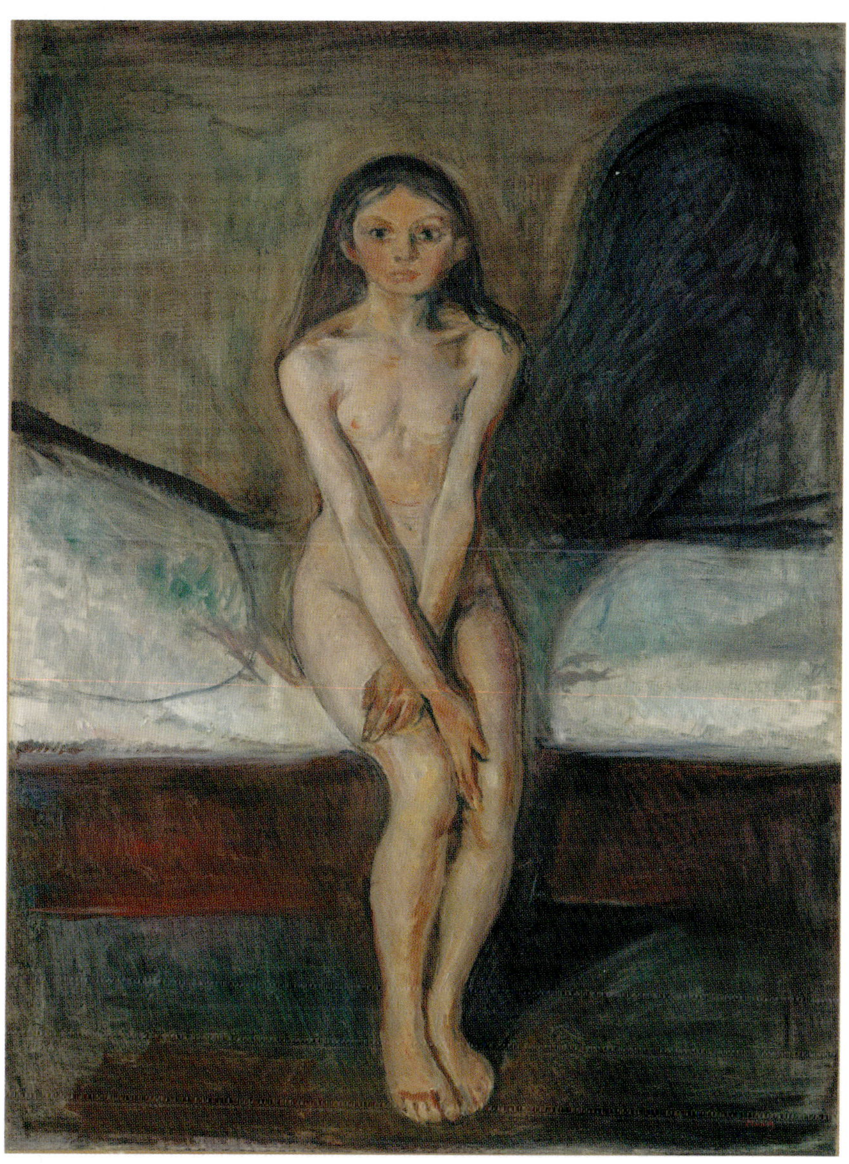

53 Edvard Munch, *Puberty*, 1894

and staring directly at the viewer. A sense of emotional and psychological power is conveyed through the starkness of the setting and the artist's use of shadows – behind the figure and under the cot – which contrast with her pale flesh and add to the sense of portentousness.

Munch received little formal training in art, which contributed to his embrace of experimental techniques and styles, especially in printmaking. He developed a spare style, characterized by the use of heightened, often jarring, colour and drawing that cared little for academic measures of correctness. In the last decade of the nineteenth century, Munch used this style to develop a series of paintings that addressed the themes of love and death, which were first exhibited in 1902 at the Berlin Secession under the title *The Frieze of Life*, though the number continued to grow subsequently. Contrary to the evocations of the Golden Age in work by Symbolists such as Puvis de Chavannes, or Matisse's bright, contemporary images of leisure, Munch's cycle of paintings is heavy with a symbolism that speaks to the profound separation of individuals in a universe fuelled by desire and the inevitability of death. The figures in *Dance of Life* (1899–1900) enact a ritualized act of sexualized contact embodied in the socially-controlling construction of formal dance – in this they are a long way from the uncontrolled frenzy of Nolde's figures in *Dance Around the Golden Calf* (1912). The threatened fulfilment of sexual desire is depicted as repulsive and grotesque in the couple at the right of the image. The two women on each side of the foreground symbolize a kind of yin yang, with all the unresolvable qualities of light and dark that this represents in western dialectical thought. This is seemingly confirmed in the appearance of the woman in red, who performs her assigned role, but who is emptied of an outward show of emotion and rendered doll-like and static. A sense of foreboding or the uncanny in this scene is reinforced by the crepuscular setting, and a claustrophobic, picture space that carries with it none of the ecstatic nature worship common in much of the German Expressionism that was influenced by Munch's work.

Flemish Expressionism

In Belgium, Expressionism emerged among a loosely affiliated artists mostly associated with the artist colony in Sint-Martens-Latem, near Ghent. Flemish Expressionism was one of dominant styles in Belgian Modernism in the 1920s and 1930s. It grew largely out of influences that included the Belgian painter James Ensor (1860–1949), who spent almost the whole of his life in the city of Ostend, and the early work of Van Gogh made in the Brabant, as well as the new art emerging from Paris. Its main protagonists included Frits Van den Berghe (1883–1939), Gustave de Smet (1877–1943), Constant Permeke (1886–1952), Albert Servaes (1883–1966), Jozef Cantré (1890–1957), and Rik Wouters (1882–1916).

Ensor's palette had burst into intense, acid colour in the late 1880s, and his style became direct and robust, usually with highly simplified figures derived from his interest in masks and popular art associated not with non-European art, but with local funfairs and the Roman Catholic festival of Carnival. Whereas in Germany it was largely the use of pure colour and immediacy of the application of paint found in Van Gogh's later work that had influenced the development of Expressionism, for the Belgians it was the gritty social commentary, focused on poor workers in the region, and an awkward, hard drawing method that seemed to reflect the harshness of his subjects' existence of his early work.

In addition, the Flemish Expressionists looked to the new art emerging in Paris. Matisse and his circle were important, but so were those working in Cubism-inspired styles. Besides paintings of bourgeois domestic interiors, Flemish Expressionist subjects focused on contemporary leisure activities and sites, popular public entertainments,
54 and the working poor. De Smet's, *De Veiei Aarde* (Fertile Ground) depicts a rural scene in rough, Expressionist handling, and muted colours that signal that everything here belongs emphatically to the earth. The prominent figure in the foreground threatens to merge with the tumescent ground, signalling his autochthonous state. Rural buildings cling to the earth, and at their centre a church speaks to a religiosity in this work.

There is also evidence of the whimsical, folksy Expressionism of Germans such as Campendonck and the French-Belarusian painter Marc Chagall, especially in work made in the mid 1920s by De Smet and Van den Berghe. Cantré's prints from the same period echo those made by artists from German Expressionism's second generation, such as Conrad Felixmüller and Constantin von Mitschke-Collande (1884–1956), and his sculpture is in the tradition of Kirchner.

The Netherlands – De Ploeg

Although Kees van Dongen had been a key member of the pre-war Expressionist circle in Paris, and Van Gogh, one of the great progenitors of Expressionism, were Dutch, the tendency did not emphatically take root in the Netherlands until the middle of

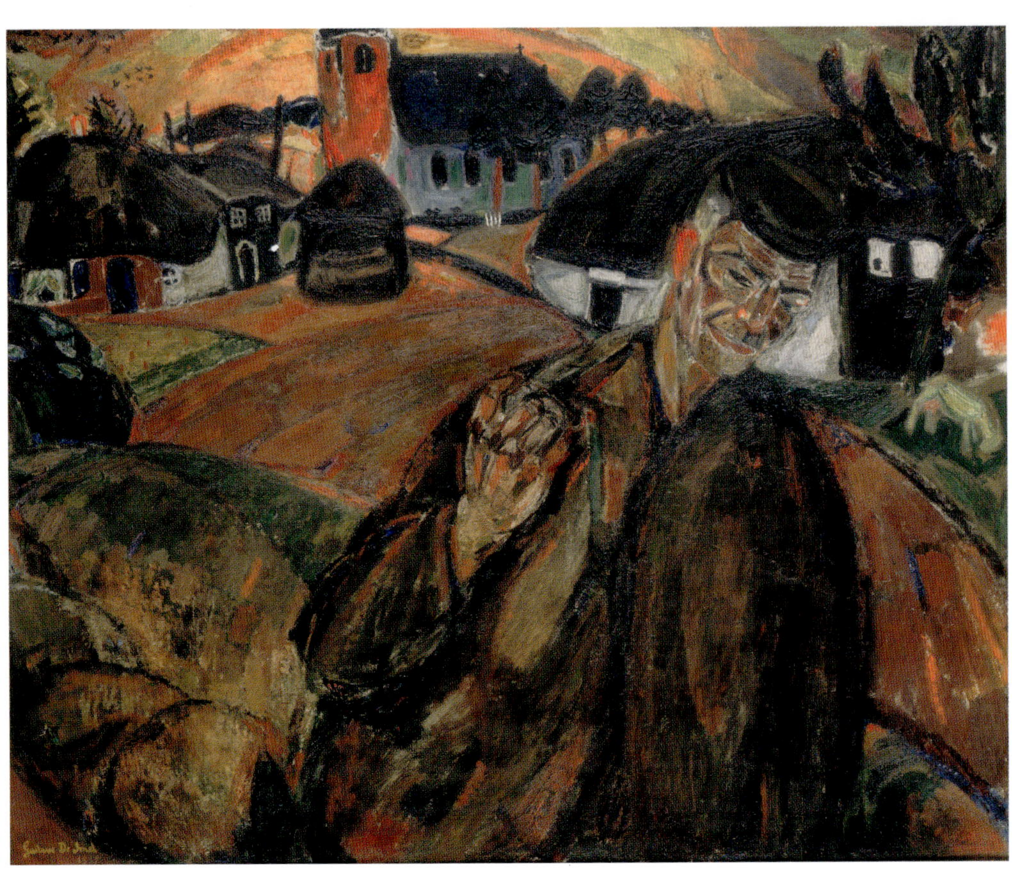

54 Gustave de Smet, *De Veiei Aarde* (Fertile Ground), 1917

the war, in the work of a group of artists working in and around the northern Dutch city of Groningen. In 1918 they formed an art association, *De Ploeg* (The Plough), with members including Jan Altink, Jan Wiegers, Johann Dijkstra, Jan van de Zee (1898–1988), George Martens (1894–1979) and Alida Pott (1888–1931), who also designed the association's logo. The metaphor of the plough signified the group's desire to establish fertile ground from which a renewal of the field of art in Groningen could grow.

De Ploeg still exists, but the period of Expressionism's dominance really belongs only to the 1920s, beginning after Wiegers's return from a stay in a sanatorium in Davos in 1921. In Switzerland he had met and befriended Kirchner, who by then was living there. The experience had a profound effect on Wiegers, who learned much from the German's attitude and practice, in painting, printmaking and carved wooden sculpture. Back in Groningen, this was added to the already foundational Expressionist influences of artists such as Van Gogh and Munch among the members of De Ploeg. Wiegers's painting style reflected the quieter, more lyrical Expressionism that characterized Kirchner's Swiss work, featuring bold planes of saturated colour, often accompanied by scratchy, hatched linear passages of paint used to define edges and features, equally in images of landscapes and figures. In common with most figurative Expressionism, the subjects chosen by Wiegers and other painters of De Ploeg tended to alternate between images of cosmopolitan individuals in urban settings, as in Wiegers's *Bohemian Interior* (1925) and his *Portrait of Kirchner in his Studio* (1925), Altink's *Portrait of Jannes de Vries* (1926), or Dijkstra's woodcut *Chez Dicque* (1926), and landscapes, including rural scenes that emphasized the fecundity of the land and a sense of visceral unity among its inhabitants. This is clear
55 in Wiegers's painting, *Landschap met rode bomen* (Landscape with Red Trees) (1922) and stark woodcuts, such as *Groningen Landscape* (1920s), in which the organic nature of the medium
56 adds to the sense of natural equilibrium. In *Merchant Woman on a Country Road*, Altink fuses a subject very familiar in Dutch art, a rustic figure in a vast, flat, rain-soaked agrarian landscape, with a distinctly modern painterly style. In this way a double sense of authenticity is claimed, via the supposed simplicity and closeness to nature of the subject and the directness and emotional honesty of the forms.

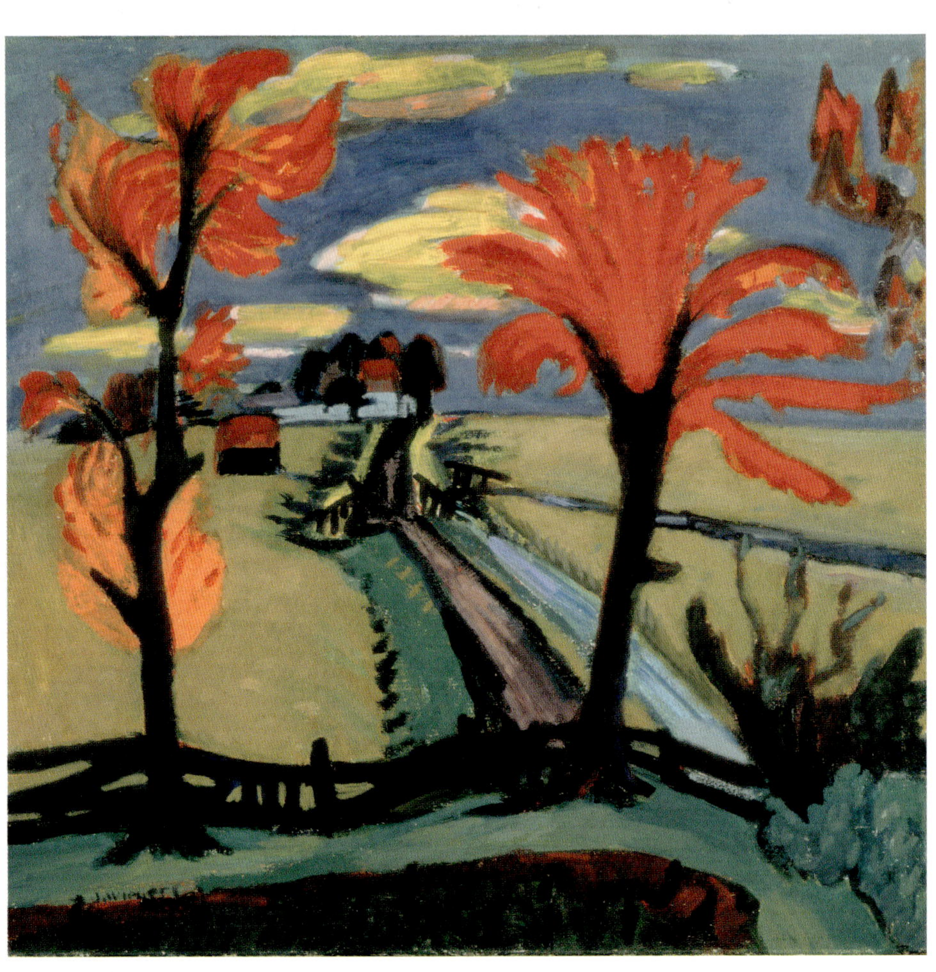

55 ABOVE Jan Wiegers, *Landschap met rode bomen (Landscape with Red Trees)*, 1922
56 OPPOSITE Jan Altink, *Koopvrouw op landweg* (Merchant Woman on Country Road), 1925

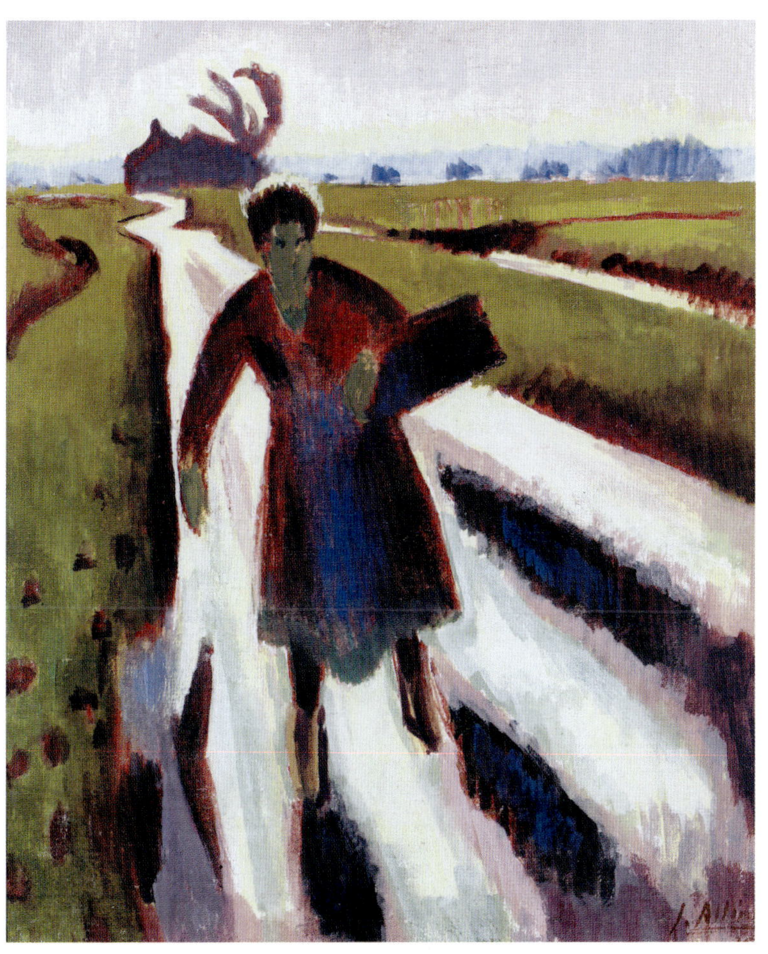

Rot-Blau

Kirchner's example was also crucially influential in Switzerland itself. Several young artists in Basel reacting against the stranglehold of the dark-toned value painting in vogue at that time were inspired by a large exhibition of Kirchner's work held at the Kunsthalle in mid-1923. As a consequence, Albert Müller and Hermann Scherer sought out Kirchner at his home near Davos and the three of them became friends. They learnt much from Kirchner's example, establishing a strong lyrical Expressionism in their work, much in the way that Wiegers did. At the end of 1924, together with another Basel artist, Paul Camenisch (1893–1970), they formed the group *Rot-Blau*. Kirchner himself was never a member, but he supported them. The reasons for choosing this name remains unclear, although these are two primary colours associated with strong emotions,

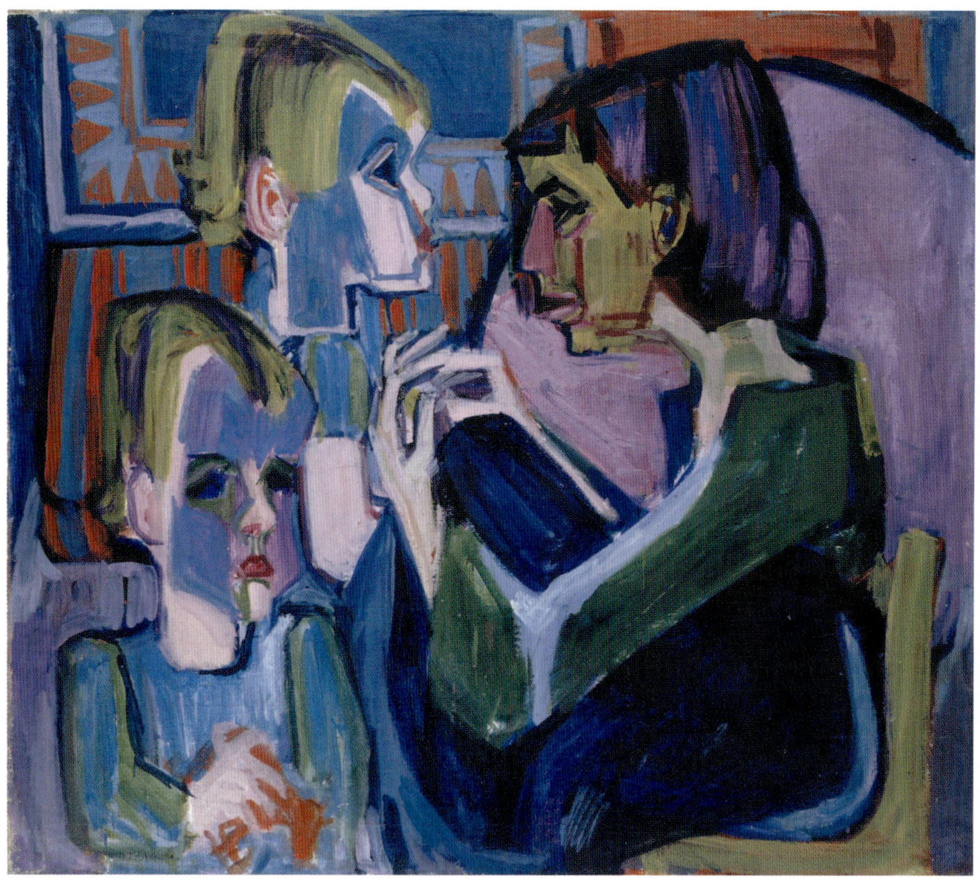

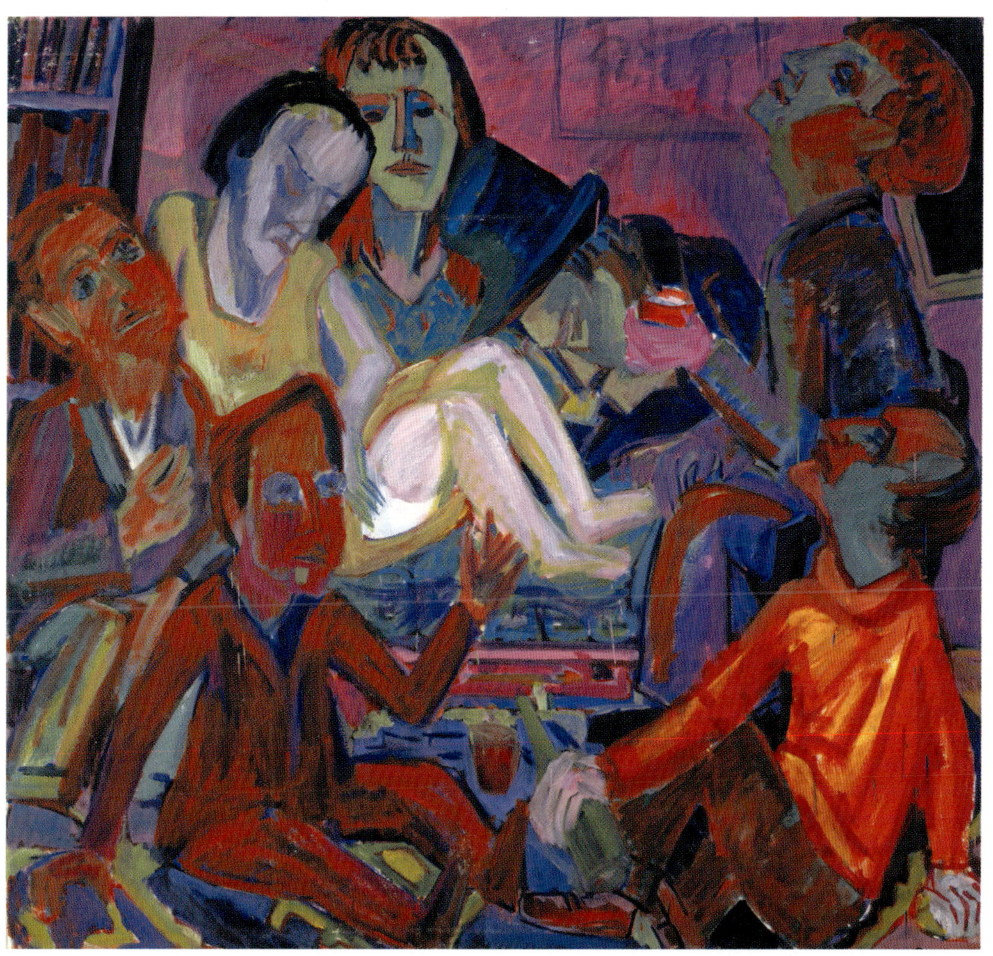

57 LEFT Albert Müller, *Mütter mit Kindern* (Mother with Children), 1925
58 ABOVE Hermann Scherer, *Atelierfest* (Party in the Studio), 1925

and there was a likely nod in the direction of the pre-war Blue Rider. Kirchner's example is strong in Rot-Blau art, although
57, 58 paintings such as Müller's *Mother with Children* (1925) and Scherer's *Party in the Studio* (1925) clearly show the characters of each individual artist. The subjects of these works are characteristically intimate, showing Müller's own family and a group of Scherer's friends in his studio respectively. Kirchner's dream of the dawn of a new generation of Swiss Expressionism was tragically cut short by the early deaths from illness of Müller and Scherer within five months of each other.

Expressionist Women across the World

We have already seen many examples of the centrality of the roles played by women in the development and dissemination of Expressionism, from artists such as Gabriele Münter, Marianne Werefkin and Erma Bossi in Munich, and Sigrid Hjertén and Siri Derkert in Sweden, to collectors such as Rosa Schapire and Galka Scheyer and the Düsseldorf dealer Johanna 'Mutter' Ey (1864–1947). This is a pattern that was repeated internationally throughout the 1920s.

In Ireland women artists were at the forefront in development of a vanguard modernist painting that was heavily indebted to Parisian Expressionist and cubo-Expressionist examples. They included Evie Hone (1894–1955), Mainie Jellett (1897–1944), and Mary Swanzy (1882–1978), all of whom studied at times in Paris. Swanzy exhibited at the *Salon des Indépendants* and developed a sustained Expressionist practice that owed much to both Cézanne and Matisse's circle and the Cubist movement, especially the likes of Robert Delaunay and André Lhote. Works
59 such as *Abstract* suggests a dense, primeval landscape, perhaps inspired by the artists wide travels, and demonstrate a cubo-Expressionist manner that is as much reminiscent of Franz Marc's later work as any Parisian precedents.

59 BELOW Mary Swanzy, *Abstract*, date unknown
60 OPPOSITE Guan Zilan, *Portrait of Miss L*, 1929

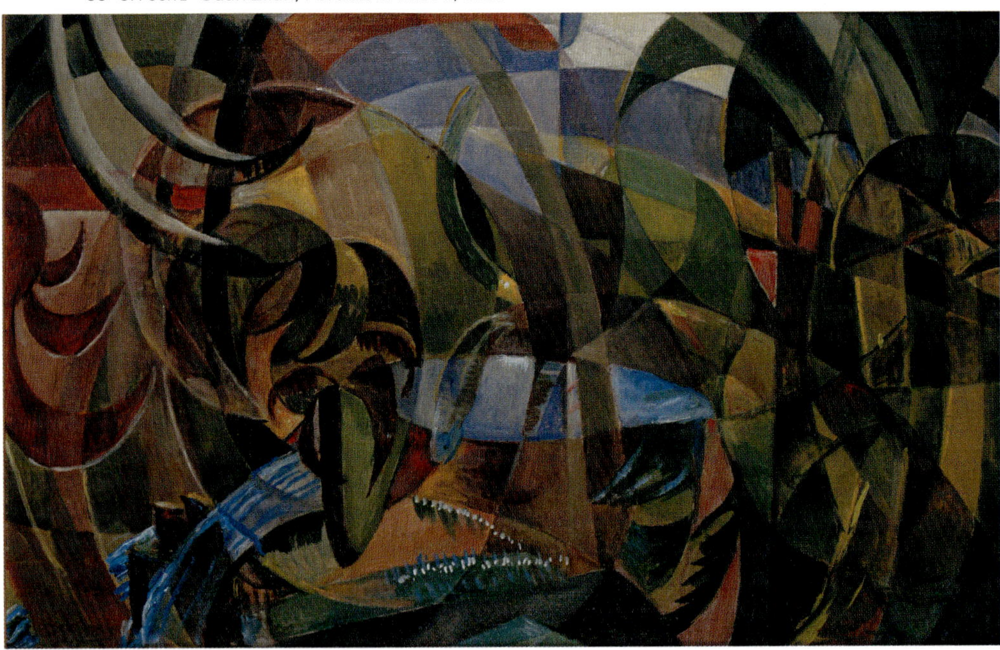

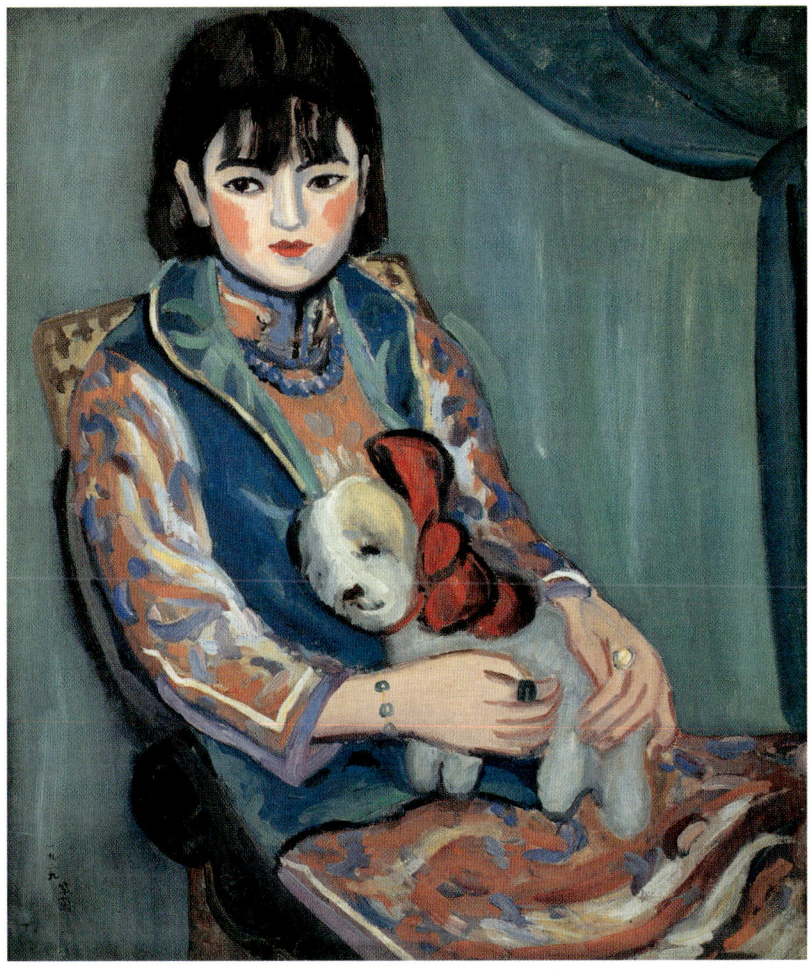

In China women artists such as Pan Yuliang (1895–1977) and
Guan Zilan (1903–1986) introduced a modernist aesthetic and
contemporary subjects to the country. Both studied overseas, Pan
in Paris and Guan in Japan, developing styles that owed much
to the example of Matisse and his circle. Guan, in particular, is
interesting because her experience of Expressionism came via
Japan, whose art world during the 1920s was at the height of an
influence of French post-Impressionism, which in turn had been
60 informed by Japonisme. Her *Portrait of Miss L* (1929) employs a
gentle Expressionist style, which together with the fashionable
clothing and self-assured stance, reinforces that sense of the
modernity of her subject.

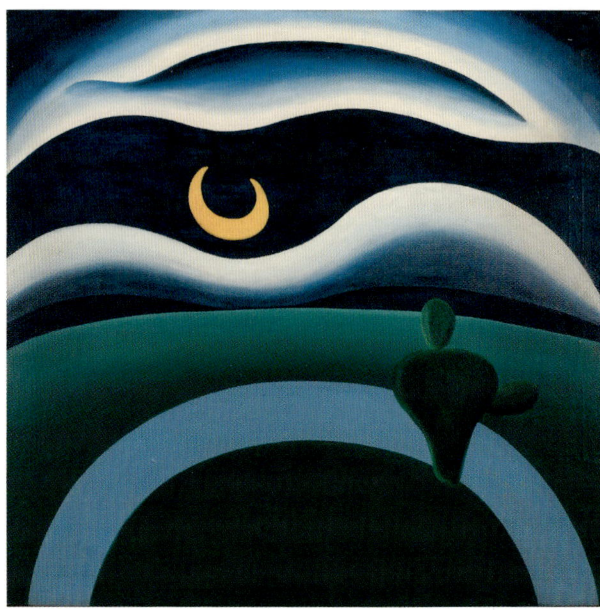

61 Tarsila do Amaral, *The Moon*, 1928

Brazil

In many countries the introduction of Expressionism marked the inception of a national modernist aesthetic, as was the case in Brazil and South Africa, for example. The Brazilian artist Anita Malfatti (1889–1964) studied in Germany between 1910–1914, where she encountered Expressionist art, notably at the 'Cologne Sonderbund Exhibition' (1912), before extending her studies in the United States. She developed a personal figurative Expressionist style that featured intense, saturated colour and the use of Cubist-style facets within the general formal structure of her paintings, as can be seen in *Tropical* (1917). She returned to Brazil in 1917, where her first exhibition caused uproar among the deeply conservative audience. The critical response was brutal, with critics attacking her not only for her avant-garde stance and style, but also on account of her gender. Yet, sympathetic critics and modernist writers leaped to Malfatti's defence, and her show came to be seen as the catalyst for seismic change in the arts in Brazil that received its first emphatic confirmation in 'Modern Art Week', in Sao Paolo in 1922. In addition to exhibitions of modernist art, the event included lectures, concerts and poetry readings, and saw the confirmation of the place of Malfatti and another woman, the
61 painter and sculptor Tarsila do Amaral (1886–1973) as leaders of the new movement in the visual arts.

South Africa

Two women – Maggie Laubser (1886–1973) and Irma Stern (1894–1966) – are widely credited as introducing a modernist aesthetic to South Africa. At that time the country was still a British colony whose economy was based on mining and farming, and the ruling class had little interest in contemporary art. Laubser and Stern's agency was probably partly a result of the fact that there were no male artists working within modernist idioms, but also because they were professional and independent. That said, at first they were met with hostility and rejection by the conservative and misanthropic South African art world, only really beginning to receive wide recognition in the 1930s.

Stern was born in the Transvaal. She was part of the German-Jewish community that had begun to develop in South Africa in the nineteenth century, though she spent most of her life between Africa and Europe, establishing a reputation as an Expressionist artist in Germany long before her work was accepted in the country of her birth. She became interested in Expressionism during her studies in Germany, which intensified after she met Max Pechstein towards the end of the First World War. Pechstein introduced her to the Berlin Expressionist circles, where she was able to construct an image of herself as an 'authentic' African and

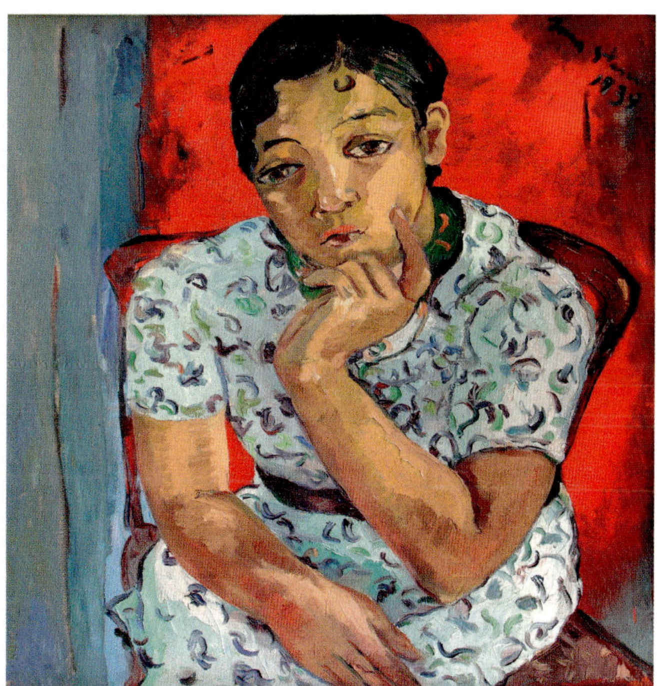

62 Irma Stern, *Girl in a Print Dress*, 1939

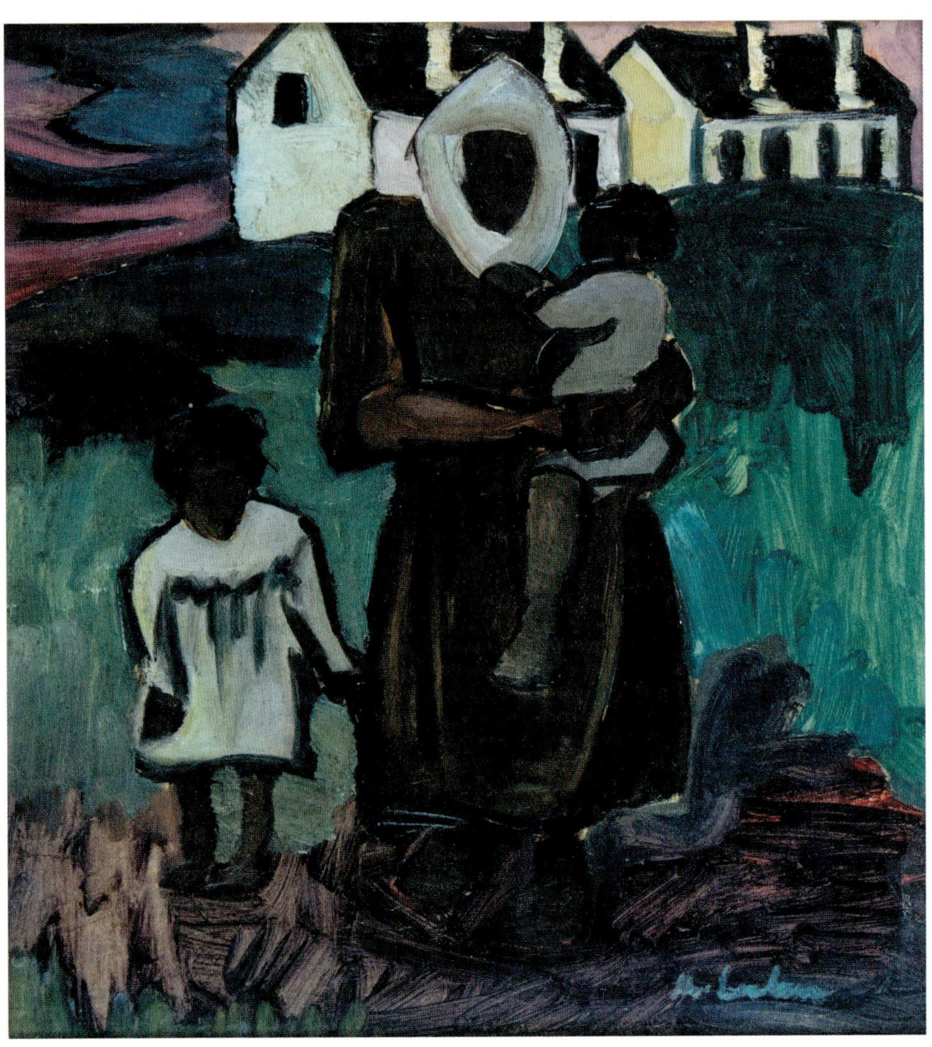

63 Maggie Laubser, *Vrou met twee kinders* (Woman with Two Children), 1928

knowledgeable about indigenous African art and culture; something which played perfectly to contemporary European exoticism and fascination with the notionally 'primitive'. She was one of only a few women who were members of the Expressionist Novembergruppe, and back in South Africa she was able to use her European modernist credentials to great effect, in contrast to the primitivizing self-image she cultivated in Germany. Early work by Stern, such as *Children Playing* (1924) is close to Pechstein's post-Brücke Expressionism, developing into a personal style that utilized saturated colour and distorted drawing, which heightened the emotional impact of her imagery, as in the powerful
62 introspection of the figure in *Girl in a Print Dress* (1939).

Laubser was born and raised in South Africa, but in 1913 she travelled to Europe where she developed her art practice, particularly in the artist colony at Laren in the Netherlands, in London, and in Germany. In Berlin she immersed herself in a study of figurative Expressionism and met the erstwhile Brücke artist, Schmidt-Rottluff, whose example – Laubser's fierce assertion to the contrary notwithstanding – was deep and long-lasting, and clear in the woodcut *Landscape with Harvesters in Wheatfield* (1926), for example. Laubser's Expressionism was, in general, a synthesis of the more painterly elements of German and Flemish models, as is
63 clear in *Woman with Two Children* (1928), which is a sensitive representation of Black South Africans without any of the primitivizing characteristic of Stern's images of indigenous peoples.

Denmark

Denmark experienced a brief flowering of intense Expressionist activity during and shortly after the First World War, facilitated in large part by the country's political neutrality. As with Sweden and Norway, the model was largely Parisian, although exhibitions organized by *Der Sturm* were also held in the Danish capital, Copenhagen in 1917 and 1918. Danish Expressionism at this time was, though, dominated by a formalist approach, more in keeping with Matisse and his circle than the metaphysics of Walden and Kandinsky. Pioneers of Danish Expressionism included artists such as Harald Giersing (1881–1927), Karl Larsen (1897–1977) and Olaf Rude (1886–1957), all of whom were associated with *Klingen* (The Blade), a magazine founded in 1917 to act as a mouthpiece for the new art. The first issue included interviews with Matisse and Picasso, and the third contained a full Danish translation of Matisse's 'Notes of a Painter'.

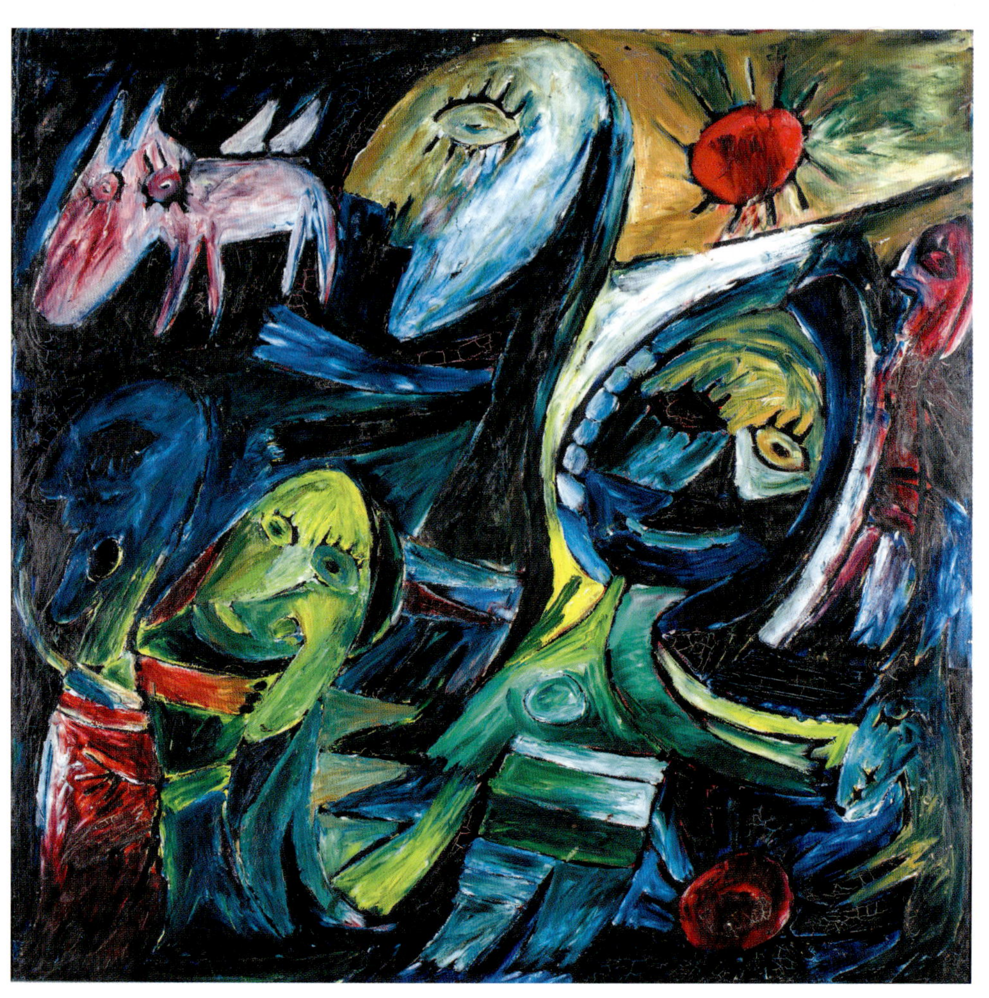

64 ABOVE Carl-Henning Pedersen, *Fantasy II*, *c*. 1943
65 OPPOSITE Egill Jacobsen, *Accumulation*, 1938

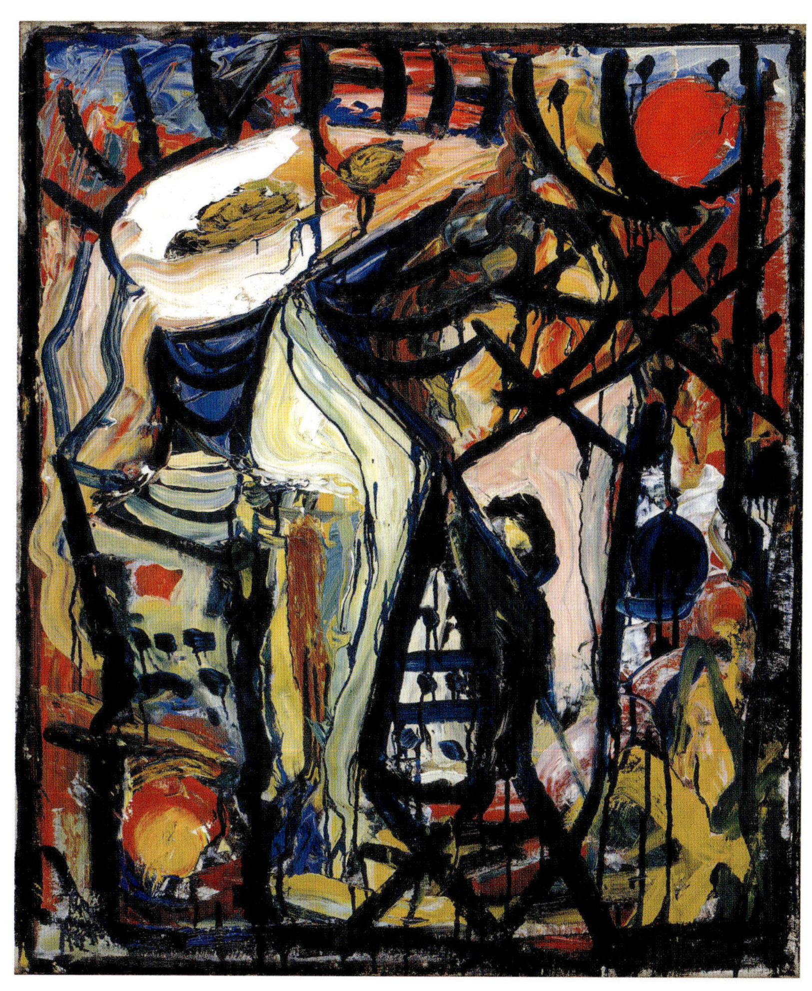

By the mid-1920s Expressionism was a spent force in Danish painting. However, it experienced a revival there in the mid-1930s out of the unlikely ranks of the Danish Abstract Surrealist group *Linien* (The Line). Unhappy with the doctrinal elements of Surrealism, the painters Ejler Bille (1910–2004) and Richard Mortensen sought instead to explore, according to Bille, an 'art in which the soul is expressed in a symbolic language generated by fantasy.' They were soon joined by other young artists, including Asger Jorn, Sonja Ferlov (1911–1984), Henry Heerup (1907–1993), Egill Jacobsen
64 (1910–1998), and Carl-Henning Pedersen (1913–2007), keen
to develop an art that was spontaneous in its production and powerful in its symbolism, whilst also leaning towards abstraction in its forms.

The breakthrough work by what would come to be known as the Danish Experimental Group was Jacobsen's
65 *Accumulation*. Painted after his return from Paris, where
he had been inspired by Picasso, and in response to the German invasion of Czechoslovakia, it spoke to, as he said, 'the struggle of people dreaming of freedom and revolution while surrounded by oppressive darkness.' Jacobsen quickly applied sweeps of liquid paint in pure colours with a large brush, obviating any possibility of finicky detail. Any mixing of paint was done on the canvas itself, and the sense that the materials are somehow working actively with the painter is further enhanced by paint streaks running and sometimes merging with parts of the surface while wet. This goes well beyond the contemporary thoughtful, intuitive abstractions of the Surrealist Joan Miró (1893–1983) in its raw spontaneity, although there are similarities with André Masson's (1896–1987) experiments with automatic methods.

In common with many avant-garde modernist artists, and especially those with Expressionist leanings, the Danish Group stated a desire to return to beginnings in their art; to offload surplus social and cultural constraints, and to regain both a primitive simplicity and universal symbolism in visual communication. In this, they were guided much more by the work and theoretical utterings of Kandinsky and Klee than Matisse or the Brücke – it is interesting that both Kandinsky's and, especially, Klee's presence as teachers at the Bauhaus in Germany also led to a generation of artists who practised a form of Abstract Expressionism in Germany throughout the
66 1930s, including Fritz Winter (1905–1976), whose *Komposition
über erste Blüten im Walde owes much to the example of both artists. Asger Jorn also worked through Klee and Kandinsky, as it were, on his way to achieving a fully independent style

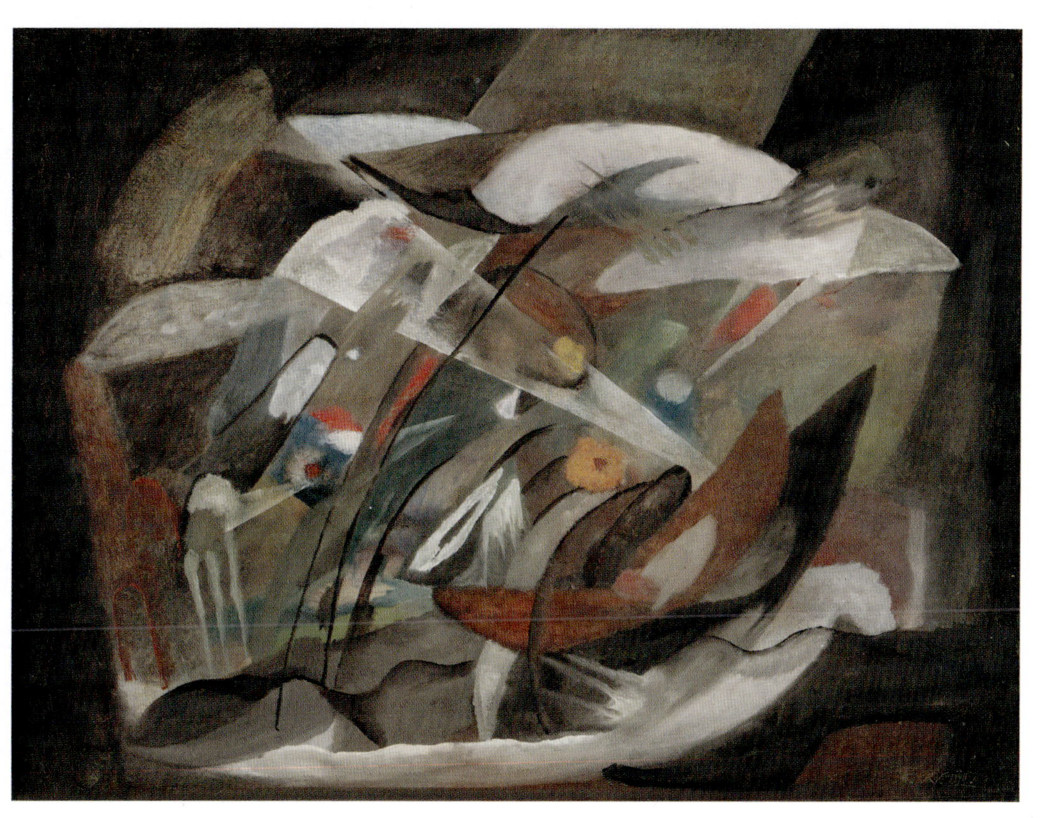

66 Fritz Winter, *Komposition über erste Blüten im Walde* (Composition on the First Blossom in the Forest), 1940

in the late 1940s. In *Untitled* (1943–44) Jorn uses facets of
colour expressively, in much the same way that Klee does in
67 *The Full Moon* (1919), and he also adopts Klee's habit of creating
ambiguous representational elements that work much like
the famous rabbit-duck illusion. The result in Jorn's image is
a feeling of primal becoming that is shrouded in a profound
sense of the uncanny.

The Danish Group were members of the *Høst* (Harvest) exhibition association and associated with the magazine *Helhesten* (Hell-Horse), which was initiated by Jorn and named for the three-legged horse from Scandinavian mythology that symbolized illness and death, and which was said to appear in times of tragedy and upheaval. It was published

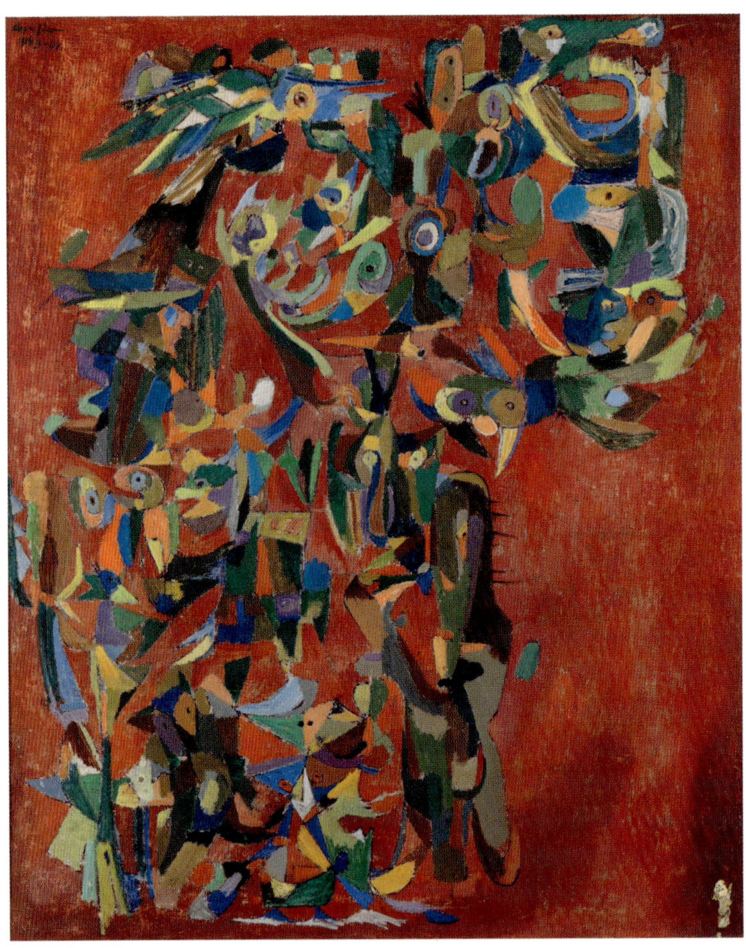

67 LEFT Asger Jorn, *Untitled*, 1943–44
68 OPPOSITE Paul Klee, *Der Vollmond* (The Full Moon), 1919

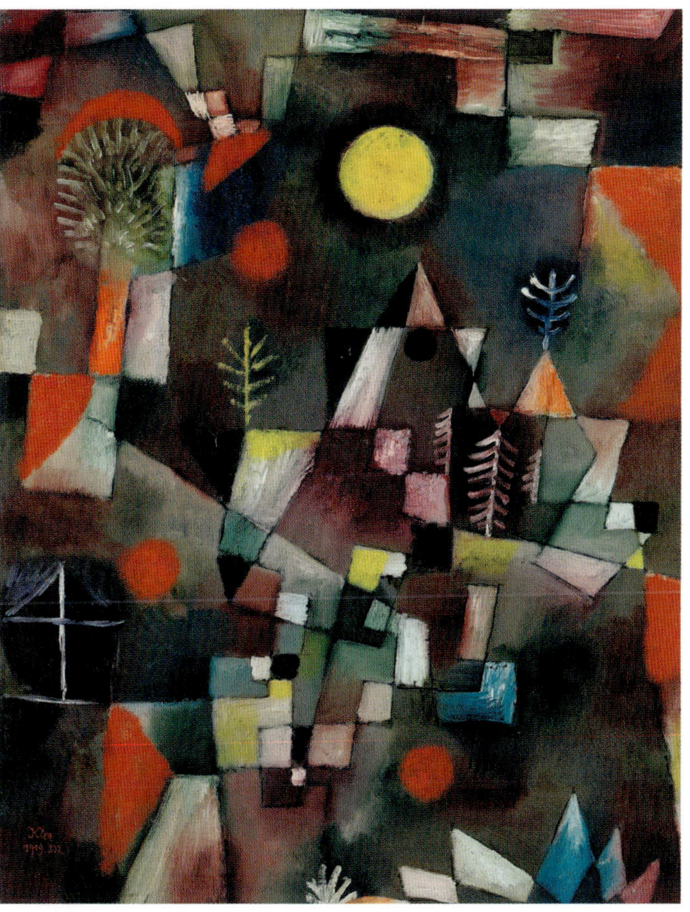

from 1941–1944, throughout the Nazi occupation of Denmark and emphasized an egalitarian approach to creativity and the consumption of art that extended the general embrace of the Danish and international folk art and culture that was already present in the thought of the group in the late 1930s. However, as the art historian Kerry Greaves has noted, '*Helhesten's* engagement with both Danish social democratic and German traditions, and the group's transformation of so-called "degenerate" art styles into an exploration of the redemptive possibilities of gestural abstraction, manifested a singular model of cultural resistance during World War II.'

In this way pre-war Modernism, and particularly German Expressionist tropes, were weaponized through a universalism that undermined Nazi myths of pan-Nordic identity. If Bille's

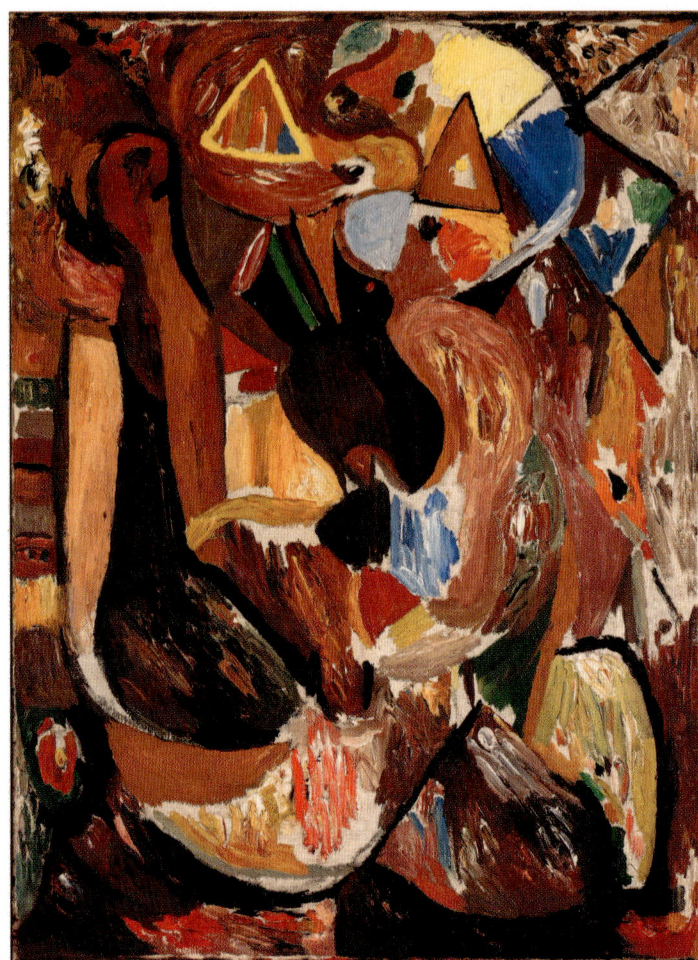

69 LEFT Ejler Bille, *Figure*, 1942
70 OPPOSITE Egill Jacobsen, *Orange Object II*, 1943

69 *Figure* seems measured in its use of an Abstract Expressionist
70 language, Jacobsen's *Orange Object II* is self-consciously childlike in its style, and in the emphasis on individual elements deemed to be important, such as eyes and nipples, which are rendered similarly – and therefore related psychologically – as red-centred starbursts. Paint is similarly applied in a consciously ham-fisted way, suggesting that here viewers are participating in something archetypally brutal; primitive and direct.

Helhesten and the work and thought of the artists associated with it was of particular importance to the emergence of a powerful strain of Expressionism in Europe in the aftermath of the Second World War that has usually been collected under the catch-all title Informal Art. It had its most visible early manifestation in the CoBrA group, which included the Danish artists among others, and whose name is an acronym derived from the initials of the capital cities of the countries from which all of its core membership was drawn, Copenhagen, Brussels and Amsterdam (see Chapter 4). Yet perhaps precisely because it was a movement that existed during a period of war and occupation, and because its members participated in the post-war reignition of the European avant-garde, it has been somewhat overlooked in dominant histories of Modernism. It is important to note, though, that the activities of *Helhesten* signal both a continuity of Expressionism and a subtle transformation

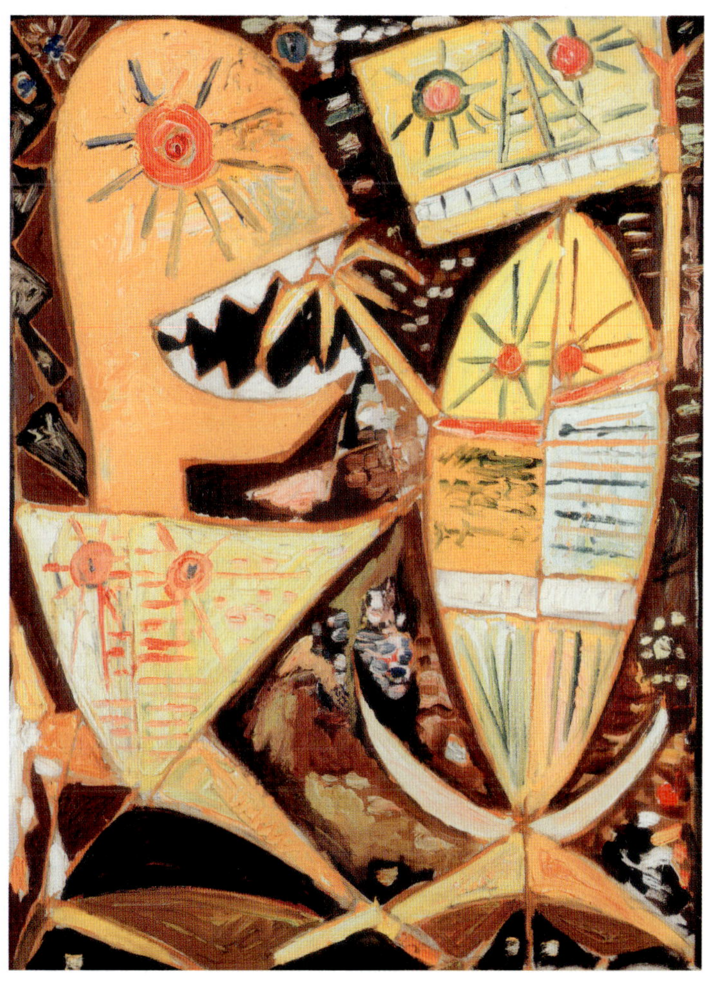

of its precepts, from representing the establishment of a self-consciously modernist sensibility to performing a self-reflexive criticality from within modernist practice.

Entartete Kunst

It may well have been that Expressionism had run its course as a major stream of modernist aesthetics by the end of the 1930s. Surrealism had become a global phenomenon and looked set to replace Expressionist notions of immediacy, spontaneity, and cosmogonic mythologizing with more measured rationalist interests in political science through Marxist theory and psychology based on the work of Sigmund Freud (1856–1939) and Théodore Flournoy (1854–1920). Expressionism in the francophone and anglophone worlds had become unambiguously connected to Germany, and the rise of Nazism in that country initially led to a general presumption that Expressionism would continue to be seen as quintessentially representative of the German or Nordic spirit. Indeed, Joseph Goebbels (1897–1945), the Nazi Minister for Propaganda championed Expressionism in exactly these terms – paintings by Nolde hung in his office – until the state turned emphatically against all forms of Modernism in the arts in 1937. At this point, a series of events took place that would lead to a recuperation of German Expressionism among Germany's enemies. Modern art, and particularly Expressionism, was declared 'degenerate' by the Nazis and brutally suppressed. Work in public museums was deaccessioned, and art from private collections – especially those owned by Jewish Germans who had not already left the country – were confiscated and sold abroad. Many modernist artists fled Germany and, subsequently, countries under German occupation, notably to the United States. Those who remained were forbidden to make art and, in the case of many who were Jewish or actively Communist, were murdered.

Not all Expressionists, though, were entirely antipathetical to the regime. For example, Nolde had been an early member of the Nazi party, and he reacted to being declared a 'degenerate' artist with letters to Goebbels and others pleading his credentials as a good 'Aryan'. The letters still exist, although in the immediate aftermath of the war concerted efforts were made to downplay his racial supremacist sympathies, and to foreground his suffering under the Nazi regime. Similarly, the Flemish Expressionist Albert Servaes was a member of Dinaso, a fascist Belgian political party, in the 1930s and an enthusiastic collaborator with the Nazis during the German occupation of Belgium.

In 1937, the great visible symbol of this sinister turn of events in German official culture was the staging of two major art exhibitions in Munich. The first was the 'Große Deutsche Kunstausstellung' (Great German Art Exhibition), held at the vast halls of the new House of German Art, designed to showcase the conservative, saccharine, academic realist works acceptable to Nazi taste. The second was 'Entartete Kunst' (Degenerate Art), held in the narrow spaces of the Archaeological Institute, which was meant a 'final' exhibition of modern art to show the visible results of what the Nazis saw as Germany's slide into degeneracy during the Weimar Republic.

More than two million people visited 'Entartete Kunst' in Munich (which remains the highest attendance ever for a modern art exhibition), and a million more in the course of its subsequent tour, which included venues in Berlin, Düsseldorf, Weimar and Vienna between 1938 and 1941. Although the Nazis insisted that these visitor numbers represented ordinary Germans keen to witness just how awful modern art was, it is generally acknowledged that most, in fact, were people going to witness, as they saw it, art that they loved probably for the last time.

The exhibition also helped to provoke a general hardening in favour of the need to protect modern art in the democratic West, even among those who didn't particularly care for it. We have already seen how the Nazi vilification of Expressionism allowed the *Helhesten* group to reclaim and weaponize it in their practice under German occupation. In Britain, which had hitherto been more or less hostile to German Expressionism, an exhibition of 'Twentieth-Century German Art' was hastily mounted at the New Burlington Galleries, London in 1938 with the intention of defending German Modernism on the world stage. It consisted of more than three hundred works by the same artists who had been included in 'Entartete Kunst' , and the opening was attended by high profile art world figures, including Picasso, the Swiss-French architect and painter Le Corbusier (1887–1965), and the Director of the National Gallery, Sir Kenneth Clark (1903–1983). A book, *Modern German Art* was also published simultaneously – the first in English on the subject – in the influential Pelican imprint.

The idea of 'degenerate art' predated the Nazis, however. Since the end of the nineteenth century the enemies of modern art had used metaphors of disease as a means of attack. Sometimes this was based on physical conditions, especially as regards accusations of supposed abnormalities of vision or motor skills. More often it was psychological, usually supposing some kind of regression to childlike states or mental pathology.

Connections had long been argued between genius and madness; the first constantly threatening to tip over into the second. So, when writers like Hungarian physician and writer Max Nordau (1849–1923) described modern art as 'degenerate' at the turn of end of the nineteenth century they were building on ideas already embedded in the popular mind. In *Entartung* (Degeneracy) (1895) Nordau embarked on a pseudo-scientific 'exposé' of modern art as a form of 'mental decay' whose influence was 'disturbing and corrupting.' The kinds of ideas he articulated, though unacceptable and anachronistic now, were often accepted at the time, when reactionary thinkers repeatedly sought to implicate social and artistic radicalism with disease, thereby rendering it in need of correction and cure. Modern artists and their apologists – and Expressionists are prominent proponents of this – often compounded the problem by voicing their *admiration* for the very qualities for which they were being attacked. Madness, in particular, was viewed romantically, and regularly held up as a state of absolute liberation whose creative mechanisms, if not its lived condition, were to be aspired to. In the early twentieth century there were public exhibitions of so-called 'psychotic' art, drawn from the collections of psychiatrists, that were widely attended and praised by artists like Klee, Arp and Ernst. The claims of using self-conscious creative strategies of 'regression' among modern artists, including Nolde, Marc, and Picasso, led to an additional charge of criminality; if these artists were not ill, went the argument, since their work is an abomination, they must be knowingly duping the public.

These kinds of attacks were relatively common in criticism of modernist art in the first three decades of the twentieth century, appearing in French and English publications as much as in German ones. However, they tended to have little physical impact beyond confirming distaste for Modernism amongst existing culturally conservative groups. However, in Germany the Nazis (and later, in the USSR under Stalin's leadership) accepted Nordau's ideas with a chilling literalness and used them to justify their policy of cultural destruction. Irrespective of their individual politics or ethnicity, modern artists were implicated through the common thread of supposed degeneracy in the Nazi's attacks on bolshevism and Judaism.

Entartete Kunst turned out – entirely unintentionally on the part of the organizers – to be a defining moment in the history of modern art. Its didactic intent, though intended to deliver a wholly negative message, nevertheless resulted in curatorial innovations, such as 'informative' wall texts and accompanying published exhibition guides, thematic hanging and the use of suggestive visual juxtapositions, all of which are now staples of temporary exhibition design. Nazi iconoclasm was not to triumph. Hitler's 'Thousand Year Reich' crumbled after only a dozen years, but only after a global conflagration that devastated Europe and produced not only the usual casualties of war, but also witnessed the systematic murder of millions of innocent people and led directly to a schism of the continent that was to last through five decades. Now widely seen as symbolic of the 'free' West, Expressionist tendencies were strong in art in the immediate aftermath of the war in much of Europe and the United States. However, in the newly constituted, DDR (German Democratic Republic), which was part of the Communist Eastern Bloc, German Expressionism came to be seen – at least at first – as almost the official art form, not only because it had become symbolic of anti-fascism, but also precisely because many Expressionists, such as Felixmüller, had pursued radical socialist and communist agendas.

Chapter 4
America Ascendant

America had produced non-figurative painters since the early days of abstraction, such as Stanton MacDonald-Wright (1890–1973), Morgan Russell (1886–1953), Stuart Davis (1892–1964), Max Weber (1881–1961), Marsden Hartley and Arthur Dove (1880–1946). However, these artists often worked abroad (particularly in Paris) or were marginalized in the context of a local art world that preferred figuration and regionalist subject matter in American art. Dove, in particular, was an important early exponent of Abstract Expressionism, followed at the end of the First World War by Hartley. The work of both artists was championed by Alfred Stieglitz (1864–1946) through his New York avant-garde gallery, 291.

Marsden Hartley had been in Paris in 1912 and Berlin from 1913 until he was forced to return home because of the war at the end of 1916. In Europe he associated with the artistic and cultural avant-garde, and he was especially taken with Kandinsky and his writings. The works Hartley
71 produced in Berlin, including *The Aero* (*c.* 1914) and *Portrait of a German Officer* (1914) utilize an Abstract Expressionist visual language. Hartley himself spoke of them in ways that echoed Kandinsky, as 'the first expression of mysticism in the modern tendency.' They can also be read as highly coded declarations of love towards a Prussian officer, Karl von Freyburg, who was killed at the front. Hartley was steeped in the transcendentalist poetry of Ralph Waldo Emerson (1803–1882) and the declarative verse of Walt Whitman, whose barely disguised homoeroticism at times must have struck a chord. Berlin provided Hartley with a space in which gay culture was relatively open, if subject to a need for careful social separation of public and private lives. In his later work, Hartley returned to a lyrical figurative Expressionism, often

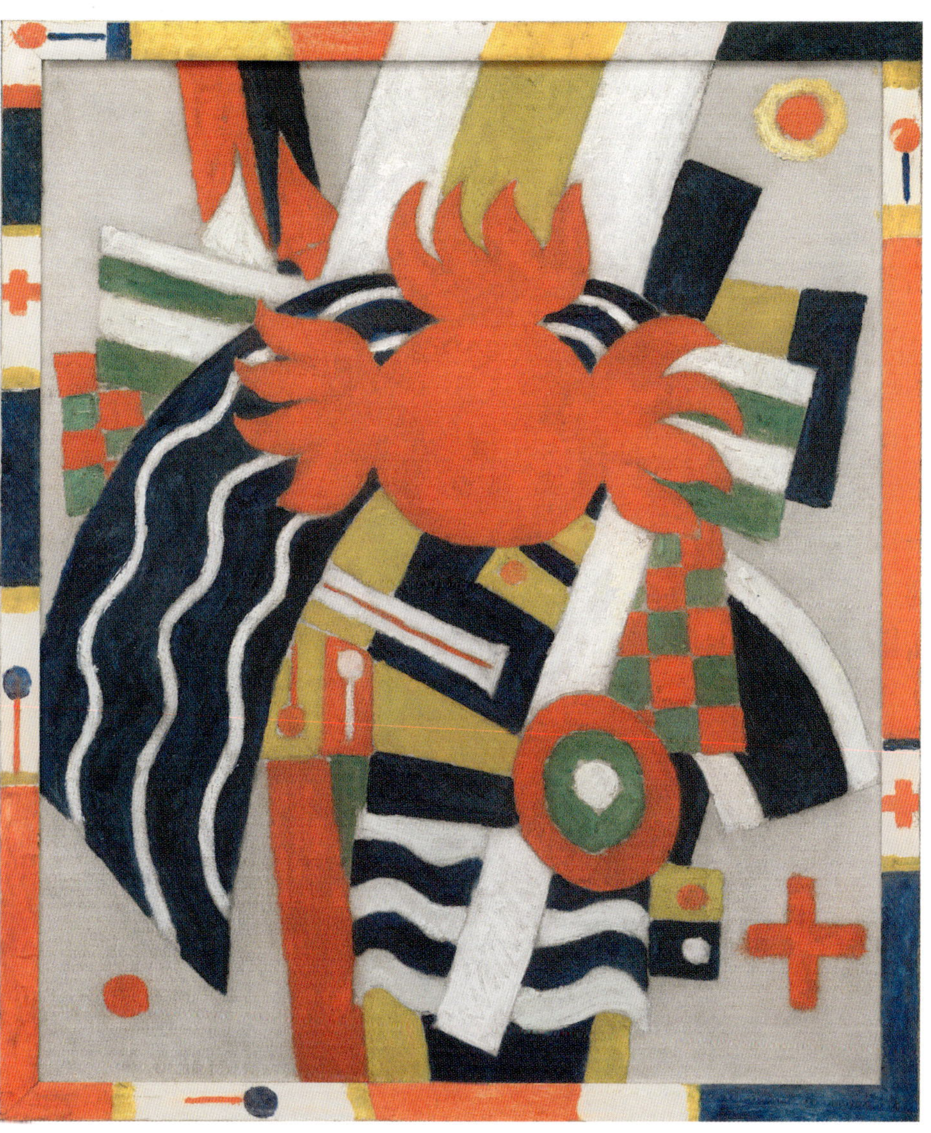

71 Marsden Hartley, *The Aero*, c. 1914

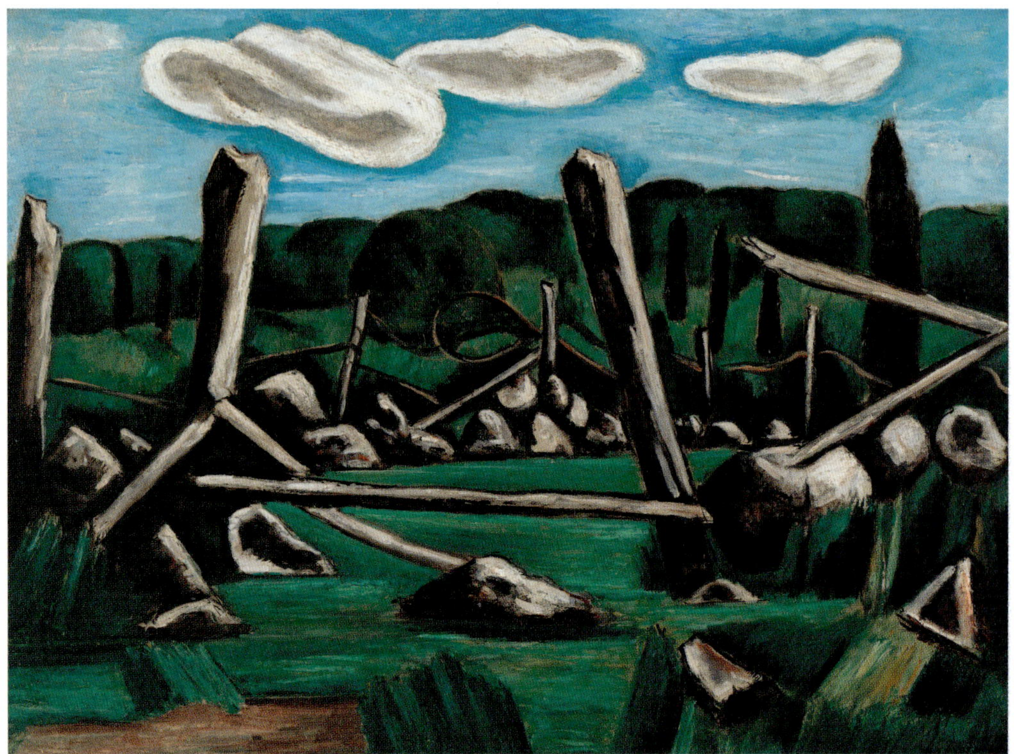

72 Marsden Hartley, *The Old Bars, Dogtown*, 1936

72 evoking the metaphysical spirit of places, as in *The Old Bars, Dogtown*. He also became much less guarded about his own sexuality, producing images of virile, athletic young men, although remarkably published criticism has only recently engaged with this aspect of his practice.

If Expressionism was far from being the dominant strain in homegrown American Modernism in the 1920s and 1930s, links to a still-live European Expressionism can be followed through émigrés like Hans Hofmann (from Germany), Arshile
73 Gorky (from Armenia) and Willem de Kooning (from the Netherlands). At the same time high-end American collectors of modernist art and new museums, such as the Barnes Foundation, Philadelphia (1922), the Museum of Modern Art (1929) and the Solomon R. Guggenheim Museum (originally named the Museum of Non-Objective Painting, 1939) in New York privileged European – and especially Parisian – Modernism.

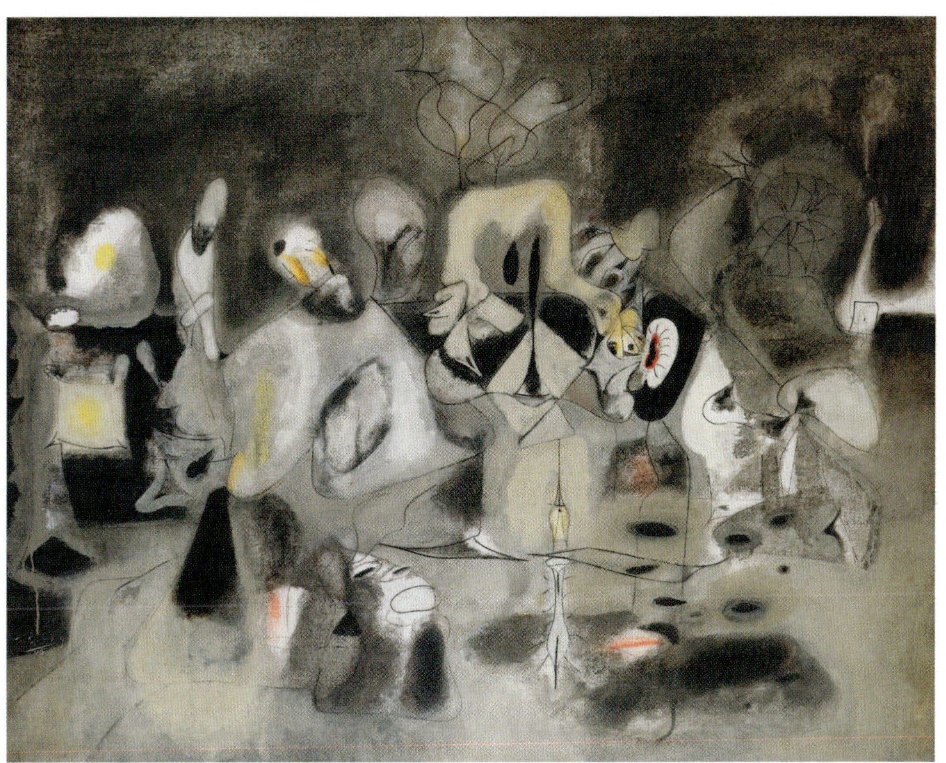

73 Arshile Gorky, *Diary of a Seducer*, 1945

Things began to change with rise of Nazism and especially the coming of war in Europe in 1939. The Second World War threw the art world in Europe into torpor and significant numbers of European artists, writers and collectors sought safety in the United States. These displacements led to a reorientation of the global art world axis and, perhaps ironically, given the number of Europeans and European artworks around, a growing self-confidence among American modernists, art dealers and museums. Moreover, the United States economy recovered much more quickly than those of European countries, which were bankrupt and mostly literally in ruins. As the American critic Clement Greenberg (1909–1994) astutely put it as early as 1948: 'the main premises of Western art have at last migrated to the United States, along with the centre of gravity of industrial production and political power.'

Abstract Expressionism

New York became the focus of a significant exile population, which meant that the Americans were able to develop their art during the early 1940s in a creative environment that included a melting pot of Expressionist art from Europe since the turn of the end of the twentieth century and a number of modernist critics and teachers. Arguably the most important of these was the German painter and educator Hans Hofmann (1880–1966), who emigrated to the United States in 1932. Hofmann had been active in the Munich avant-garde, and in 1915 opened a school that built on the ideas of Cézanne and French and German Expressionism. He continued teaching after he relocated to America, first at the Art Students League of New York, and subsequently in his own schools in New York City and Provincetown, Massachusetts. His pupils included some of the future key figures of Abstract Expressionism, such as Lee Krasner and Helen Frankenthaler (1928–2011), although the influence of his ideas went much wider among New York artists and critics, especially Jackson Pollock (1912–1956) via Krasner, and Clement Greenberg via Frankenthaler.

Another important émigré figure was the British painter and printmaker Stanley William Hayter (1901–1988). Although best known as a Surrealist, Hayter's practice contained much in common with Expressionist views of creativity and picture-making. Hayter had established Atelier 17, ostensibly a printmaking studio, in Paris in 1933, which he subsequently transplanted to New York in 1940 in rooms at the New School. Atelier 17 was a space devoted to experiment and conversation. Established artists were allowed to use it at any time, and although it was, theoretically, a teaching facility, student learning occurred largely through immersion in a common environment of practice, rather than by any didactic method. At various moments until Hayter returned to Paris in 1950, students at Atelier 17 might rub shoulders, and interact with, already established modernist giants, such as André Masson, Joan Miró, and Yves Tanguy (1900–1955). At the same time, young American artists hungry to assimilate at first hand something of the culture of European Modernism, such as Robert Motherwell (1915–1991), William Baziotes (1912–1963), and Pollock, were drawn to this honeypot.

The stage was set for the emergence of a homegrown modern movement that critics would measure in terms of its difference to European sensibilities rather than its indebtedness, in spite of several of its key figures being émigrés, such as Arshile Gorky (1904–1948) from Armenia,

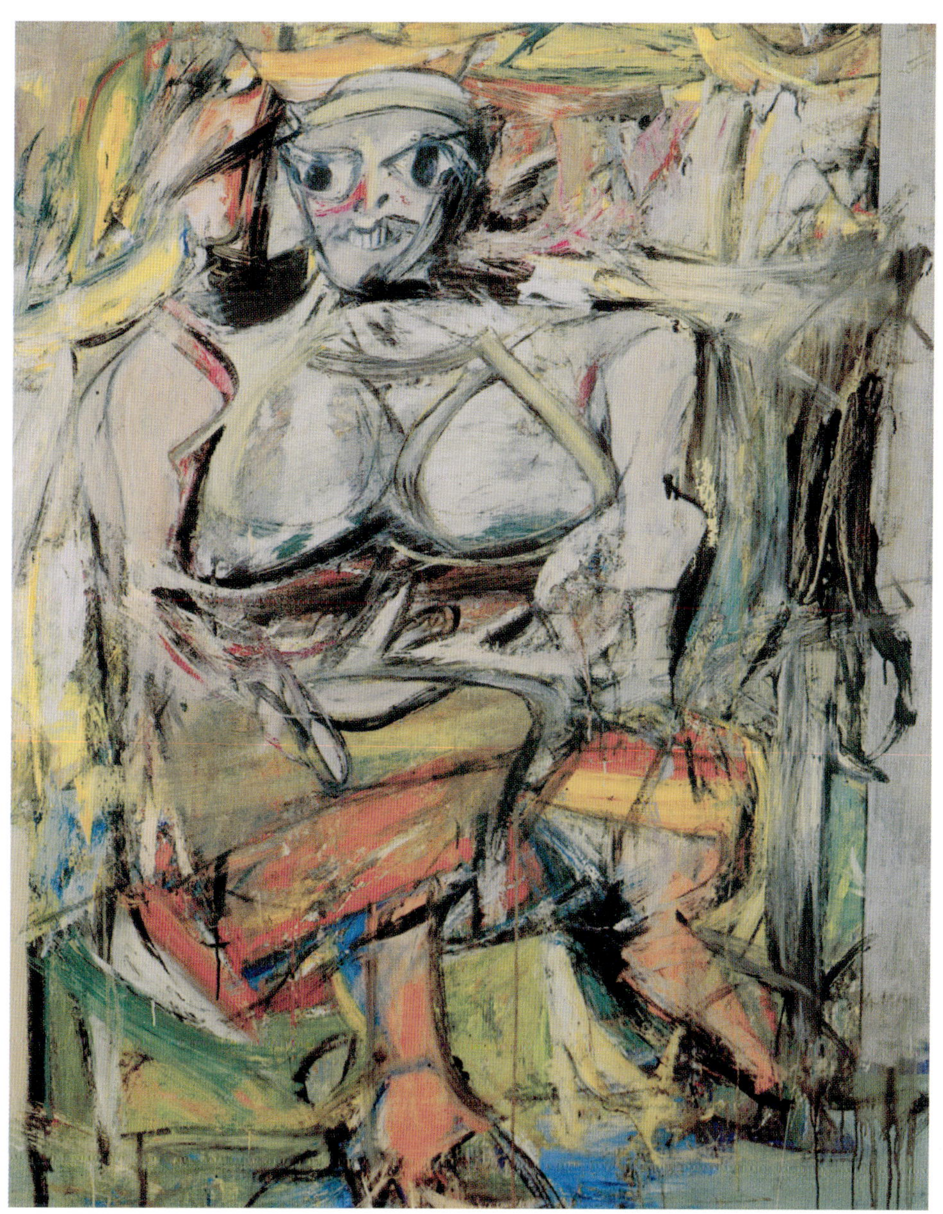

74 Willem de Kooning, *Woman I*, 1950–52

74 Mark Rothko from Latvia, Willem de Kooning (1904–1997) from the Netherlands, and Janet Sobel (1893–1968) from Ukraine. Crucially, the much vaunted 'Americanness' of this new art was linked to a belief in its ability to communicate internationally, in line with a renewed political and cultural self-confidence in the United States. The previous European – and especially Parisian – monopoly on art and culture was declared to have been broken and 'Abstract Expressionists' – alternatively known as the 'New York School' or 'American Action Painters' – like Pollock, Mark Rothko, De Kooning, Motherwell, Adolph Gottlieb (1903–1974) and Barnett Newman (1905–1970) – quickly became household names, achieving almost superstar status in the 1950s, and their work came to be regarded as representative of specifically 'American' values – usually in opposition to Communist ones, associated with the USSR and Eastern Bloc – in international, government-sponsored exhibitions in the Cold War.

Abstract Expressionism is generally seen as an East Coast movement, although there were 'Abstract Expressionist' groups in Chicago, the American Northwest and on the West Coast. It has also generally been viewed as overwhelmingly the preserve of white, heterosexual men. Yet, at the time and in retrospect, we can see that some of its most interesting – and prominent – practitioners were women, such as Krasner,
75 Frankenthaler, Elaine de Kooning (1918–1989), Grace Hartigan
(1922–2008) and Joan Mitchell, and people of colour, such as
76 Hale A. Woodruff (1900–1980) and Norman Lewis (1909–1979). The critical and art-historical privileging of white men was a direct result of the ways in which contemporary critics and subsequent art historians constructed the narrative.

Overall the Abstract Expressionists had in common left-wing political leanings – at least in their youths – and many had been involved with the Federal Arts Project in the 1930s, which was one of the work-relief schemes that was part of President Roosevelt's New Deal after the Great Depression. By the time the United States entered the Second World War in 1942, though, none of them can be said to have been actively pursuing a politicized art. Cut off from the physical proximity of fascist Europe and then more or less isolated by war, they already saw themselves as philosophically, as well as physically, distanced from the Old World. Typically, Barnett Newman regarded this a loss, but also as an opportunity to enact a kind of artistic renaissance. In 1948 he said, 'Everything in Europe is so highly civilized. The artist in America is, by comparison, like a barbarian. He does not have the superfine sensibility toward the object that dominates European feeling. He does

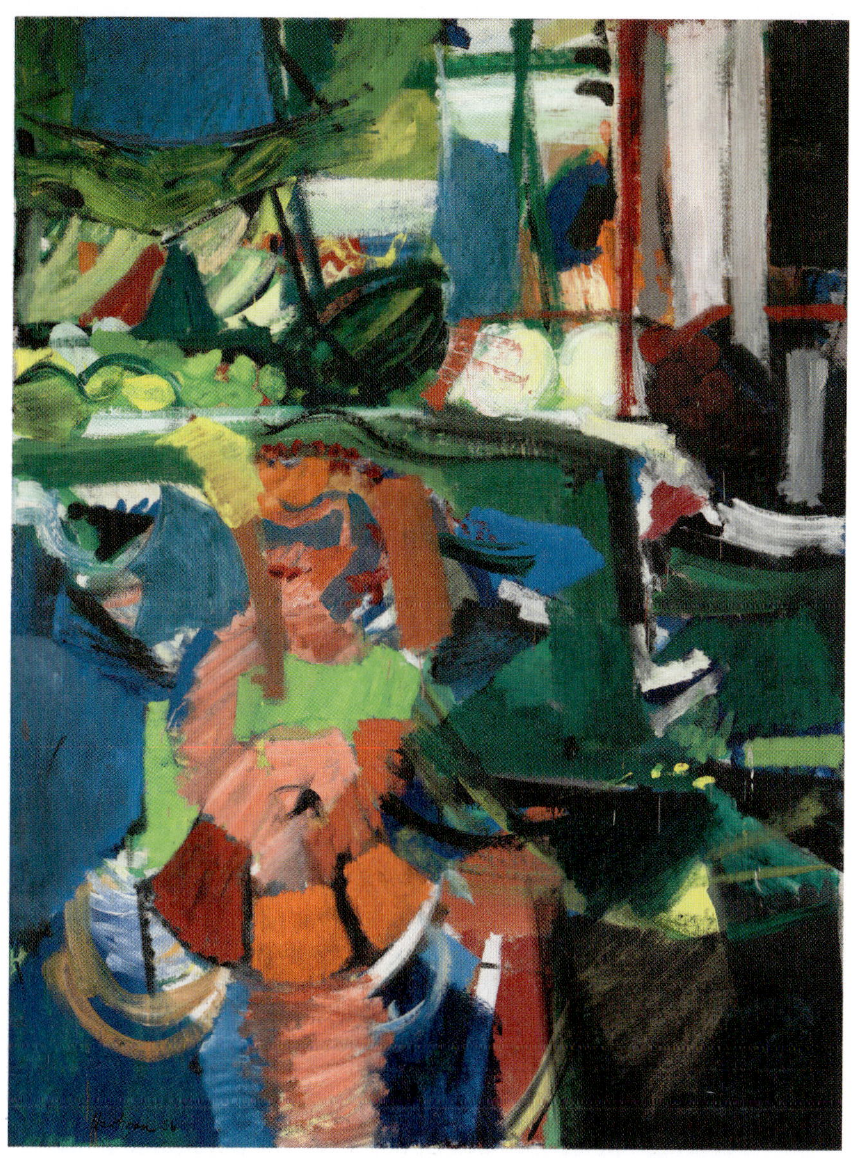

75 Grace Hartigan, *Summer Street*, 1956

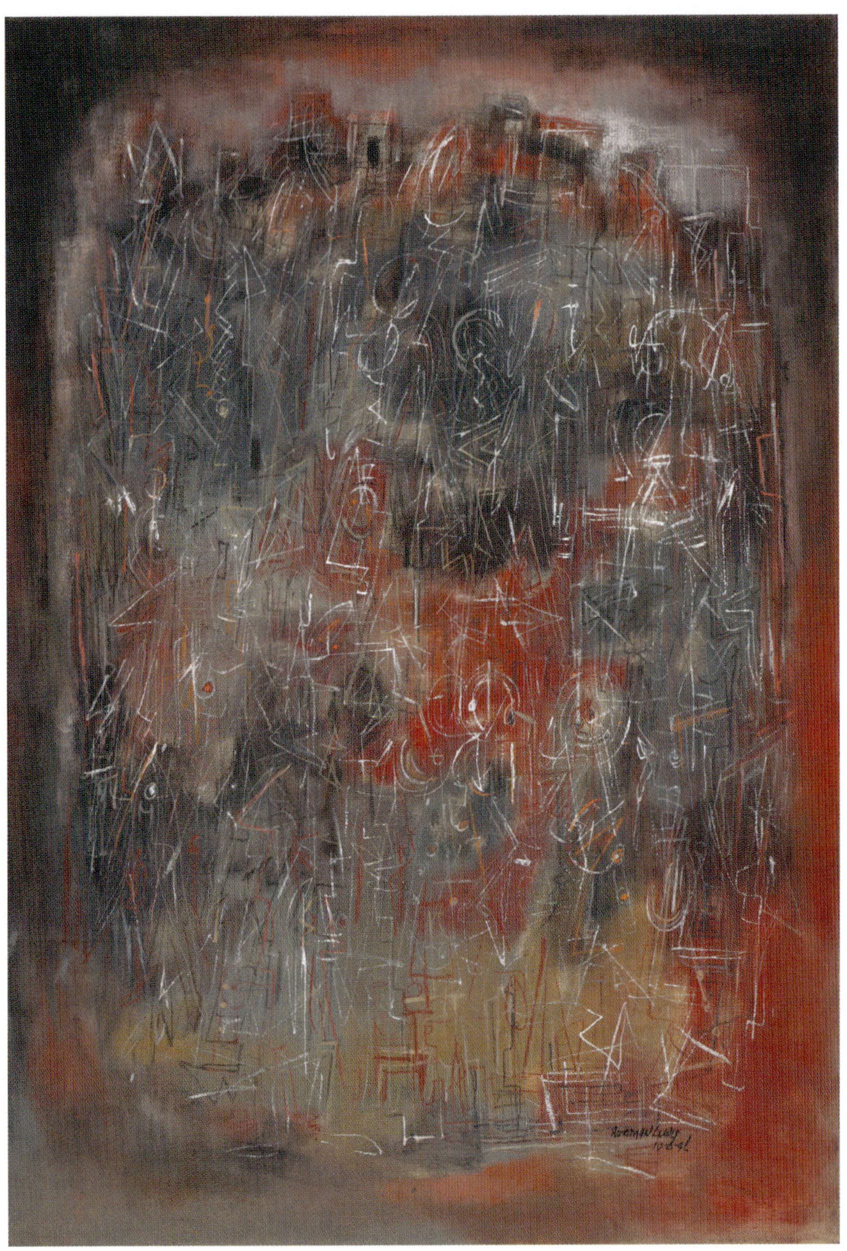

76 Norman Lewis, *Multitudes*, 1946

not even have the objects. This then is our opportunity, free of the ancient paraphernalia, to come closer to the sources of the tragic emotion. Shall we not, as artists, search out the new objects for its image?' Reflecting a little later in 1960, Gottlieb went even further, invoking similar language to that used at the beginning of the century to justify the New Painting, claiming that in order to move forward as artists, it had been 'necessary' to destroy 'the concept of what constituted a good painting...the measuring rod with which paintings were judged.'

Painters like Rothko, Pollock, Gottlieb, Newman, Lewis and Sobel shared the view that the purpose of art was to uncover essences, to purify the image in order that it might speak in universal terms. As Lewis said, 'I am a loner and paint out of a certain self-imposed remoteness. When I'm at work, I usually remove my state of mind from the Negro environment I live in. I paint what's inside...Being a Negro, of course, is part of what I feel, but in expressing all of which I am artistically, I often find myself in a visionary world.' Thus, in a painting like *Prehistory* (1952) Lewis exchanges the particularities of contemporary New York City for a generalized primordial soup of life's earliest beginnings. Amorphous, vaguely animate forms that are on the verge of coming into being ebb and flow in an indeterminate pictorial space. In other paintings, such as *Harlem Turns White* (1955), viewers are seemingly witness to the visionary moment of disintegration of mundane appearances.

The primitivizing desire to uncover essences was also supported by a tendency in work and thought of the Abstract Expressionists to resituate humanity as part of an organically unfolding and vital Nature, rather than being the centre around which nature must revolve. Like the Surrealists before them, they believed that the revelation of universal themes could come from an examination of the self, continuing romantic notions of the artist as seer and culture shaper, and therefore as a pioneer and outsider, at the cutting edge of things – and thus likely to be socially isolated and misunderstood. Newman claimed: 'Instead of making cathedrals out of Christ, man, or "life", we are making it out of ourselves, out of our own feelings.' The Americans believed strongly in the potential for a direct, unmediated art, which is epitomized by Motherwell's assertion that, 'The need is for felt experience – intense, immoderate, direct, subtle, unified, warm, vivid, rhythmic.' This brought them
77 closer to German post-Expressionists like Willi Baumeister (1889–1955), Ernst Wilhelm Nay, Fritz Winter and, of course, Hans Hofmann, who proved himself one of the great late

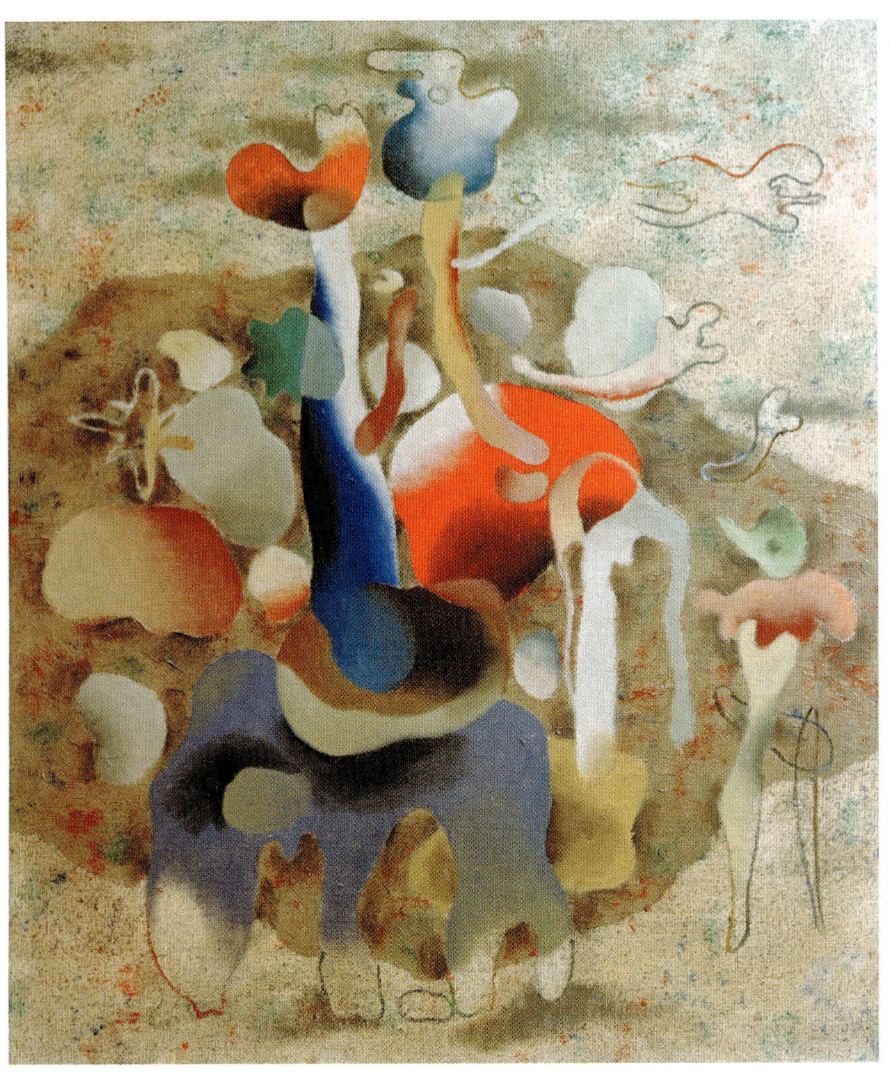

77 Willi Baumeister, *Steingarten II* (Stone Garden II), 1939

developers of twentieth-century art when, in his seventh decade, he became recognized not only as a teacher, but also as being an important exponent of Abstract Expressionism in his own right.

Like the mythic pioneers of the American West hymned by Whitman, the New York painters saw themselves as plunging into uncharted territory, but this time these were solitary voyages into the psychic interior of each one, much in keeping with the ways in which Klee had described the creative process in his teaching at the Bauhaus. As Clyfford Still (1904–1980) said in 1952, 'We are now committed to an unqualified act, not illustrating outworn myths or contemporary alibis. One must accept total responsibility for what he (*sic.*) executes.' Abstract Expressionist art can look like a very odd collection of very different types when looked at together, yet it is precisely the artists' insistent individualism, identifiable in their restless search for signature painting styles particular not to any 'school' but to each individual, that perhaps provides their strongest connection as a group.

The individualism of the Abstract Expressionist group is one reason why they never organized as a unified movement. They occasionally organized group exhibitions, as with the now legendary 'Ninth Street Show' (1951), which in many ways marked the public debut of Abstract Expressionism, and included among others, Frankenthaler, Mitchell, Hartigan,
78 Pollock, Elaine and Willem de Kooning, Motherwell and Newman. They remained loosely affiliated, though, more through their social activities, which included a culture of heavy drinking, often centred around the Cedar Tavern in Greenwich Village, fuelled by stereotypical machismo behaviours amongst some of the men. This contributed to its received image as white hetero, and obscured – was likely meant to obscure – a more complexly gendered experience among some of them, including Pollock, whose hard drinking and braggadocio masked trauma inflicted by his brothers and others from his early years owing to his 'sensitive' personality and a likely less binary sexuality. Many of the Abstract Expressionists also shared dealers, such as Peggy Guggenheim (1898–1979), Betty Parsons (1900–1982) and Sidney Janis (1896–1989).

Internalization of the creative impulse also helps to explain why the New York School painters came to develop styles that leaned towards the non-figurative. The apparent abandonment of the object is often related to the artists' primitivizing interest in myth and mystical views of nature. Rothko said in 1945: 'If previous abstractions paralleled the scientific and objective preoccupations of our times, ours are finding a pictorial equivalent for man's (*sic.*) new knowledge and consciousness of his more complex inner self.' They favoured the universalizing theories of culture of Swiss psychologist C. G. Jung (1875–1961) against the Surrealists' obsession with the rational materialism of the Austrian psychiatrist Sigmund Freud. Instead of the alienation at the heart of Freud's view of the modern psyche, Jung – whose thought was often consumed by the artists in pop media form, rather than through direct knowledge of his work, although Pollock underwent a period of Jungian analysis in the late 1930s – appeared to offer ways of gaining authentic access to primitive states of consciousness and thereby of connecting with the universe. He believed that by taking stock of one's dreams and analysing 'primitive' and 'archaic' mythology, it might become possible once again for people to participate in the unfolding natural drama, as had humans in the state of nature. This is one of the things that connects the Americans with the early Expressionism of artists such as Kirchner, Heckel, Nolde, Marc, Kandinsky, and particularly Klee.

In the paintings of Newman, Gottlieb, Pollock, Krasner and Mark Tobey (1890–1976), for example, figures and objects were replaced with archetypal symbols, which go beyond representation, but which are therefore less easily categorized in the world of things outside of the works. This was, then, to be seen less as non-objective art and more as a kind of profound realism in which descriptive images were replaced by symbolic figures and archetypes. Figure-ground opposition was brought into play in paintings, although in a pictorial space that was insistently shallow and often articulated by reliance on the grid.

Gottlieb's so-called 'pictographs'– a term commonly used in the American context to describe Southwest Native American
79 imagery – such as *Pursuer and Pursued* (1946–47), *Vigil* (1948) and *Ashes of Phoenix* (1948) are among the most interesting use of the grid as a painterly device in Abstract Expressionism. They derive in part from indigenous American sources, especially the textiles and carvings of the Chilkat, Kwakiutl, and Tlingit peoples, although other equally strong influences mentioned by Gottlieb included predella panels from Renaissance altarpieces, and the Cubist grids of the Uruguayan painter Joaquin Torres-Garcia (1874–1949). The division of the picture surface further emphasized its flatness, while at the same time allowing Gottlieb to present imagery in a serial way,

78 OPPOSITE Jackson Pollock, *Full Fathom Five*, 1946

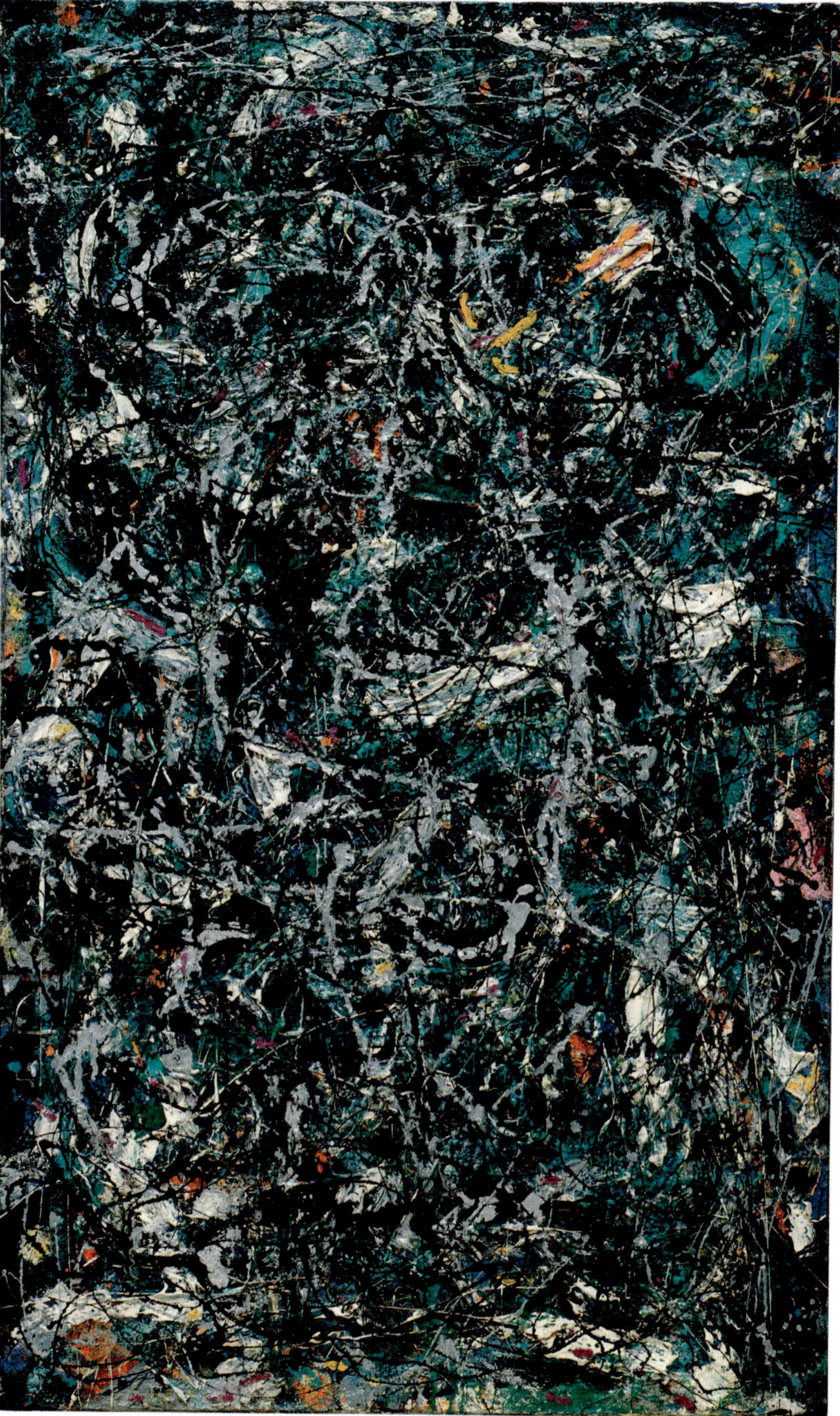

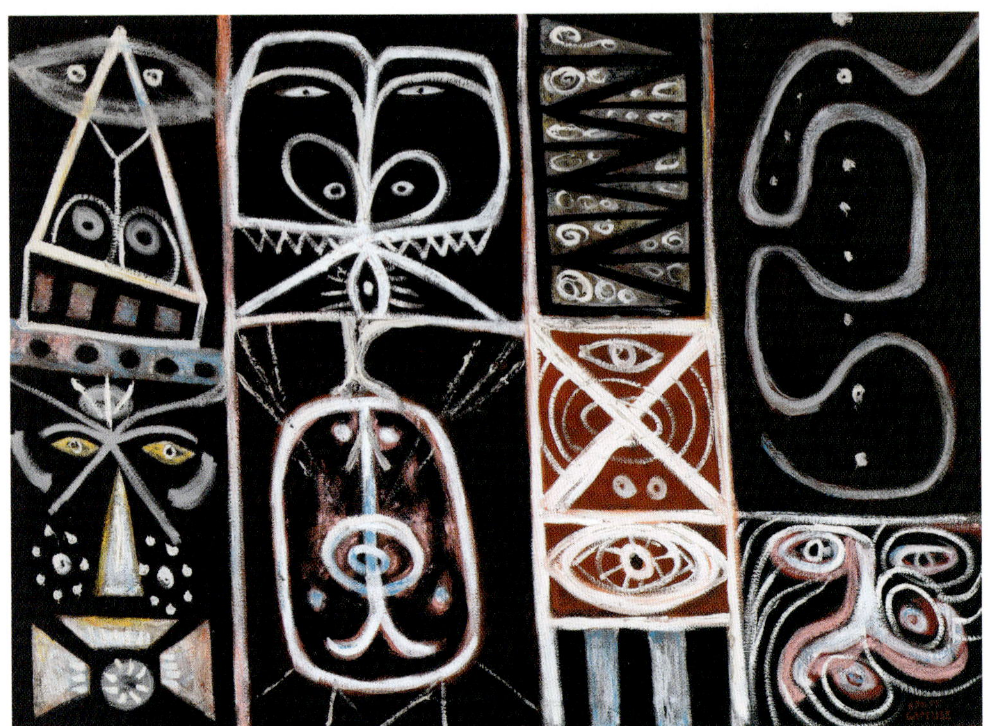

79 Adolph Gottlieb, *Vigil*, 1948

thereby resisting the temptation to read it as narrative. In 1951 he used the metaphor of the way the stereotypical American family unit occupied a house to explain what he was trying to achieve in his painting: 'People frequently ask why my canvases are compartmentalized. No one ever asks this about a house. A man with a large family would not choose to live in a one room house....I am like a man with a large family and must have many rooms. The children of my imagination occupy the various compartments of my painting, each independent and occupying its own space. At the same time they have the proper atmosphere in which to function together, in harmony and as a unified group.'

The primitivism of the Abstract Expressionists was at the same time more universalizing in its mythic sources than most pre-war European Modernism and more self-consciously 'American' in its spread of interest in so-called 'primitive' cultures. In place of African and Oceanic art they looked to indigenous material culture from North America and ancient Pre-Colombian art, usually supported by some level of anthropological knowledge. However, 'primitive' art styles were less important than the ideas that they represented. In 'The Ideographic Picture' (1947), Newman argued that in the hands of the 'primitive' artist the abstract shape was a 'living thing...a carrier of the awesome feelings he (*sic.*) felt before the terror of the unknowable.' And, in common with Rothko, he suggested that Abstract Expressionism had a 'spiritual kinship with primitive and archaic art.' For his part Pollock, who grew up in the American West, argued for the 'reasonableness' of Native American art: 'I have always been very impressed with the plastic qualities of American Indian art. The Indians have the true painter's approach in their capacity to get hold of appropriate images, and in their understanding of what constitutes painterly subject matter. Their colour is essentially Western, their vision has the basic universality of all real art.'

Writing in the wake of the war in 1947, Newman, who was often seen as the theorist of the loosely affiliated group, claimed that their abstraction did not constitute a turning away from the world, but rather an attempt to make something real of people's incomprehension in the face of the horror of their time: 'Our obsessive, subterranean, and pictographic images are the expression of the neurosis which is our reality. To my mind certain so-called abstraction is no abstraction at all. On the contrary, it is the realism of our time.'

80 Earlier works by Rothko, such as *Entombment, I,* display a concern with organic forms that speak to an interest in the primordial forces of growth and movement that characterize

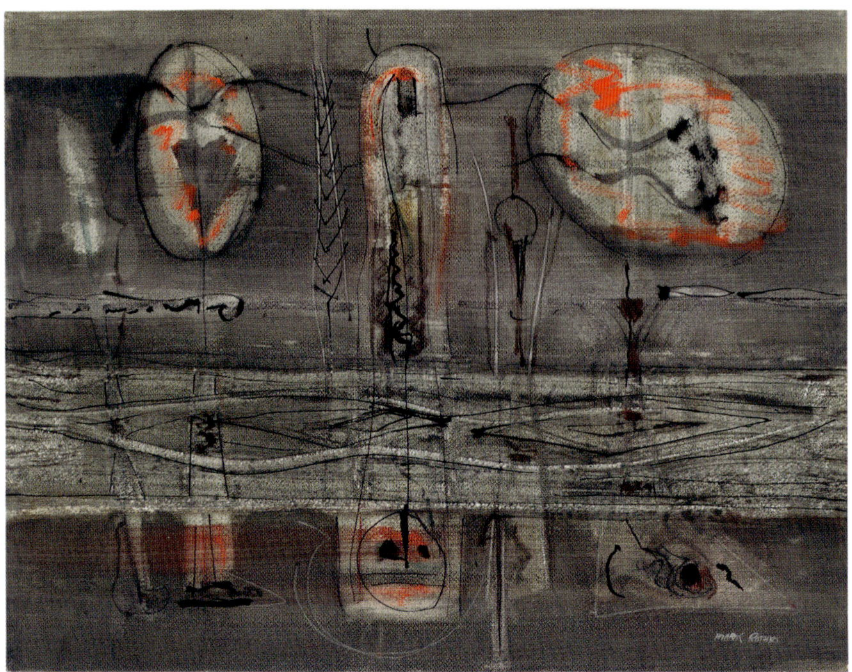

80 ABOVE Mark Rothko, *Entombment, I*, 1946
81 OPPOSITE Mark Rothko, *1957 # 20*, 1957

natural creation. But in his and Newman's mature paintings in particular formal simplicity was taken to similar extremes of modernist predecessors like Kazimir Malevich and Piet Mondrian (1872–1944) – who spent the last four years of his life living and working in New York. The Americans nevertheless maintained an insistently painterly touch in their work, related to earlier Expressionism. Newman's signature 'zipper' motif and Rothko's 'floating', indistinct rectangles were merely a kind of basic structure on which colour could be applied to emotive
81 ends. Rothko's *Red on Maroon* (1959) and *1957 #20*, and Newman's *Cathedra* (1951) are contemplative works before which viewers must abandon themselves to an intuitive or emotional response. The necessity of 'feeling' the content of such work is often underscored by their use of very large canvases approaching the dimensions of murals, so that viewers experience a sense of being enveloped by these colour fields.

The generally large scale of Abstract Expressionist paintings also emphasized their gestural qualities, implicating through the residue of their actions that is evident in the works the physicality of the artist's body as agent. This is clear in the bold,

direct mark-making in paintings by Willem de Kooning, Pollock, Krasner, Hartigan and Mitchell, for example, but it is no less if more subtly present in the more subdued practices of Newman, Rothko, Still and Frankenthaler.

If the imaginative reconstruction of the process of making a painting is an important part of the human content of much Abstract Expressionism, it was famously valorized in the writings of the critic Harold Rosenberg (1906–1978), who coined the term 'action painting' to describe it. In 1952 he wrote: 'At a certain moment the canvas began to appear to one American painter after another as an arena in which to act – rather than as a space in which to reproduce, analyse, or "express" an object, actual or imagined. What was to go on the canvas was not a picture but an event. The painter no longer approached his (*sic.*) easel with an image in his mind; he went up to it with his material in his hand to do something to that other piece of material in front of him. The image would be the result of this encounter.' Rosenberg's gendered narrative notwithstanding, his words are equally relevant to Abstract Expressionist women.

Several artists in New York at this time experimented with drip painting techniques as ways of developing more immediate, automatic processes, including Stanley William Hayter, Norman Lewis, and Janet Sobel, which necessitated reorientation of the canvas onto a horizontal surface. Sobel produced a number of
82 remarkable works around 1945, including *Untitled* (*c.* 1946–48), in which a free-flowing lattice of dripped liquid enamel paint seemingly dances around and over a vaguely figurative oil paint base. Her innovation was twofold, both in terms of the experimentalism of her technique and her use of enamel paint, intended for commercial, rather than fine art use. It was probably works such as this one that Pollock saw at this time, and which led him to experimenting with, and significantly extending, the technique.

Pollock's method entailed keeping the brush above his canvas when applying paint, which demanded a high level of painterly directness and reliance on intuitive decision-making that brought the performative aspect of painting into stark relief. Similarly, his decision to work on the floor of his Long Island studio on huge pieces of unstretched canvas meant that he was forced quite literally to enter the 'arena' of the picture ground. In
83 *Number 1, 1948* and *Number 1, 1950 (Lavender Mist)*, for example, representational symbols are replaced by the raw residue of the artist's presence – including distinct handprints in the upper left part of *Number 1, 1948*. Similarly, there is a directness and spontaneity in the drip technique, which suggests parallels with the improvization structures and syncopation of the jazz

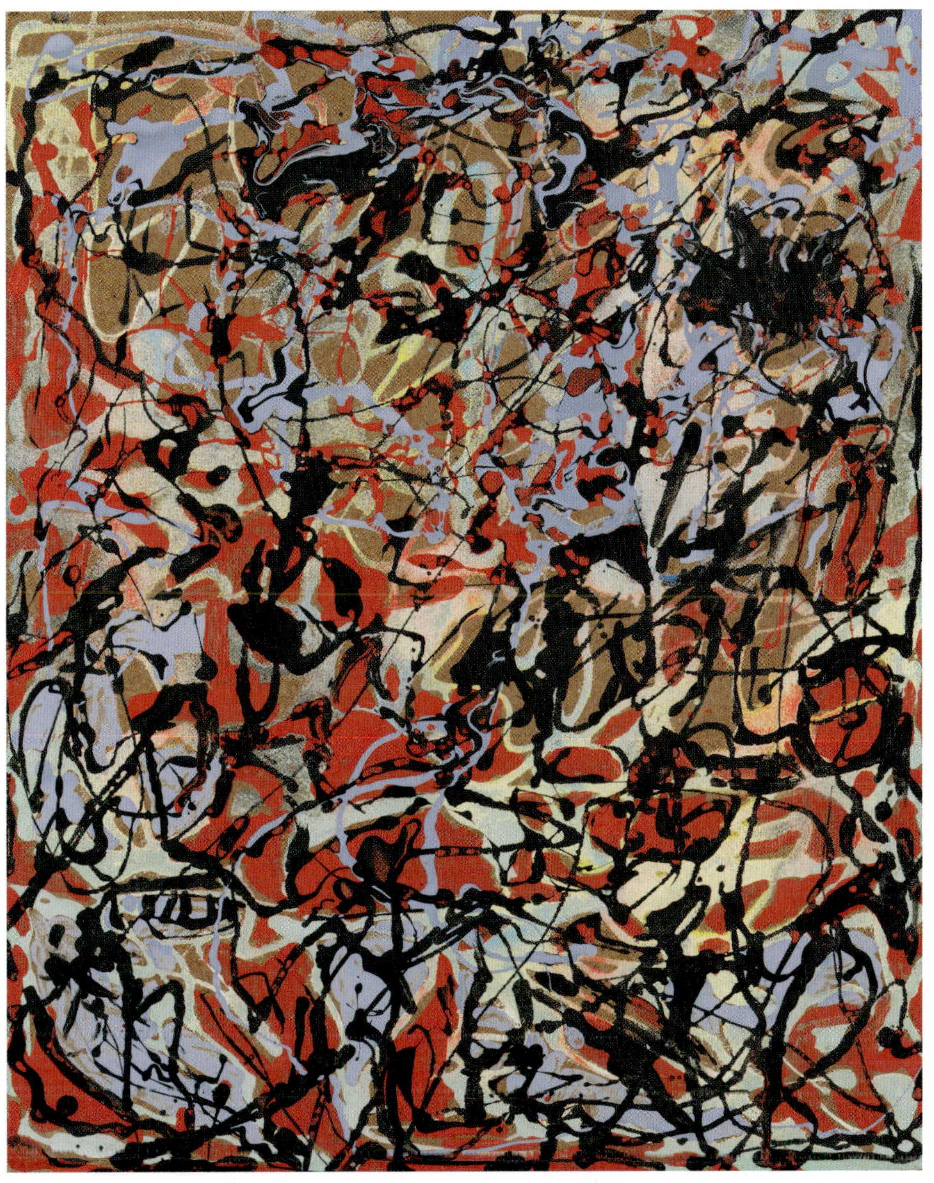

82 Janet Sobel, *Untitled*, c. 1946–48

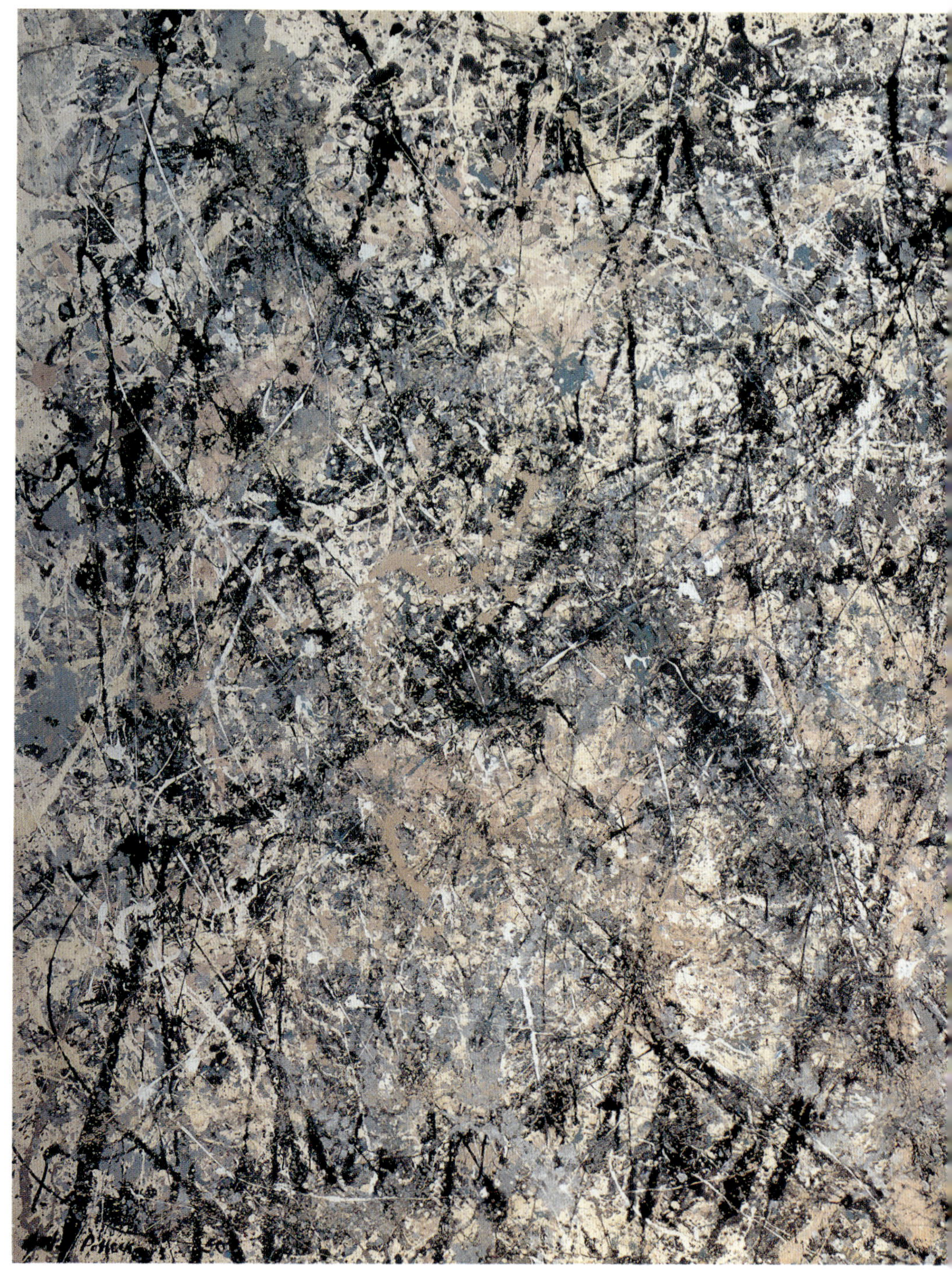

83 Jackson Pollock, *Number 1, 1950 (Lavender Mist)*, 1950

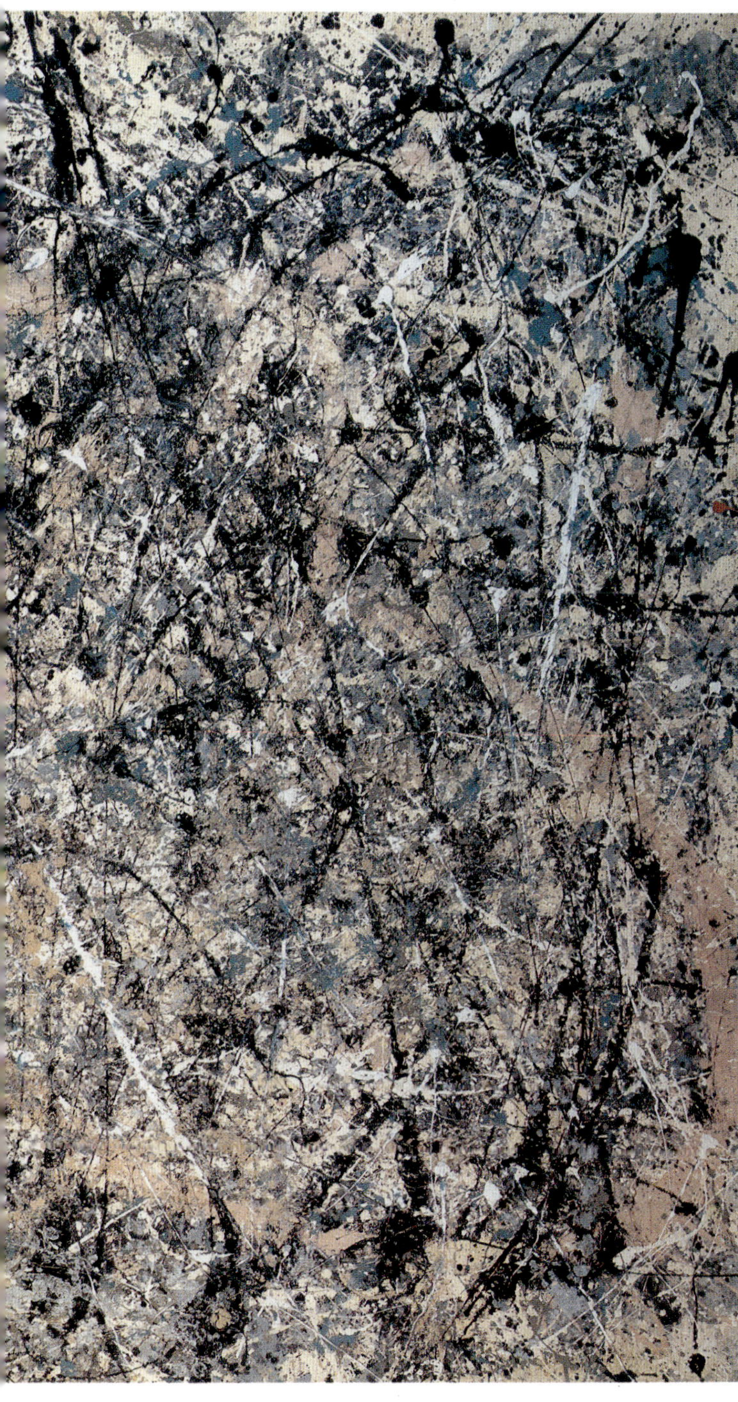

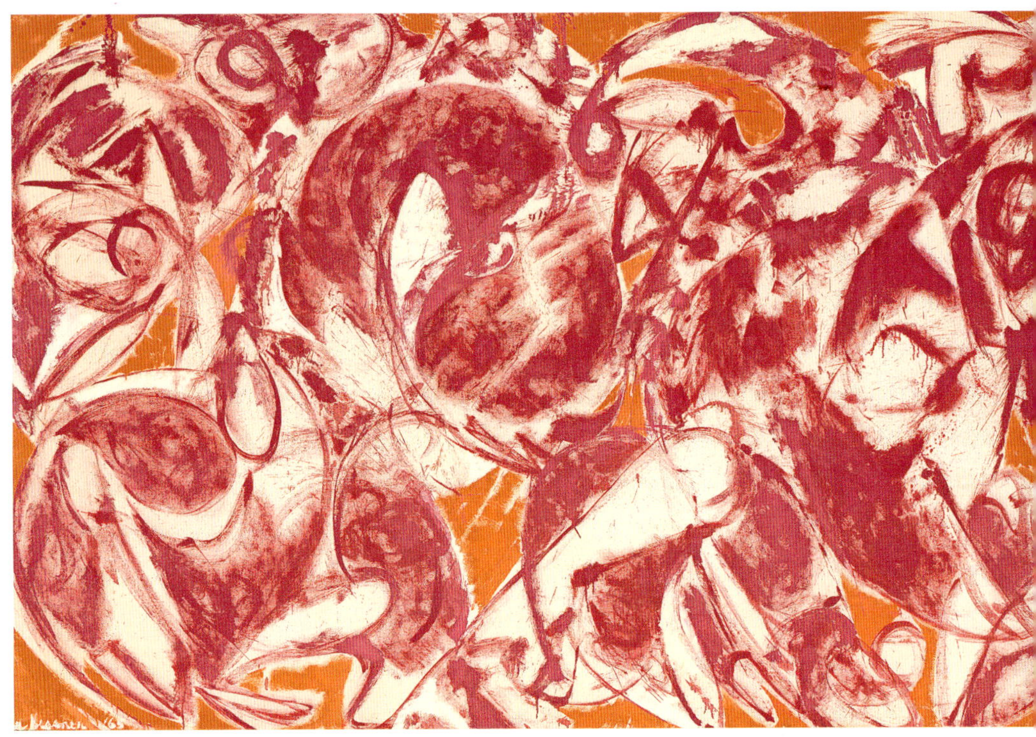

records that he liked to play while working. Pollock said that, because the brush did not touch the surface, it gave him the freedom to 'move about the canvas, with greater ease' and to express an 'inner world – in other words – expressing the energy, the motion, and other inner forces,' and so attaining briefly that elusive union of the conscious and unconscious realms to which he aspired. 'On the floor,' he said, 'I am more at ease. I feel nearer, more a part of the painting, since this way I can walk around it, work from the four sides and literally be in the painting.' This he said, was akin to the method of the 'Indian sand painters' of the American West: 'When I am in my painting, I'm not aware of what I'm doing. It is only after a sort of "get acquainted" period that I see what I have been about. I have no fears about making changes, destroying the image, etc., because the painting has a life of its own. I try to let it come through. It is only when I lose contact with the painting that the result is a mess. Otherwise, there is pure harmony, an easy give and take, and the painting comes out well.'

The sense of witnessing the encapsulation of a complex unfolding movement, coupled with the revelation of personal

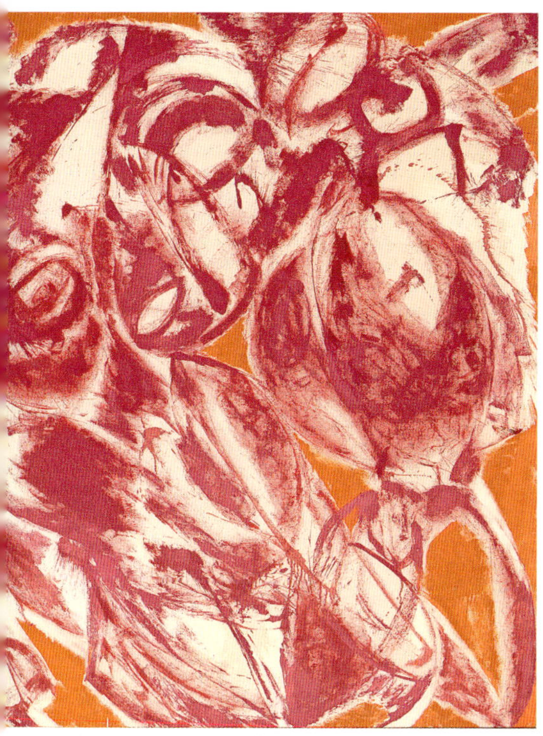

84 Lee Krasner, *Combat*, 1965

history through a kind of physical, biological memory is intensified by the generally large size of the drip paintings and the range of colour, which also suggests metaphoric replacement of the large open spaces of Pollock's unsettled early years in Wyoming, Arizona and California, rather than his mature experience of the streets of New York City: 'I enjoy working big and whenever I have a chance, I do it whether it is practical or not....I feel more at home in a big area.' Pollock's friend, Clement Greenberg typically saw the reasons for the increase in scale in Abstract Expressionist painting as a purely painterly imperative. In his essay, '"American-Type" Painting' (1955) Greenberg argued that, 'the Abstract Expressionists were being compelled to do huge canvases by the fact that they had increasingly renounced an illusion of depth within which they could develop pictorial incident without crowding; the flattening of the surfaces of their canvases compelled them to move along the picture plane laterally and seek in its sheer physical size the space necessary for the telling of their kind of pictorial story.' This is amply illustrated in Krasner's huge,
84 powerful image, *Combat* (1965).

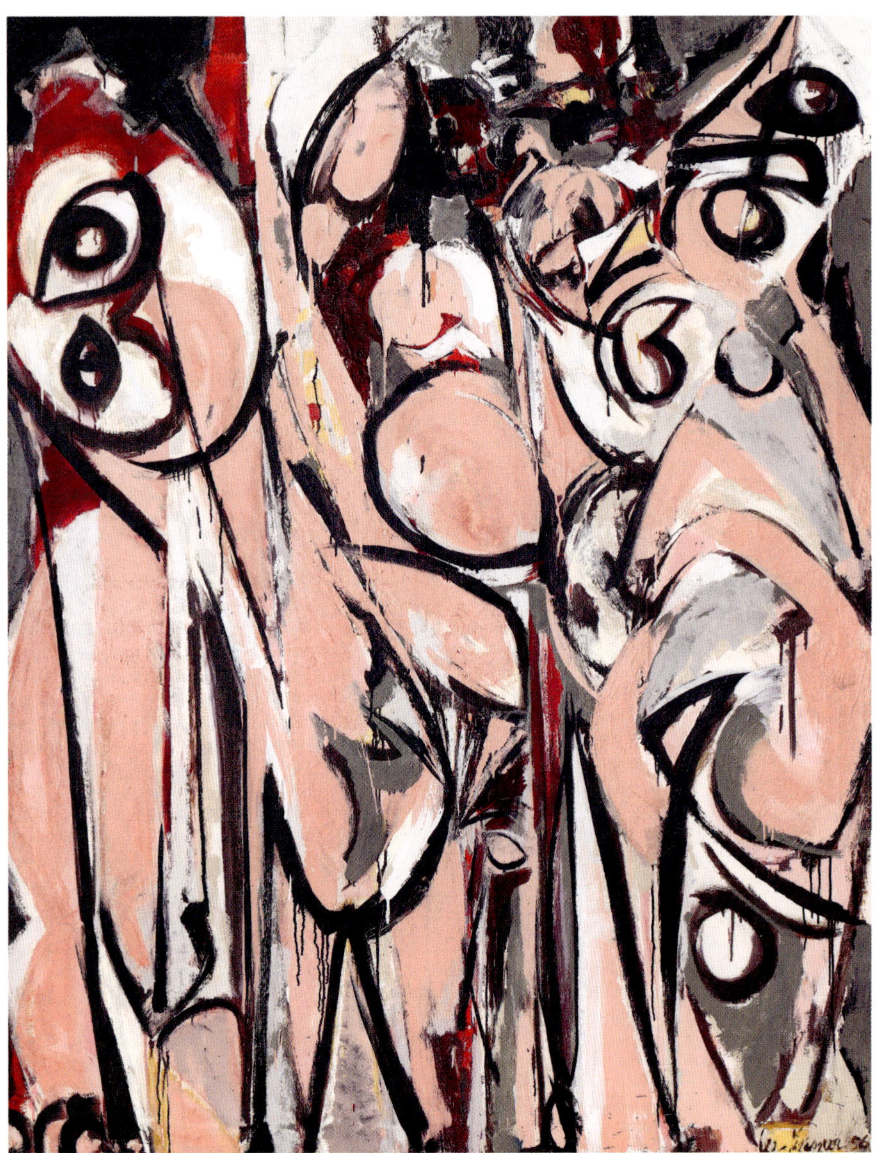

85 Lee Krasner, *Three in Two*, 1956

The Abstract Expressionists' common interest in Jungian psychology helped to reinforce their belief that all art worthy of the name stems from the unconscious, and that it therefore contained within it the possibility of communicating directly with the viewer at this more primitive level. Gottlieb was typical of them all when he said, 'When I'm painting, I'm completely preoccupied with the technical problems. Furthermore, before I even start to paint, I have to get myself charged, and this is something I can only feel in a vague way. When I feel that I'm fully charged and ready to let go on the canvas, I'm not in a position to view myself in an objective way. I have to let my feelings go and it's only afterwards that I become aware of what my feelings really were. And for me this is one of the fascinations and great experiences of painting.' However, where Gottlieb, Newman, Gorky and Rothko understood the unconscious largely as a storehouse of symbols linking past and present, Pollock and, to some extent, Krasner, regarded it as a wilder, more mysterious region of the mind populated by mythic and religious symbols. In their work it is often much more difficult to separate art and life. In place of the tragic subjects and pantheistic organicism found in work by the first four artists in the 1940s, they developed
86 personal iconographies in works such as Pollock's *Guardians of the Secret* (1943) and *Totem Lesson I* (1944), and Krasner's
85 *Three in Two* (1956), that is related much more directly to contemporary ethnographic descriptions of the magical operations of many traditional cultures across the planet. These works are replete with archetypal imagery derived from many sources, both visual and literary. Most important, though, is the creation of private symbols that lies behind the appropriation of mythic elements.

A New Academy

The rise of American Abstract Expressionism was supported by intense critical engagement with its products – by artists and writers alike – and the patronage of galleries and dealers committed to modernist art. Unsurprisingly, as the reputations of painters like Pollock and De Kooning grew, their work was quickly exhibited in, and acquired by the two major New York public modern art spaces, the Museum of Modern Art and the Guggenheim Museum. This institutionalizing of Abstract Expressionism was accompanied by the institutionalizing of a particular theory of modernist art represented by the critical writings of Clement Greenberg and later Michael Fried (b. 1939). Greenberg's close relationships with the artists of the New York School helped both to represent

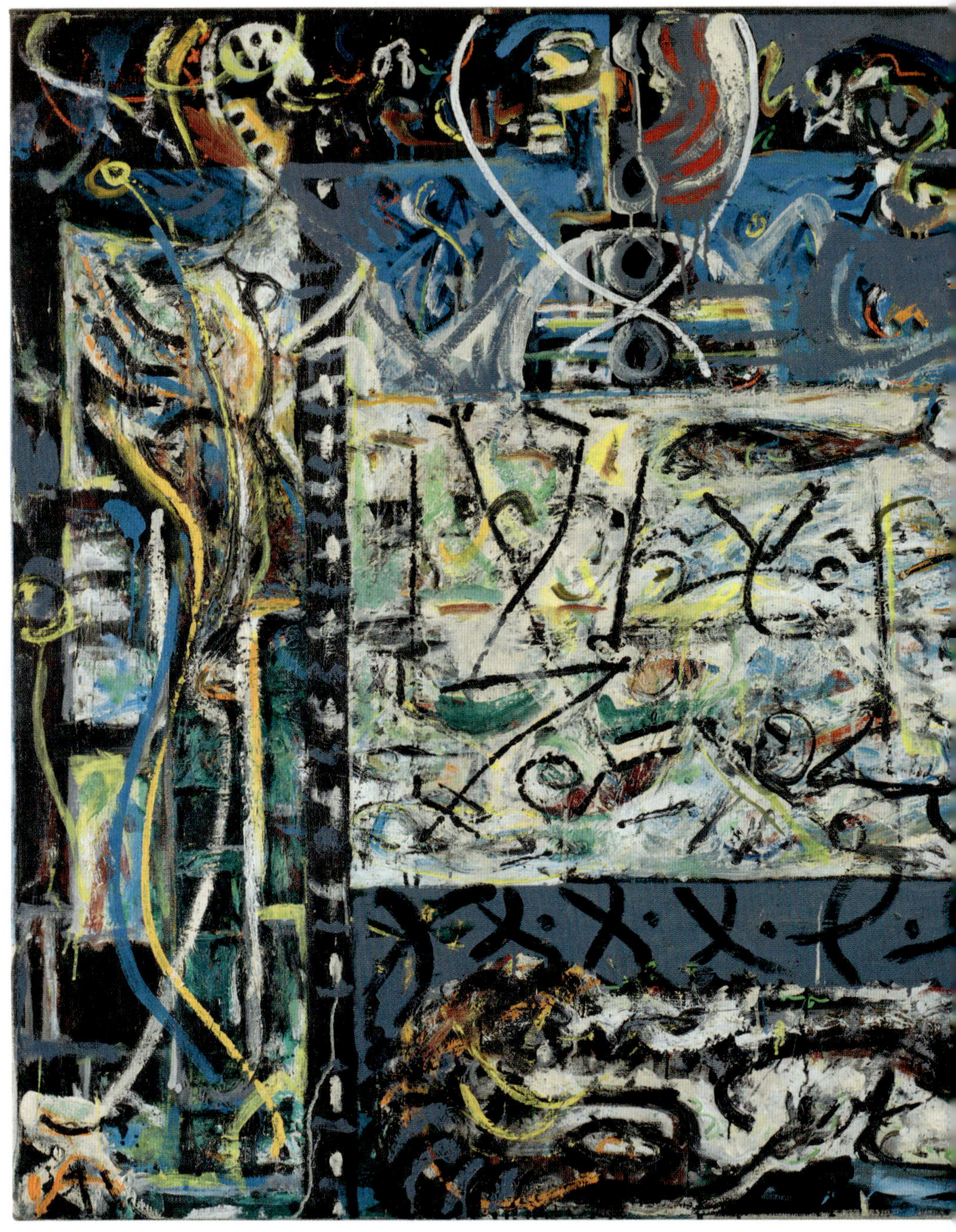

86 Jackson Pollock, *Guardians of the Secret*, 1943

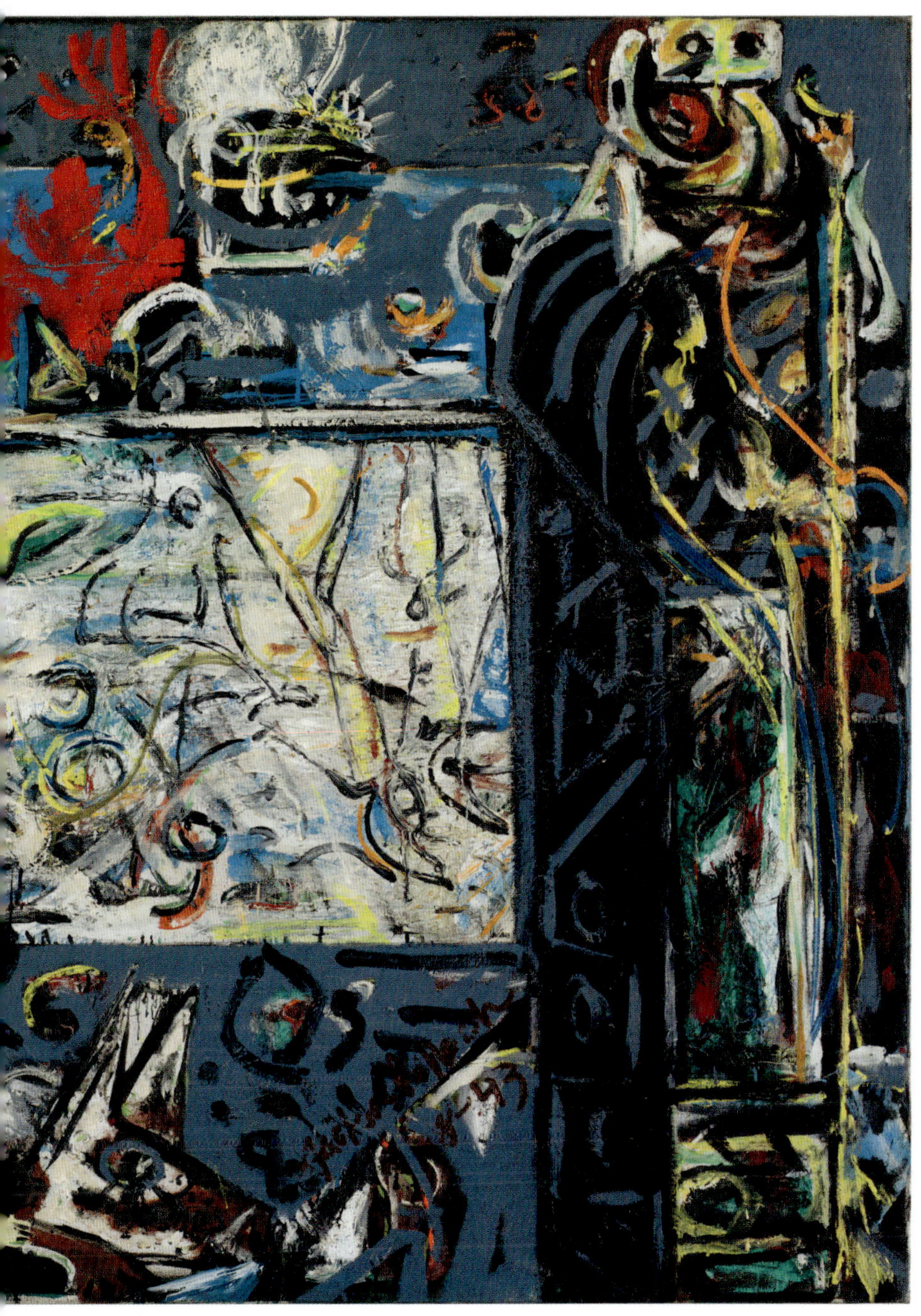

Abstract Expressionism to the art world and to shape it as it developed in the 1950s. His emphasis on formal issues as opposed to questions of narrative or even metaphysical content moved discourse about Abstract Expressionism away from psychological interpretation – clear in Rothko's, Gottlieb's and Newman's pronouncements in the 1940s, for example – and towards questions of art's relationship to itself. This emphasis on art's autonomy – in other words, the fact that it need not rely on any other thing out there in the world to define it or to justify its existence – proved terrifically important in both practice and criticism in the final four decades of the twentieth century, partly because it helped complete the process of the institutionalization of Modernism, and partly because it energized fiercely opposed debates about what constitutes the 'proper' nature of artistic practice.

Greenberg's 'Modernist Painting' (1960) was the culmination of his thinking about modern art since 1939 and is one of the clearest and most precise critical articulations of the modernist-formalist project. Originally a radio broadcast and published a year later, 'Modernist Painting' sought to define Modernism as a particular tendency, whose origins could be traced to eighteenth-century Enlightenment thought, and which was characteristically 'self-critical' – that is, he argued, it develops and understands itself as a discipline by testing itself against discourse within the parameters only of the discipline. Revealing his Marxist-Hegelian roots, Greenberg produced a historicist model of a more or less linear development over the course of a century towards a 'purified' modernist practice that was now evident in certain 'advanced' work. Modernism's triumph, therefore, had occurred in the present that Greenberg himself inhabited. As Fried put it in 1965: 'Roughly speaking, the history of painting from Manet through Synthetic Cubism and Matisse may be characterized in terms of the gradual withdrawal of painting from the task of representing reality...in favour of an increasing preoccupation with problems intrinsic to painting itself.' Whilst it began in clearly Expressionist views of art, this process culminated, he believed, in the work that was purely formalist and self-critical, as epitomized in the practice of painters such as Morris Louis (1912–1962), Kenneth Noland (1924–2010), and Jules Olitski (1922–2007).

Greenberg's account of Modernism as 'self-critical' rejects social and historical interpretation and the relevance of politics to practice. Yet political interests and engagement had been a staple of the modernist avant-garde. The denial of this dimension effectively neutralized, after the event, any social threat inherent in an art practice that needed to see itself as being in a state of permanent revolution. This probably had more relevance in the United States than anywhere else in the West in the post-war period owing to an institutional fear of Communism that often bordered on the hysterical and resulted at times in physical suppression of individuals and groups with Communist 'sympathies'. Given the generally leftist political views of the avant-garde – not to mention Greenberg's own Marxist past – it is easy to see how the 'depoliticizing' of Modernism might be seen as an imperative. However, though it might no longer be politically subversive, Modernism's critical function remained an essential part of its identity, though transformed into self-criticism. In this form Modernism was easily absorbed into the institutions of democratic states, including the art schools, where the rhetoric of self-critical art subversion became a cornerstone of the new academy.

Greenberg's key assumption was that all art forms had qualities that are unique only to them and that a 'pure' art could only be attained by getting rid of all those things that are extraneous to it. As he put it in 'Modernist Painting': 'The task of self-criticism became to eliminate from the effects of each art any and every effect that might conceivably be borrowed from or by the medium of any other art.' He argued that the only unique condition of painting was 'flatness, two-dimensionality.' As a result, he regarded illusionistic painting as the least true to the medium, since it used art(fullness) 'to conceal art,' so that viewers see objects in three-dimensional space before they recognize it as pigment on a flat surface. Modernism, on the other hand, calls attention to its condition as art: 'One is made aware of the flatness of their pictures before, instead of after, being made aware of what the flatness contains.' This is essentially anti-Expressionist, where value is placed on the psychological possibilities inherent in the art object and direct communication to viewers of states of mind.

Greenberg did not see abstraction as a necessary quality of modernist painting, but he did regard it as a logical step since abstraction was least likely to encourage associations with physical things outside the picture and destroy the assertion of its flatness. This is because, as he pointed out, 'All recognizable entities (including pictures themselves) exist in three-dimensional space, and the barest suggestion of a recognizable entity suffices to call up associations of that kind of space.' Such associations were less likely to happen when viewing a Rothko or Mitchell abstract than, say, a still life by Matisse or a late garden painting by Monet. Yet, Greenberg also recognized that human perception instinctively searches for

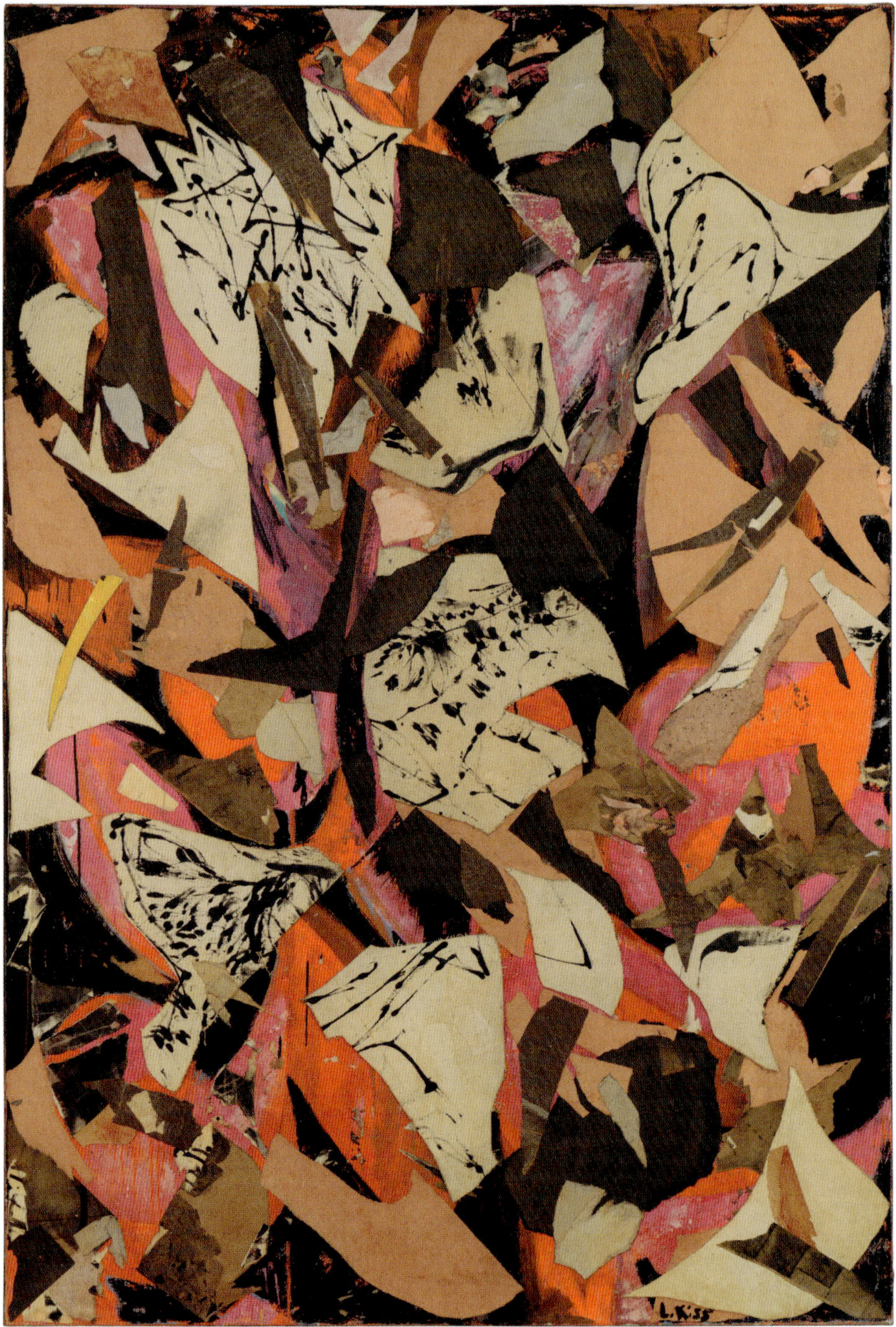

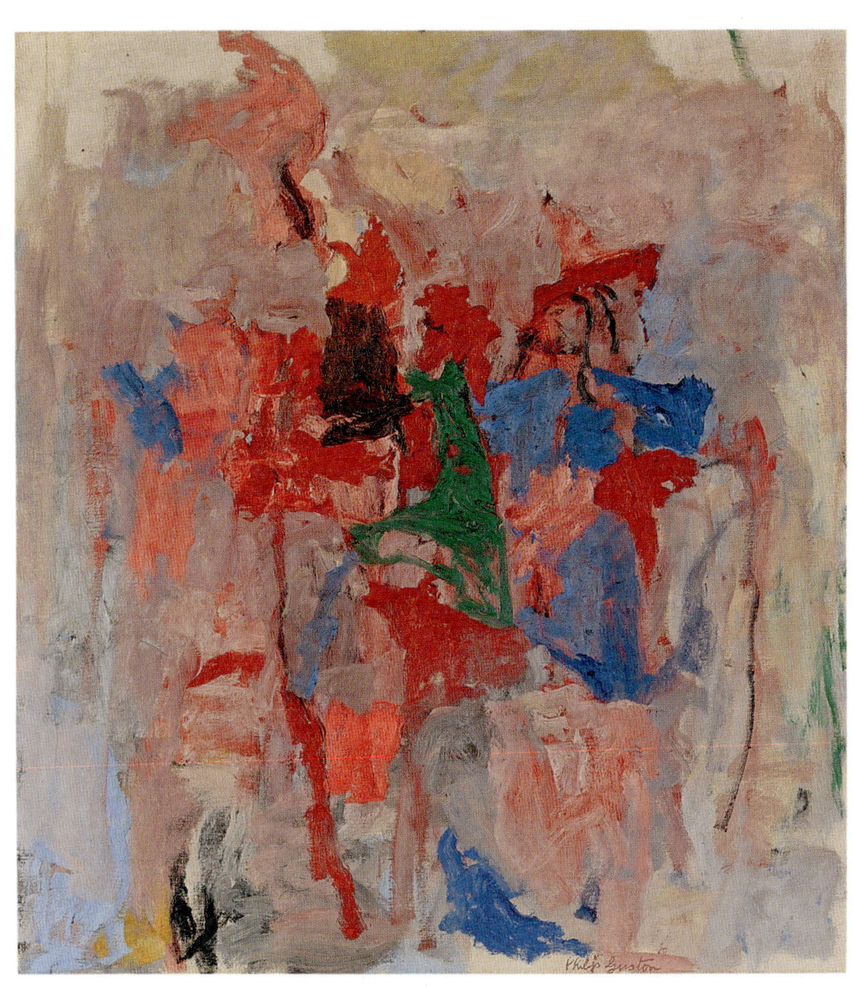

87 OPPOSTE Lee Krasner, *Bald Eagle*, 1955
88 ABOVE Philip Guston, *Processional*, 1957

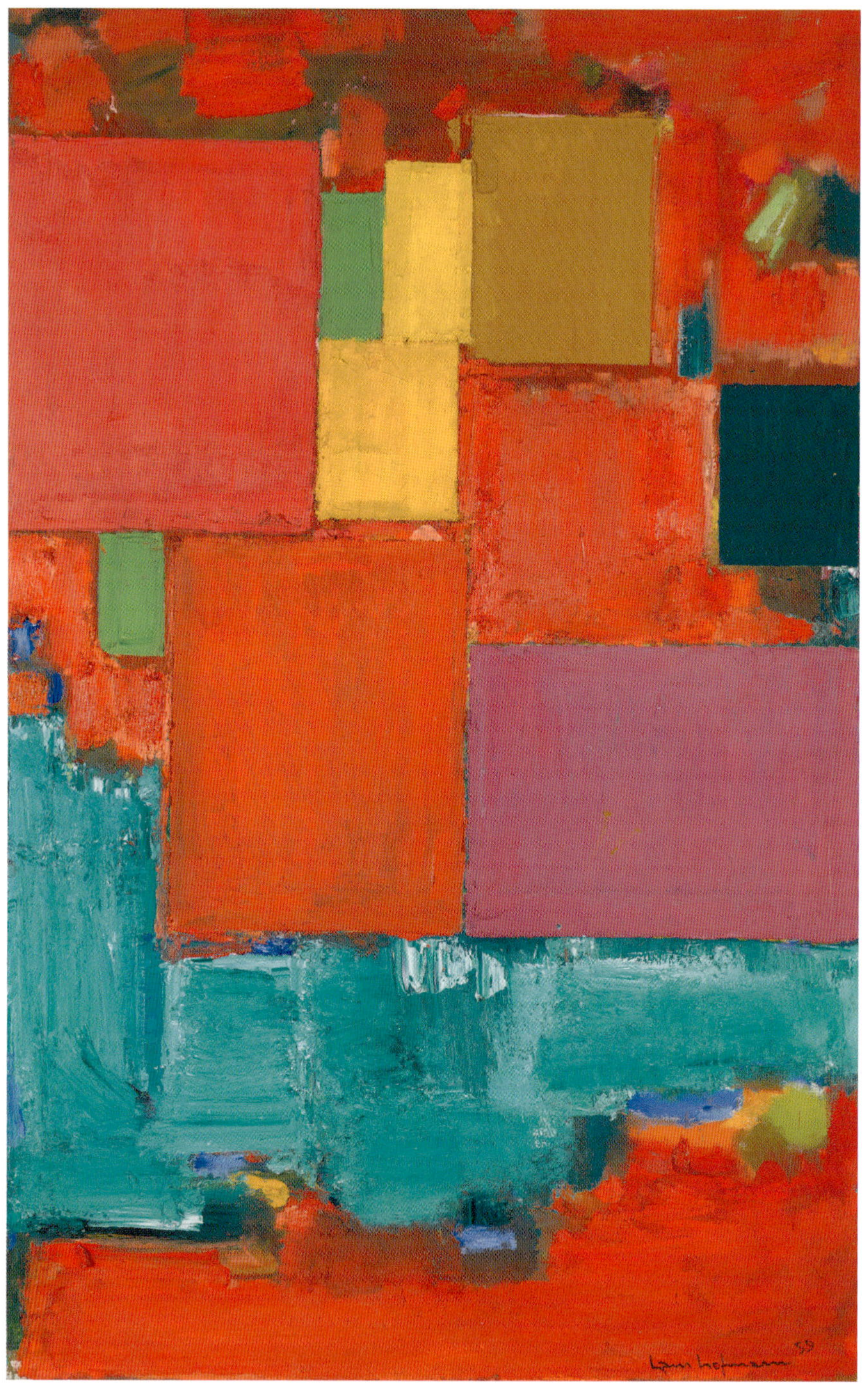

89 Hans Hofmann, *Pompeii*, 1959

shape and pattern. Even when faced with non-objective images
a process of 'seeing-in' occurs in which viewers unconsciously
search for familiar objects in pictures.

Even in Abstract Expressionist painting, space is not
excluded. The dense, all-over webs of a drip painting by
Pollock, *Autumn Rhythm (Number 30)* (1950) and the bold collage
87 cut-up elements that constitute Krasner's *Bald Eagle* (1955)
are both suggestive of a complex, shallow spatial terrain,
comparable to Cubist *passage*. Rothko's and Newman's colour
fields, meanwhile, seemingly consist of vast, indeterminate
88, 89 voids, and Hofmann and Philip Guston's (1913–1980)
abstractions have a kind of optical 'push and pull', in which
space and movement are suggested by colour and form.
Absolute flatness was therefore regarded, said Greenberg, as
an ideal towards which painting should aspire: 'The flatness
towards which Modernist painting orients itself can never be
an utter flatness,' he wrote, but importantly, the kind of space
it permitted was now purely 'optical', as opposed to 'sculptural'
– that is, an illusion of three-dimensional space: 'Where the
Old Masters created an illusion of space into which one could
imagine oneself walking, the illusion created by a Modernist
is one into which one can only look, can travel through only
with the eye.'

One of the painters who perhaps first came closest to
achieving this purely optical painting in the early 1950s was
90 Helen Frankenthaler. Like many abstract painters she relied
on controlled accident in the development of a piece and was
hypersensitive to modulations of colour and form on the
surface of her canvases. Paint was usually poured or thrown
onto the surface, but then worked into with 'rags or brushes
to form the so-called accident into my aesthetic.' In this way
her paintings grew organically, as it were. This method could
result in a successful outcome – either quickly, or sometimes
over a long period – or a disaster, which was subsequently
scrapped. The artist's judgment is necessarily exercised
throughout such a process of making, according to each piece's
formal organization, so that once again we are faced with art
concerning itself wholly with art.

Frankenthaler's innovation, which had widespread repercussions on modernist painting for two decades, was the technique of applying very thin paint onto unprimed canvas so that it soaked into the surface, making paint and ground a single entity. Her painting *Mountains and Sea* (1952) has become almost talismanic, since this was the work that Morris Louis and Kenneth Noland were inspired by when they visited her studio with Greenberg in 1953. They began to experiment with

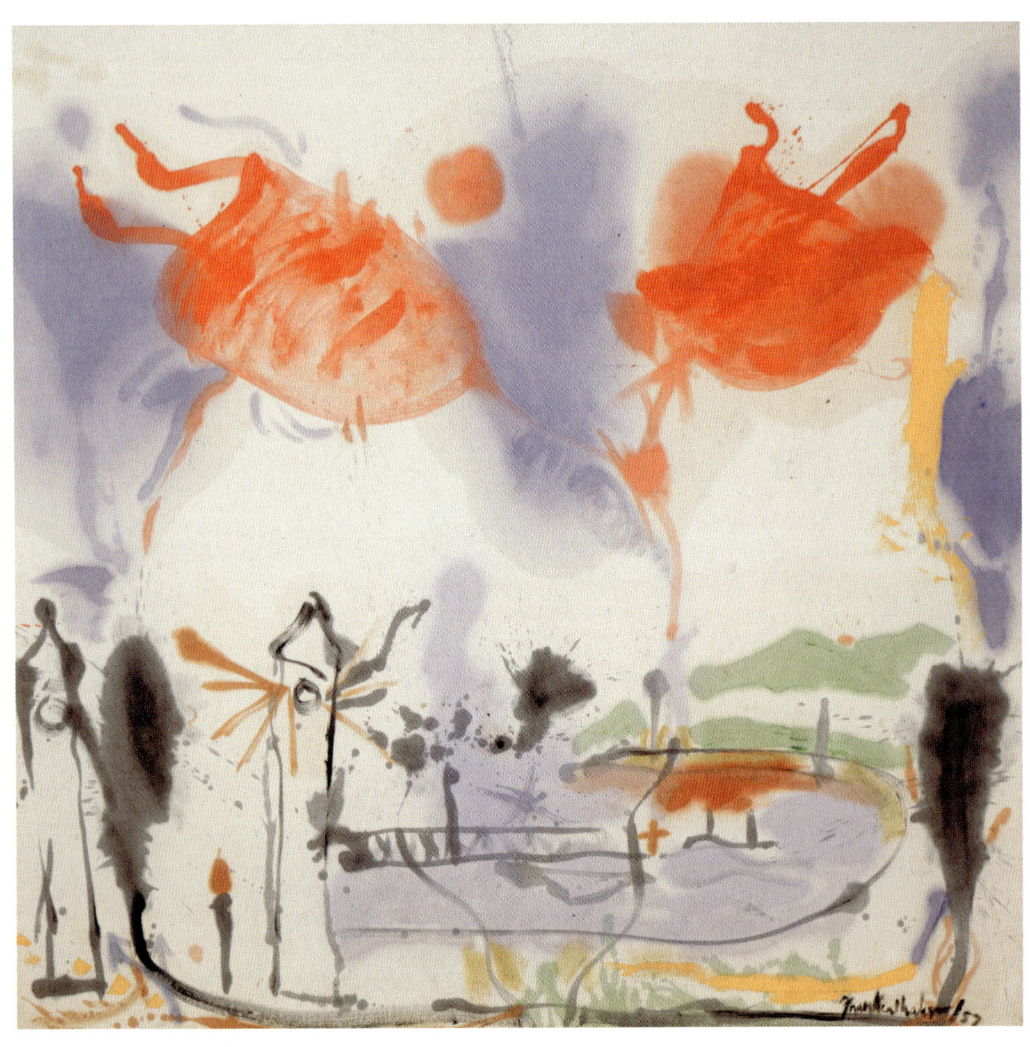

90 Helen Frankenthaler, *Round Trip*, 1957

staining techniques using the relatively newly invented acrylic resin paints. The advantage of acrylic over oil paint is that it maintains a much higher degree of colour saturation when thinned to a liquid. Louis produced a series of vast paintings in which paint was poured onto slightly tilted, raw canvas, so that gravity rather than the artist's gesture created form. In works like *Tet* (1958) and *Golden Age* (1958), colours overlap and merge forming the ground into flat 'veils', whilst in others, like *Pi* (1960) and *Beta Kappa* (1961), the lines of pigment retain their separate identity, but operate as marginalia around a dominant expanse of bare canvas. Noland later wrote: 'We were making abstract art, but we wanted to simplify the selection of materials, and to use them in a very economical way. To get to raw canvas, to use the canvas unstretched – to use it in more basic or fundamental ways, to use it as fabric rather than as a stretched surface.' From an American perspective, at least, these developments appeared to sound a death knell for any continued relevance for gestural Expressionism in painting.

Post-War Expressionism in Europe

American Abstract Expressionism has come to dominate accounts of post-war abstraction and Expressionism to the extent that the general spread of something like a dominant Expressionist tendency – both abstract and figurative – across Western Europe tends nowadays to be overlooked. Another contributing factor is the common subsuming of European post-war Expressionism under the broader heading of '*art informel*' in art historical narratives. This was a term invented by the influential French critic Michel Tapié (1909–1987) to describe work in an exhibition he curated in Lille, France in 1952. Titled, *Un art autre* (Art of Another Kind), it included
91 artists from Wols, Jean Fautrier (1898–1964), and Jean Dubuffet, to Karel Appel and Willem de Kooning, as well as others not closely aligned with Expressionist practice such as Henri Michaux, whose automatic paintings drew heavily on
92 Surrealist and Far Eastern practices, as in *Peintre à l'encre de Chine* (1961–62).

Tapié's reason for inventing yet another new term was driven partly by a desire to differentiate post-war European painting from what he regarded as its now tainted forebears, but it is also part of that patricidal desire in Modernism to be seen to be supplanting the old with the new. Yet when the British poet and critic Herbert Read wrote about western Modernism in general at the end of the 1950s, his declaration that Abstract Expressionism 'has been the characteristic style

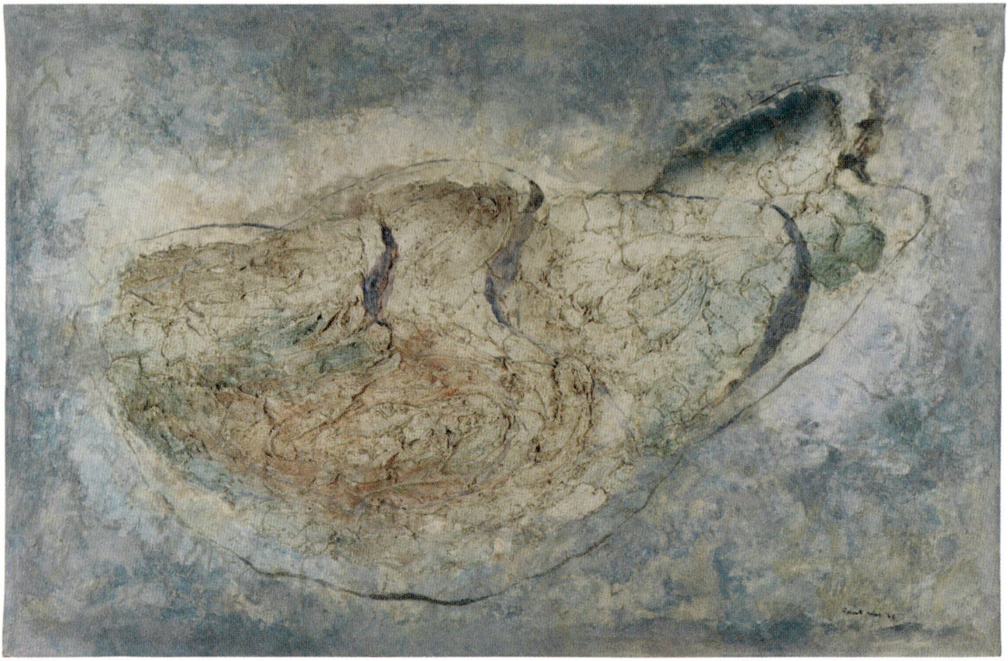

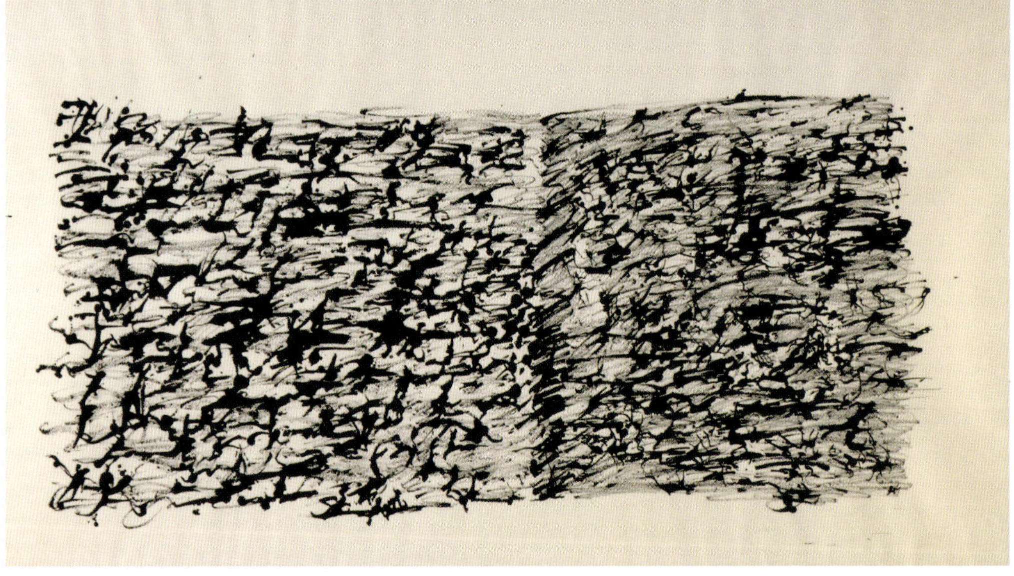

91 TOP Jean Fautrier, *Femme douce*, 1946
92 ABOVE Henri Michaux, *Peintre à l'encre de Chine*, 1961–62
93 OPPOSITE Alan Davie, *Image of the Fish God No.2*, 1956

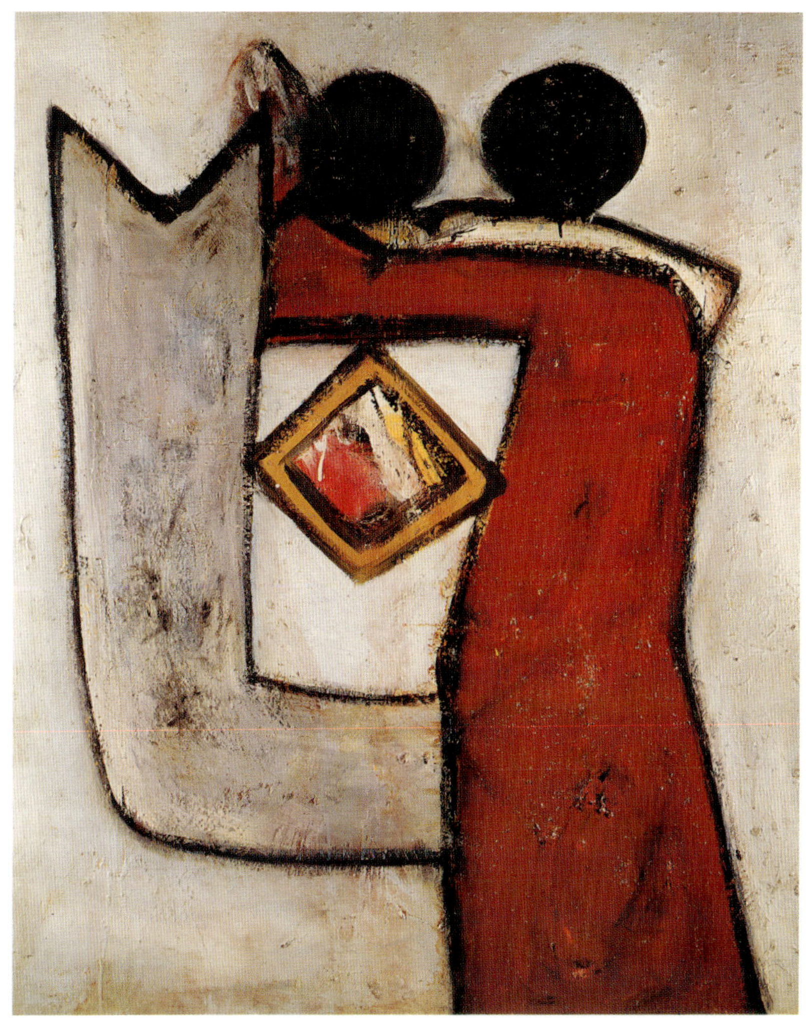

of the period since the Second World War,' must have seemed
at the time like a truism. Besides Appel and Dubuffet, others
such as, Pierre Soulages (1919–2022), Jean Bazaine (1904–2001),
93 Hans Hartung (1904–1989), Jean-Paul Riopelle (1923–2002), Alan
Davie (1920–2014) and Asger Jorn were producing paintings in
the 1940s and 1950s that paralleled the various concerns of the
American Abstract Expressionists, while others such as, Francis
Bacon, Leon Kossoff (1926–2019) and Frank Auerbach (b. 1931),
were forging a more distinctly figurative Expressionist reaction
to the times in which they lived.

European Abstract Expressionism remained, overall, more closely wedded to the easel and was more domestic in scale. As a result, it was less inclined to the kind of vigorous physicality of painters like Elaine and Willem de Kooning, Joan Mitchell, Krasner and Pollock. Exceptions include Appel, Dubuffet, Jorn, and Roger Hilton (1911–1975), all of whom took their already established Expressionist styles onto another level of scale and physicality after they experienced the work of the Americans. In Britain especially, though, at this time another kind of abstraction that was altogether quieter and more lyrical was also prominent. It tended toward the pastoral rather than the urban, growing out of pre-war neo-romanticism, which itself had reached back beyond Expressionism to the nineteenth century and looked to the long tradition of evocative landscape painting in Britain. Often centred around activity in the long-established artists' colony in St. Ives, Cornwall, and with emphasis on the painterly organization of colour conceived as simultaneously decorative and richly allusive of place, work by Peter Lanyon (1918–1964), Patrick Heron (1920–1999), Terry Frost (1915–2003), Ivan Hitchens (1893–1979) and later Howard Hodgkin (1932–2017) and Albert Irvin (1922–2015) established an abidingly popular seam of Abstract Expressionist practice.

CoBrA

One of the first, and certainly most prominent, organized groups to emerge in Europe after 1945 was emphatically Expressionist, albeit informed by Surrealism, which had been the dominant modernist tendency in most of Europe in the years immediately before the war. CoBrA represents an unlikely synthesis of elements: theory and practice; myth and dialectical materialism; Expressionism and anti-formalism. At its root, though, was a deep shared commitment to the importance of the human condition (compare this with Marc's 'animalization' of art), and to embracing the brute and physical world as an organic, living thing that participates actively in the general world-drama.

CoBrA is an acronym derived from the initials of the capital cities of the native countries of its core members: Copenhagen, Brussels, and Amsterdam. It was invented by the Belgian painter and poet Christian Dotremont (1922–1979) in November 1948 as the title for a journal whose original purpose was to provide a focus for the Dutch and Danish Experimental Groups and the Belgian Centre for Revolutionary Surrealism, but it came to describe a wider group of artists united by left-wing politics and devotion to radical experimentation in art and literature. CoBrA's major figures included, in the Netherlands, Karel Appel,

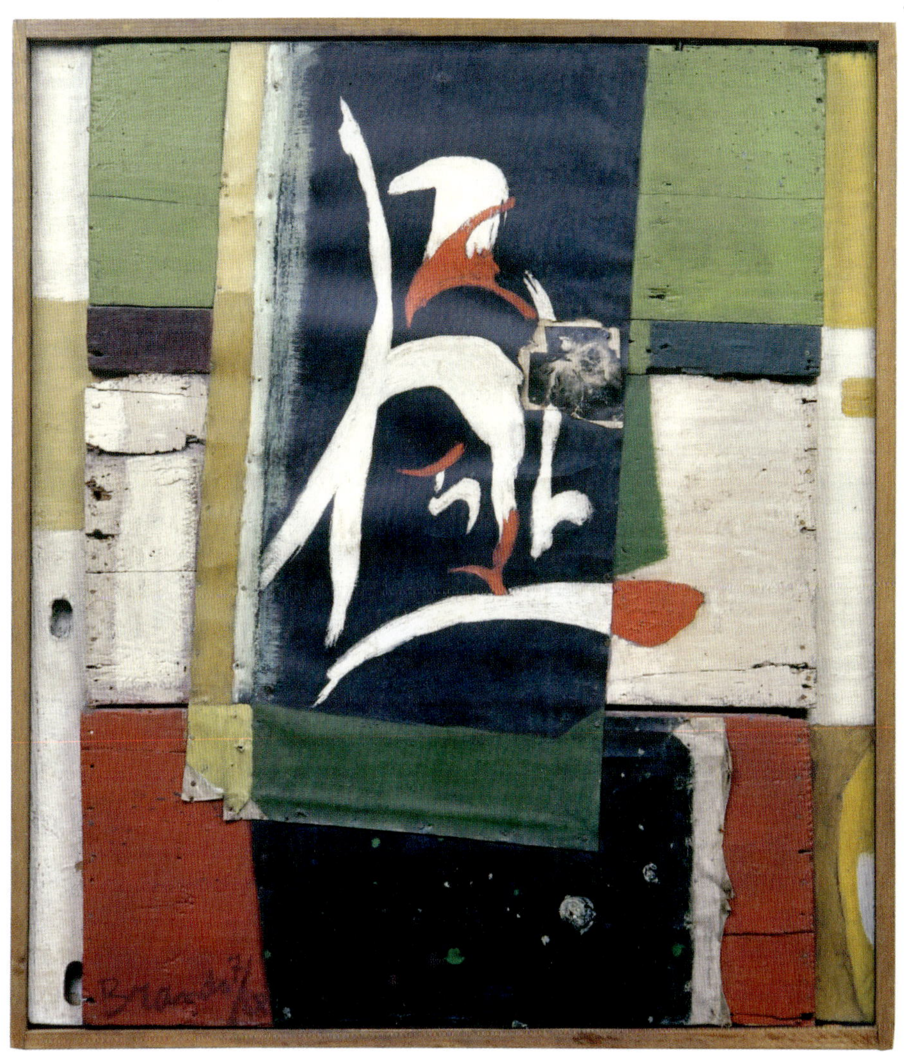

94 Eugène Brands, *Sign in Orion*, 1948

94 Eugène Brands (1913–2002), Constant, Corneille (Guillaume Cornelis van Beverloo) (1922–2010), Lotti van der Gaag (1923–1999), Anton Rooskens (1906–1976), Lucebert (1924–1994) and Theo Wolvecamp (1925–1992); in Denmark, Asger Jorn, Carl-Henning Pedersen, Egill Jacobsen, Ejler Bille, Henry Heerup
95 and Else Alfelt (1910–1974); in Belgium, Christian Dotremont,
96 Pierre Alechinsky (b. 1927), and Pol Bury (1922–2005). Only eight issues of *CoBrA* were published between 1949 and 1951, supported by a small number of other publications and some group exhibitions, including a major exhibition in 1949 at the Stedelijk Museum in Amsterdam, and another in 1951 at the Palais des Beaux-Arts in Liège, Belgium, which signalled the end of the movement. Although its existence as a coherent group was short-lived, CoBrA's international impact and influence were significant, and its core figures continued to be prominent in the contemporary art world.

Dotremont, who from the beginning was CoBrA's most vociferous propagandist, described it as a 'simplist, experimental movement,' where simplism is viewed as the 'extremism of experimentation,' based on a fundamental

95 Else Alfelt, *Jorden – Vandet og Bjergene*, 1952

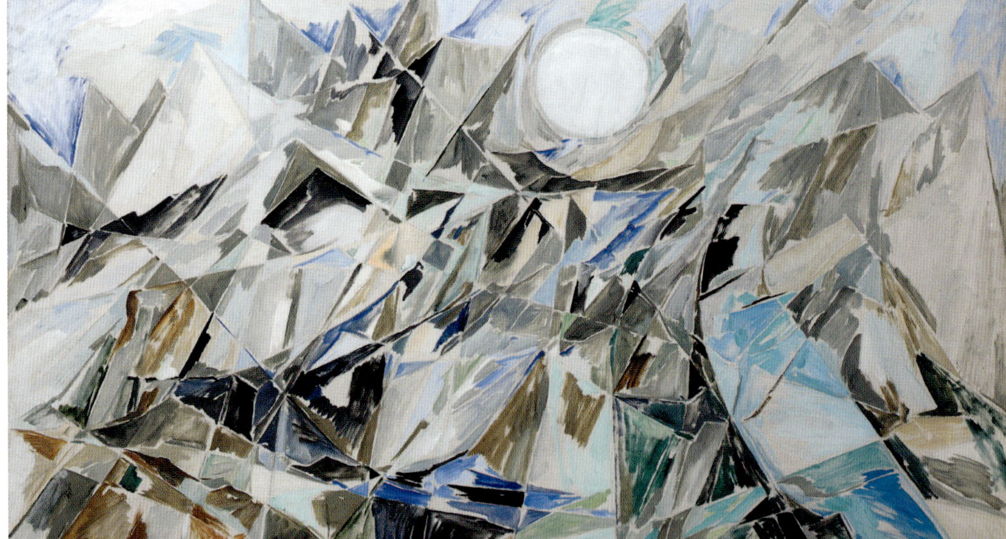

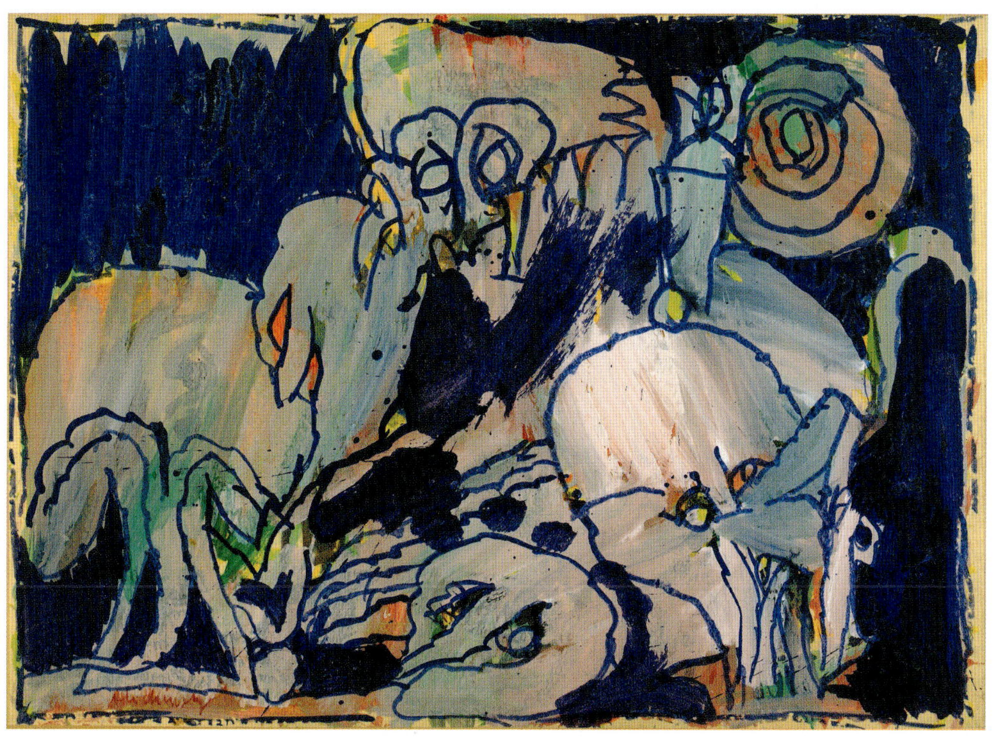

96 Pierre Alechinsky, *Le bleu de Methylène* (Methylene Blue), 1974

rejection of the idea of linear development in art and ideas. In one respect this relied on the pre-war Surrealist interest in looking outside the accepted cultural canon for artistic precedent and influence, but CoBrA also rejected Surrealist tendencies to attempt to replace old systems and structures with new ones. Continual experimentation in art (like perpetual revolution in politics) implies not only dynamism, but also the necessity to accept nothing as a stable precedent for creative development. Where Dotremont's language has an aura of 'theory', Alechinsky put it more lyrically, saying that CoBrA tried to be 'happily unselfconscious' in its art: 'intelligence and creative thought are ignited in the encounter with the unknown, the unexpected, the accidental, disorder, the absurd and the impossible.' At the heart of this is a commitment to the idea that play is a fundamental element in the development of culture, as laid out in the Dutch cultural theorist, Johan Huizinga's (1872–1945) influential book, *Homo Ludens* (1938). Huizinga introduced '*ludens*', which is the present participle of the Latin verb for play

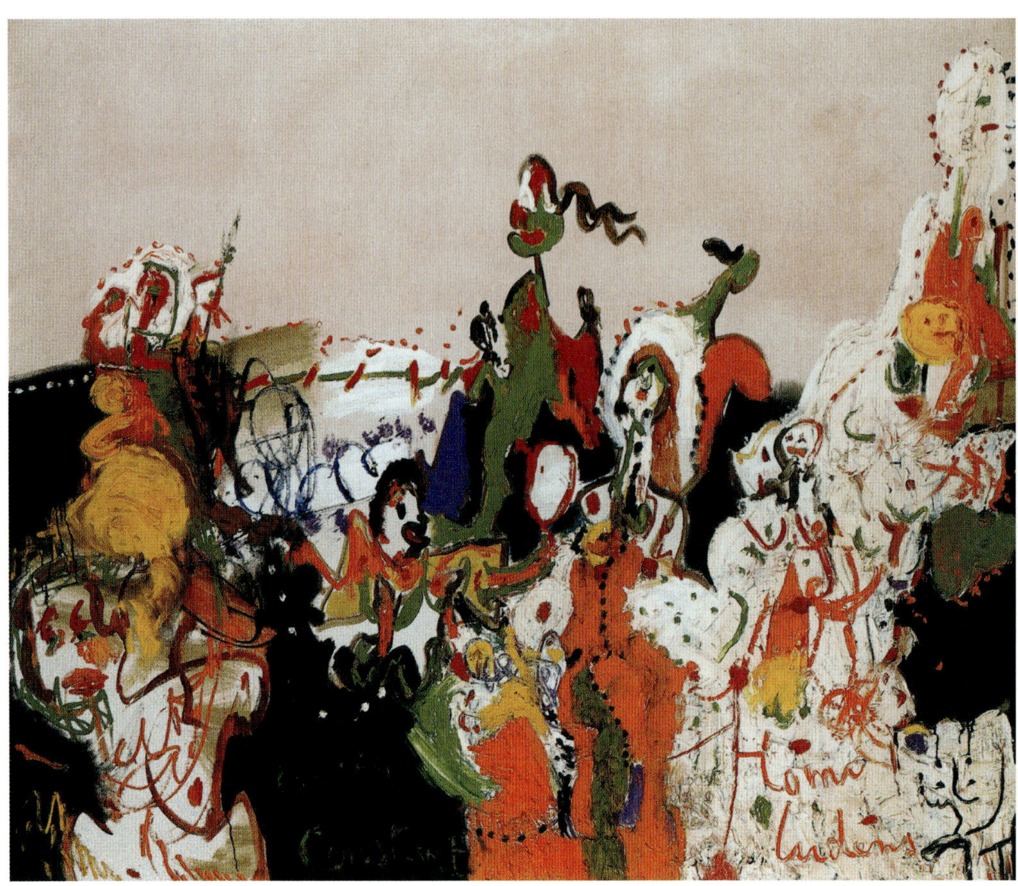

97 Constant, *Homo Ludens*, 1964

(as well as 'school' and 'practice'), in his definition of the crucial, defining characteristic of modern humans, in contrast to the formulation *Homo sapiens*, in which emphasis is placed on rationality or wisdom. He argued that, 'Genuine, pure play is one of the main bases of civilization.' And at a time when the values of a European 'civilization' that had led to the unspeakable horrors of the Holocaust and the Second World War were being seriously questioned by many, Huizinga's belief in the primacy of play and its location outside of 'ordinary' life offered the possibility of cultural change generated from within. Moreover, he had argued that because 'all play is voluntary activity,' it is in itself 'freedom.' Little wonder, then, that 'freedom' and 'play' are leitmotivs of classic CoBrA art, celebrated not least in Constant's later carnival-like image

97 of tumultuous activity, *Homo Ludens*, which was named for Huizinga's treatise.

Asger Jorn typically talked in 1949 about CoBrA's experimentalism in terms of a suspension of linear thought: 'The purpose of our experimentation is to allow thought to be expressed spontaneously, without being ruled by reason. This irrational spontaneity allows us to access the vital source of our life. Our aim is to escape the rule of reason – which is and always has been nothing other than the idealized rule of the bourgeoisie – in order to achieve the reign of life.' There is an underlying primitivism to these positions, which is the glue that holds CoBrA together more than any other thing. Its impulses, both aesthetic and political, came from a shared dissatisfaction with the ruling culture of its seemingly culturally moribund post-war present. Not for the first time in the twentieth century, the artists' call was to supplant rationality; that tyranny of logic and reasonableness that can explain away atrocity and which exemplified 'civilization'. In true Romantic fashion, they argued that the status quo would be replaced by a culture of 'the people'. Not the industrialized masses, but the people at their most candid and unpolluted, 'nourished only by a natural and therefore general urge to expression,' as Constant put it. This kind of cultural primitivism characteristically identifies the good with that which is 'natural' or 'according to nature.'

CoBrA's primitivism was defined, on one hand, by an obsession with the tabula rasa. It insisted always on the idea of creating from beginnings born out of play, since culture, as Huizinga argued, 'arises in and as play, and never leaves it.' There is also a strong sense of the necessity of breaking free of the accumulated shackles of European civilization. CoBrA looked backwards for its inspirations and guidance, either literally, to ancient and primitive folk culture – its lore and its objects – or metaphorically, to the beginnings of culture, represented by the child, or to the unconscious, which they regarded as primitive consciousness. They approached the latter in two ways: by personal explorations of unconscious operations, using strategies like automatism (in common with their contemporaries in the United States); and through an interest in the creative products of people with psychiatric illnesses, whose conditions they regarded as 'liberating' insofar as they believed in the now outdated idea that psychotic experiences resulted in a desirable relinquishing of control by the rational, 'civilized' mind. Having apparently found themselves 'cut free from the past' by the destructive circumstances of recent history, Rooskens asserted in 1948,

'Only primitive beings, children and psychopaths could count on our sympathy.'

The Danish artists, probably more than any of the others, were steeped in knowledge of folklore and mythology that they used as a repository for continual reinvention, drawn as it was from their activities with *Helhesten* during the Nazi occupation
70 of Denmark (see Chapter 3). Paintings like Jacobsen's *Orange Object II* (1943) and Pedersen's *Starred Heads* (1949) and
99 *Mennesker og den gule stjerne* (1950) all refer in their forms and primeval atmosphere to ancient, often archetypal themes. Jorn, too, drew deeply from this same cup in images like *Aganak* (1950), although his affinity with the mythical forces of a distant geographical past is probably most forcefully and suggestively in later near-abstract paintings like *Deuil troublé* (1957) and
98 *Instructive Extruction of a Konstructif Destruction* (1966). As he said in 1950: 'I work with the primordial cells from which life itself originated, in the days when it all began.'

The snake has a long history as archetype and mythological symbol. CoBrA was much more than a witty acronym, for the

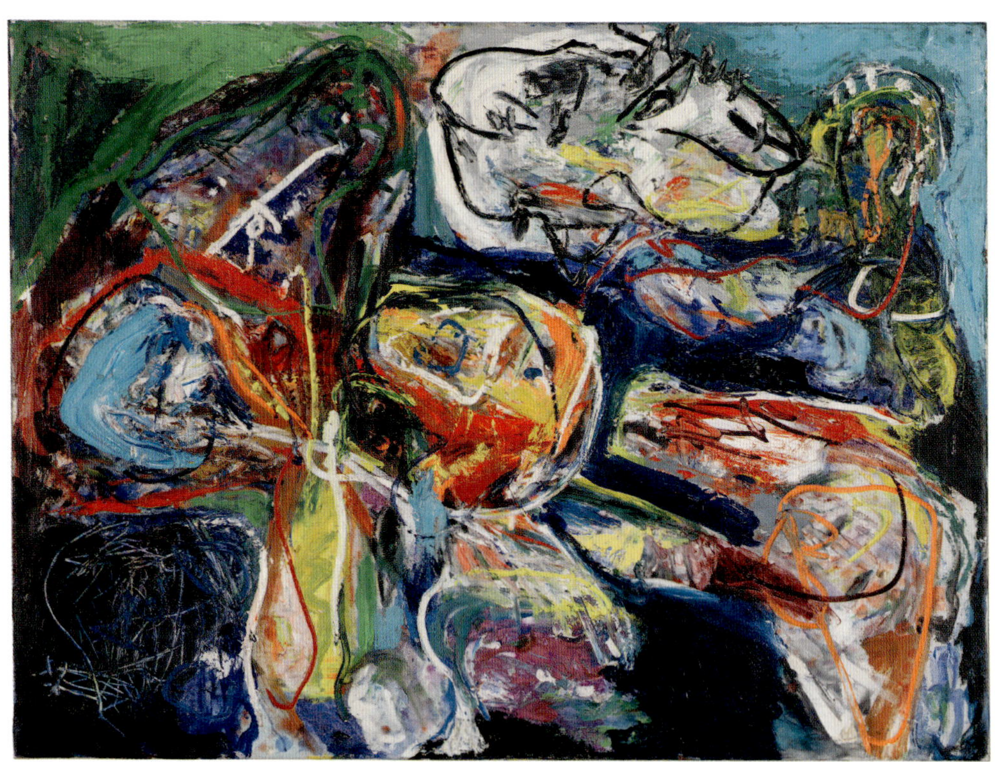

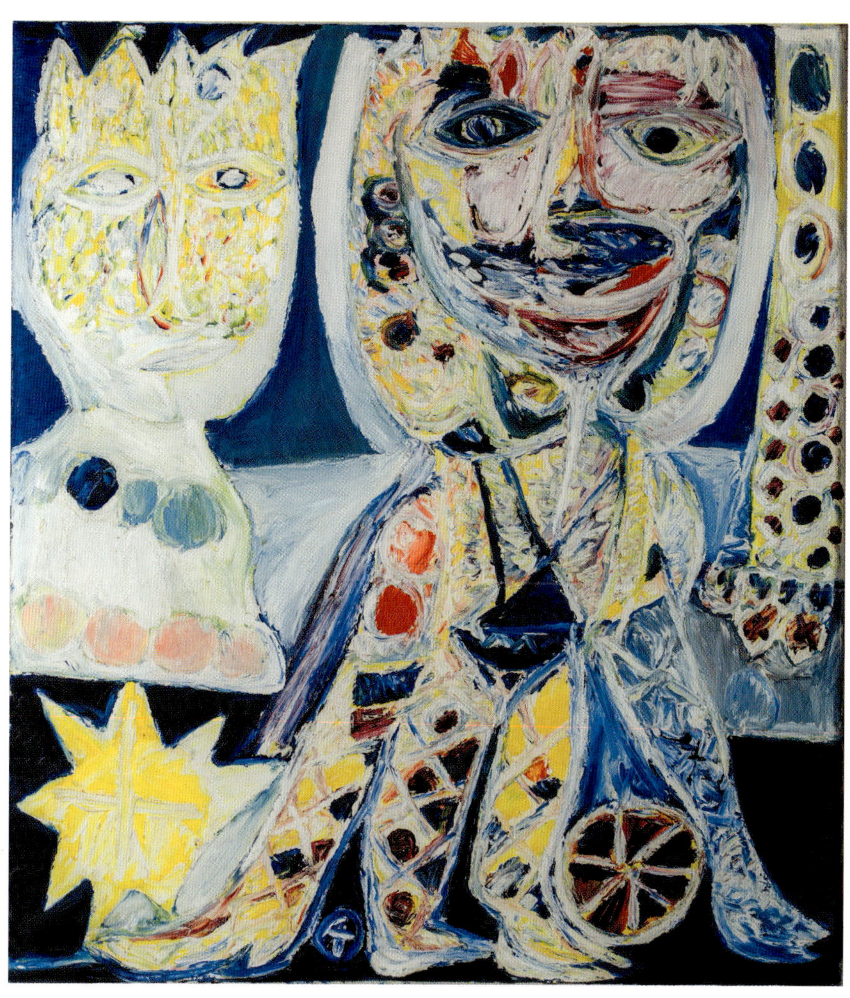

98 OPPOSITE Asger Jorn, *Instructive Extruction of a Konstructif Destruction* (sic.), 1966
99 ABOVE Carl-Henning Pedersen, *Mennesker og den gule stjerne*, 1950

snake was a favoured device for many of its future members even before the formation of the group. The Danes were aware of the importance of the snake in Scandinavian antiquity. Jorn had even studied the Edda, the main source on Norse mythology, written down in Iceland in the thirteenth century. For Dotremont, the snake was almost a personal talisman, and its link to labyrinths, knots, arabesques, wheels and spirals make it a consistent presence in CoBrA art, from Jorn's *La lune et des animaux* (1950) to Alechinsky's *Le vert naissant* (1960), which is all writhing, serpentine form.

Despite continuous recourse to the written word, the CoBrA project is marked by an anti-intellectualism that is a factor of its rejection of the culture of the immediate past. Its texts encouraged experimentation and the participation of the viewer in the work, where the aspiration towards a vaguely defined 'freedom' was a constant. In that new, post-war era, Constant argued in a 1948 manifesto, 'Art means everything.' But art's most important task was not aesthetic or formal, it was primal: 'the activation of the urge to create.' Jorn summed the project up well: 'Our experimenting is geared to the uninhibited expression of thought beyond the control of reason. Through this irrational spontaneity we have reached the vital source of being. Our aim is to escape the tyranny of reason so as eventually to establish the sovereignty of life.' Yet, this very embrace of collective individual freedom carries the seeds of its own demise, destined, it seems, to end in the structures of professional careers and system building in one's practice that denies finally the commitment to continuous experimentalism and undifferentiation that CoBrA espoused.

At times all the CoBrA artists manifestly struggled to make artworks that were in fact vitalist; that is, objects which carried the chaotic energy of the artistic process forward with them, as 'real' organic things in themselves. Even at their most abstract
100 and physical, as in Appel's *Archaic Life* (1961), there is no escape, finally, from the sense that these paintings are mediated things, whose materiality is shot through with traces of the artists' performative encounter with their materials.

Arguments about the existence of a shared fundamental drive to expression led to experiments with collaborative working and 'interspecialization', as they put it. This was an attempt to further suppress the expression of individual personality in order that works might speak with a voice that was more universal. In their writing, the CoBrA artists more often attempted to give form to their universalism through the language of dialectical materialism as the group attempted to reach out to the great undifferentiated mass of

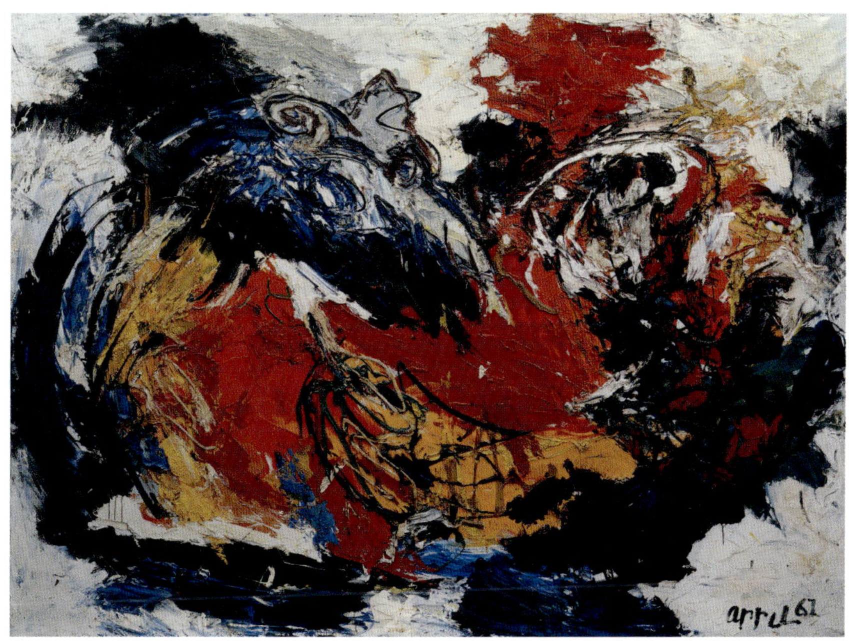

100 Karel Appel, *Archaic Life*, 1961

'the people'. Indeed, Constant and Jorn continued to have an active, if idiosyncratic engagement with Marxist philosophy and politics throughout their lives. But 'interspecialization' can also be viewed in primitivizing terms as evidence of a longing for further regression to earlier, simpler states of existence based on the Darwinist precept that evolution (of the individual organism and of cultures) proceeds from relatively homogeneity to heterogeneity, marked by a high degree of specialization in the function of constituent parts. CoBrA's reversal of this notion is highlighted in Dotremont's description of a group summer sojourn at Bregnerød, near Copenhagen in 1949, which culminated in the decoration of part of the Art Academy's weekend summerhouse in which they were staying: 'In Bregnerød, the non-painters painted, the non-sculptors sculpted...the non-poets wrote, the Danes spoke French, the francophones spoke a pidgin language where the nouns were essentially Danish, the adjectives English and the verbs German.' This was repeated at the end of November that year when Appel, Constant and Corneille decorated the ceramist Erik Nyholm's (1911–1990) home in Silkeborg, Denmark.

At the same time Appel, Constant and Corneille, Jorn and Nyholm executed a so-called 'Cobramodification'. Part of its

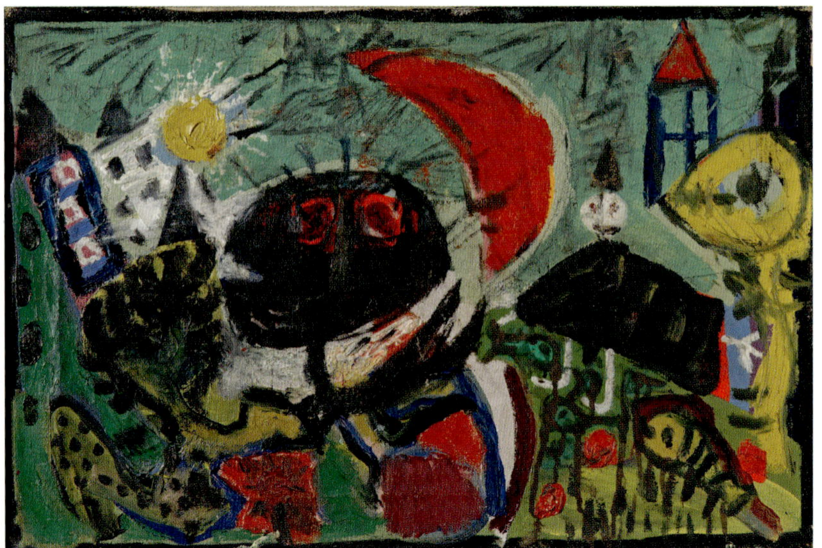

101 ABOVE Asger Jorn (with Constant, Karel Appel, Erik Nyholm and Corneille), *Cobra-modification (on a painting by Richard Mortensen)*, 1949
102 OPPOSITE Karel Appel, *Questioning Children*, 1949

significance lies in it being a piece of cultural vandalism. The five artists literally obliterated a painting by another artist, Richard Mortensen (1910–1993), whose fashionable hard abstract style had developed under the influence of Kandinsky in the 1930s. In this way they supplanted symbolically, as they saw it, the individual and elitist with the collaborative and participative. The destructive gesture contained in the act of
101 making *Cobra-modification* not only necessarily supplanted Mortensen's painting, but crucially overlays it, burying it, as it were. *Cobra-modification* might be seen more properly as obstructive, rather than destructive; a metaphor for CoBrA's play-based activism. *Homo ludens* here comes to the fore. Jorn's later modifications, which he called *peinture détournée* ('diverted' or 'hijacked' paintings), perhaps lay out the dialectic more clearly. Since in these works, such as *Le canard quiétant* (1959) and *Le bon berger* (1959–60), which were most often based on paintings by unknown artists bought from thrift stores, the original images remain visible *and* important elements. For Jorn, such a process was part of an active participation in the life of objects, and therefore society, read as a necessarily vital and changing thing that was always in danger of ossification. In 1959 he wrote, 'Be modern, collectors, museums. If you have old paintings, do not despair. Retain your memories,

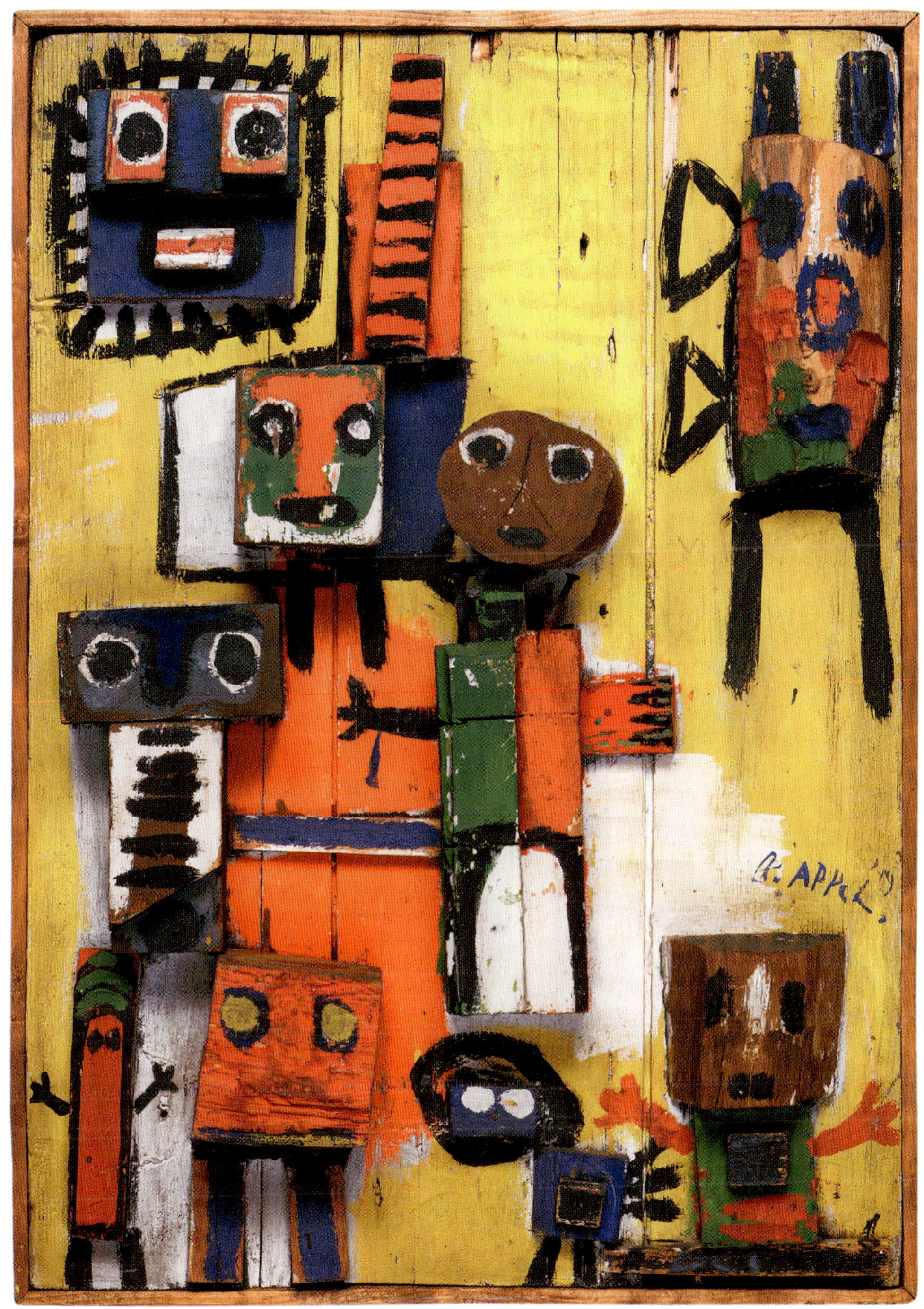

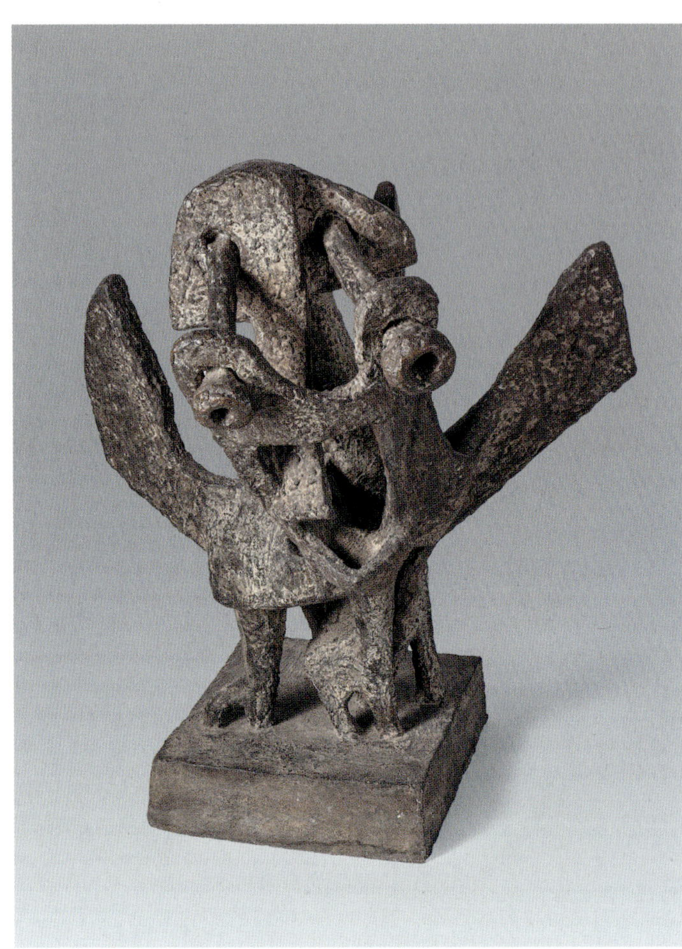

103 Lotti van der Gaag, *Bird of Prey*, 1952

but *détourn* them so that they correspond with your era. Why reject the old if you can modernize it with a few strokes of the brush? This casts a bit of contemporaneity on your old culture'. It is a choice, he argued, between being consigned to history or being part of the processes that produce history: 'There remain only two possibilities for us in Europe: to be sacrificed or to sacrifice. It is up to you to choose between the historical monument and the act that merits it.'

The aspiration towards 'freedom' resulted in a characteristic ham-fistedness in the execution of CoBrA works in all media, from paintings, like Constant's *Bird Idyll* (1948) and Corneille's
102 *Oiseau de Paris* (1948), to sculpture, like Appel's *Questioning*
103 *Children* (1949) and Lotti van der Gaag's *Bird of Prey* (1952), and

books, like *Goed morgen Haan* (Good Morning Rooster, 1949) by Constant and Gerrit Kouwenaar (1923–2014). CoBrA works often have a rough, unfinished look, indicative of a kind of urgency to make a statement spontaneously in order to be able to move on, leaving behind an object that embodies the process of its production, thereby enabling imaginative work by the active viewer. This is made clear in different ways. For example, the physical elements that make up reliefs like Brand's *Sign in Orion* (1948) and Appel's *The Bridge* (1948) remain discreetly identifiable units, even as they function together as representation. Similarly, the physical scratching and gouging into the surfaces of works like Appel's untitled terracotta sculptures from 1954 and Lucebert's *Weeping Woman* (1960) constitute a readily identifiable residue of the physicality of their production, which can be compared to contemporary work by artists like Dubuffet and Fautrier.

A tension between abstraction and figuration can be traced throughout CoBrA, especially in later works by Appel, Jorn and Rooskens. Of all the CoBrA artists who engaged with non-objective art, Jorn in particular never entirely dispensed with figuration as the underpinning for his process-driven explorations in paint. Indeed, in the cases of all the artists during the CoBrA period proper, and in common with most pre-war Expressionism, visual communication was driven primarily from a baseline of highly simplified and stylized figurative representation.

Paint was often urgently applied in a mass of lines and drips, slicing through a thick impasto. Rough, simplified forms were used, which was part of that desire to strip away the complexities of 'civilized' European views of the world to rediscover some more primitive, and therefore 'authentic' feeling. Expression takes precedence over style, resulting in images with little or no pictorial depth that asserted their presence as objects through the evident physicality and apparent spontaneity of their production. Jorn characteristically described this in revolutionary terms: 'The purpose of our experimentation is to allow thought to be expressed spontaneously, without being ruled by reason. This irrational spontaneity allows us to access the vital source of our life. Our aim is to escape the rule of reason – which is and always has been nothing other than the idealized rule of the bourgeoisie – in order to achieve the reign of life.' Constant argued that this was bound up in the dynamic, fluid process of the encounter between artist, materials and the engaged viewer: 'As far as we are concerned, the true source of art can only be found in matter. We are painters and for us materialism is, first and foremost, a sensual experience of the world and sensual experience of the paint.'

Emphasis on spontaneity and the 'unmediated' nature of authentic creativity gave rise to a belief that CoBrA shared with Abstract Expressionism, namely that art comes from the unconscious. Wolvecamp declared, 'I start with a spot of colour, with the materials, I do not know where I am going. I improvise and, in the almost automatic act of painting, I feel that I am liberating myself. When I paint, I do not judge what I've done – that comes later. What suggests forms and ideas to me is the contact with the materials.'

CoBrA, especially in the case of its Nordic members, showed an interest in indigenous folk art and popular culture that was common with early Expressionism and Romanticism. Typically, the CoBrA artists were attracted to several groups separated by time and cultural identity, who were perceived as sharing similarly 'primitive' ways of life, that were based on notions of communal living and a sense of being wedded to 'the soil'. For some, like the urbanite Appel, this was little more than an abstraction to which one might aspire, but for someone like Jorn, who came from the relatively isolated, rural Danish region of Jutland, there was an immediacy to such notions, including the continued physical presence in the landscape of relics from the area's pagan and early Christian past. Either way, the underlying idea presumed that prehistoric, pagan and early Christian northern European cultures occupy a similar intellectual space as contemporary or near contemporary peasant cultures, and even, sometimes, urban popular culture (where the latter signifies the vital, 'simple' culture of the masses, finding pictorial form in graffiti, for example). The desire to find the 'natural man' in these geographically local 'primitive' groups, existing in a state of relative freedom was compelling enough among the artists to result in a tendency for them to overlook the highly structured and, in many respects, inflexible and hierarchic base of such societies. Thus, Constant raised the supposed 'vitality' and 'freedom' of folk art against the elitism of 'bourgeois' high culture, as he heralded a new mass art, 'nourished only by a natural and therefore general urge to expression,' in which 'the genius of the people...replaces individual performance.'

In line with their own claim to the greater affect of 'generalized' representation, CoBrA artists perceived the naive imagery of folk art and the supposedly socially 'liberated' art of psychiatric patients as representative of an unconscious will to present archetypes. A characteristic of much folk art, as well as work by people living with schizophrenia, is a tendency to mix image and text (though the two are connected only by a lack of a sense of needing to maintain the purity of image and text through its conventional separation in high art). This ranges from runic inscriptions on stones through text laid on top of pictures in Christian votive pieces, and fusions of image and dissociative and textual neologisms in the works by mental health patients that they had seen. Dotremont claimed that they played a part – mainly by association – in the development of the CoBrA 'word-image'. Collaborative works like Dotremont and Jean-Michel Atlan's (1913–1960) book, *Le Transformes* (1950) and Dotremont and Jorn's painting, *I Rise, You Rise, We Dream* (1948) typically fuse word and image in a lyrical way, whereas Alechinsky and Dotremont's *Seismographic Armful* (1972) is redolent of the dissociative element characteristic of much schizophrenic work.

The CoBrA artists were aware of art by psychiatric patients, through texts such *Bildnerei der Geisteskranken* (Artistry of the Mentally Ill, 1922) by the German psychiatrist and art historian Hans Prinzhorn (1886–1933), and through occasional exhibitions arranged under the auspices of the psychiatric profession in France. In general, though, before 1950 it was a romantic idea of 'madness' rather than its creative productions that drove CoBrA's interest, mediated perhaps to some degree by their common interest in the work of Paul Klee, who had visited the Prinzhorn Collection in Heidelberg in person.

In the case of CoBrA's French contemporary Jean Dubuffet, Prinzhorn's book had been the touchstone for the collection of psychiatric and marginal arts that he began around 1940, and to which in 1949 he gave the name *'Art Brut'* (Raw Art) – Tapié was a member of his *Compagnie de l'Art Brut* and ran the small gallery in Paris in which Dubuffet showed his collection, located in the basement of the Galerie René Drouin. Jorn, Constant, Corneille and Appel, became familiar with Dubuffet's collection through Drouin's gallery, and in 1950 Appel visited a major exhibition of 'psychopathological art' at the Sainte-Anne psychiatric hospital several times. He bought the catalogue and read through it. He then began to make additions and drawn interventions, in a process not unlike Jorn's *détourn*. In this case, Appel disrupted and at times obliterated the learned, explanatory medical texts with primitive, Expressionist images that seemingly arise from those primal regions of consciousness over which psychiatry attempts to exercise power, and in doing so attempted to reclaim the territory of 'madness' for 'freedom'.

CoBrA's concern for the 'primitive' was above all a concern for directness of expression and the ability to experiment unhindered by high art precedents and intellectualization. The 'primitive' was found, therefore, wherever this directness was perceived, though nowhere was it more evident than in the art of children. In this aspect of their primitivism, they went much further than Matisse, the Blue Rider and even Paul Klee. Probably the only other comparable artist at the time was Dubuffet, who had begun collecting children's drawings in 1939, and who gloried in the naivety of children's art, whilst bringing a distinctly adult sensibility to childlike images such as *Touring Club* (1946) and *The Will to Power* (1946). Their interest stemmed from an essentially Rousseauean belief that children are not so much imperfect versions of adults requiring 'correction', but 'natural' beings with an enormous potential for development. This was reflected in the extent of the influence of the Kindergarten movement, which emphasizes the educational necessity of self-activity and play, and where picture-making is an essential aspect. The child is the primitive par excellence in all evolutionist models of cultural development, and for CoBrA, the purest evidence of the 'primitive' was to be found in an examination of childhood and the art of children. Constant argued typically that, 'The child knows of no law other than its spontaneous sensation of life and feels no need to express anything else.' The developmental potential of each child might also be seen through Huizinga's lens as the ground for eternally repeating, generation after generation, individual cases of the general, formative play impulse at work. In this sense the child, as the pure embodiment of *Homo Ludens*, symbolizes freedom itself.

The experience of child art lay behind the free experimentation underpinning paintings such as Appel's *People and Animals* (1949) and Eugène Brands's *Painting C* (1951), whose playful, exuberant qualities set them apart from the post-war existentialist gloom more common in European art at this time. Play, too, was central to the two CoBrA collaborative projects in Bregnerød and Silkeborg. This optimistic embrace of play and the collective project also separates the CoBrA project from Dubuffet's solitude and pessimism. Child art also provides one of CoBrA's most direct formal precedents. Comparisons can be made, for example, between drawings by children reproduced in *Cobra 4* and Constant's *Bird Idyll* and Appel's *Beast* (1952), particularly in the expressive distortion of forms and the use of scribble. Appel's early polychrome sculptures, made from trash, nailed together and roughly painted, *Figure* (1947), *Drift in the Attic* (1947), *The Bridge* (1948), and *Questioning Children* (1949), all speak with the directness and tragi-comic innocence of very young children – or adults traumatized by the experience of war and its aftermath – struggling to make visual sense of the world in a manner that is at once spontaneous, guileless and sublime. It is no coincidence that several of Appel's works have the title 'Questioning Children', including the mural he painted for the canteen of Amsterdam's town hall in 1949. Its reference to hungry refugees was not lost among diners whose objections to its subject matter and modernist style caused it to be covered over.

CoBrA turned their interest to the art of very young children, whose visual and motor skills are much less developed than older ones. However, CoBrA's infantilism should not be seen as a literal attempt to regress to childhood, but as part of that same primitivizing desire to gain access to original creative forces that Picasso had attempted through adopting the forms of certain types of African sculpture in his work forty years earlier. Like Klee before them, the CoBrA artists were aware that their recovery of childhood took place at a highly sophisticated level. As Alechinsky said, 'It takes years to find the childlike inside oneself. At the outset, one is an old man. CoBrA is a form of art which heads towards childhood, tries to recover folk art and child art for itself. With the means available to adults, non-naive means. It is not naivety which is required.'

Avant Garde after Auschwitz

The German sociologist and philosopher Theodor Adorno (1903–1969) famously said that 'to write lyric poetry after Auschwitz is barbaric.' In the wake of the physical and cultural destructiveness of the Second World War and the almost unimaginable human horrors perpetrated by Hitler and Stalin, the utopian ideals of both the artistic right and left seemed hopelessly ill-founded. How could art still be possible? To concentrate on aesthetics and formalism was to avoid facing a thing that had been revealed as the living, darkest aspect of western culture. Yet to represent suffering artistically was to risk transfiguring it in a 'hideous affirmation' precisely because of the artist's cultural complicity, whatever their political stance. 'The notion of a "message" in art, even when politically radical,' Adorno wrote, 'already contains an accommodation to the world.' An obvious response would have been to stop producing art altogether, although this was not Adorno's solution. Another possible response was to retreat into cynicism – a charge which has been levelled at much of the progressive art of the second half of the century

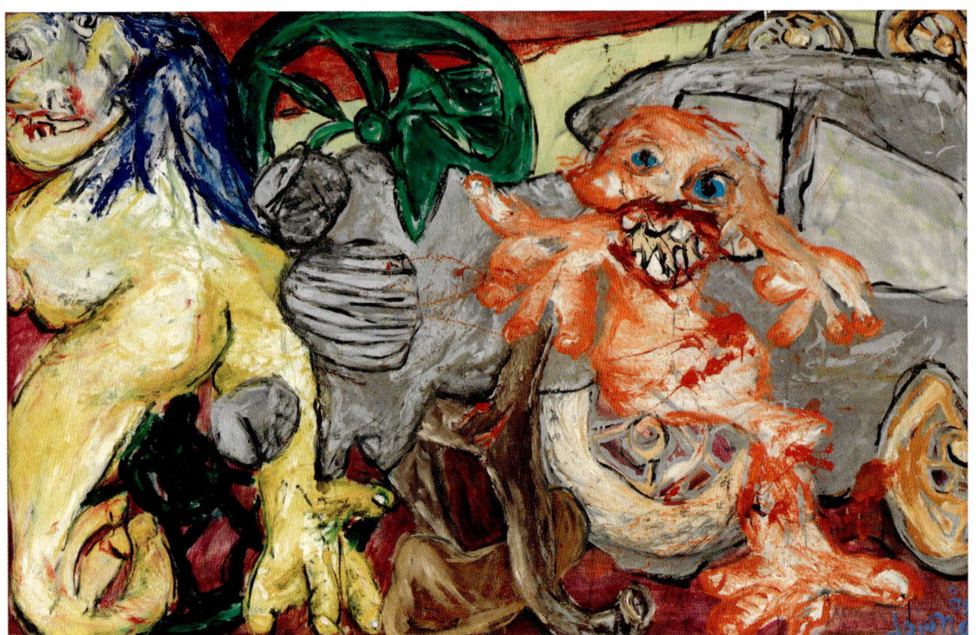

104 Jacqueline de Jong, *Rencontre Accidentel* (Accidental Painting), 1964

by hostile critics. Adorno himself fixed on autonomous art as
the only radical possibility precisely because of its oppositional
stance towards a troubled reality, and because he regarded
such 'nonconceptual' objects as embodied knowledge. Another
unexplored possibility, though, was the dystopian figurative art
that grew out of pre-war avant-gardism. It was characterized by
fierce individualism and a wilful attempt to occupy a creative
and intellectual space at the edges of culture, whilst remaining
very much within it physically. In this way, artists like Dubuffet,
Francis Bacon, Leon Golub (1922–2004), Edward Burra (1905–
104 1976) and later Philip Guston, Maria Lassnig and Jacqueline de
Jong (1939–2024) produced figurative paintings that embodied
a politics of representation, and which undermined and went
far beyond the ideological reportage supposed in Adorno's
definition of 'committed' art.

105 Bacon was a mercurial figure. At a time when it was a
criminal offence in the UK, Bacon was openly gay. He was
equally at home with the aristocracy and art world glitterati
as he was with Soho bohemians and the shady working-
class underworld of London's East End, and he wove easily
between these very different worlds. His painting focused
overwhelmingly on the individual figure – often male sexual

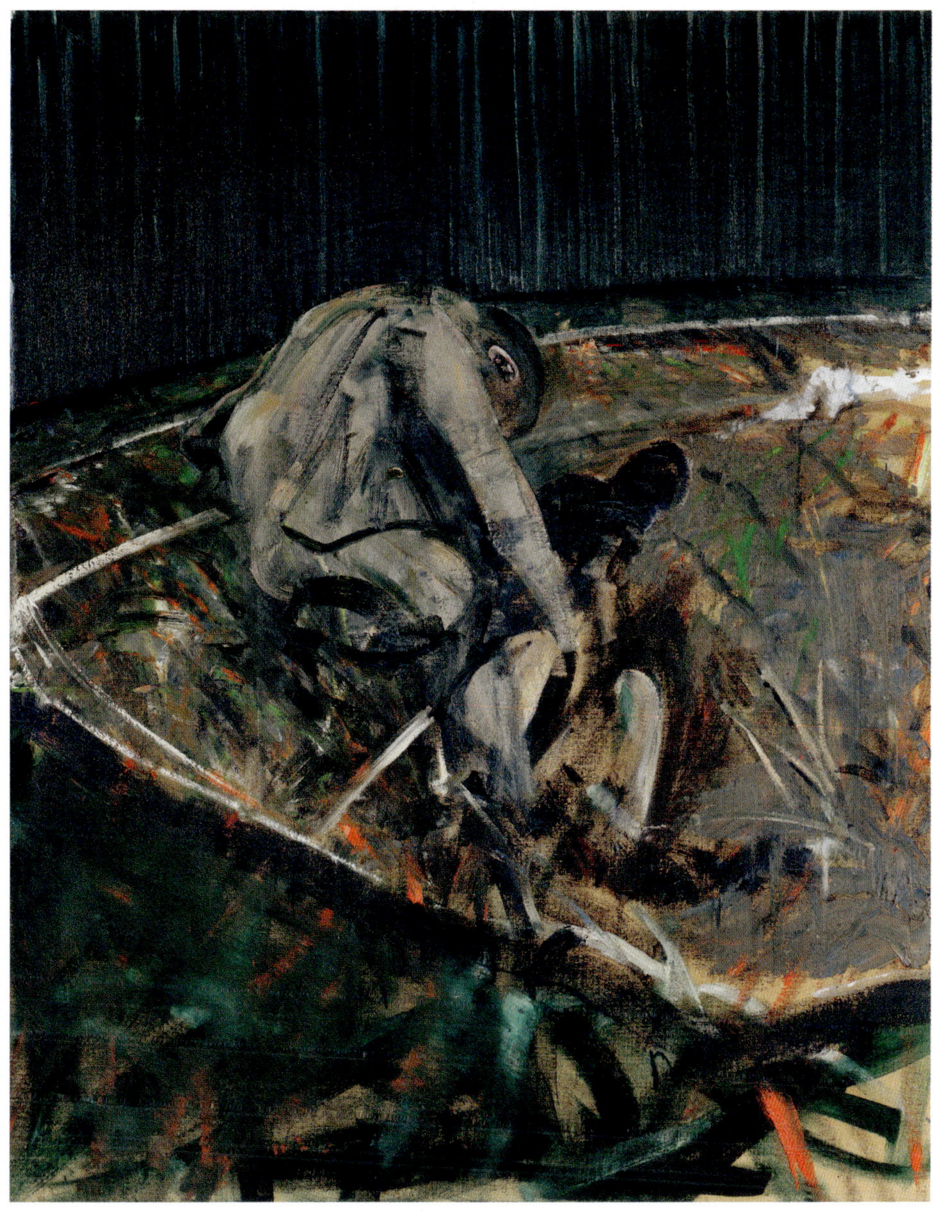

105 Francis Bacon, *Figures in a Landscape*, 1956–57

partners – isolated in space and often bound up in a fragmentary tubular architecture that referred pictorially to modernist interior design. Bodies are characteristically distorted and shattered in ways that seem very distant from the aesthetic fragmentation of figures and objects in Cubist art, and much closer to Expressionists from Germany's second generation, whose own work also emerged from a near-apocalyptic situation of war, social upheaval and disease. Bacon matter-of-factly described his painting as, 'an attempt to bring the figurative thing up onto the nervous system more violently and more poignantly.' His work emphasizes the abject qualities of human existence, our brute nature. The profound silence of the painting medium provides the perfect ground for laying out the unheeded drama of an existence that is futile even as we try to make of it something meaningful, as had Munch half a century earlier. The existential 'joke' of meaninglessness is grimly confirmed in Bacon's occasional use of religious figures as subject matter – such as the *Study After Velazquez's Portrait of Pope Innocent X* (1953) – and his adoption of traditional Christian devotional forms such as the diptych and triptych. His figures wrestle against animality, sometimes apparently literally, as in *Figures in a Landscape* (1956–57). They struggle to remain whole against the forces of chaos, often caught at the moment where dissolution threatens. Panic terror is Bacon's leitmotiv, epitomized in the soundless primal scream that is often the focal point in his paintings, sometimes actually obliterating the cranium of the figure, which is the seat of human intellect. Yet, despite his own intensive lifestyle, Bacon's visual source material consisted almost exclusively of – besides his memory – mediated images: photographs and photographic reproductions of other art.

Brutism

In Paris, artists like Dubuffet and Fautrier led the way in turning artmaking into a base, physical act. Dubuffet's paintings from the 1940s are essays in *haute pâte*, spiked with non-art materials like coal and stones, their dense surfaces scratched and gauged as though bearing the evidence of an attack. Moreover, these assaults were committed in the act of representation, including portraits of his friends and associates, such as *Monsieur Plume Botanical Piece (Portrait of Henri Michaux)* (1946) and *Dhôtel with a Tinge of Apricot* (1947). The humanity of the resulting figures is saved ultimately only by Dubuffet's knack of imbuing his images with an equally pointed wit and humour. There is a kind of methodical violence
106 in Dubuffet's *Corps de dames series* (1950–51), whilst the women painted by the Willem de Kooning from around the same time emerge in a more painterly way through a dynamic process of

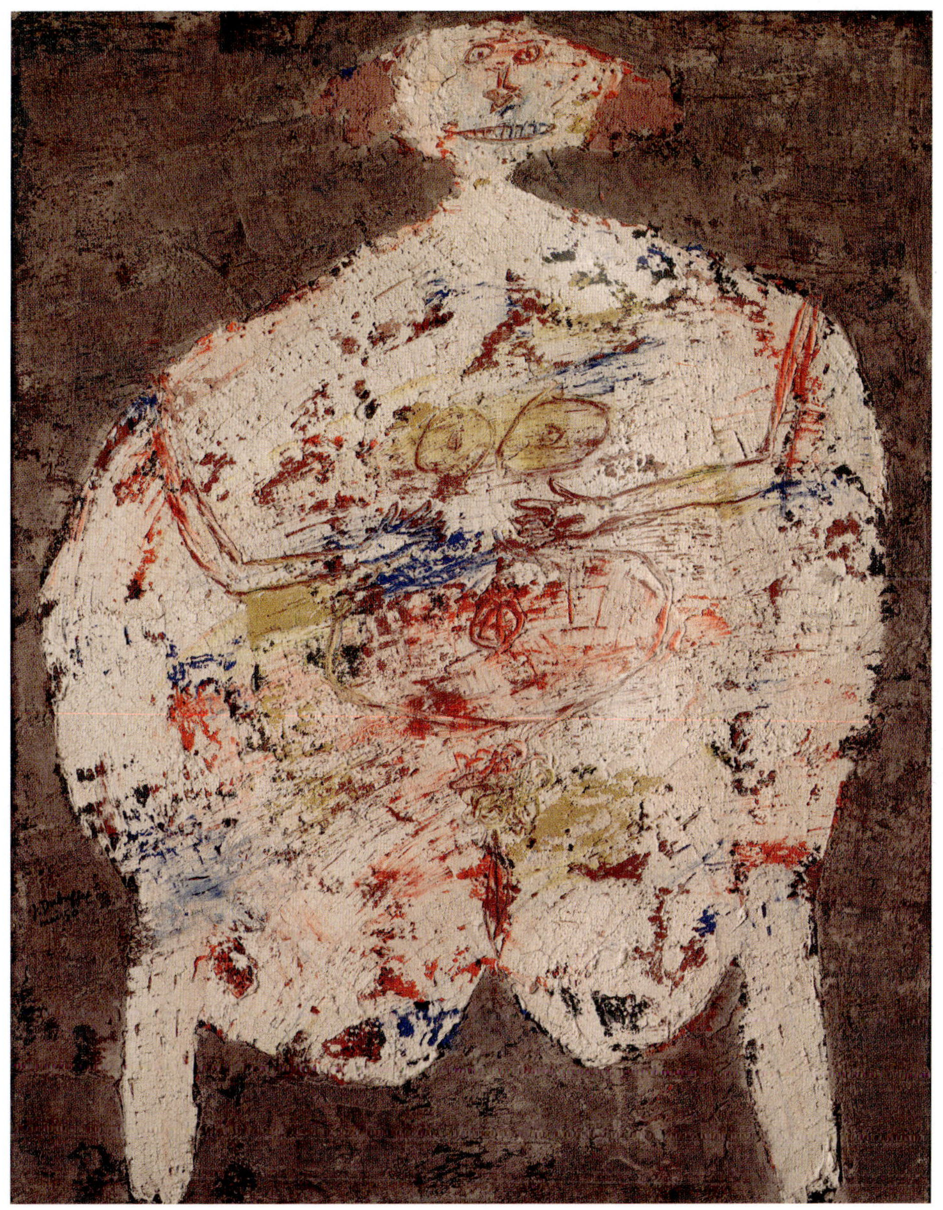

106 Jean Dubuffet, *Corps de dame, Jardin fleuri* (Lady's Body, Flower Garden), 1950

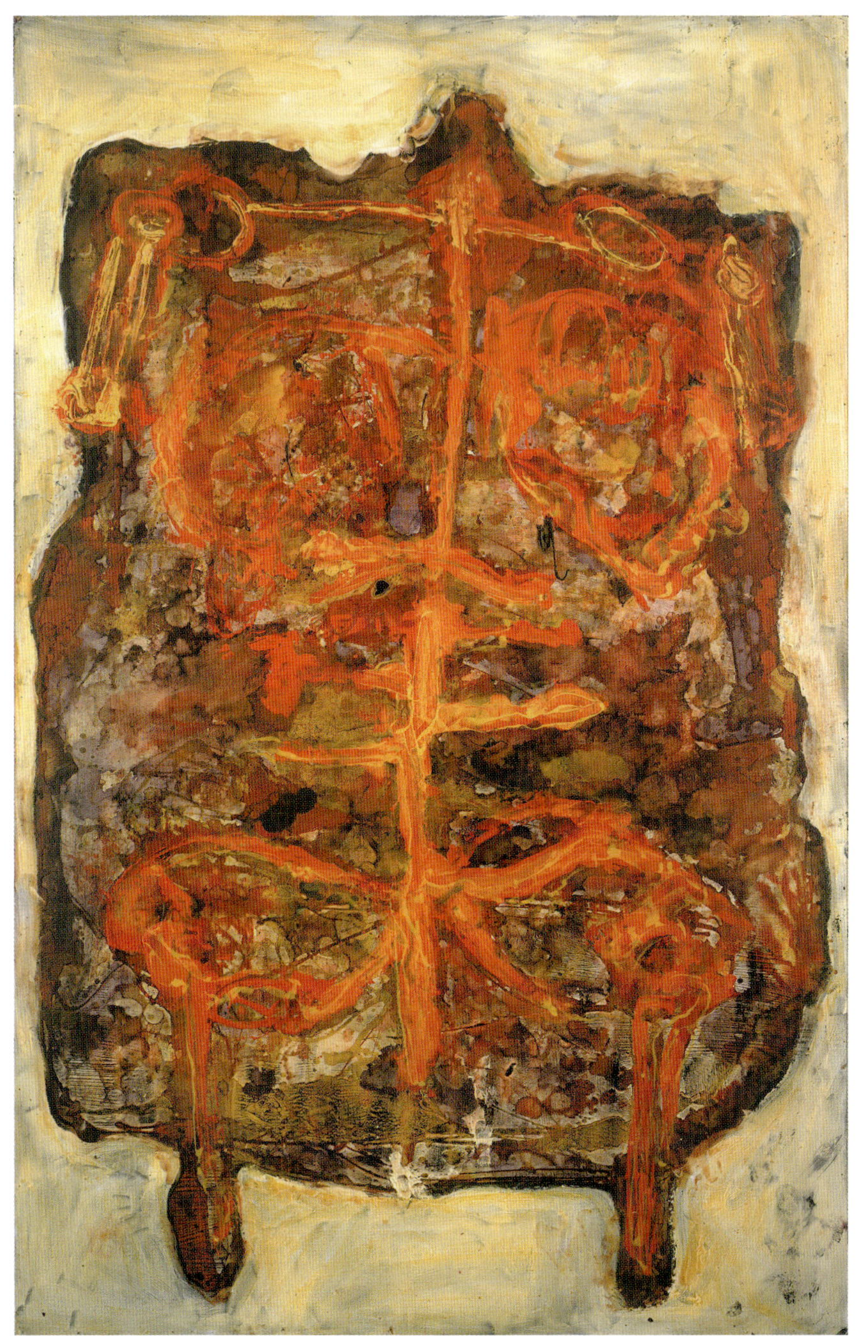

107 Magda Cordell, *Figure 59*, *c.* 1958

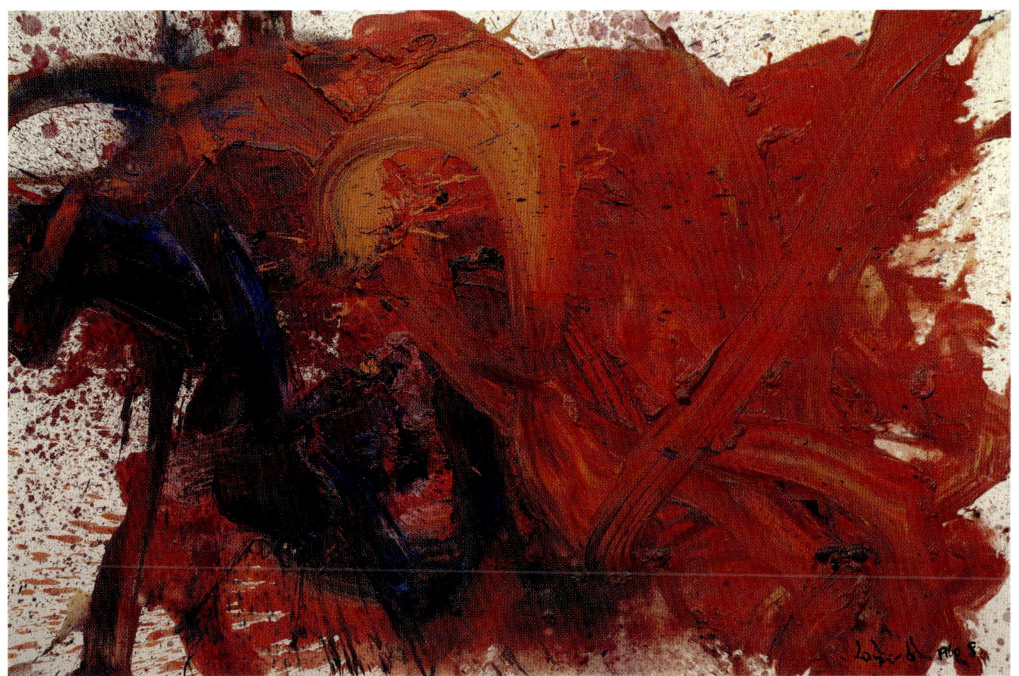

108 Kazuo Shiraga, *Golden Wings Brushing the Clouds Incarnated from Earthly Wide Star (Chikatsusei Maunkinshi)*, 1960

107 addition and scraping. Magda Cordell (1921–2008), a British-based Hungarian artist, who was a founding member of the Independent Group, from which Pop Art developed in Britain also worked in a primalist, Abstract Expressionist style. Her explorations of the female form, though, possess a sensitivity to the subject arising from her lived gender experience, mirroring work developed by others such as Maria Lassnig and Nancy Spero, and providing something of an antidote to Dubuffet's and De Kooning's misanthropic aggressivism.

Appel took this gesturalism to its extreme point, which was captured in *De werkelijkheid van Karel Appel* (The Reality of Karel Appel), a film made by Jan Vrijman in 1963, which in some ways is a rather self-conscious melodramatic response to Hans Namuth's famous 1951 film of Pollock at work. Appel slashes and slaps paint with a large palette knife, then rushes at and attacks his canvas in mock-serious battle. Against a background of *musique barbare* (barbaric music) performed by the jazz musician Dizzy Gillespie he tells viewers, 'I paint like a barbarian, in a barbaric age.' The film builds up to a febrile crescendo of music and action, with Appel shouting repeatedly in English, 'I do not paint, I hit!'

Brutalism was taken to a further level by the Japanese
painter Kazuo Shiraga (1924–2008). To Pollock's dripping,
Appel's hitting, and Dubuffet's scratching, Shiraga added
the technique of painting with one's feet. Shiraga was a
member of the Japanese post-war artists association, Gutai,
and was a pioneering experimentalist, employing a range of
contemporary art media, such as performance, installation and
conceptualism. He is best known for his foot paintings, which
caught the attention of people like Tapié, and which led to him
being embraced in Europe as a fellow traveller in *art informel.*
Shiraga's first foot paintings were meant as performance art
pieces, with the emphasis being on immediacy approaching
as far as possible unmediated actions of primitive smearing
of liquid paint. After 1959, though, he began using the same
108 technique in his studio to create paintings, such as *Golden
Wings Brushing the Clouds Incarnated from Earthly Wide Star
(Chikatsusei Maunkinshi)* (1960), whose apparently formless
physicality stands in stark contrast to its complex title, which
refers to the famous fourteenth-century Chinese novel *Shuihu
zhuan* (Water Margin), which follows the feats of outlaw Song
Jiang and his band of accomplices.

Expressionist Survivals

By the end of the 1950s, the centre of the global contemporary
art world had effectively moved to New York, supplanting
Paris. Much more than a cultural shift, the change of axis was
underpinned by a seismic shift in the location of the economies
of the art world. In New York Abstract Expressionism remained
the dominant tendency in contemporary art, with painters
such as Guston, Mitchell and Frankenthaler making important
contributions during this period. Another American, Sam
Middleton (1927–2015) was also influential, but this time in the
Netherlands, rather than his native country. Middleton grew
up in New York and developed an Abstract Expressionist style
influenced by his experience of jazz music in Harlem. However,
his experience of racism and a lack of opportunity for Black
artists led him, like several others at the time, to relocate to
the Netherlands, a country he perceived to be entirely more
109 tolerant. *Come Sunday* (1962) is a good example of Middleton's
early Dutch period Expressionism.

A 'long Abstract Expressionism', lasting well into the 1960s can be discerned in many parts of the world, although increasingly submerged beneath new waves of contemporary art that became dominant in both critical and art historical narratives and the market, beginning with the emergence of Pop Art in London in the mid-1950s and soon after in New York.

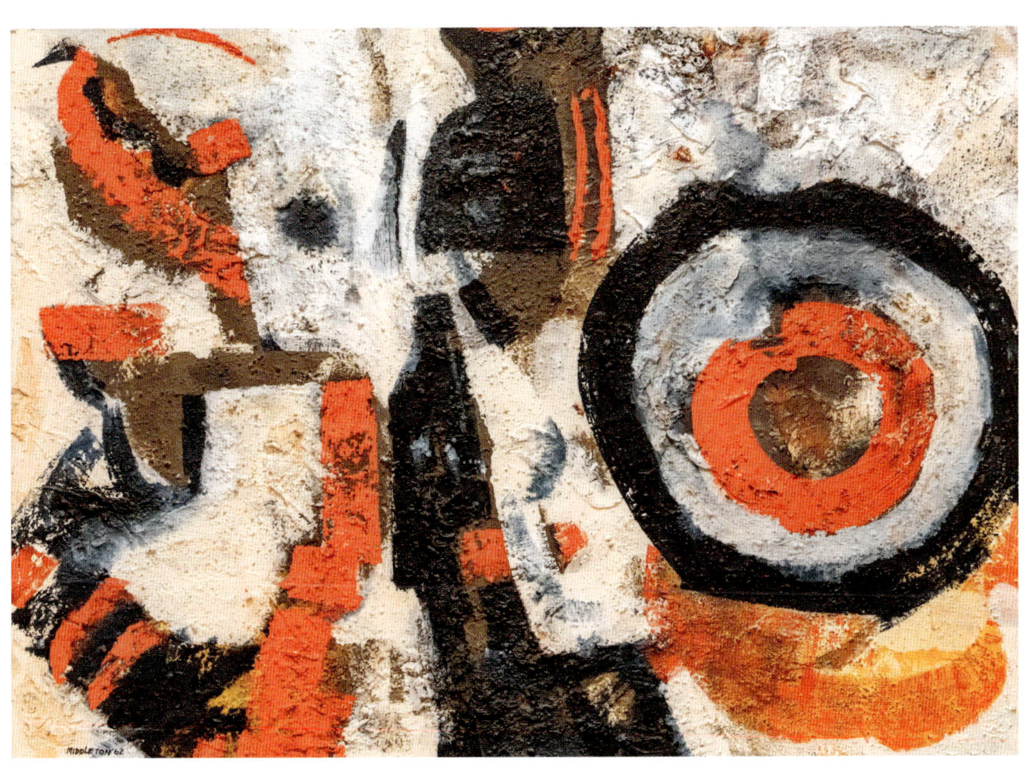

109 Sam Middleton, *Come Sunday*, 1962

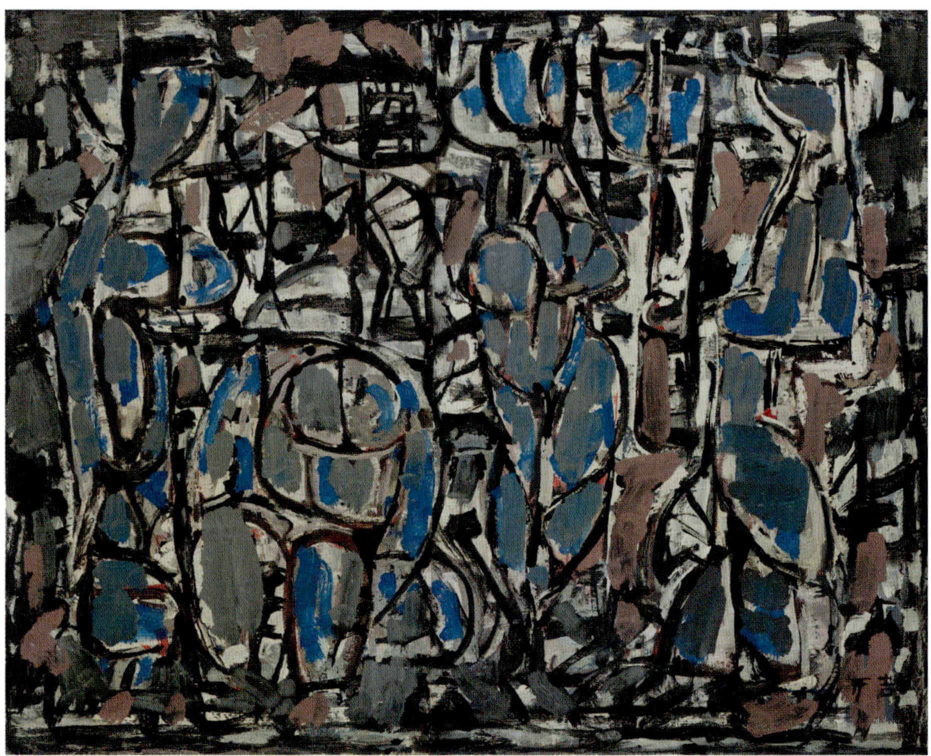

110 Ian Fairweather, *The Pool*, 1959

Often these Expressionists were unconnected to artists groups,
which added to the forgetfulness of an art world that found it
much easier to deal with current collective 'isms'. The Scottish-
110 Australian artist Ian Fairweather (1891–1974), for example,
whose work was steeped in a knowledge of Far Eastern
cultures, as well as European Modernism, created his now
much-lauded late Abstract Expressionist work living in
primitive conditions in near-isolation on Bribie Island in
111 Queensland, Australia. Another Australian, John Olsen
(1928–2023) produced a sustained body of compelling and
important Abstract Expressionist works after experiences in
Europe in the 1950s, including at Hayter's Atelier 17, which by
then had relocated back from New York to Paris. Yet, in spite
of his near-canonical status in his own country, and perhaps
because he never actively courted European or American
markets, his work remains largely unknown outside Australia.

112 Others include the Korean artist Wook-Kyung Choi
(1940–1985) and the British painter Gillian Ayres. Choi lived

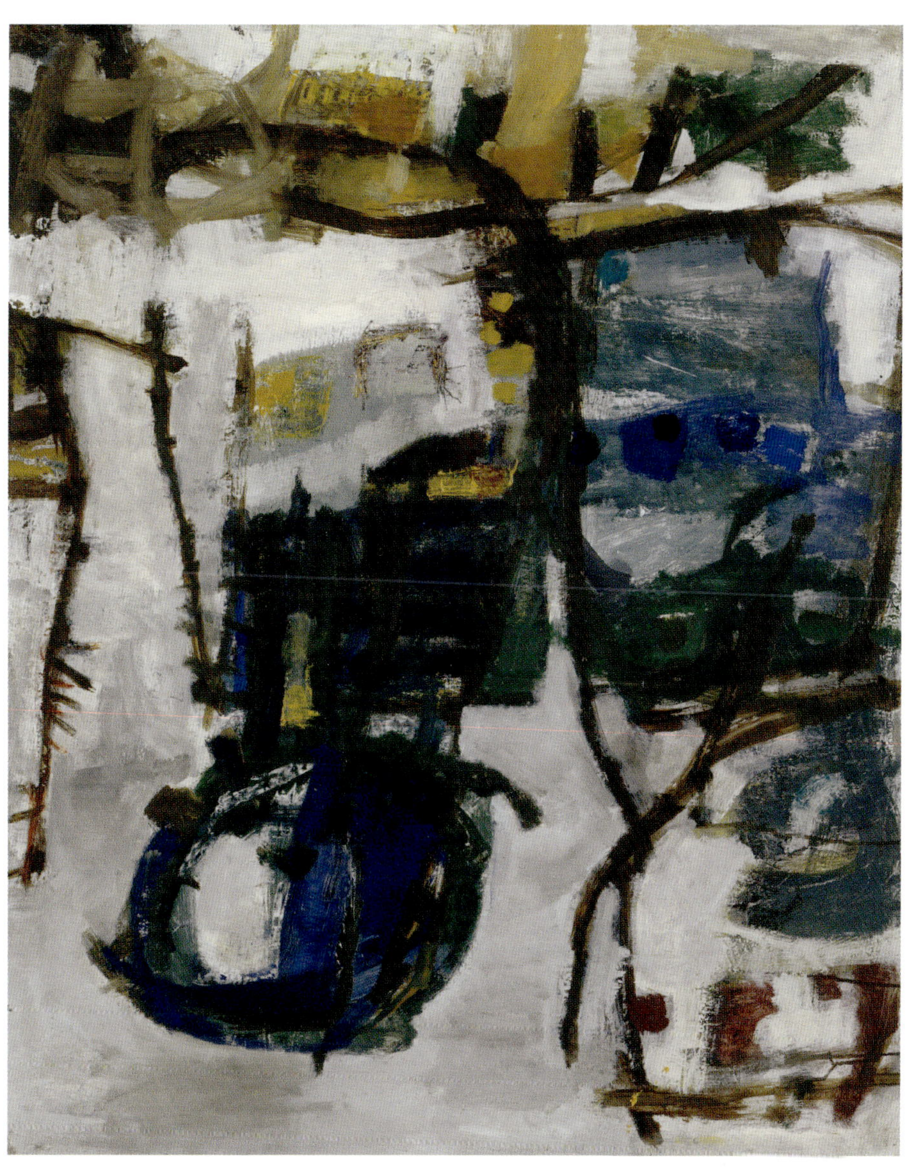

111 John Olsen, *Dylan's Country*, 1957

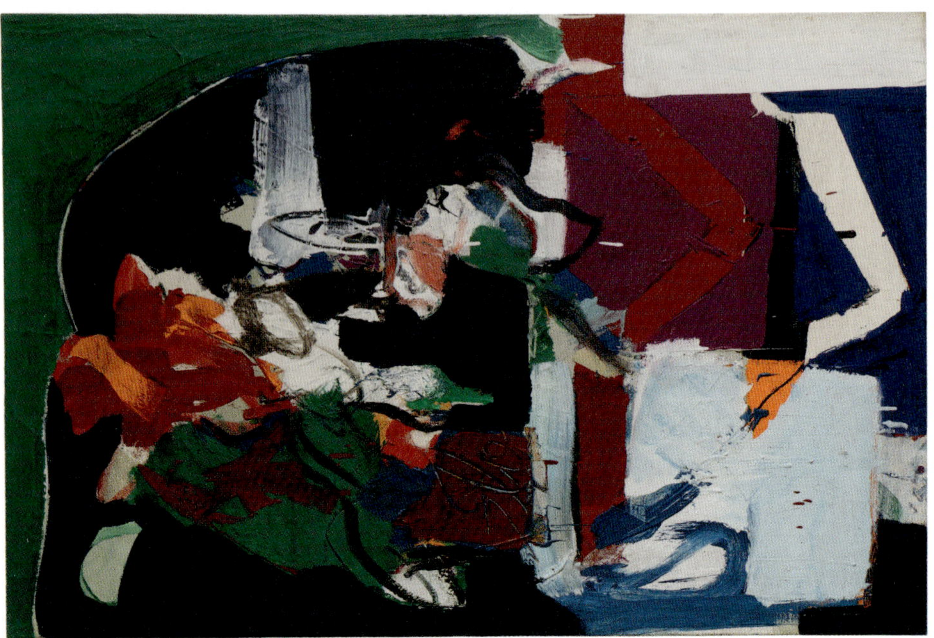

112 Wook-Kyung Choi, *Untitled*, c. 1960s

in the United States from 1963, where she developed a bold Abstract Expressionist style that nevertheless preserved narrative elements, as with some of the Americans, such as Grace Hartigan. Choi's sense of self-identity was an important part of her creative drive. As she said, 'my experiences, as a woman and a painter, serve as a daily source for the creative inspiration necessary for my work. My paintings are collaged bits of time from my past and present experiences...but I am not simply telling stories. I am trying to express, visually, my experience of the moment lived. I hope to share, to communicate, and to create an empathy for the experience.' Unfortunately, her return to Korea in 1978 occurred just before interest in Expressionism in Europe and America was rekindled with the appearance of a new generation of 'Neo-Expressionist' painters, and her premature death in 1985 further suppressed the global reception of her work.

Chapter 5
Expressionism After Modernism

Modernism's endgame in the 1960s saw minimalist abstraction competing with Pop Art figuration. In place of the much-vaunted 'authenticity' of the autograph gesture of Abstract Expressionism, both tendencies argued that style was socially constructed, and they embraced a fully mediated way of representing the world that often included literal appropriations of commodity items and objects from popular culture into their works. Reality could be mediated not only by its representation in artworks, but also by artists working with *representations* of things and events (especially through photography and film), rather than being witness to them at first hand. There is a sense that all images are 'screened' – that is, already printed, broadcast or in some way produced and consumed. The evolutionary project of modernist avant-garde art seemed to have been completed, leaving behind a culture that had proved utterly resistant to its aesthetically driven revolutionary fervour and a toolkit of media and styles that was now available for use by an emergent 'postmodern' art, whose progressiveness was, in turn, based on how the elements from that toolkit were put to use – although there were glorious maverick exceptions to this attitude, as with the American artist Don van Vliet (1941–2010), who had originally found cult fame as Captain Beefheart for his idiosyncratic, experimental blues music. After 1982, though, he devoted himself entirely to painting, producing a body of powerful, direct Expressionist works without any care for critical attention or commercial success.

The 1970s had seemed to be the decade of concept and new media art, emphatically rejecting the possibility of authentic autograph gestural practice. Yet, its close seemed to signal the re-emergence of painting, and in particular expressivist

painting, as an authentic activity, which was heralded in 1981 by an ambitious exhibition at the Royal Academy of Arts, London, curated by Norman Rosenthal, Nicholas Serota and Christos Joachimides. Aptly titled 'A New Spirit in Painting', it sprang from an observation that a generation of younger artists were strongly favouring the easel over other media, and that this in turn validated and provided a space for artists from the previous generation who had doggedly committed themselves to the practice of painting in a decade when they had all but been ignored by dominant art world narratives. The Royal Academy show included thirty-eight artists, mostly aged between around forty and fifty years old, and mainly from the United States, the United Kingdom and Germany, including several who would rise spectacularly to prominence in the early 1980s, such as Julian Schnabel (b. 1951), Georg Baselitz (b. 1938), Rainer Fetting (b. 1949), and Anselm Kiefer (b. 1945). The older generation was represented by figures such as Francis Bacon, Willem de Kooning and Picasso, who was represented by powerful Expressionist paintings made near the end of his life that had been widely ridiculed by critics when they were
113 first exhibited. Paintings such as Picasso's *Femme nue au collier*, for example, suddenly seemed emblematic of the vigorous, intuitive Expressionism of this younger generation of artists.

While not all the painting in the Royal Academy show could be characterized as Expressionist – post-pop paintings by David Hockney (b. 1937) and Andy Warhol (1928–1987) were included, for example – the overwhelming sense was of an Expressionist resurgence. However, although it brought painting back into focus, it was also notable for a complete absence of women. Prominent mid-career artists such as the Gillian Ayres from Britain or Maria Lassnig from Austria, and emerging ones such as Elvira Bach from Germany, who one might reasonably expect to have been there, were overlooked, thereby skewing public perception of the 'new' painting and contributing further to the myth of Expressionism as the preserve of male machismo – Bacon's and Hockney's (unexamined) gay sexuality notwithstanding.

Neo-Expressionism

Neo-Expressionism quickly came into use as the general term to describe a fairly wide range of practices springing from often different engagements with past Expressionist manifestations, including besides those already mentioned
114 artists such as A. R. Penck and Franz Hitzler (b. 1946) in Germany, John Walker (b. 1939) and John Bellany (1942–2013) in Britain, and Per Kirkeby (1938–2018) in Denmark. What did

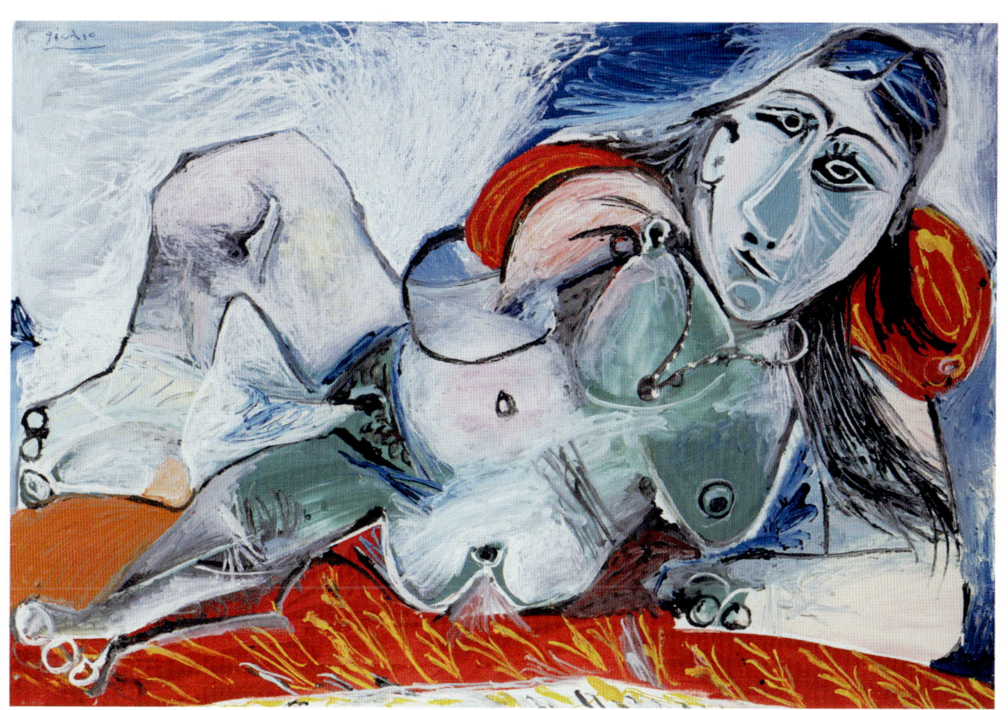

113 Pablo Picasso, *Femme nue au collier* (Nude Woman with Necklace), 1968

connect them, though, was a common conscious adoption of one or more of the already-existent visual languages of Expressionism. In that sense, at least, they were 'postmodern' – a term that was widely used throughout the 1980s, but which slowly came to be replaced by the rather more vague 'contemporary art', which is nowadays the general designation of all putatively 'progressive' art made since around 1970.

Maria Lassnig had been influential in the introduction of *art informel* into Austria in the 1950s, but her lasting contribution relates to her development of the concept of 'body awareness'. In her work, Lassnig attempted to express physical perceptions visually, from the inside out, so to speak. This was not meant in a symbolic or empathic way, but what she herself felt. As a result, Lassnig's subject had to be herself, performing a blurring between feeling and representation that chimed with much emerging feminist art at the time. Since her work is about subject rather than object, physical sensation rather than emotion, her images are often unsettling in both form and
115 colour, as in *Die Last des Fleisches* (The Burden of Flesh, 1973). In a 2008 interview Lassnig described her method as an almost

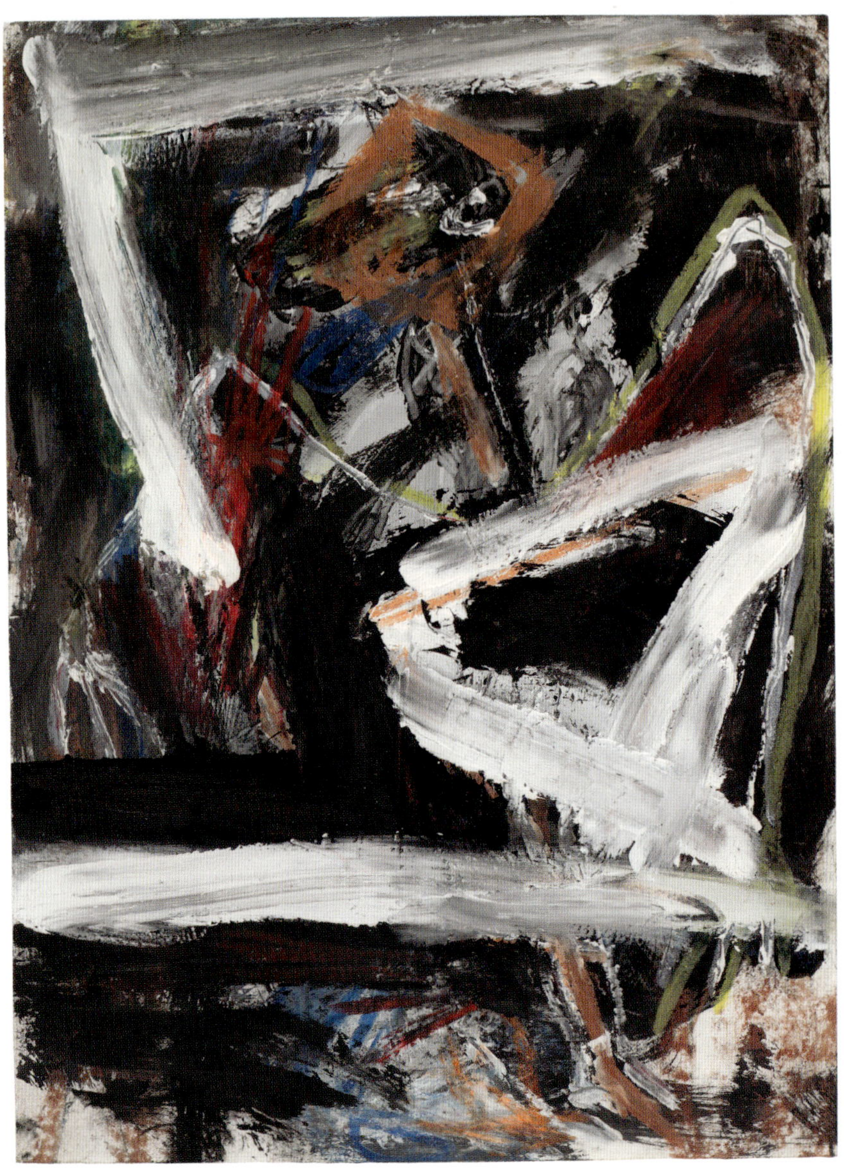

114 Franz Hitzler, *Untitled*, 1978

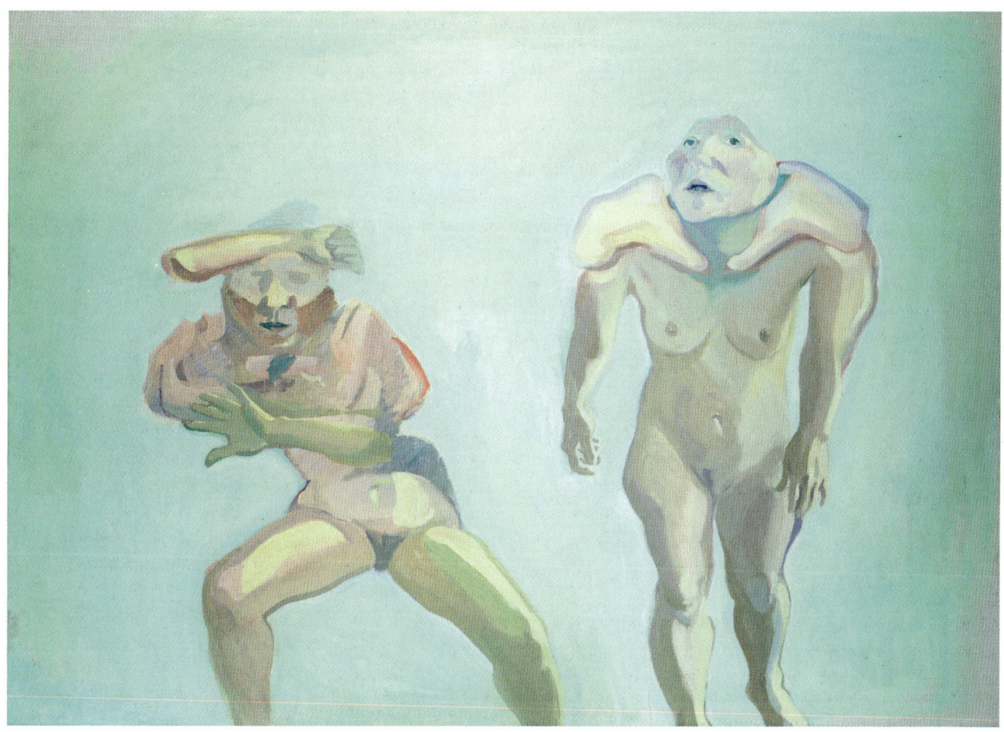

115 Maria Lassnig, *Die Last des Fleisches* (The Burden of the Flesh), 1973

automatic process, which she began by directing her attention towards herself: 'I do not aim for the 'big emotions' when I'm working but concentrate on small feelings: sensations in the skin or in the nerves, all of which one feels. I became interested in all this early on and tried to fix these sensations in straightforward brushstrokes, because in the body they are changing continuously. You have to be quick when painting like this, because the next minute you might not have the same feeling anymore.' Lassnig was closely associated with progressive Viennese groups, including Actionism while in Austria. However, she spent most of the 1960s and 1970s in Paris and New York, and separation from the Austrian contemporary art world perhaps helps explain why she has often been overlooked in art historical surveys, beyond gender bias.

One of Lassnig's close Viennese friends was Arnulf Rainer, who was also involved in Actionism and whose work is centred around the human body and psychology. A core part of his practice centres around scribbled interventions on photographs

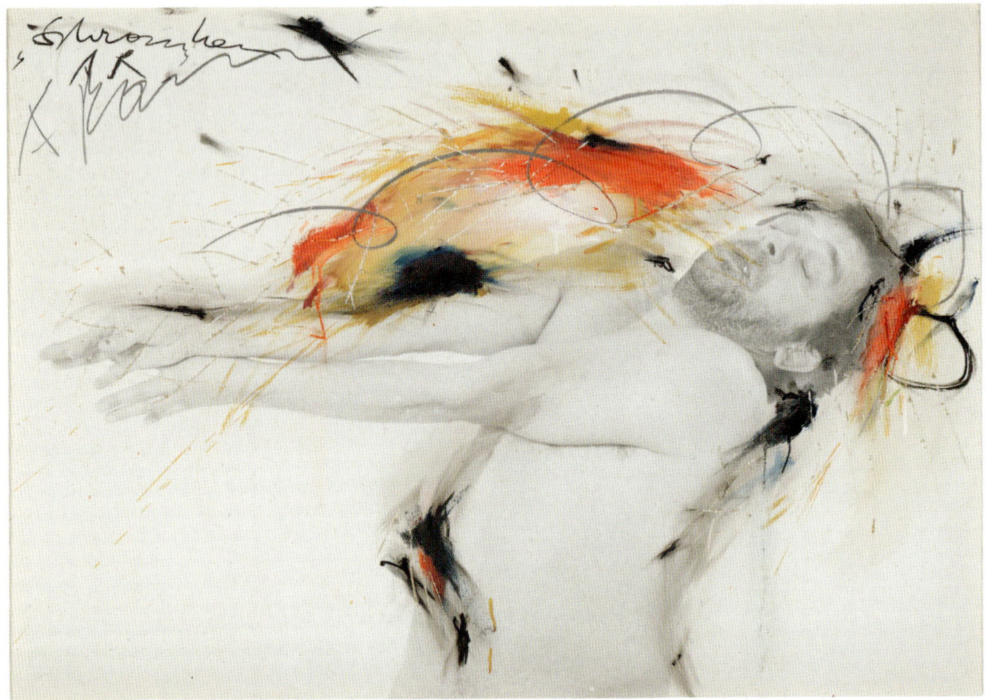

116 ABOVE Arnulf Rainer, *Schranken* (Barrier), 1974/75
117 OPPOSITE Arnulf Rainer, *Cross*, 1986

of his own and other bodies, in so-called 'overpaintings', as in
116 *Schranken* (Barrier). Rainer's method was partly developed via
117 his experience of art made by mental patients, which he began
to collect in the 1960s. At times he collaborated with artists with chronic mental health conditions from the so-called Artists' House, established in the grounds of the psychiatric hospital in Gugging, near Vienna, which was set up by the psychiatrist Leo Navratil (1921–2006), who had in turn been influenced by his involvement with Viennese avant-garde artists, including Rainer, Georg Eisler (1928–1998) and Alfred Hrdlicka (1928–2009).

Rainer's method of overpainting recalls the scribble of severely autistic mental patients, such as the Gugging artist Max (Rudolf Liemberger) (1937–1988), and includes a series based on photographs of the late sculpture of Franz Xaver Messerschmidt (1736–1783) consisting of strange physiognomic studies produced when Messerschmidt was suffering from a form of paranoid schizophrenia. Rainer's

experiments with alcohol and hallucinatory drugs and his series of simulations of the facial distortions of catatonics led him to develop an affinity with the psychotic state that has guided his production since. As Rainer said in 1987, 'I devote myself to the contemplation of a concise, minimal form of overpainting. But this cannot hold my interest indefinitely: sometimes the swarming of the faces around and within my head is just too insistent. Cause: perhaps a dearth of close personal contacts, perhaps some individual stress? Are these the paranoiac's familiar hallucinations of mocking faces, the menacing leers, the piercing unnerving stares, the faces that come too close to one's own?'

In Germany, Ursula Schultze-Bluhm (1921–1999), known simply as Ursula, developed ways of working in painting and constructed sculptural objects that was closer in form and iconography to psychiatric art itself. In works such
118 as *Eines Nachts, im Park Monceau um 23 Uhr*, an Abstract Expressionist handling of paint simultaneously coalesces into a hallucinatory figuration in which the entire surface is packed with throbbing life that spins between the primal and earthy and the celestial. Similarities between highly symbolic, though often-hermetic imagery characteristic of
119 schizophrenic drawings are even clearer in *Meine Berlin-Träume in Mittenwalde*, in which experience and fantasy collide in a vortex of automatic marks that conjure a malevolent dominant form with eyes of some dripping vegetal stuff, and which is constructed entirely from smaller discreet elements recognizable as birds, buildings and plants.

The German artist Georg Baselitz has also interrogated pathological states in his work and is a collector of psychiatric art. Baselitz was emblematic of many young German artists' rejection around 1960 of what they saw in their divided country as an imposed internationalism, in the form of Abstraction in capitalist West Germany and Socialist Realism in communist East Germany. Along with contemporaries such as Jörg Immendorff (1945–2007) and Markus Lüpertz (b. 1941) he insisted on exercising memory about his country's recent history and critical engagement with a cultural tradition smothered by collective historical amnesia. They refused to accept either the imposed certainties of communist collectivism or the sanitized individualism of American-style democracy. In its place they proposed an aggressive, painterly figuration that owed as much to art by mental patients as it did to early German Expressionist precedents, such as Kirchner, Nolde and Dix. Nolde, of course had a complicated relationship to Germany's recent past because of his Nazi sympathies, while Dix had suffered the double indignity of being declared a degenerate artist in the 1930s and after the war being regarded as representing a direct link to a German romantic tradition that post-war Germany wanted to bury because of its twisted appropriation by the Nazis.

Baselitz blasted onto the scene with two 'Pandemonium' manifestoes (1961, 1962), written with the painter Eugen Schönebeck (b. 1936), and a Berlin exhibition of his 'Neo-Expressionist' figurative work in 1963 that saw the confiscation of two paintings on the grounds of obscenity. One of these, the proto-punk *Die große Nacht im Eimer* (Great Night Down the Drain, 1962–63), depicts a full-frontal semi-naked man clutching his horse-like phallus, and behind him another, prone figure is slumped. More than anything the painting became a symbol for the illusory nature of the freedom that democracy was supposed to have brought to the new German Federal Republic. As Baselitz wryly noted, 'The wonderful thing about the 1950s and 60s was the general feeling that all the doors were open. People said: there's no problem, we're all free. We live in a free society. There's no need to demolish anything, there are no taboos. And then came this ridiculous picture.'

If there are visual similarities to psychotic art in Baselitz's early artwork, including the compulsive late drawings produced by the French playwright and actor Antonin Artaud (1896–1948) after he was hospitalized for a severe psychiatric collapse, the Pandemonium manifestoes read like schizophrenic writing. They are at once messianic, scatological, profound and syncopated, with psychological content that takes them into Surrealism's darkest and most fearful realms. They are an assault on amiability: 'In me the brewers of poison, the annihilators, the degenerates. Have attained a place of honour....We have blasphemy on our side!' And in the face of Germany's national amnesia, Baselitz and Schönebeck screamed: 'I am warped, bloated and sodden with memories. The destinies that make no one look up: I have them all on record.'

Baselitz and his contemporaries were painters of contemporary life, but also traded in cultural memory and recognizably Germanic symbols – the oak, the eagle and a particular range of types of landscape. Instead of rootless internationalism they chose an art wedded to place, and against the mass-produced, branded objects familiar in Pop Art they chose handwork. Lüpertz went so far as to claim Nietzschean ideas as central tenets in his works, at a time when the philosopher was banished from discourse even in university departments of philosophy in Germany and the United States.

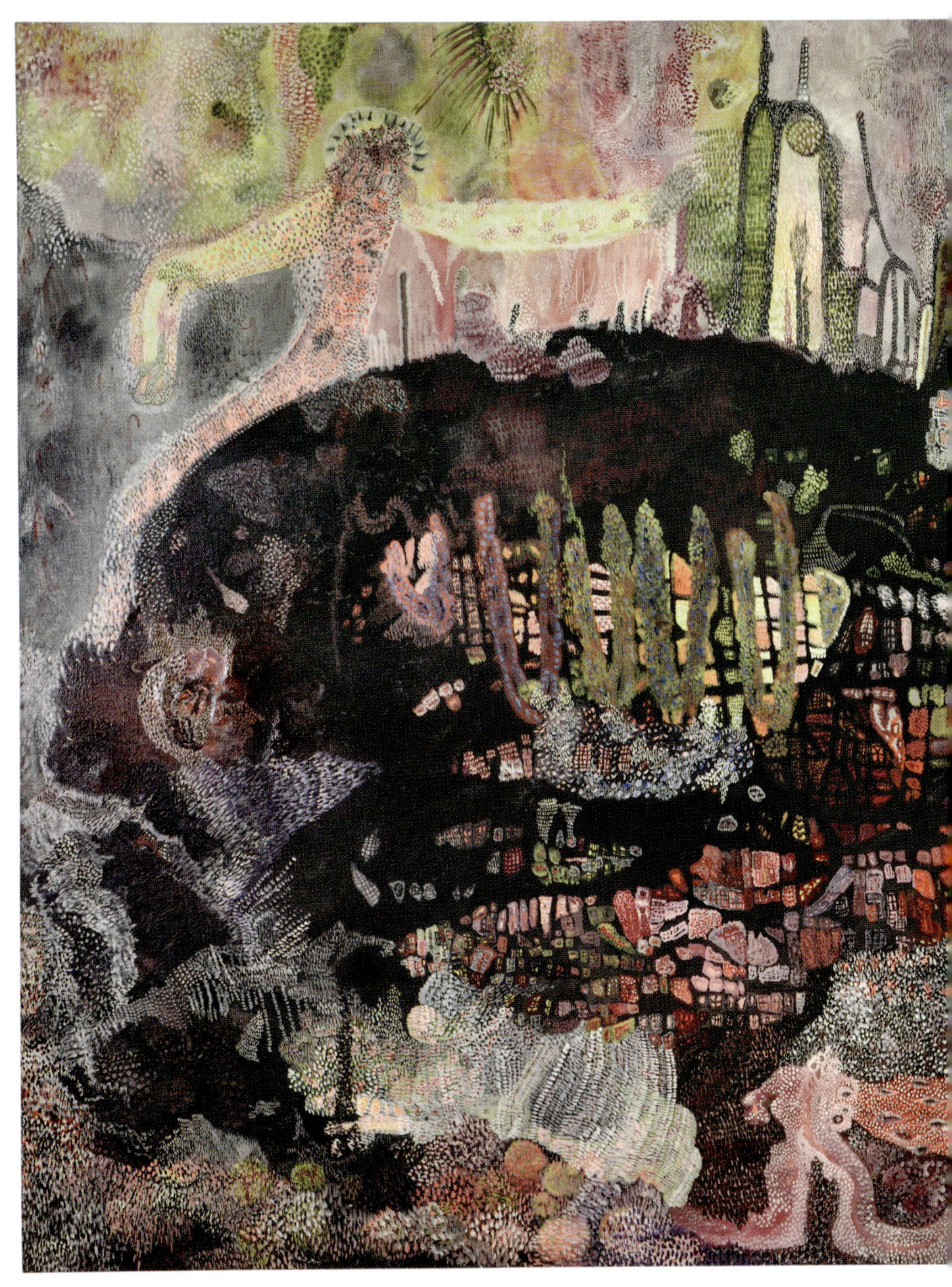

118 Ursula Schultze-Bluhm, *Eines Nachts, im Park Monceau um 23 Uhr* (One Night, in Monceau Park at 11 p.m.), 1961

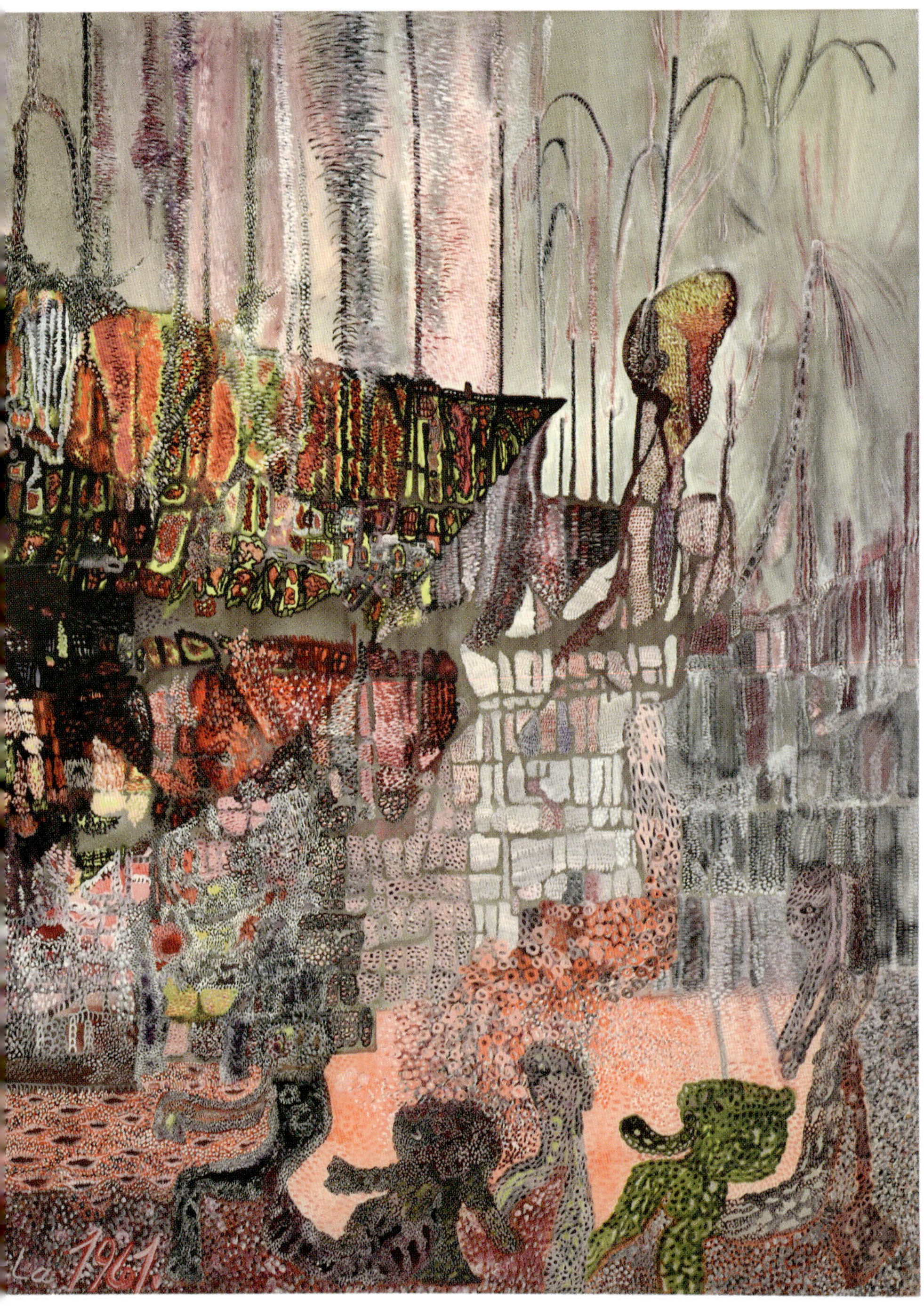
La 1961

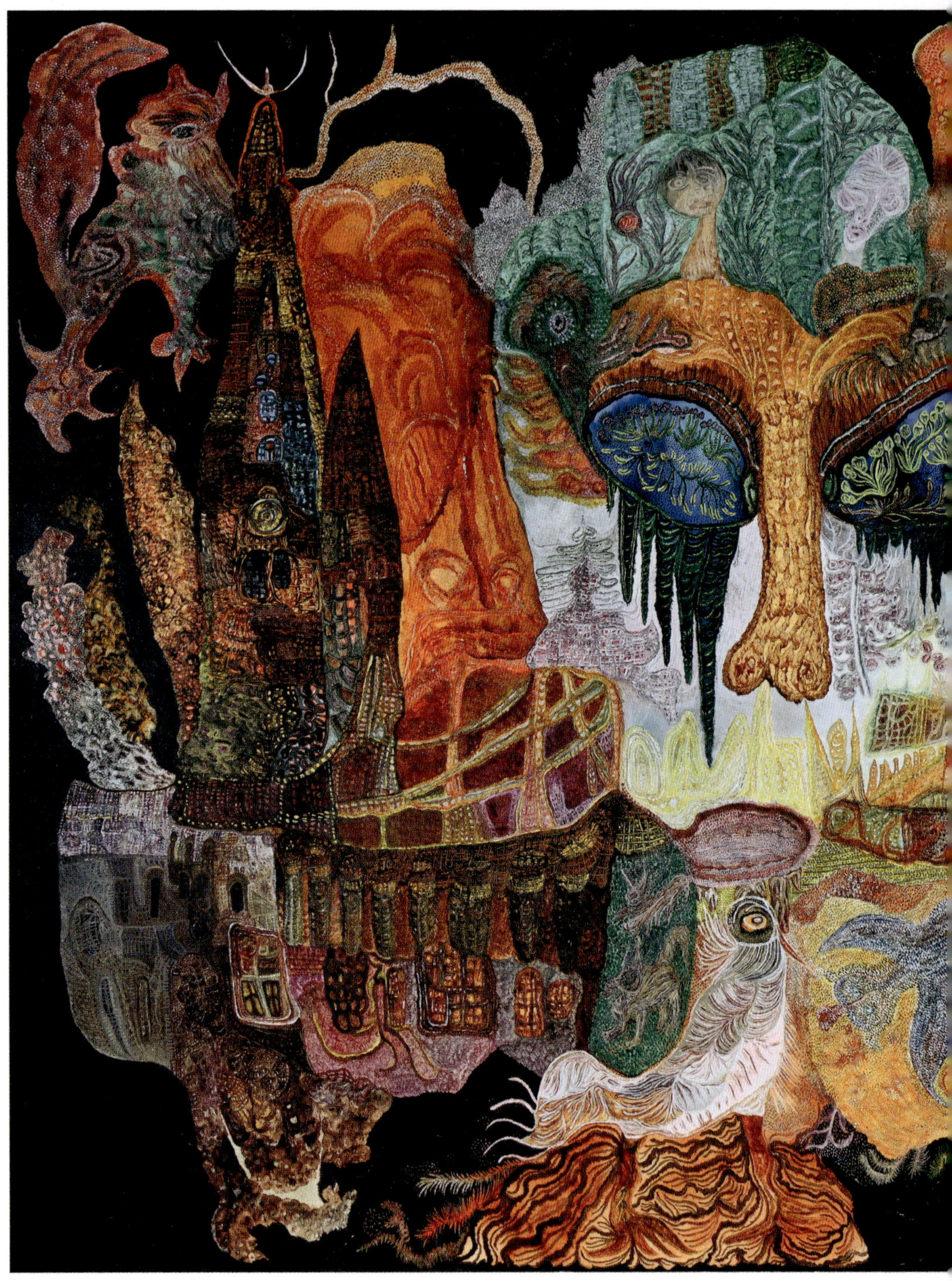

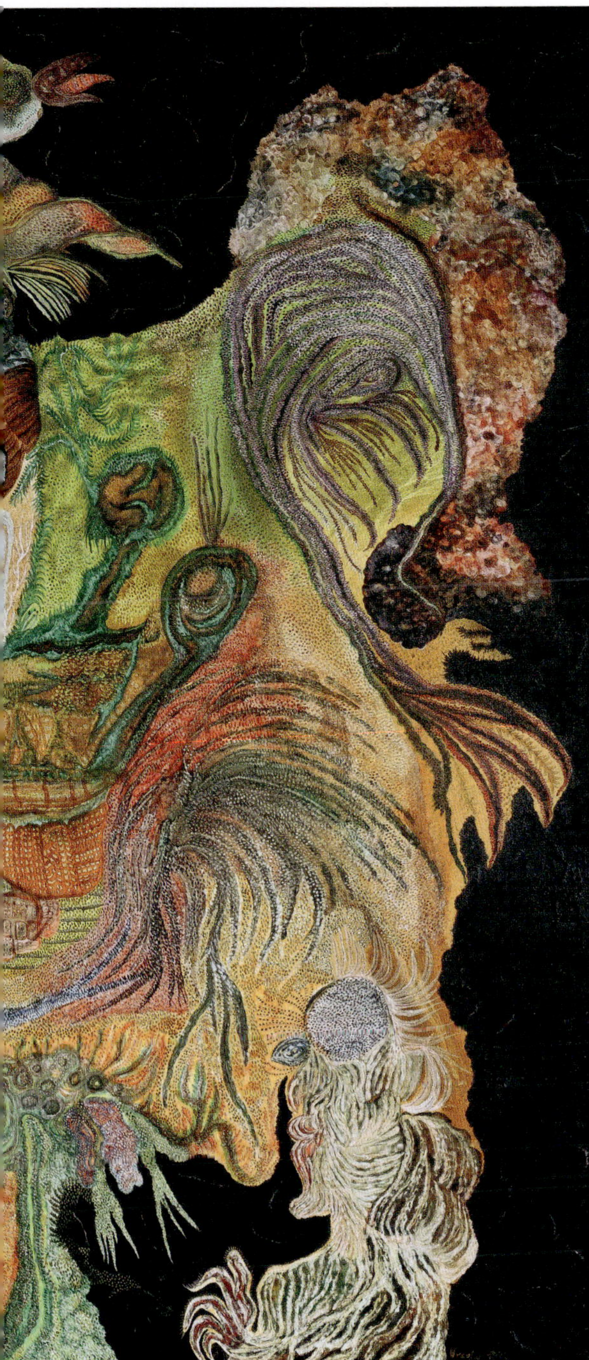

119 Ursula Schultze-Bluhm, *Meine Berlin-Träume in Mittenwalde* (My Berlin Dreams in Mittenwalde), 1977

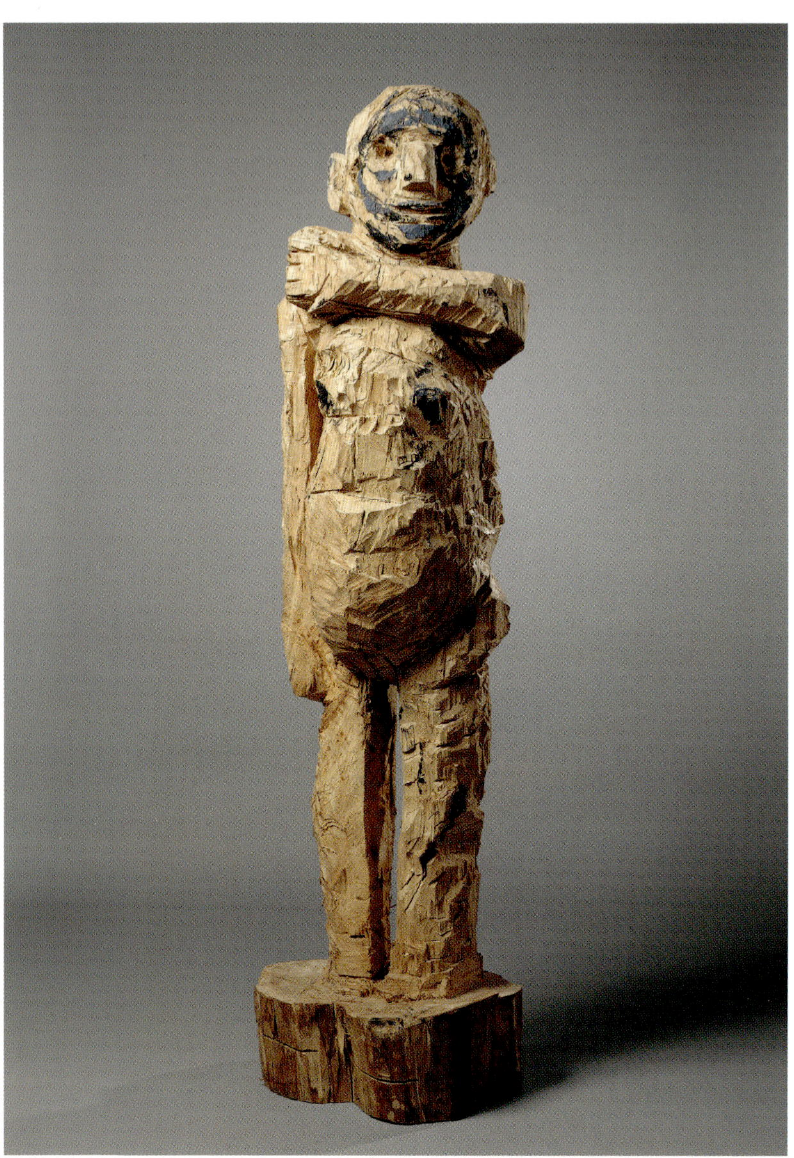

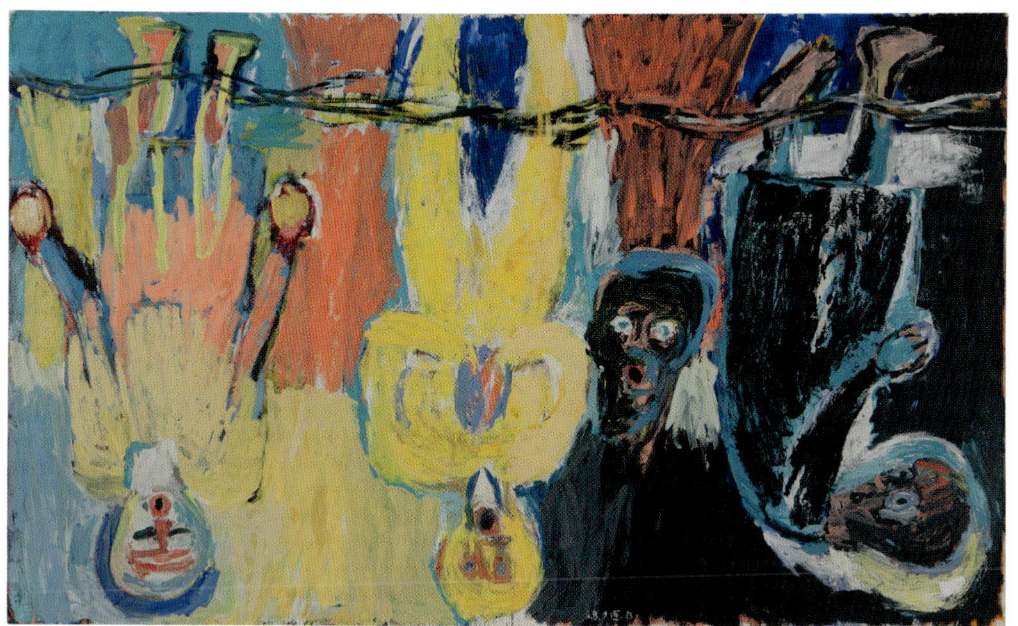

120 OPPOSITE Georg Baselitz, *Untitled*, 1982–3
121 ABOVE Georg Baselitz, *Der Brückechor (The Brücke Choir)*, 1983

Yet, although their art was clearly oppositional and seemingly packed with meaningful content, they were consistently reluctant to describe their intentions, leaving viewers to infer meaning for themselves. Baselitz's view was that this was because authentic artists are social outsiders: 'The artist works in an entirely irresponsible manner. His (*sic.*) relation to society is anti-social, and his only duty is to maintain his composure, in respect of himself and his work.' This is unsettling in itself but must have been doubly so in the 1960s and 70s, when discourse *about* art *by* artists reached new levels of intensity. Baselitz responded with a progressively brutalized figuration that often made the much vaunted 'directness' of early twentieth-century
121 Expressionists appear well-mannered, in works such as *The*
120 *Brücke Choir* and *Untitled* which are a kind of late examination
of German Expressionism, especially Munch and the Brücke artists Kirchner and Nolde. In 1969 he had begun producing paintings in which the motif was inverted, while remaining entirely figurative. The result was striking, further challenging the normative impulse to 'read' the painting as image.

Neo-Expressionism's second generation in Germany was more exuberant. Artists like Rainer Fetting, Elvira Bach,
122 Helmut Middendorf (b. 1953) and the brothers Albert Oehlen

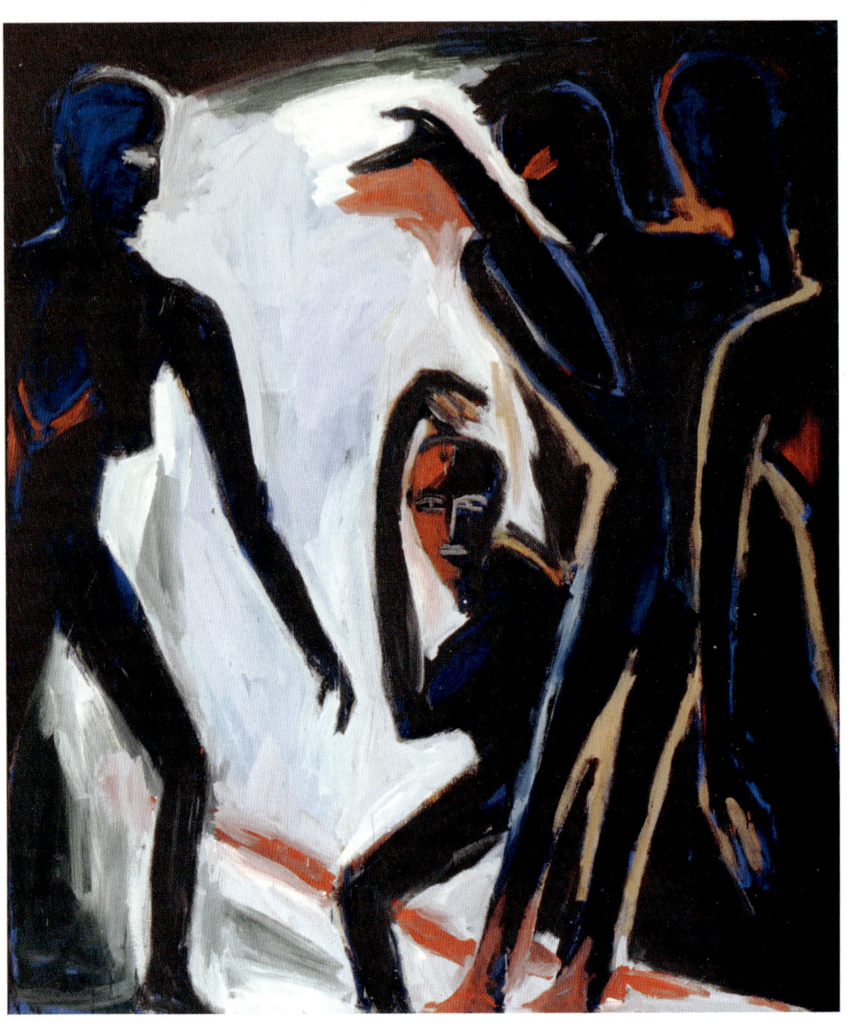

122 ABOVE Helmut Middendorf, *Großstadteingeborene* (Natives of the Big City), 1982
123 OPPOSITE Markus Oehlen, *Untitled*, 1984

123 (b. 1954) and Markus Oehlen (b. 1956) occupied a West German space that had begun to confront the past more openly and which was optimistic, self-confident and open. Their painting was a strident expression of contemporary youth – a culture of punk rock and extrovert sexuality that in many ways mirrored the permissive subculture in Berlin in the 1920s. Although their work was usually larger and more vigorously and directly executed, it is closer in character to that of the Brücke and many Second-Generation German Expressionists than to older contemporaries like Baselitz and Schönebeck. They are usually described as *Neue Wilden* (New Savages), echoing characterizations of the New Art by Franz Marc in the *Blue Rider Almanac* in 1912, although their form of direct painting seems to go much further into primal depths than Expressionists at the beginning of the twentieth century.

The Neue Wilden not only shared Brücke's commitment to Expressionist figuration but also a love of popular entertainment – cafés, the variety theatre, and the dance hall for Brücke; nightclubs, punk rock gigs, and the movies for the Neue Wilden – as in Middendorf's *Electric Night* (1979) and
124 Fetting's *Drummer and Guitarist* (1979). Elvira Bach was one of

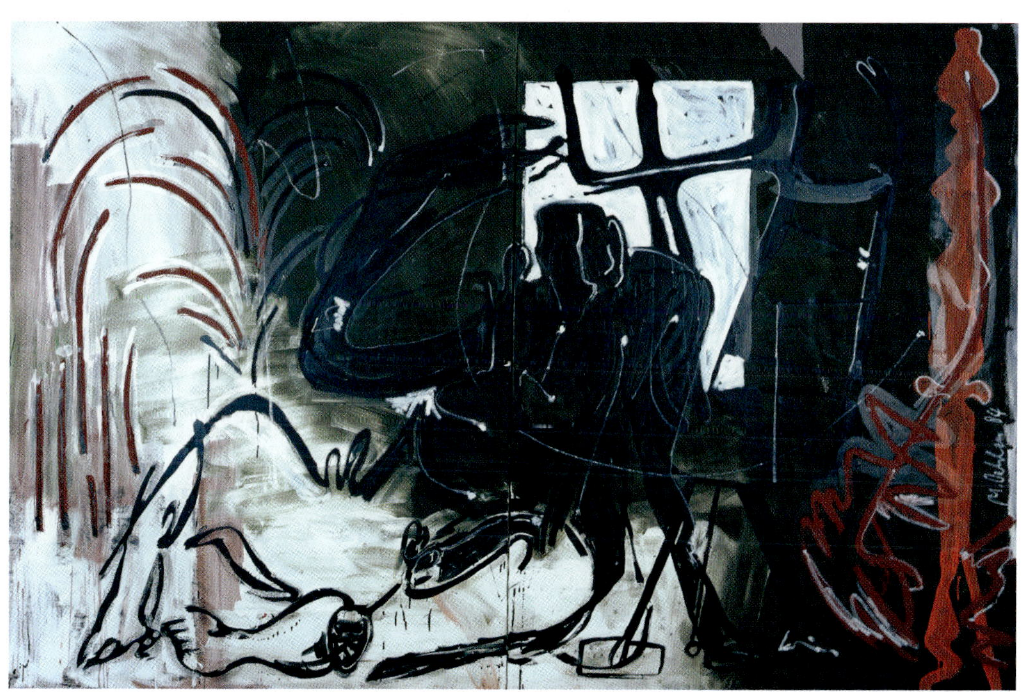

the few women to emerge as an important figure in this milieu. This was no doubt partly because of contemporary feminist strictures on painting being irredeemably bound up with phallocentric power play, yet she engaged with the medium precisely to present strong, independent urban women, as in
125 *Letting Go* (1991) and *Schwarz und Bleich* (1985). 'I wanted to show the woman as an individual,' she said, 'not imbedded in the group or together with other people. That was my experience, anyway. By exhibiting myself, just like my paintings. Observing myself. What are the reactions? Can you do that, are you allowed to do that, as a woman, stand at the bar like that, beautifully dressed? The women figures developed out of these experiences. I was interested in that, without a man, without a girlfriend, to just go somewhere alone, unprotected.'

Another figure who enjoyed an extraordinary rise to prominence in the context of the Neo-Expressionist moment was Anselm Kiefer. Like Baselitz his work is very physical and even more richly iconographical. Its origins, though, are in

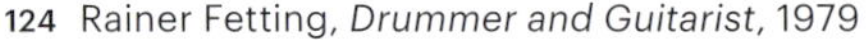

124 Rainer Fetting, *Drummer and Guitarist*, 1979

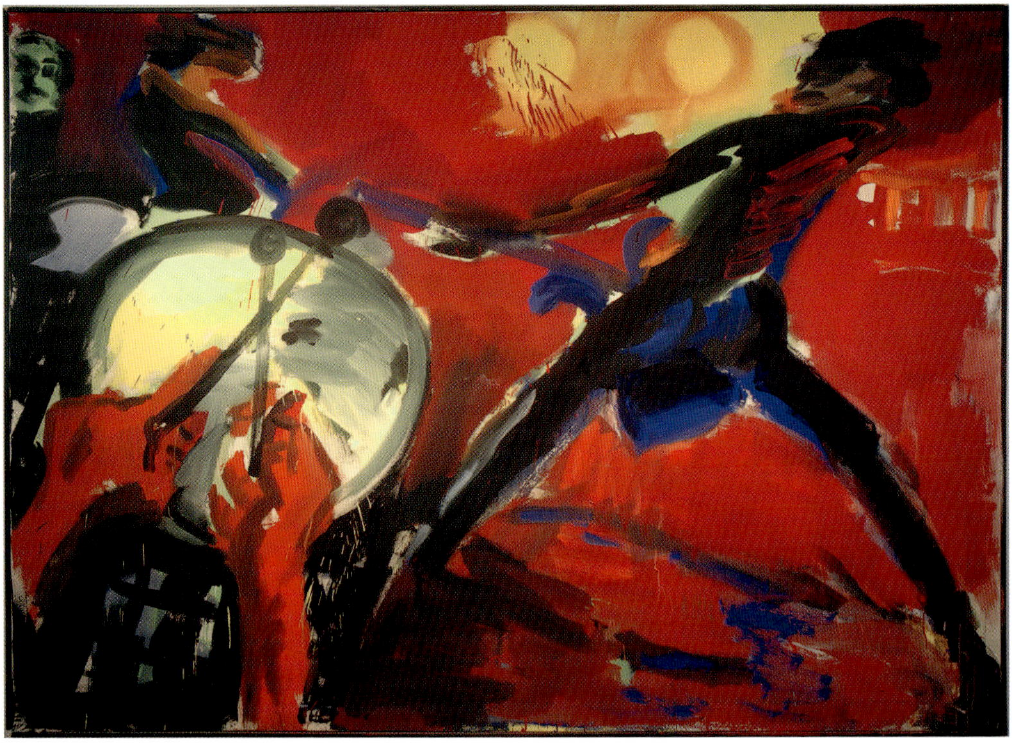

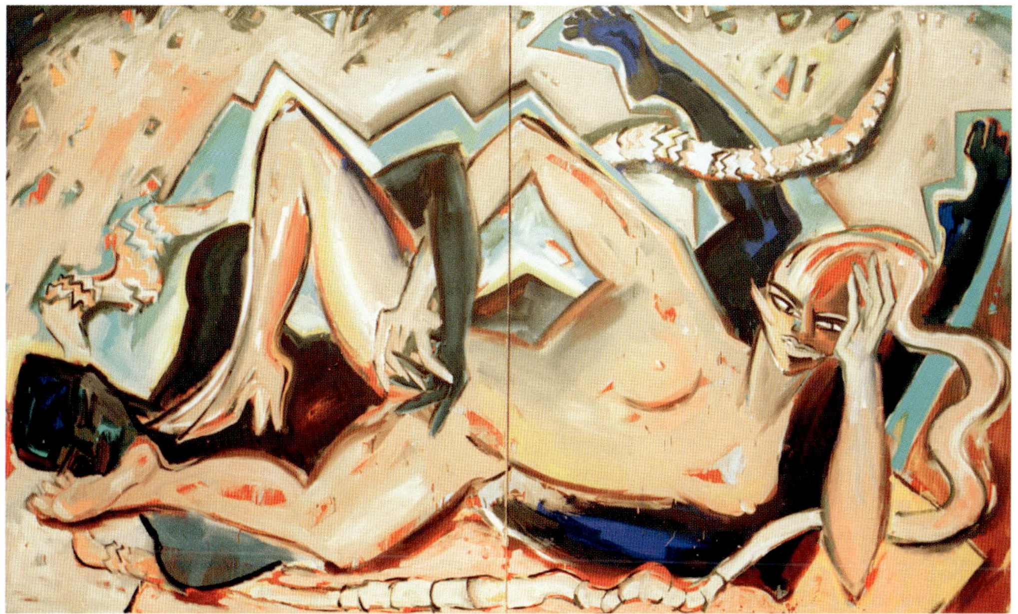

125 Elvira Bach, *Schwarz und Bleich*, 1985

1960s conceptualism, and in particular show the influence of his teacher, Joseph Beuys (1921–1986), whose practice privileged the mythic function of objects, usually integrated into quasi-shamanic performances, although Kiefer's later highly physical integration of objects into paintings was prefigured by Bernard Schultze (1915–2005) in works such as
126 *rifrost* (1958). Germanic subject matter pervades Kiefer's work, from historical association to evocations of culture and place. Episodes and characters from the ancient German sagas, mediated at times through the lens of Wagner, were fused with troubled national memories: in early works such as *Parsifal* (1973) the 'flame' of memory is consigned to an attic, like a moribund object that is nevertheless too painful to part with entirely. For many years his insistence on exploring Germany's repressed Romantic subconscious, wound up as it was with
127 the terrible spectre of its recent history, in works such as *Ways of World Wisdom: The Battle of Hermann* (1978), made his work embarrassing to his fellow countrymen, as was demonstrated by the unremittingly hostile response of German critics to his inclusion in the Venice Biennale in 1980. Remarkably, the opposite was true of critics from elsewhere, most notably the Americans, who saw in his work an honest and serious

confrontation of difficult themes that transcended the local and the personal.

Kiefer is a history painter on a grand scale. At times risking grandiloquence in his later installation work, he has typically pursued his practice through making paintings, woodcuts, sculptures and unique, handmade books. By the early 1980s he was already using a characteristically wide range of materials, such as lead, straw, wire, hair, earth and other pieces of organic and inorganic debris, which additionally announced the works' physical presence as sculptural objects. Like German forebears such as the Expressionist Nolde and Romantic Caspar David Friedrich, Kiefer is a supreme landscape painter. His subjects are sometimes the same as those of Friedrich and Nolde, although the pantheistic embrace of the soil that is strong in the first two is replaced by alienation in Kiefer, giving his landscapes an awful beauty that is at once physically and emotionally distant and overwhelming, as in *Emanation*

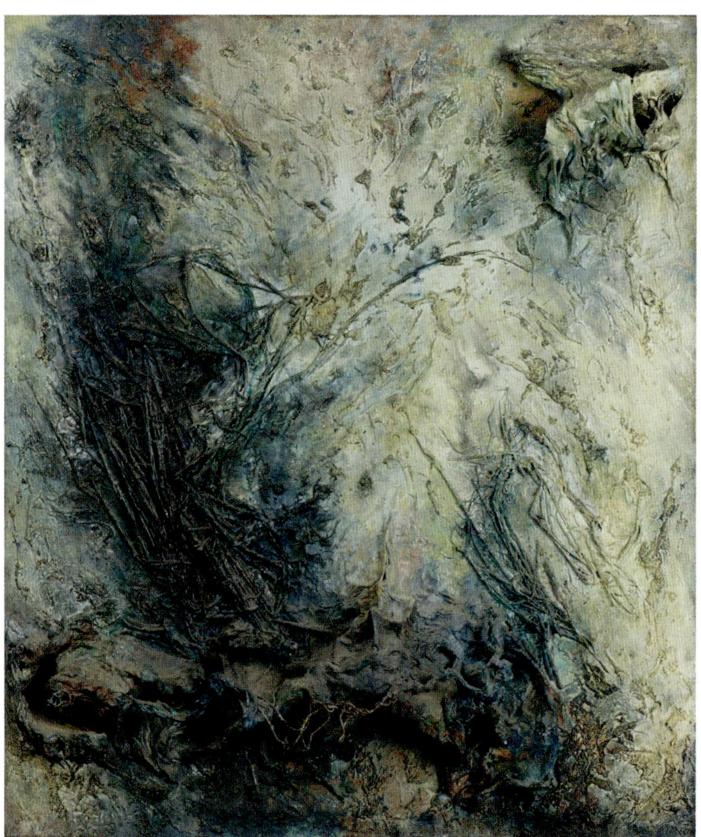

126 LEFT Bernard Schultze, *rifrost*, 1958
127 OPPOSITE Anselm Kiefer, *Ways of World Wisdom: The Battle of Hermann*, 1978

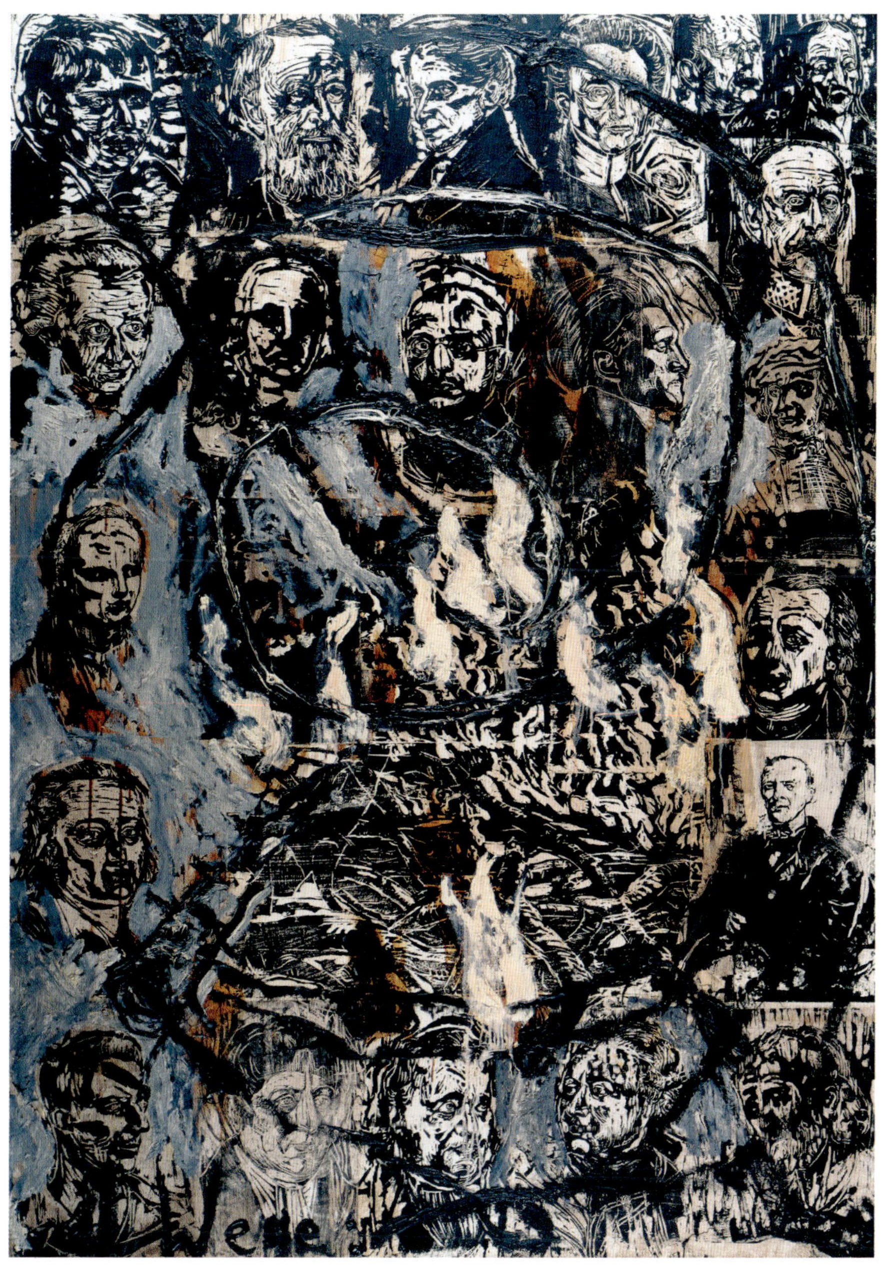

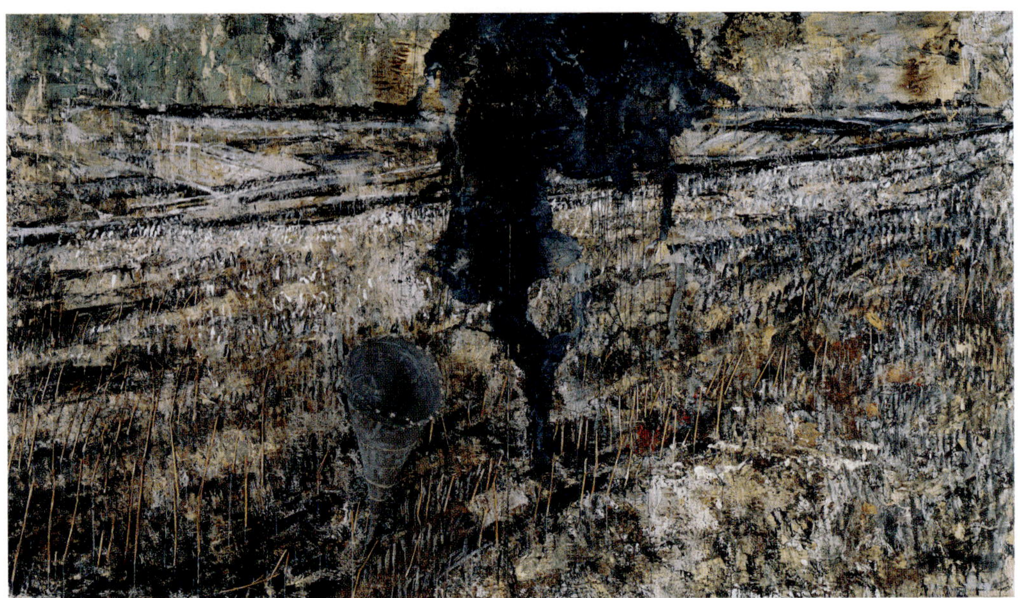

128 Anselm Kiefer, *Emanation*, 1982–86

(1982–86). Paintings like *Heath of the Brandenburg March* (1974), which depicts a desolate landscape, with the title written in large letters across its surface, contain multi-layered associations for Germans that were mostly painful after 1945, but which are not readily apparent to viewers from other countries. Similarly, the painting *Eisensteig* (1986) incorporates olive branches, iron and lead which is emblematic of the multivalent emotions surrounding travel. Yet, in this context it is impossible not to be reminded of the railways that transported millions of people to their deaths in concentration camps by the Nazis.

Kiefer's books are essentially visual, with text used only rarely, and then in a similar manner to in his paintings. Early books like *Operation Sea Lion* (1975) and *Sand of the Brandenburg March I* (1977) characteristically mix photographs, often staged in the artist's studio in mock-heroic style, with interventions in paint, sand, oil and glue. Around the mid-1980s Kiefer began making books with lead pages. *Zweistromland – The High Priestess* (1985–89) is a sculptural installation consisting of nearly two hundred lead books. Its scale is huge and the books impossibly heavy and unwieldy. But they are functional as books, nevertheless. The effect is to re-impose on the book the order of preciousness it once unambiguously possessed as rare container of knowledge, in contrast to the throwaway commodity it has become. Kiefer's intellectual sources are varied, ranging from books on philosophy, history, alchemy, and the Kabbalah to ancient Babylonian and Nordic mythologies. They are often fused in richly associative subjects that have shape-shifted throughout history, producing a kind of mythic space which deals in time as synchronic rather than diachronic. The most obvious example is that of Lilith, a powerful, chaotic and rebellious figure who appears, among other places, in Babylonian myth, Jewish daemonology, and early Christian mystical writings.

The early prominence of painters such as Julian Schnabel and David Salle (b. 1952) notwithstanding, in the United States Jean-Michel Basquiat provided the most compelling and intense example of a Neo-Expressionist aesthetic. Born to middle-class Puerto Rican and Haitian parents, his home life was troubled, and Basquiat left to eke out a precarious existence in Lower Manhattan at the age of seventeen. His meteoric rise to fame began in 1980 after he emerged from the New York underground street art and emerging hip-hop music scenes, fuelled by enthusiastic responses to his work by critics, gallerists and members of New York's contemporary cultural scene.

Part of Basquiat's allure was the directness and spontaneity of his work, which brought the visual language of the street onto the pristine walls of the art gallery spaces, and the sheer freshness of his visual language. Basquiat was also incredibly charismatic, which also added to opportunities for creating useful networks and generating public interest that were essential aspects of career development for artists at a time when New York was obsessed with celebrity. Unfortunately, the emerging mythos of Basquiat was also based on primitivizing and racist constructions that conflated descriptions of his behaviours and imagery as savage outpourings of New York underground culture and stereotypes of Blackness.

Basquiat engaged with these issues head-on in his work, reflecting forcefully on the legacies of colonialism and slavery that were still all too apparent in contemporary life. He worked quickly, mixing image, text and scribbled gestural marks in ways that bring signs and message crashing together in a mass of neologism, derailment and echolalia,
129, 130 as in *Kings of Egypt II* and *Notary*. The orientation of his pictures is to flatness, with every mark operating across a two-dimensional plane, including figuration, which is always resolutely primitive. It is for the viewer to piece together each unruly matrix – or perhaps to respond in purely formal terms? Fame and wealth intensified, rather than relieved

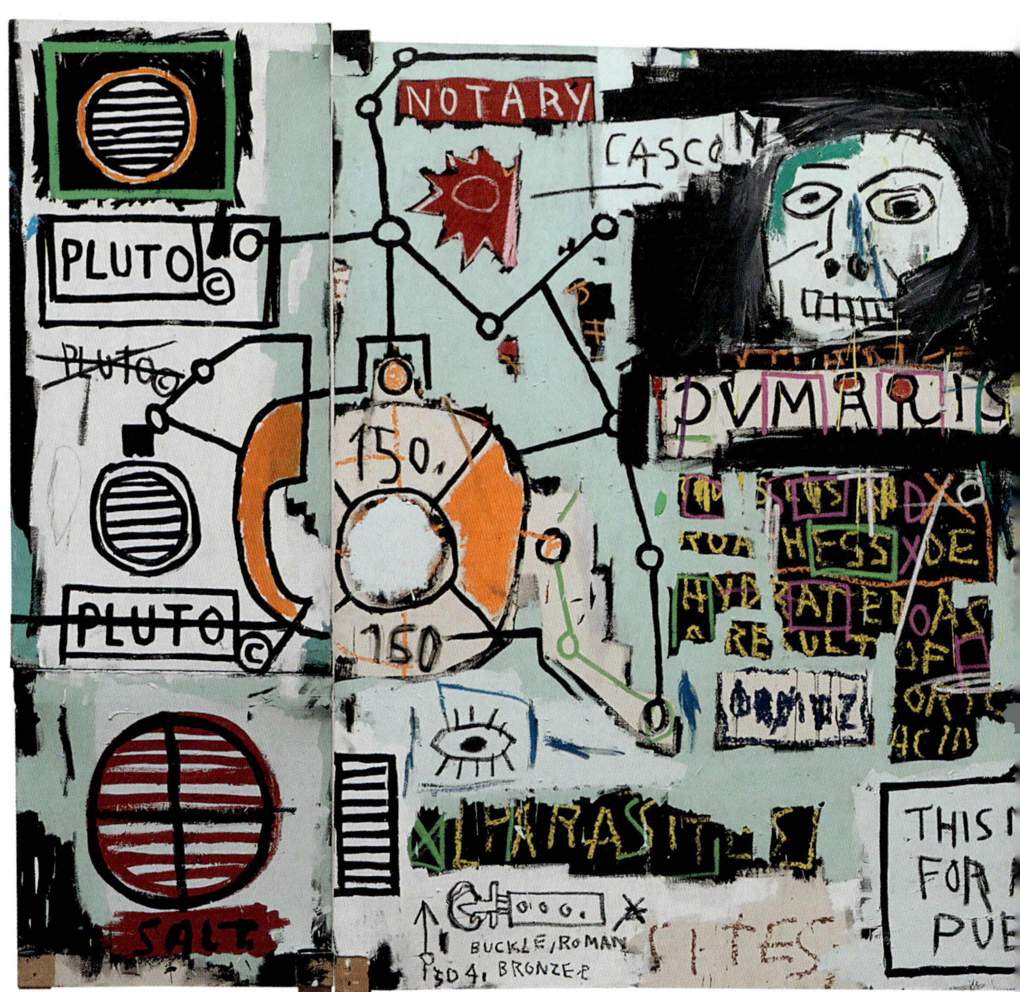

129 Jean-Michel Basquiat, *Notary*, 1983

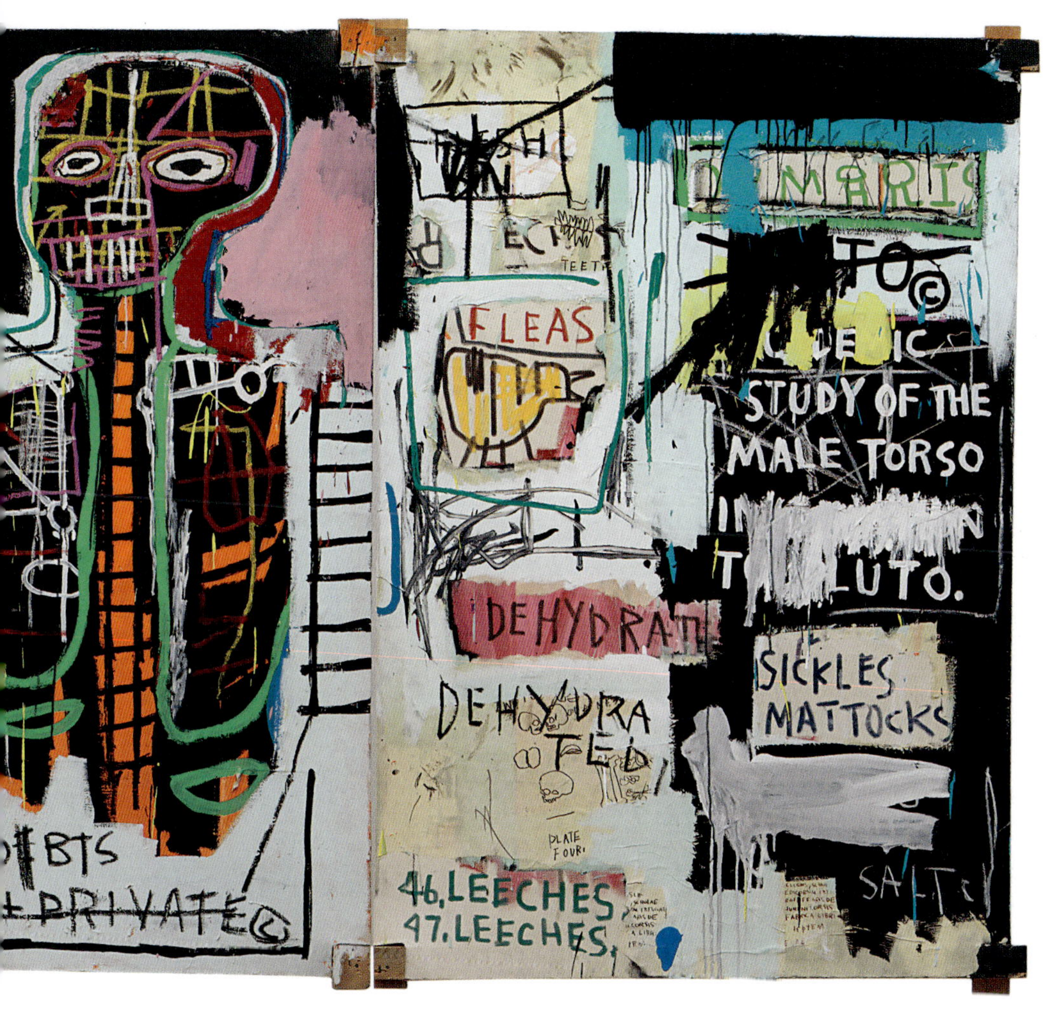
FLEAS
STUDY OF THE
MALE TORSO
LUTO.
SICKLES
MATTOCKS
PLATE
FOUR
46. LEECHES.
47. LEECHES.
PRIVATE©

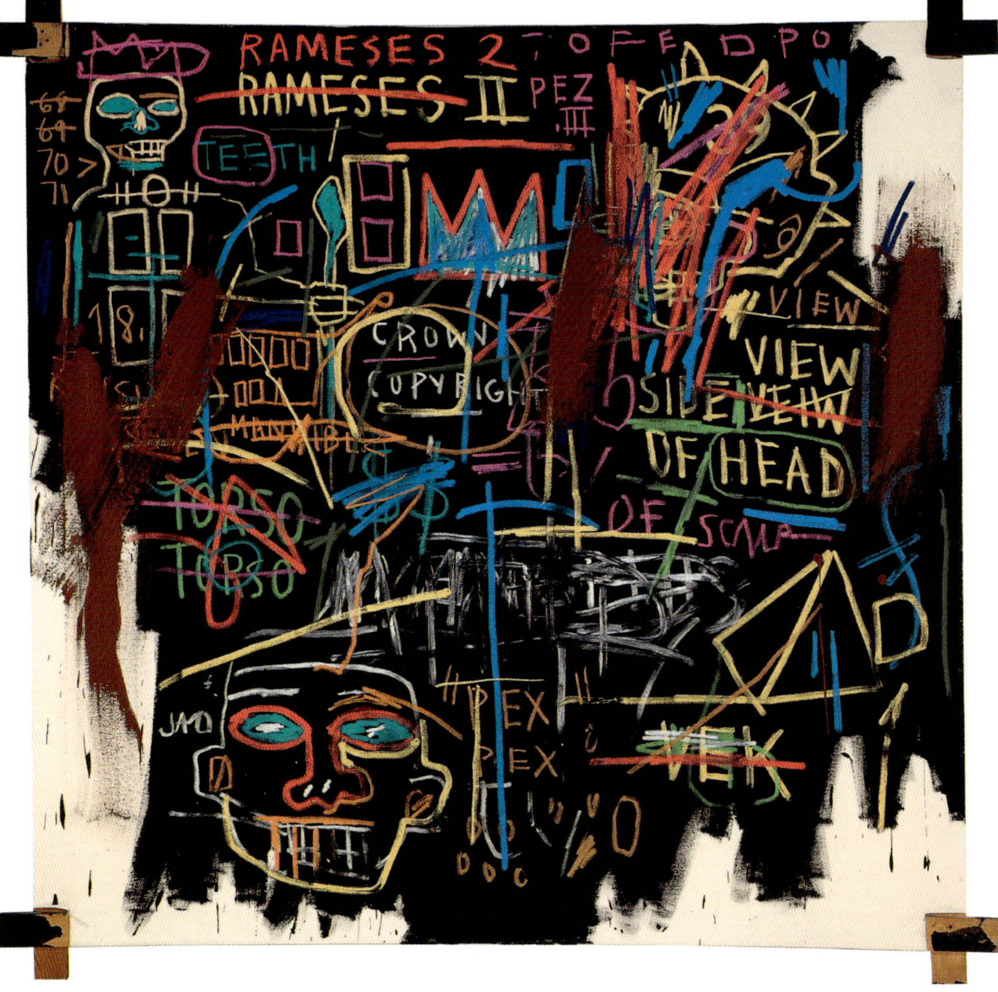

130 Jean-Michel Basquiat, *Kings of Egypt II*, 1982

Basquiat's troubled relationship with the world. An already-present paranoid tendency deepened (presumably not helped by prodigious cocaine use), so that he inferred tokenization by supporters even when the dominant attitude was celebration. Paradoxically, Basquiat cultivated the image of wildness, even as he increasingly self-medicated. His death from a heroin overdose at the age of twenty-seven provided something like an apotheosis.

Where Expressionism Dare Not Tread

The contemporary critical response to Neo-Expressionism in the United States was mostly dismissive. The writer Craig Owens, for example, recognized the legitimacy of what he saw as the sincere, if utopian project of early Expressionism: 'Expressionism was an attack on convention (this is what characterizes it as a modernist movement), specifically, on those conventions which subject unconscious impulses to the laws of form and thereby rationalize them, transform them into images.... The Expressionists, however, abandoned the simulation of emotion in favour of its seismographic registration.' But he rejected its supposed re-emergence in 1980s new art, accusing Neo-Expressionism, on the contrary, of being 'Expressionism...reduced to convention.'

At the height of the First World War in 1916, Hermann Bahr wrote in his book *Expressionism*, 'This is the vital point – that man should find himself again....he has become the tool of his own work, and he has no more sense, since he serves the machine. It has stolen him away from his soul. And now the soul demands his return. This is the vital point. All that we experience is the strenuous battle between the soul and the machine for the possession of man. We no longer live, we are lived.' Art – and specifically a metaphysical Expressionist art – was to be the means by which this restoration might be effected, he argued. In the view of the highly influential critic and academic, Hal Foster, such ideas cannot be legitimately applied to the current moment, because, he said, 'However real alienation is today, the crisis of the individual versus society is largely a cliché, as is the crisis of high versus low culture.' This is, however, a highly privileged view of the cultural moment, arguably representative as much of Foster's intellectual milieu and interest in minimal and concept art over Modernism in general and Expressionism in particular.

In 'The Expressive Fallacy' (1983) Foster scathingly wrote: 'Neo-Expressionism: the very term signals that Expressionism is a "gestuary" or largely self-aware act.' On one hand, he rightly pointed to the 'rhetorical nature' of Expressionism and its status as a visual language: 'Expressionism is a paradox: a type of representation that asserts *presence* – of the artist, of the real. Of course, this Expressionist presence is by proxy only.' On the other hand, the materialism underpinning Foster's worldview does not allow for idealism or metaphysics. 'Neo-Expressionism,' he argued, 'occurs as one more belated attempt to recentre the self in art,' in spite of revelations that 'subjectivity has proven to be no more exempt from reification and fragmentation than objective reality.' Such critique presupposes highly self-aware practices, conducted at least as much with an eye to historical precedence as to the immediate demands of visual communication. As Foster said, 'Far from a return to history (as is so ideologically posed), recent culture attests to an extraordinary *loss* of history – or rather a displacement of it by the pseudo-historical.' Artists, in general, he argued, 'only *seem* to prize open history...in fact, they give us hallucinations of the historical, masks of these moments. In short, they return to us our most cherished forms – as kitsch.' At best, the appearance of Neo-Expressionism is a 'problematic response' to the loss 'of the historical, the real, and of the subject.'

An Other Expressionism

There is a rich vein of art from the American South that shares many of the fundamental qualities of Expressionism, but
131 which does not go by that name, including the painters Purvis Young (1943–2010), Sam Doyle (1906–1985), Mary Tillman Smith (1905–1995) and William Hawkins (1895–1990). It is by turns content-laden, enunciatory and often deliberately obscured or veiled in its messaging. It was created after the Civil Rights movement ended, although many of those who made it lived through it, close to the epicentre of the struggle, before finding their vocation as full-time artists. Much of the work is an open response to that struggle. All of it speaks powerfully to aspects of the history and lived experience of being African American in the South. This was an art that developed originally in response to the need for displaced, enslaved and commodified cultural groups to record, preserve and disseminate specific ideas and information, while avoiding detection by those holding power. As a result, much before the middle of last century was ephemeral and is now lost.

If Basquiat's rise to fame was meteoric and came early, recognition by the mainstream contemporary art world for almost all these artists came only after their deaths. They were, like Basquiat self-taught, though not necessarily by choice. Opportunities for higher education for Black people

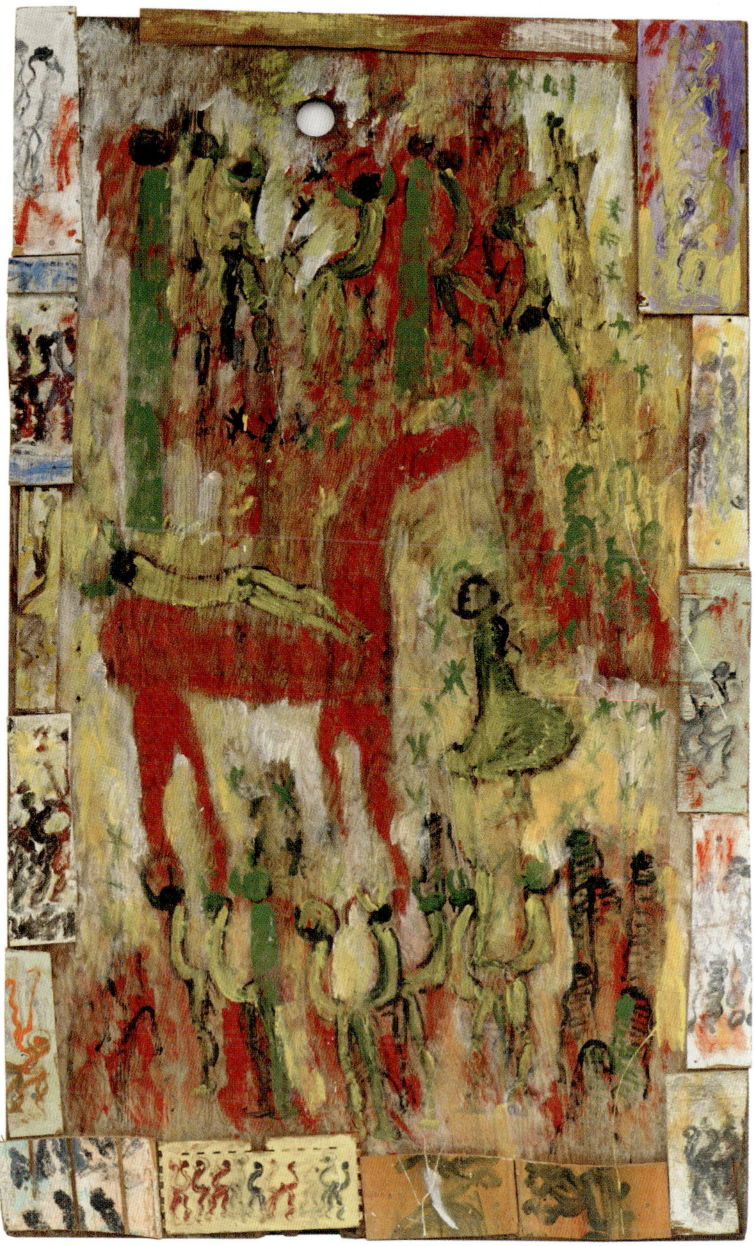

131 Purvis Young, *Carrying the Angel to the People*, 1994

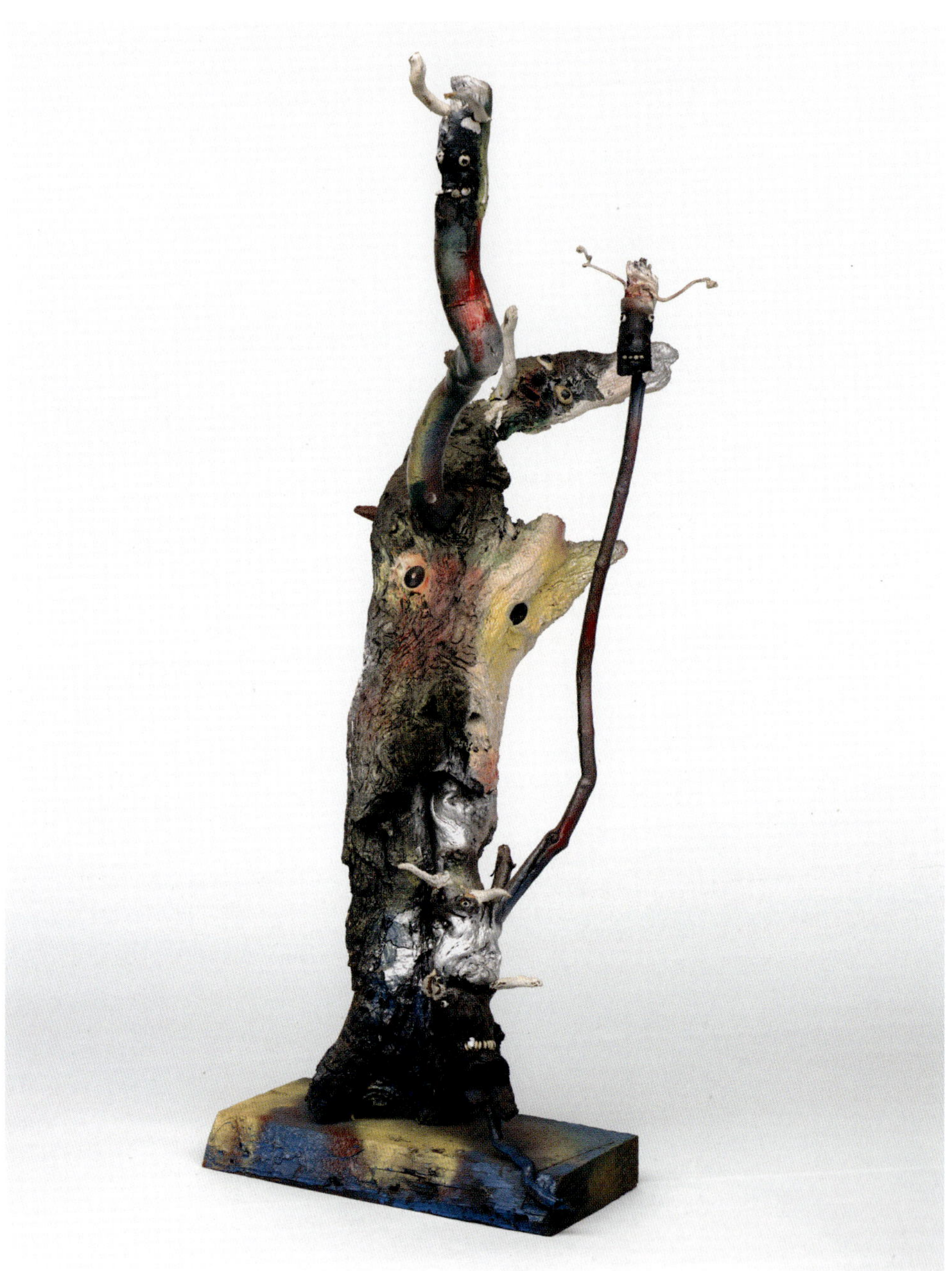

132 Bessie Harvey, *Seven Faces of Eve*, 1987

of their generation in the South were notoriously few. This lent their work ingenuity and freshness born out of the need to improvise skills and materials. Also, many of them, including Thornton Dial (1928–2016), Mose Tolliver (1924–2006) and Joe Minter (b. 1943), came to artmaking later in life, after retirement or injury led to them leaving regular blue-collar jobs. Similarly, and notwithstanding continued strong residual racism in the United States and an unfinished project for achieving social equity, advances in education and opportunity have resulted in significant change in the lives of Black people in the South that have largely removed the conditions in which that art was produced. As a result, the most intense period of production was broadly around three decades or so, from the 1970s. While it mirrors to some degree the period of Neo-Expressionism, this is coincidental. Neither the self-taught Americans nor the Neo-Expressionists knew of the other's existence.

Many of these artists came from the area in and around Birmingham, Alabama, including Dial, Minter, Lonnie Holley (b. 1950) and Ronald Lockett (1965–1998). In their art representation was primarily dealt with as sign. What was most important was not that things were represented mimetically through technical skill or emotionally through expressive handling of materials, but that things in the works stood metonymically for things in the world. Thus, in Lockett's *Traps* (1989) fragments of actual fence fixed over deer fashioned out of found wood and tin cutout represent 'traps'; in *Last Supper* (1986) a found piece of wood fixed to an image denotes a table; and in Dial's *Farmer's Wife and the Colored Graveyard* (2005) pieces of corrugated iron, domestic ornaments and items of clothing function synecdochally.

The Birmingham group shared with other African American
132 self-taught artists, such as Bessie Harvey (1929–1994), Emmer Sewell (1934–2022) and Dinah Young (b. 1932), an organicist, essentially metaphysical attitude to their materials, including found objects, believing that even commodity objects are vessels capable of containing human experience and history through use (and abuse), making things that are used up and broken in their utilitarian function doubly powerful in their symbolic life incorporated in art. As Dial said, 'Everything I pick up be something that done did somebody good in their lifetime. So I am picking up on their spirit.' Beginning as simple necessity, born of poverty, Dial eschewed the new and unused, and found significance beyond mere form in broken and discarded things. It is, in part, a basis of the once common yardshow, characteristic of Southern African American

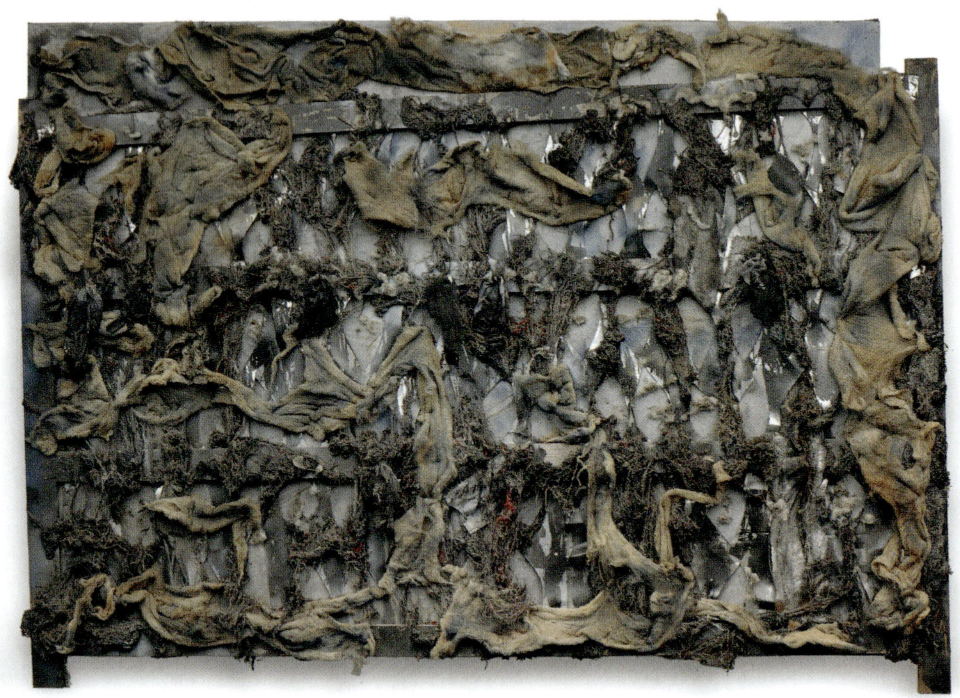

133 Thornton Dial, *Shadows of the Field*, 2008

properties. At one level things are seen to have conjural potential, inanimate at first but capable of being activated by performative means. More prosaically, perhaps, it might be said that in the art of Dial and Lockett there exists an embodied telling of history through material objects that are capable of speaking their message through skilled (that is, creative) interlocutors. It is not, then, so much in seeing importance and use in the things people throw away as seeing things that people have used as imbued with their own experiences and desires, as well as those of their particular social and cultural contexts.

Without knowing anything of theories of Expressionism Thornton Dial employed a modality that was essentially expressionist. To be successful a work must literally embody the person of the artist, transmogrified through the materials: 'The piece is going to have Mr Dial in it, under it, and over it, and everybody can know it.' Dial shared a concern with freedom, both as personal creative liberation and social justice, with Expressionists from throughout the twentieth century. 'My art is evidence of my freedom,' he said, 'When I start any piece of art I can pick up anything I want to pick up....I start with

whatever fits with my idea, things I will find anywhere. I gather up things from around. I see the pieces in my mind before I start, but after you start making it you see more that need to go in it.' Similarly, Dial's treatment of historical narrative, through means that are highly personal, at times idiosyncratic, and invoke spirit, chimed with Expressionism, but clashed with an art-world moment in which the 'death of history' was a buzz phrase. Dial, on the contrary, sensed no loss of history, instead part of his project is a *reclaiming* of history: 'My art is talking about the power. It is talking about the coalmines and the ore mines and the steel mills. It is talking about the government, and the unions, and the people that controls the hills and the mountains. The power of the United States is the fuel that carries the United States on. It carries everything, the mills and factories and stores and houses. I try to show how the Negroes have worked in all these different places and have come to help make the power of the United States what it is today.' This included, of course, the shadow of slavery and the Jim Crow South, which Dial dealt with brilliantly in works such as
134 *Graveyard Traveller/Selma Bridge* (1992), *Cotton Field Sky Still*
133 *Over Our Head* (2001), and *Shadows of the Field* (2008).

Ronald Lockett shared these Expressionist concerns. In the last four or so years of his life he abandoned painting almost completely for a kind of collage and constructivist technique that utilized found sheet metals from around

134 Thornton Dial, *Graveyard Traveller / Selma Bridge*, 1992

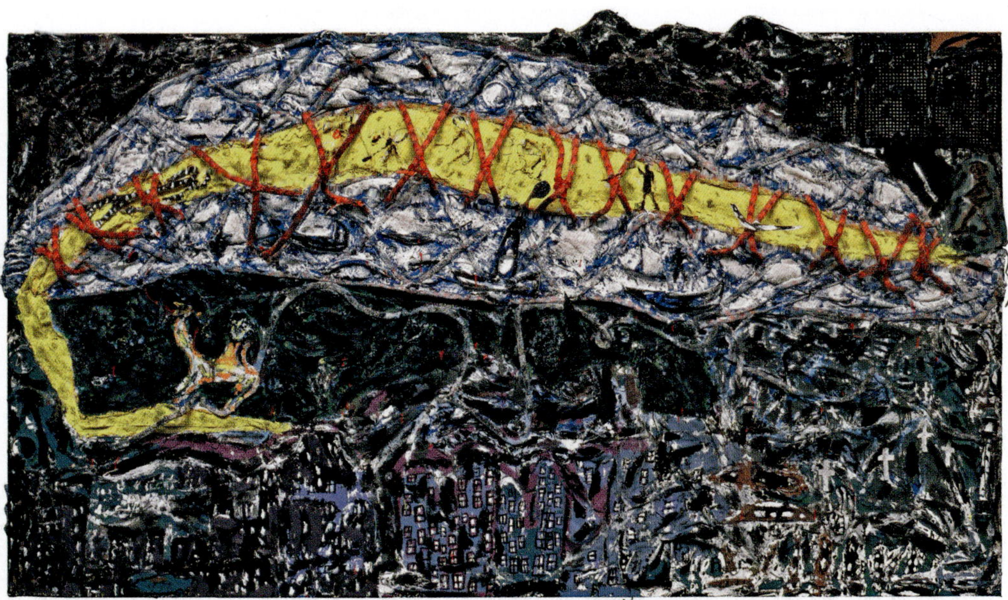

his neighbourhood in Bessemer, Alabama. Once parts of buildings, these materials were already subtly coloured through oxidization, and the weathering of paint applied years before. Aptly, his new medium was *of* his place, both literally and metaphorically, as representative of the rust belt that the area around Birmingham became in the 1980s, as the steel and construction industries on which it had been built faltered and failed. Sheets of tin, nailed onto sheets of weathered plywood or wooden frames, became the ground of pictures from their first
135 utilization. In some pieces, like *Once Something Has Lived it Can Never Really Die* (1996), Lockett fixed the same traced, clipped-tin cutouts of deer and painted branches that are common to earlier *Traps* pictures. More often, he used a new method to create his familiar iconography of deer, buffalo, wolves and figures, using punched-out holes, with strips of tin overlaid and held with flathead nails to develop his forms. In the end, the ground became the work, as in *Oklahoma* (1995), *The Enemy Among Us* (1995) and *Sarah Lockett's Roses* (1997). Inspired by his experience of the Southern African American quilting tradition, and like the Abstract Expressionists Rothko, Still and Hofmann, Lockett's pictorial arena became the image in itself. And like them, the ground-as-image retained its representational force. Here are things that begin in individual human emotion and engagement with the physical and quotidian, but which make of it something transcendent and universal.

Although artists such as Dial, Lockett, Harvey and Holley were clearly highly intelligent and completely committed to their practices, their formal education was negligible, and they had developed and worked without contact with the dominant art world. For a long time, they were inscribed into discourses of ethnicity, the self-taught, outsider and the vernacular. Yet Dial, for example, was the contemporary of the great post-war generation of white southern artists like Robert Rauschenberg (1925–2008) and Jasper Johns (b. 1930). Why was he not also in their pantheon? The answer is partly because, whereas Rauschenberg and Johns embarked on their careers in their twenties, achieving wide recognition early on, Dial was in his late fifties when he fully embraced his calling as artist, after forty years of blue-collar toil. By the time Dial emerged onto the art scene around 1990, the way in which he breathed his art to life was rather unfashionable, sharing many more affinities with the *art informel* of the decades after the Second World War than the increasingly paradigmatic neo-conceptualism of the last two decades of the twentieth century. Moreover, the Neo-Expressionism of the 1980s, to which Dial's work has its most immediate visual comparators in American art had

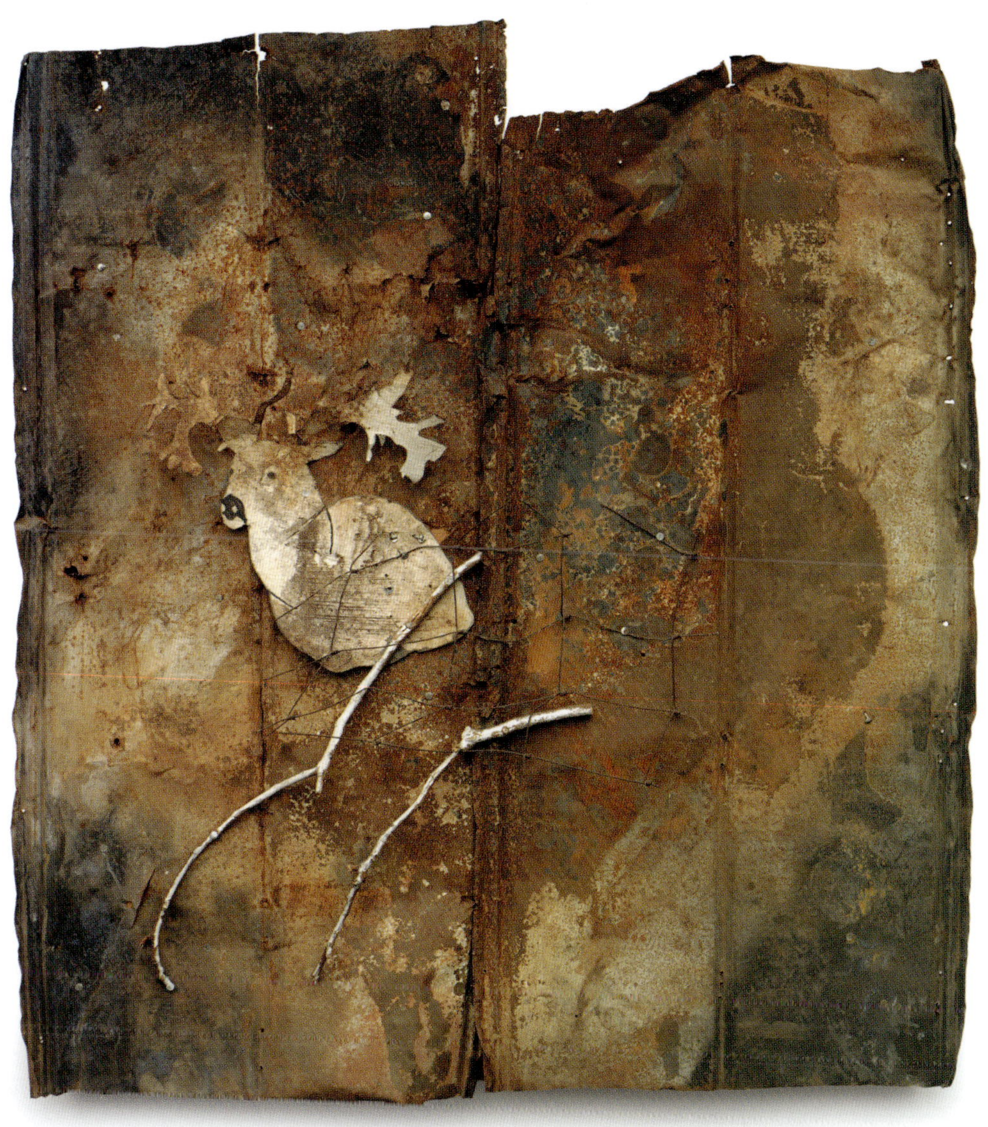

135 Ronald Lockett, *Once Something Has Lived it Can Never Really Die*, 1996

been stopped in its tracks; its (anti-) theoretical underpinnings called to account, as we have seen, by influential critics like Hal Foster, Craig Owens and Benjamin Buchloh and its market value negatively impacted more than most by the financial crash of the late 1980s. The reputations of the Neo-Expressionists like Julian Schnabel and David Salle dipped spectacularly, and post-conceptual art gained an ascendance that is yet to be toppled. So, Dial's arrival on the scene, at the mature age of sixty-two made his work almost impossible to accommodate into narratives of contemporary art at that moment. It was only with the advent of sweeping institutional changes in American museums, driven primarily by sustained public calls for greater accountability, acknowledgement of cultural diversity, and the need for equity, that a space opened to accommodate this art, so that it might now properly take its place in the art historical narrative.

A Contemporary Expressionism?

At the close of the first quarter of the twenty-first century, painting is once again highly visible in contemporary art. A great deal of it has a clear expressionist feel, characterized by directness of touch and a concern for emotional communication over technical polish. Arguably some of the most powerful work has come from women and people of colour who have confidently adopted painterly languages for so long associated stereotypically with white male preserves. This was partly driven by the punk aesthetic that ushered in the German Neue Wilden and near-contemporaries such as Tracey Emin (b. 1963) in Britain, who emerged from a neo-conceptualist aesthetic as part of the YBA (Young British Artists) phenomenon in the late 1980s, but whose sustained commitment to a candid, spontaneous drawing and painting practice led her to become something of a touchstone for many of the new generation of Expressionist-oriented artists. Another important factor lies in a reclaiming and owning of Expressionist primitivist tropes to engage in embodied cultural critique. To some extent the example of Basquiat is a kind of touchstone – and his brand of image-making is now enormously popular. But in Europe especially, there are precedents of artists from the first postcolonial Black diaspora who reclaimed their own cultural forms and imagery through styles related to European Expressionism.

The Surinamese-Javanese artist Soeki Irodikromo (1945–
136 2020) provides a good early example. Works such as *Untitled*
(1971), completed when Suriname was still a Dutch colony,
combine themes and motifs from Javanese mythology and

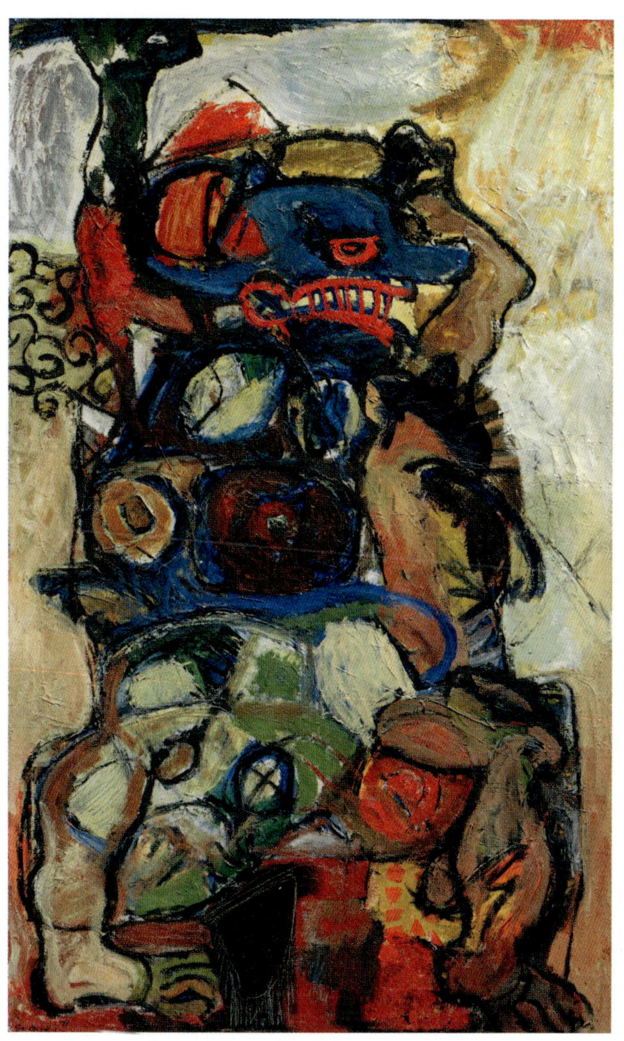

136 Soeki Irodikromo, *Untitled*, 1971

an Expressionist approach to painting influenced by CoBrA. Irodikromo studied in both in Suriname's capital, Paramaribo and Rotterdam. His practice, though, remained based in his home country, whose rich cultural diversity – built since the seventeenth century successively from African slaves, Indian and Javanese contract workers, as well as Dutch colonists and its indigenous population – he celebrated and accommodated in his paintings. Another Surinamese artist Erwin de Vries (1929–2018) found success in the Netherlands originally through portrait sculpture and monuments – indeed he is probably best

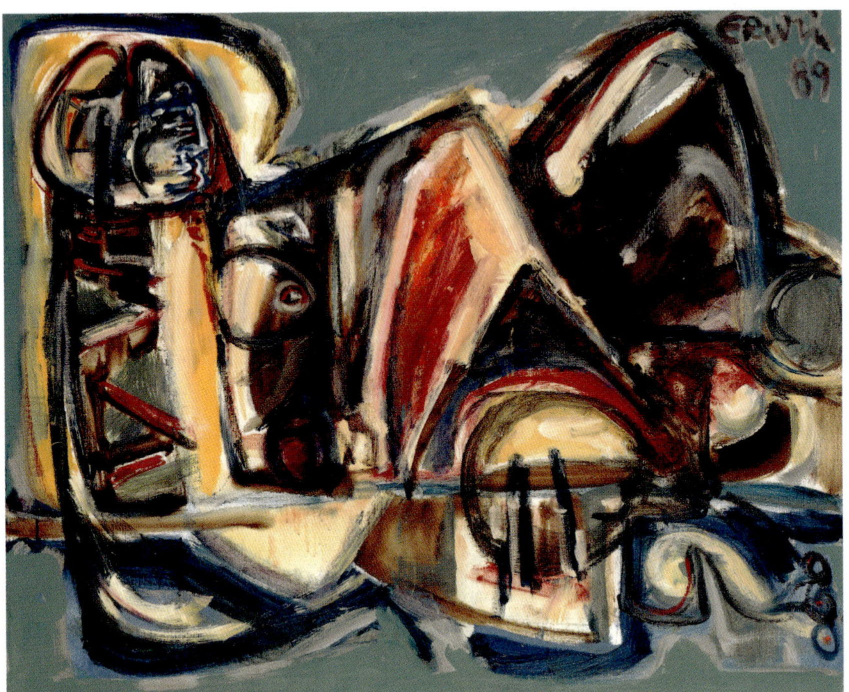

137 Erwin de Vries, *Mexican Woman in Profile*, 1989

known for his National Slavery Monument in Amsterdam. At times, though, his painting was a rich mix of cultural forms,
137 with European Modernism at its core. His *Mexican Woman in Profile* (1989) delivers a punchy Neo-Expressionism that has its roots on CoBrA and Picasso's late Expressionist nudes.

Like many other European countries in the postcolonial period, the population of those born in The Netherlands has grown to include a significant number of people with diverse backgrounds. Where Black artists like Sam Middleton had earlier settled in The Netherlands to escape the racism and lack of opportunity in the United States, new generations of Dutch people of colour have sought to speak about their own experiences of racism and structural inequality in their country. Cultural hybridity and a keen sense of the importance of valuing diversity are at the core of their practices, and their imagery and techniques are as likely as not to draw on and utilize the languages of Expressionism. The Dutch artist Iris Kensmil is of Surinamese descent. In her work she draws on her own experience of being a Black European, engaging in an activist practice that speaks to feminism and celebrates

historical moments in the struggle against Black oppression
138 in a voice that is authentic and visually powerful. *Mellow Dance* (2007) utilizes a figurative Expressionism to speak to the relevance of Black American pop culture. Her work is diverse, drawing, as she says, 'on the European tradition of painting and drawing, on contemporary concepts of image and artist's strategies, and on the history behind my world of experience as a person with black skin.' Like Irodikromo, Michael Tedja (b. 1971) also references CoBrA in his work, although in his case this is done in a highly deliberate way, which places his contemporary use of the expressionist idiom squarely in the context of intentionally choosing an available visual language with the intention of it being recognized as such, with all its
139 attendant cultural resonances. Works such as *Narrow Escape* (2002) seek to replace bourgeois rituals in art with an apparent spontaneity that recalls CoBrA's much vaunted 'freedom'. The work is underpinned, though, by a highly knowing use of cultural and historical reference.

At times activist employment of a direct, figurative expression can result in physical threat to the life of the artist,

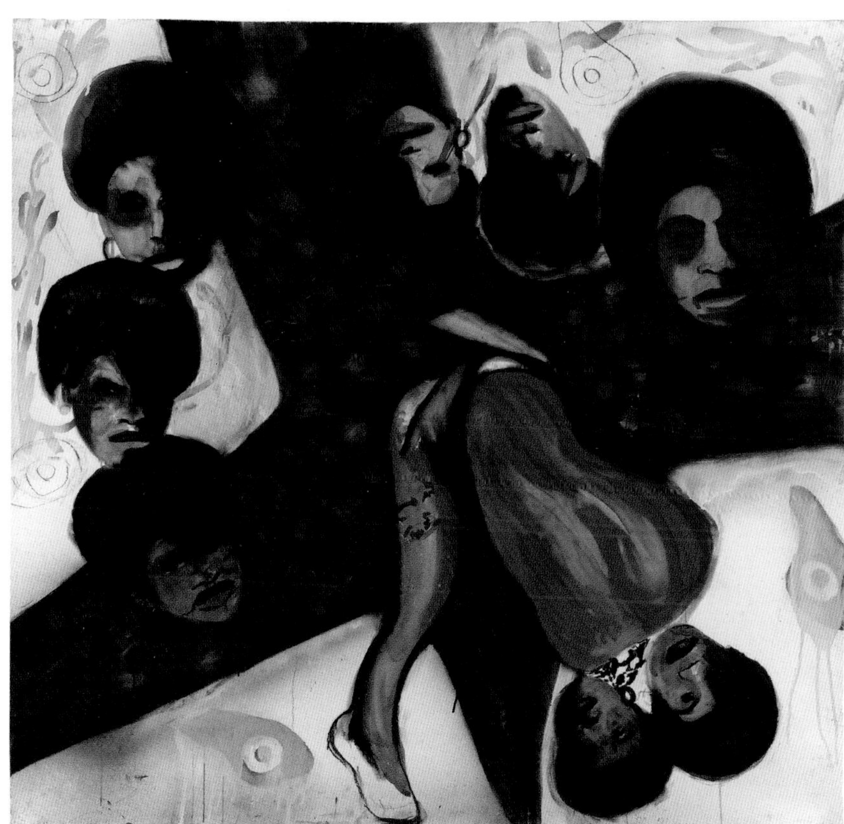

138 Iris Kensmil, *Mellow Dance*, 2007

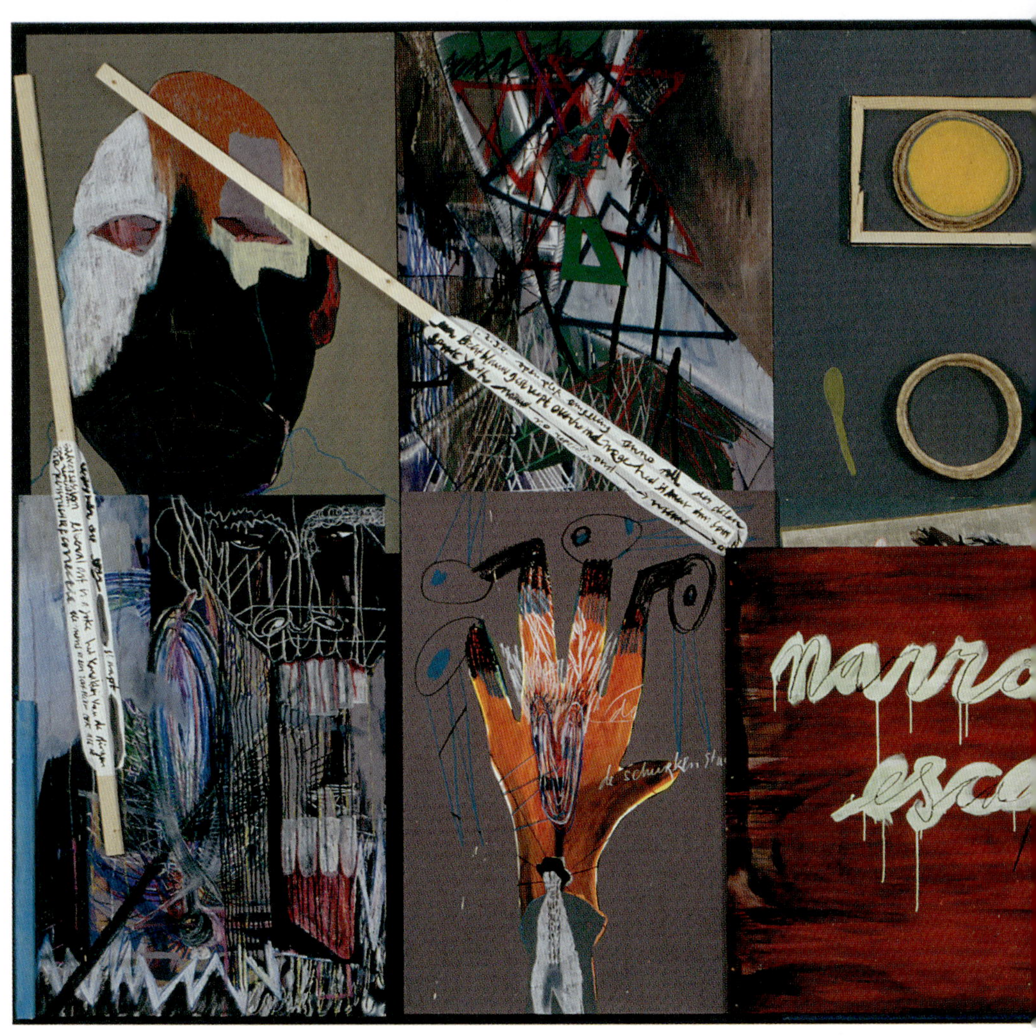

139 Michael Tedja, *Narrow Escape*, 2002

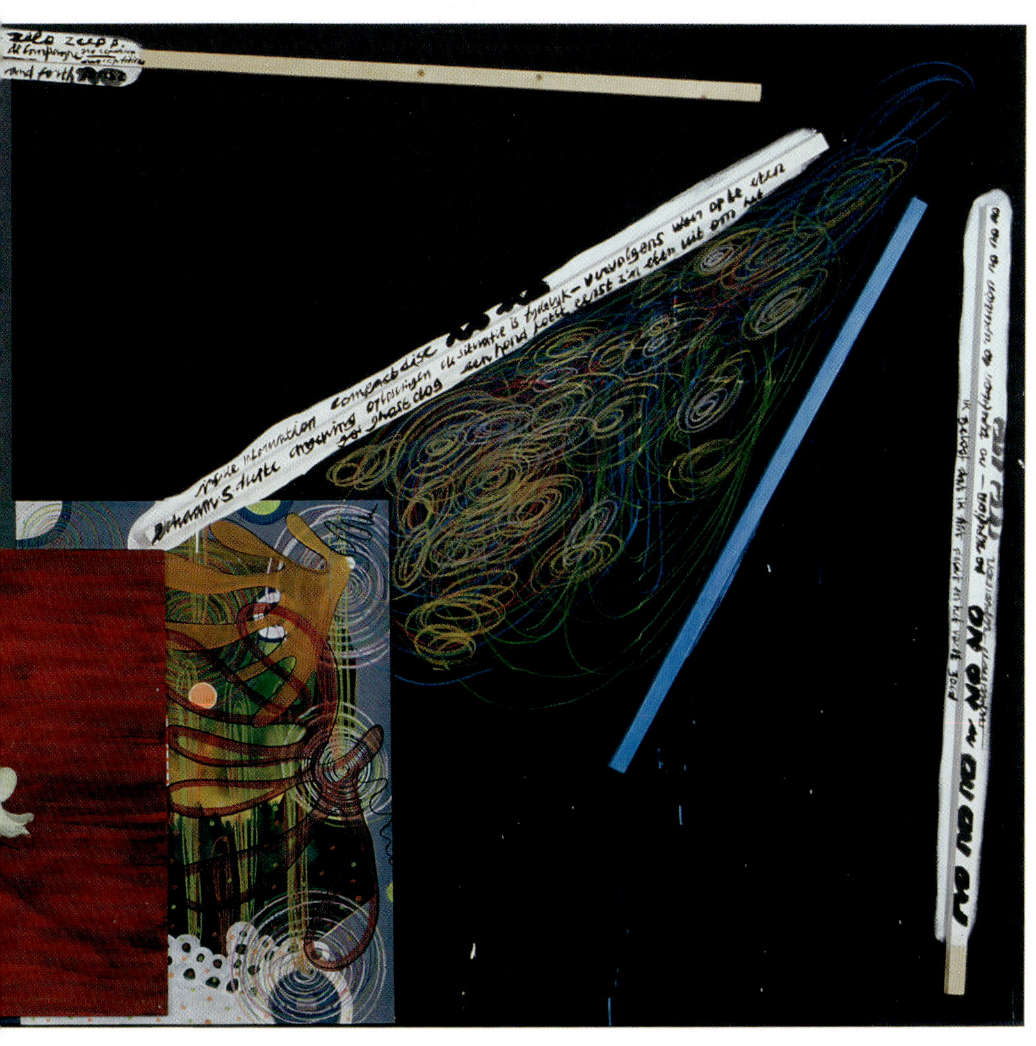

as has been the case with Dutch-Moroccan painter Rachid Ben Ali (b. 1978). His paintings characteristically mix image and text aimed at confronting viewers with social inequity and enacting acts of cultural resistance. He received death threats from Islamist militants after he exhibited works questioning the violent political acts of ruling powers in Iran, resulting in the need for bodyguards for his safety.

Much twenty-first century Expressionism, though, is related more to the individual concerns of artists, who at times appropriate multiple Expressionist languages to speak to histories of art and gendered power structures. The British artist Cecily Brown (b. 1969) makes large, bold paintings that are densely worked and occupy a liminal space where abstraction and figuration meet. Her toolkit of painterly precedents includes not only Abstract Expressionists such as Willem de Kooning, Krasner and Gillian Ayres, but also old masters such as Rubens and Rembrandt. Her methodology, though, is uncontrived. She has only a vague idea of where she wants a painting to end up at the beginning, and her decision-making throughout the process is intuitive rather than intellectual. As she said, 'I want to make forms that are either just dissolving or in the process of just becoming something and to play with the relationship between the eye and the brain.' The eroticism and sexuality in
140 *Trouble in Paradise* is as much a result of Brown's handling of form and colour as it is of the forever nascent figuration that packs the surface. The British painter Lydia Gifford (b. 1979) also emphasizes the importance of intuition in her process, producing a kind of painterly Expressionism in a tradition reaching back through Ayres to Bomberg. Gifford at times paints on domestic textiles that have, as she says, 'a direct and intimate relationship to the body,' such as towels, bedsheets and clothing. She perceives tactile memory in these used materials: 'Bodies, the body gone, the body grown, grief, love, the changing body, ageing, loss, pain, joy and desire.'

The work of artists such Arnaldo Roche Rabell (1955–2018) and Eddie Martinez is much closer to the practices of first-generation Neo-Expressionism. The American artist Martinez makes large-scale, vigorous paintings, with visual languages and iconography that are appropriated at will from a heady mix of sources, from high art precedents such as CoBrA, Guston, Schnabel and
141 Basquiat to street art and popular culture, such as *Outer Worlder*. Although Martinez draws on an index of mediated images, as with Basquiat, the emphasis is on speed and immediacy of image-making in an attempt to achieve some kind of expressive authenticity through directness and spontaneity. Roche Rabell was born and raised in Puerto Rico and after completing an

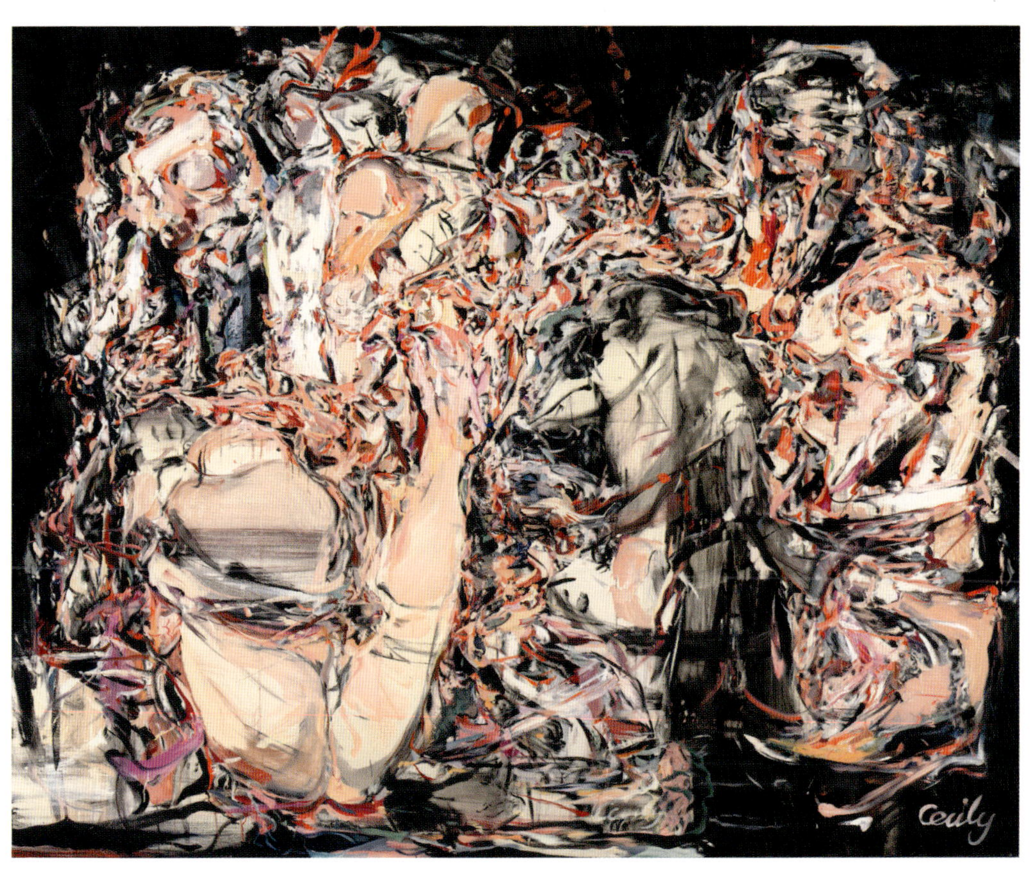

140 Cecily Brown, *Trouble in Paradise*, 1999

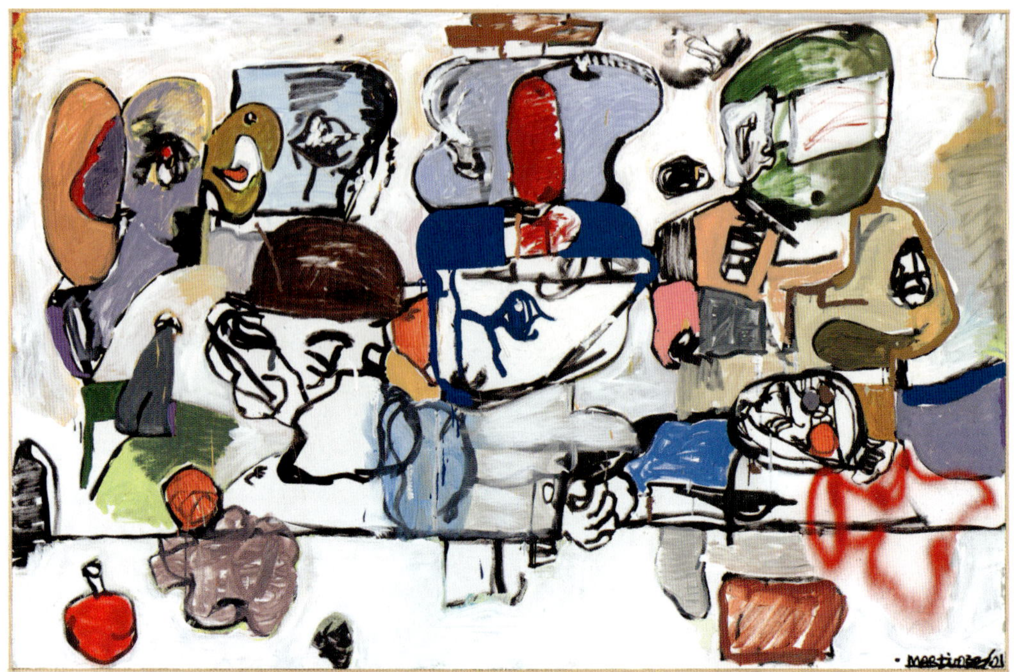

141 Eddie Martinez, *Outer Worlder*, 2021

MFA at the Art Institute of Chicago, split his time between
Puerto Rico and the mainland United States. His work reflects
something of that duality, in terms of both subject matter and
142 technique. Paintings such as *The Subconscious Knows How to Kill
His Son* (1993) exhibit a characteristically vigorous handling of
paint, including violent scraping that accentuates the nightmare
violence of the image.

The painter Tu Hongtao (b. 1976) provides another interesting variation on the possibilities of a contemporary Expressionism. He grew up in southwestern China during a period of rapid social and economic change, initially adopting a neo-pop style that was popular in both the Chinese and international contemporary art markets at the turn of the century. By 2010 he had shifted his focus to paintings that bring together European abstract Expressionist painting practices and the spatial conventions of traditional Chinese landscape ink painting. This performs a sort of inversion of the paths taken by some of the Abstract Expressionists and others such as the Scottish-Australian Ian
Fairweather. The destination, however, was similar, with paintings
143 such as Tu's *Wind Through the Valley* (2018–19) employing an
intuitive, layered mark-making from which a more spiritual sense

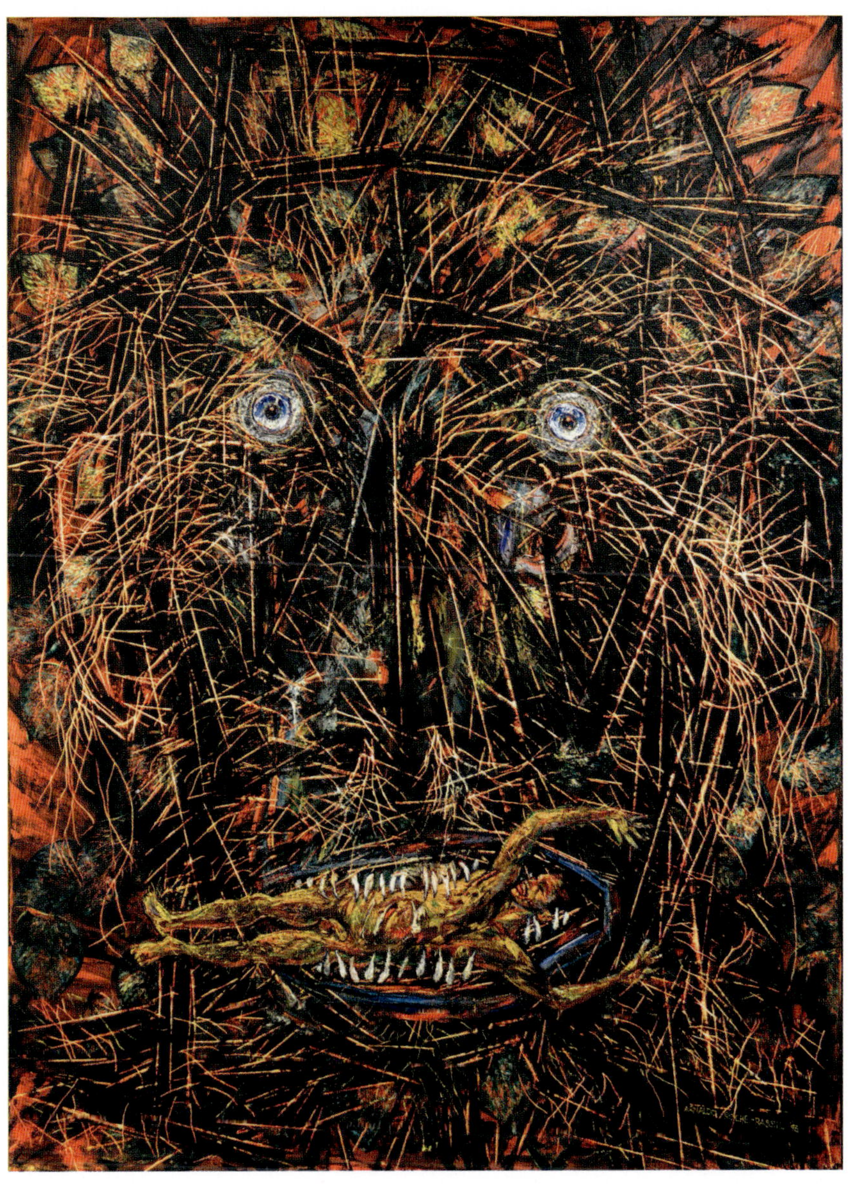

142 Arnaldo Roche Rabell, *The Subconscious Knows How to Kill His Son*, 1993

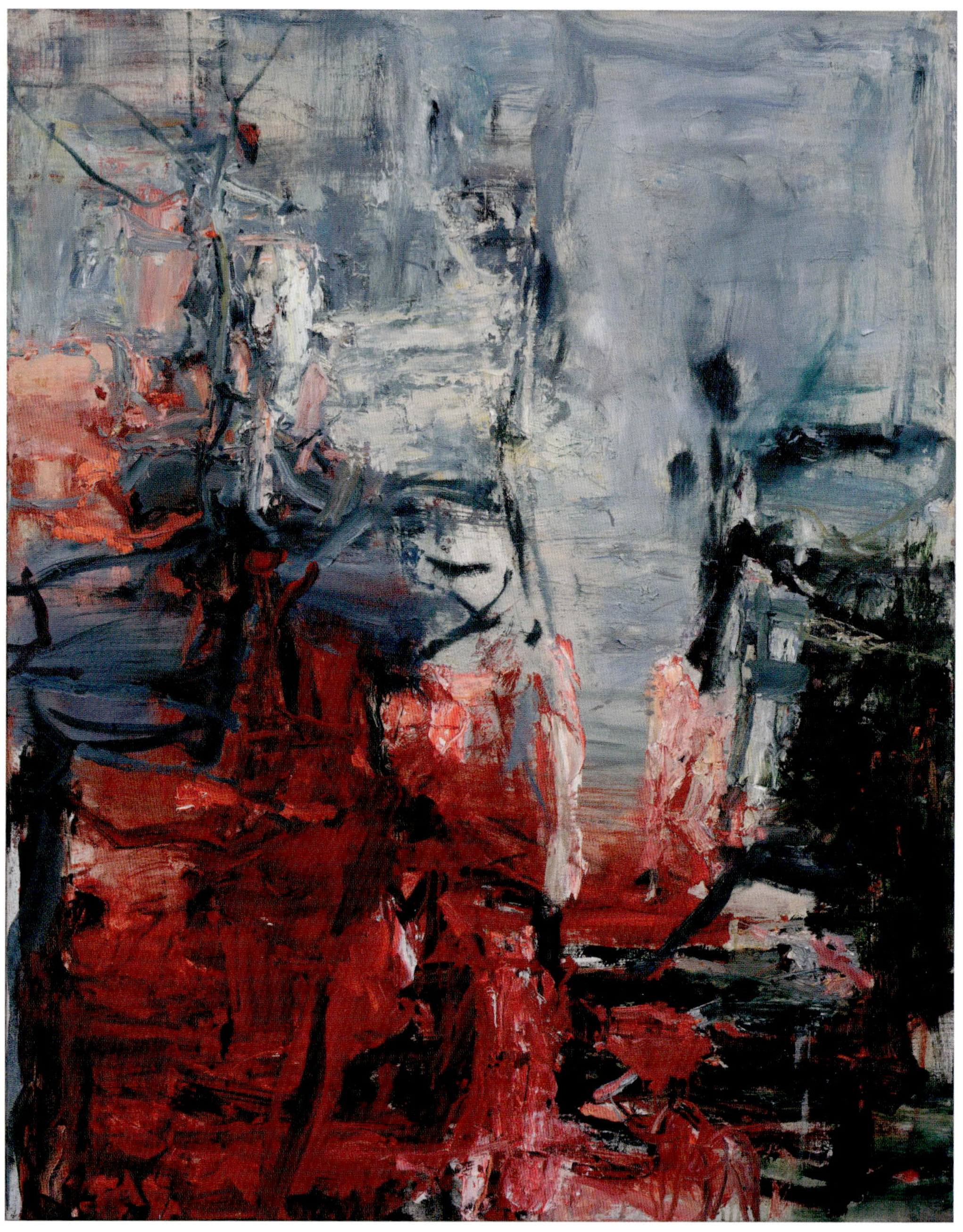

143 Tu Hongtao, *Wind Through the Valley*, 2018–19

of space and place emerges. In a world dominated by technology and the easily consumed mediated image, these are paintings that viewers feels as much as they see.

Coda

The memory of new work by two artists sticks out from my regular visits to commercial galleries in Cork Street, London as an art student in the early 1980s. The first were paintings by Jean Dubuffet executed in a direct, graphic style using only black, white, blue and red. They seemed to me exuberant and energetic, full of eager questing. It was, then, quite a surprise to discover that they were the work of a person already in his eighties. The others were recent works by John Walker. At a time when it was still unusual to find good contemporary Expressionist painting in blue-chip London galleries, Walker's work was refreshing, and I responded directly to the way in which he handled paint and the push and pull he achieved between figuration and abstraction. Four decades later I encountered his new work again in a gallery in the same London street. As with Dubuffet previously, here was a person now in his eighties creating paintings that exude freshness and vitality. In works
144 such as *Clock and Shell* and *Black Pond* (2022), Walker employs an Expressionist painterly lexicon that reaches all the way back to Matisse, but which is infused with the contemporary and a powerful feeling of a sense of place, and specifically of the part of New England that the artist has called home since 1989.

If Walker's work appears to prove that the sincere Expressionist gesture remains a possibility in contemporary art, there are other artists near the beginning of their careers who point to that possibility existing and perhaps gaining strength in the future. Jadé Fadojutimi (b.1993) and Zhang Zipiao (b.1993) both make vigorous paintings whose hallmarks are urgent mixes of calligraphic mark-making and gestural sweeps of liquid paint that speak to Expressionist sensibility. Although apparently abstract at first sight, there is figuration that is either nascent or disguised in works such as Fadojutimi's *An Empathic Revolution* (2022) and *A Permeable*
145 *Existence* (2022) and Zhang's *Pomegranate 05* (2021) and *Brain 04* (2023) that speaks in their very embodiment to the artists' inner experience. Like Kandinsky, Fadojutimi experiences synaesthesia, which means that for her colours literally have both emotional and physical affect, adding to the sense that here are paintings that might have the power to communicate powerfully and directly with viewers at a visceral level. The process of painting is for her intense, requiring periods of introspection before bursting into action, echoing the almost

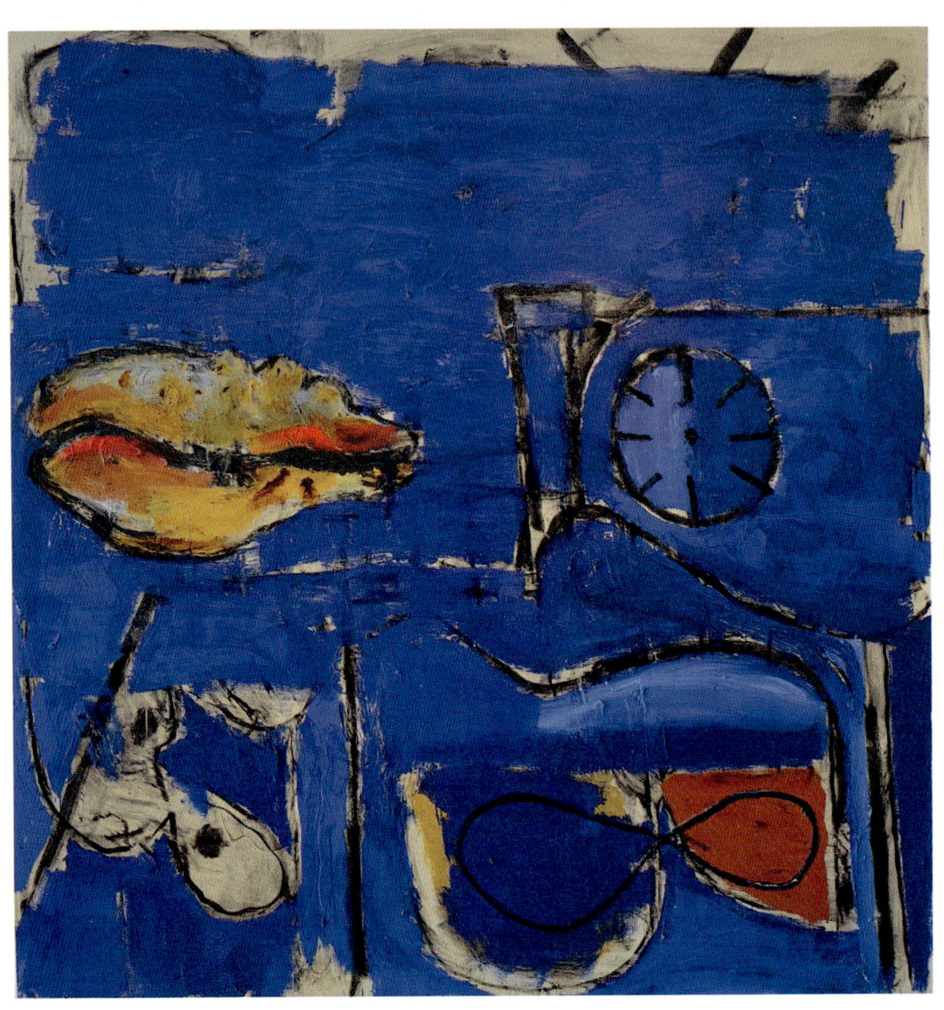

144 ABOVE John Walker, *Clock and Shell*, 2022
145 OPPOSITE Zhang Zipiao, *Brain 04*, 2023

ritualistic performative practices of artists such as Pollock, Mitchell and Frankenthaler. Zhang similarly approaches painting with intense emotion and energy, inspired in part by early experiences of seeing images of surgeries on screen over the shoulder of her doctor mother, and later through Francis Bacon's visceral expressionism. The sense of urgency and an overwhelming urge to create is central to Expressionist aesthetics, from the quiet contemplative habits of Matisse or Rothko to the performative approaches of Pollock or Mitchell. If a lot of artists working in an Expressionist idiom today are women that might be because they feel able to appropriate and exploit that language precisely to reclaim it from its gendered past, whereas for a man this could be more problematic. That contemporary viewers react as strongly and immediately to the tangible residue of Fadojutumi's and Zhang's creative operations – the art object – as to those of their expressionist forebears is surely a hopeful sign for the future.

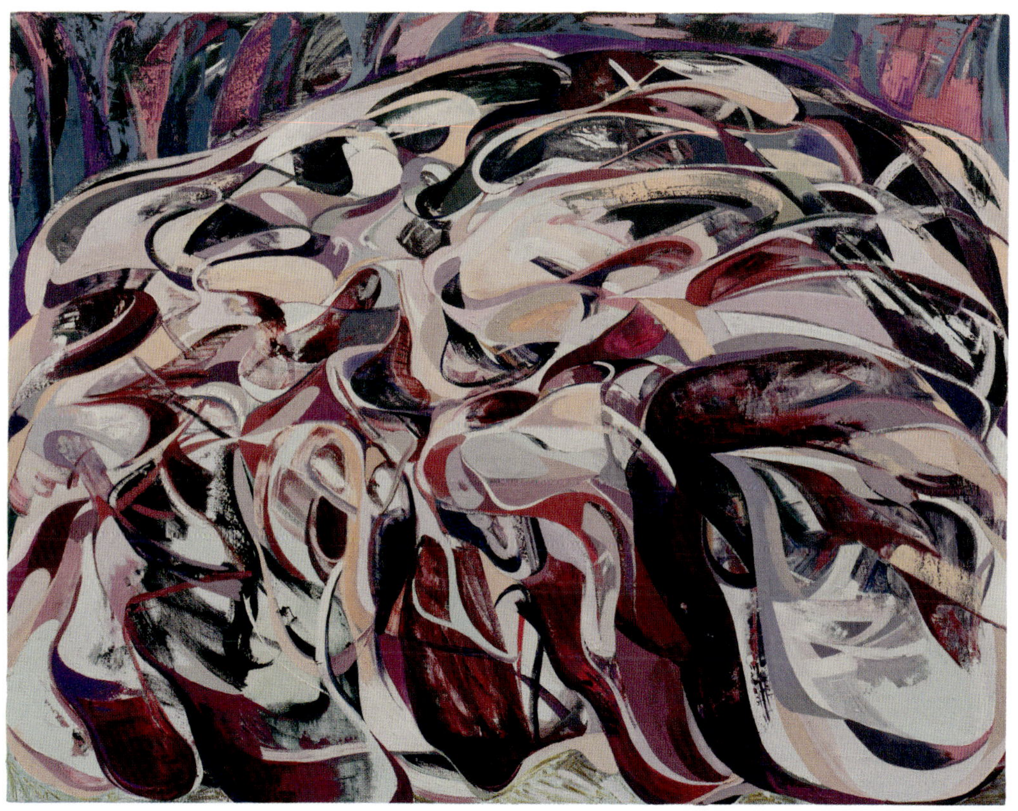

Acknowledgments

This project has been very long in its gestation, and thus many people deserve thanks for their help, support and inspiration along the way. First, and most importantly, I owe a profound debt of gratitude to my family, especially Nicky, Anna, Teresa, Lile, Sophie and Tilly. The experience of August Wiedmann's teaching at Goldsmiths, University of London was foundational to my interest in expressionism, which was deepened subsequently during postgraduate study at the University of Essex with Peter Vergo. The department at Essex at that time was a hothouse of ideas, expertise and bonhomie. Those who touched me intellectually and as friends are too many to name here in full. My thanks go to them all, in particular Neil Cox, John M. Nash, Brett Gorvy, Christian Weikop, Dorothy Price and Shulamith Behr. Other colleagues who provided insights and support along the way include Gill Perry, Paul Wood, Mieke Rijnders, Roger Cardinal, William Arnett and Bernard Herman. The person who first got me thinking that expressionism might be bigger and more connected than received art history suggests was Donald E. Gordon, whose books I first read long ago, but who sadly I never had the opportunity to meet. Thanks are also due to everyone at Thames and Hudson for their support and work, including Mohara Gill, Yasmin Garcha, Ilona de Nemethy Sanigar and especially Roger Thorp, who believed in this project from the start.

Select Bibliography and Further Reading

This bibliography is primarily a list of sources used for the quotations in this book and a selection of some of the more important contributions to the discourse on expressionism in the past century or so. Except in a limited number of cases sources have been restricted to those available in English. Tellingly most available books on expressionism are devoted to just one of the named expressionist 'movements' covered in dominant art histories, notably German Expressionism, American Abstract Expressionism and CoBrA, with Fauvism generally considered outside the context of expressionism. The voices of artists and their contemporary critics have been important to the construction of the narrative in this book, and much of this conversation has since been collected in anthologies of primary sources. The ones that have been most useful to this project are listed here. Monographs of individual artists have not been included since even a highly selective list would run to many pages. Books on many of the artists discussed are readily available and good information on all of them is freely accessible online, including in many cases the artists' own websites or ones set up by their estates or foundations.

Anthologies of Primary Sources

Flam, Jack D., ed., *Matisse on Art*, Oxford, 1984

Flam, Jack and Deutch, Miriam, eds, *Primitivism and Twentieth-Century Art: A Documentary History*, Berkeley and London, 2003

Frascina, Francis and Harrison, Charles, eds, *Modern Art and Modernism: A Critical Anthology*, London, 1982

Harrison, Charles and Wood, Paul, eds, *Art in Theory 1900–2000: An Anthology of Changing Ideas* (2nd Edition), Oxford, 2002

Kandinsky, Wassily and Marc, Franz, eds, *The Blaue Reiter Almanac*, New York, 1989

Lindsay, Kenneth and Vergo, Peter, eds, *Kandinsky: Complete Writings on Art*, New York, 1994

Long, Rose-Carol Washton, ed., *German Expressionism: Documents from the End of the Wilhelmine Empire to the Rise of National Socialism*, Berkeley and London, 1995

Miesel, Victor H., ed., *Voices of German Expressionism*, London, 2003

Shapiro, David and Cécile, eds, *Abstract Expressionism, a critical record*, Cambridge, 1990

Select Bibliography

Akinsha, Konstantin, *Russian Modernism: Cross-Currents of German and Russian Art, 1907–1917*, Munich, 2015

Anfam, David, *Abstract Expressionism*, London, 1990

Anfam, David and Davidson, Susan, *Abstract Expressionism*, London, 2016

Arnett, William and Paul, eds, *Souls Grown Deep*, 2 vols, Atlanta, 2000/2001

Ashton, Dore, *The New York School: A Cultural Reckoning*, Harmondsworth, 1983

Bahr, Herman, *Expressionism*, London, 1925

Barkan, Elazar and Bush, Ronald, eds, *Prehistories of the Future: The Primitivist Project and the Culture of Modernism*, Stanford, 1995

Barron, Stephanie, ed., *German Expressionism 1915–1925: The Second Generation*, Munich, 1988

Barron, Stephanie, ed., *"Degenerate Art" – The Fate of the Avant Garde in Nazi Germany*, Los Angeles, 1991

Barron, Stephanie and Dube, Wolf-Dieter, eds, *German Expressionism: Art and Society 1909–1923*, London, 1997

Behr, Shulamith, Fanning, David and Jarman, Douglas, *Expressionism Reassessed*, Manchester, 1993

Behr, Shulamith, *Women Expressionists*, Oxford, 1988

Behr, Shulamith, *Women Artists in Expressionism: From Empire to Emancipation*, Princeton, 2022

Benson, Timothy O., *Expressionist Utopias: Paradise, Metropolis, Architectural Fantasy*, Los Angeles, 1993

Bronner, Stephen Eric and Kellner, Douglas, eds, *Passion and Rebellion: The Expressionist Heritage*, New York, 1988
Cardinal, Roger, *Expressionism*, London, 1984
Cheney, Sheldon, *Expressionism in Art*, New York, 1934
Clutton-Brock, A[rthur], 'The Post-Impressionists', *The Burlington Magazine*, 18, January 1911
Darwent, Charles, *Surrealists in New York: Atelier 17 and the Birth of Abstract Expressionism*, London, 2023
Dodenhoff, Benjamin and Heinlein, Ramona, eds, *The Invention of the Neue Wilde: Painting and Subculture Around 1980*, Berlin, 2019
Duncan, Carol, 'Virility and Domination in Early 20th Century Vanguard Painting,' *Artforum*, December 1973
Einstein, Carl, *Carl Einstein: Selected Writings on Art*, Chicago, 2020
Elderfield, John, *The Wild Beasts: Fauvism and Its Affinities*, New York, 1984
Elger, Dietmar, *Expressionism*, Cologne, 2003
Fechter, Paul, *Expressionismus*, Munich, 1914
Finger, Anke and Shoults, Julie, eds, *Women in German Expressionism: Gender, Sexuality and Activism*, Ann Arbor, 2023
Foster, Hal, 'The Expressive Fallacy', *Art in America*, January 1983
Fry, Roger, 'Children's Drawings', *The Burlington Magazine*, 30, June 1917
Gabriel, Mary, *Ninth Street Women: Lee Krasner, Elaine de Kooning, Grace Hartigan, Joan Mitchell and Helen Frankenthaler: Five Painters and the Movement that Changed Modern Art*, New York, 2019
Gibson, Ann Eden, 'Abstract Expressionism's Evasion of Language,' *Art Journal*, Fall 1988
Gibson, Ann Eden, *Abstract Expressionism: Other Politics*, New Haven and London, 1997
Gilman, Sander L., *Difference and Pathology: Stereotypes of Sexuality, Race and Madness*, Ithaca, 1985
Goldwater, Robert, *Primitivism in Modern Art*, Cambridge, MA., 1986
Gombrich, E. H., *The Preference for the Primitive*, London, 2002
Gordon, Donald E., 'On the Origin of the Word "Expressionism"', *Journal of the Warburg and Courtauld Institutes*, 29, 1966
Gordon, Donald E., *Expressionism: Art & Idea*, New Haven and London, 1987
Greaves, Kerry, 'Hell-Horse: Radical Art and Resistance in Nazi-Occupied Denmark', *Oxford Art Journal*, March 2014
Green, Christopher, *Art Made Modern: Roger Fry's Vision of Art*, London, 1999
Guilbaut, Serge, *How New York Stole the Idea of Modern Art: Abstract Expressionism, Freedom and the Cold War*, Chicago, 1983
Haks, Frans and Bartelink, Nicolette, *De Ploeg – Verzameld in Het Groninger Museum*, Groningen, 1993
Heller, Reinhold, *Confronting Identities in German Art: Myths, Reactions, Reflections*, Chicago, 2002
Herbert, Barry, *German Expressionism: Die Brücke and Der Blaue Reiter*, London, 1983
Herbert, James D., *Fauve Painting – The Making of Cultural Politics*, New Haven and London, 1992
Hobbs, Robert and Levin, Gail, *Abstract Expressionism: The Formative Years*, Ithaca, 1981
Hoberg, Annegret, *Wassily Kandinsky and Gabriele Münter*, Munich, 1994
Höchdorfer, Achim, '1,000 Words: Maria Lassnig', interview in *Artforum*, 46/10, Summer 2008, pp. 404–07
Huizinga, Johan, *Homo Ludens: A Study of the Play Element in Culture*, Boston, 1955
Klingsöhr-Leroy, Cathrin, ed., *Der Große Widerspruch: Franz Marc zwischen Delaunay und Rousseau*, Kochel, 2009
Kurczynski, Karen, 'Expression as Vandalism: Asger Jorn's "Modifications"', *RES: Anthropology and Aesthetics*, Spring-Autumn 2008
Kuspit, Donald B., 'An Appeal for Empathy', *Art in America*, November 1984
Kuspit, Donald and Waldman, Diane, *The New Subjectivism: Art in the 1980's*, New York, 1993
Joachimides, Christos M., Rosenthal, Norman, and Schmied, Wieland, eds, *German Art in the Twentieth Century: Painting and Sculpture 1905–1985*, London, 1985
Joachimides, Christos M., Rosenthal, Norman, and Serota, Nicholas, *A New Spirit in Painting*, London, 1981
Lambert, Jean-Clarence, *Cobra*, London, 1983
Landau, Ellen G., *Reading Abstract Expressionism: Context and Critique*, Newhaven, 2005
Landau, Ellen G., and Joan M. Marter, *Abstract Expressionism: The Women*, London, 2023
Leja, Michael, *Reframing Abstract Expressionism: Subjectivity and Painting in the 1940s*, Newhaven, 1993
Lloyd, Jill, *German Expressionism: Primitivism and Modernity*, New Haven and London, 1991
Lovejoy, Arthur O. and Boas, George, *Primitivism and Related Ideas in Antiquity*, Baltimore, 1997

Lübbren, Nina, *Rural Artists' Colonies in Europe 1870–1910*, Manchester, 2001

Lynton, Norbert, Gage, John et al, *Towards a New Art: Essays on the Background to Abstract Art, 1910–20*, London, 1980

Malychava, Tanja and Wünsche, Isabel, *Marianne Werefkin and the Women Artists in Her Circle*, Leiden, 2017

Marter, Joan and Chanzit, Gwen, *Women of Abstract Expressionism*, New Haven and London, 2016

Marter, Joan, ed., *Abstract Expressionism: The International Context*, New Brunswick, NJ, 2004

Masheck, Joseph, '"Primitive" authenticity and German Expressionism', *RES*, Autumn 1982

Meyers, Bernard S., *Expressionism: A Generation in Revolt*, London, 1963

Mühling, Matthias, Hoberg, Annegret, and Straetmans, eds, *Group Dynamics: The Blue Rider*, Munich, 2021

Nordau, Max, *Degeneration*, Eastford, CT, 2014

Owens, Craig, 'Honor, Power and the Love of Women', *Art in America*, January 1983

Pauwels, Peter, De Raedt, Thijs, and Tempel, Benno, *Vlaams Expressionisme. Heerlijke herinneringen*, The Hague, 2023

Perkins, G. C., 'Expressionism in German Painting 1910–1920', *Germania*, 3/1, 1964

Pickar, Gertrud and Webb, Karl Eugen, eds, *Expressionism Reconsidered*, Munich, 1979

Price, Dorothy, ed., *German Expressionism: Der Blaue Reiter and its Legacies*, Manchester, 2020

Price, Dorothy et al., *Making Modernism: Paula Modersohn-Becker, Käthe Kollwitz, Gabrielle Münter, Marianne Werefkin*, London, 2022

Raabe, Paul, ed., *The Era of German Expressionism*, London, 1974

Ratcliff, Carter, 'The Short Life of the Sincere Stroke', *Art in America*, January 1983

Rewald, John, *Studies in Post-Impressionism*, London, 1986

Rhodes, Colin, *Primitivism and Modern Art*, London, 1994

Rhodes, Colin, 'Primitivism: The Primordium Lost and Found and Reinvented', in Zilman, Kitty and Van Damme, Wilfried, eds, *World Art Studies: Exploring Concepts and Approaches*, Amsterdam, 2008

Rhodes, Colin, 'Cobra', in Martis, Adi, ed., *Stedelijk Collection Reflections: Reflections on the Collection of the Stedelijk Museum Amsterdam*, Amsterdam, 2012

Rhodes, Colin, 'Expressionist Dial: Or Thinking Around Canonicity', in Herman, Bernard L., ed., *'They Say You Can't Draw!' Thornton Dial, Sr., First Works-On-Paper, 1990–1991*, Chapel Hill, NC, 2012

Rijnders, Mieke and Martis, Adi, eds, *Expressionisme en primitivisme in de beelende kunst van twintigste eeuw*, Heerlen, 1998

Rosenblum, Robert, *Modern Painting and the Northern Romantic Tradition: Friedrich to Rothko*, London, 1975

Rubin, William, ed., *Primitivism in 20th Century Art: Affinity of the Tribal and Modern*, 2 vols, New York, 1984

Sandler, Irving, *The Triumph of American Painting: A History of Abstract Expressionism*, London, 1976

Sandler, Irving, *Abstract Expressionism and the American Experience: A Re-evaluation*, New York, 2009

Selz, Peter, *German Expressionist Painting*, Berkeley and London, 1974

Smith, Laura, ed. *Action, Gesture, Paint: Women Artists and Global Abstraction 1940–1970*, London, 2023

Sidlina, Natalia, ed., *Expressionists: Kandinsky, Münter and the Blue Rider*, London, 2024

Stevens, MaryAnne, *After Impressionism: Inventing Modern Art*, New Haven and London, 2023

Stokvis, Willemijn, *Cobra: The Last Avant-Garde Movement of the Twentieth Century*, Aldershot, 2004

Sydow, Eckart von, *Die deutsche expressionistische Kultur und Malerei*, Berlin, 1919

Tapié, Michel, *Un Art Autre*, Paris, 1952

Thoene, Peter, *Modern German Art*, Harmondsworth, 1938

Torgovnik, Marianna, *Gone Primitive: Savage Intellects, Modern Lives*, Chicago, 1990

Vergo, Peter, *Art in Vienna 1898–1918: Klimt, Kokoschka, Schiele and their Contemporaries*, Oxford, 1981

Viatte, Germain and Cousseau, Henry-Claude, *Aftermath: France 1945–54. New Images of Man*, London, 1982

Vogt, Paul, *Expressionism: German Painting 1905–1920*, New York, 1980

Wasensteiner, Lucy, *The Twentieth Century German Art Exhibition: Answering Degenerate Art in 1930's London*, 2018

Washton, Rose-Carol, 'Kandinsky's Paintings on Glass', *Artforum*, February 1967

Weinstein, Joan, *The End of Expressionism: Art and the November Revolution in Germany 1918–19*, Chicago, 1990

Welling, Dolf, *The Expressionists: The Art of Prewar Expressionism in the Netherlands*, Amsterdam, 1968
Werenskiold, Marit, *The Concept of Expressionism: Origin and Metamorphosis*, Oslo, 1984
Weikop, Christian, ed., *New Perspectives on Brücke Expressionism: Bridging History*, Surrey, 2011
Whitfield, Sarah, *Fauvism*, London, 1991
Whitford, Frank, *Expressionism*, London, 1970
Wiedmann, August, *Romantic Roots in Modern Art*, Woking, 1979
Wiedmann, August, *The German Quest for Primal Origins in Art, Culture, and Politics 1900–1933: Die 'Flucht in Urzustände*, Lewiston, 1995
Willett, John, *Expressionism*, London, 1970
Worringer, Wilhelm, *Abstraction and Empathy: A Contribution to the Psychology of Style*, Chicago, 1997
Worringer, Wilhelm, *Form in Gothic*, London 1927
Wünsche, Isabel, ed., *The Routledge Companion to Expressionism in a Transnational Context*, London, 2019

List of Illustrations

Dimensions are in centimetres, followed by inches, height before width before depth

1 Irma Stern, *Girl in a Print Dress*, 1939. Oil, 69 × 66.5 (27¼ × 26¼). Courtesy of the Trustees of the Irma Stern Collection, Cape Town. © The Irma Stern Trust, DACS 2024

2 Gabriele Münter, *Sinnende (Sensitive)*, 1917. Oil on canvas, 66 × 99.5 (26 × 39¼). Städtische Galerie im Lenbachhaus und Kunstbau, Munich, Gabriele Münter Stiftung 1957. © DACS 2024

3 Wols, *Grenade bleue (The Blue Grenade)*, 1946. Oil on canvas, 46 × 33 (17⅜ × 13). Centre Pompidou, Paris, MNAM-CCI (AM 1971-4)

4 Gillian Ayres, *Sun Up*, 1960. Oil on canvas, 122 × 91.5 (48⅛ × 36⅛). Photo Victoria Art Gallery, Bath, North East Somerset Council. © The Estate of Gillian Ayres

5 Joan Mitchell, *Piano mécanique*, 1957. Oil on canvas, 198.12 × 317.183 (78 × 124⅞). National Gallery of Art, Washington, DC. © Estate of Joan Mitchell

6 Paul Gauguin, *Contes barbares (Barbarian Tales)*, 1902, Oil on canvas, 150 × 109 × 8 (59⅛ × 43¼ × 3). Museum Folkwang, acquired in 1903/04 for the Museum Folkwang, Hagen, since 1922 Essen (Inv. G 54.)

7 Vincent van Gogh, *Le parc de l'hôpital, à Saint-Rémy (A Corner of the Asylum and the Garden with a Heavy, Sawed-Off tree)*, 1889. Oil on canvas, 75 × 93.5 (29⅝ × 36⅞). Museum Folkwang. Inv. G 64. Acquired 1905 for the Museum Folkwang, Hagen, since 1922 Essen

8 Maurice de Vlaminck, *Les Coteaux de Rueil*, 1906. Oil on canvas, 48 × 56 (19 × 22⅛). Centre Pompidou, Paris, MNAM-CCI (Inv. AM 2675 P). © ADAGP, Paris and DACS, London 2024

9 Henri Matisse, *Femme au chapeau* (Woman with a Hat), 1905. Oil on canvas, 80.65 × 59.69 (31¾ × 23⅜). Collection SFMOMA San Francisco Museum of Modern Art, bequest of Elise S. Haas

10 Henri Matisse, *Le Luxe I*, 1907. 210 × 138 × 2.4 (82¾ × 54⅜ × 1). Centre Pompidou, MNAM-CCI (AM 2586 P)

11 Émilie Charmy, *L'Éstaque*, *c.* 1910. Oil on canvas, 57.3 × 73.7 (22½ × 29). The Art Institute of Chicago/Art Resource, NY/Scala, Florence. © ADAGP, Paris and DACS, London 2024

12 Henri Matisse, *The Moroccans*, 1916–17. Oil on canvas, 181.3 × 279.4 (71⅜ × 110). Museum of Modern Art, New York, Gift of Mr. and Mrs. Samuel A. Marx

13 Erich Heckel, *Brickworks*, 1907. Oil on canvas, 68 × 86 (26⅞ × 33⅞). Thyssen-Bornemisza Collection, Inv. 579 (1965.12). © DACS 2024

14 Emil Nolde, *Dance Around the Golden Calf*, 1910. Oil on canvas, 87.5 × 105 (34½ × 41⅜). Photo Scala, Florence/bpk, Bildagentur fuer Kunst, Kultur und Geschichte, Berlin. © Nolde Stiftung Seebüll

15 Erich Heckel, *Badende am Waldteich (Bathers at the Forest Pond)*, 1909. 82.2 × 96.2 (32⅜ × 37⅞). National Museum, Oslo (Loan from Sparebankstiftelsen DNB 2015) Photo Børre Høstland. © DACS 2024

16 Oskar Kokoschka, The Bride of the Wind, 1914. Oil on canvas, 181 × 220 (46½ × 86⅝) Kunstmuseum, Basel. © Fondation Oskar Kokoschka/DACS 2024

17 Karl Schmidt-Rottluff, *Three Nudes (Dune Painting from Nidden)*, 1913. Oil on canvas, 98 × 106.5 (38⅝ × 42). Staatliche Museen zu Berlin, Nationalgalerie. 1949 Purchase from the Galerie Schüler, Berlin, by the State of Berlin for the Gallery of the 20th Century (West). © DACS 2024

18 Ernst Ludwig Kirchner, *Women on Potsdamer Platz*, 1914. Woodcut on wove cardboard, 57.6 × 39 (22¾ × 15⅜). Städel Museum, Acquired in 1948 as a donation from the heirs of the Carl Hagemann estate

19 Max Pechstein, *In den Dünen (In the Dunes)*, 1911. Oil on canvas, 76 × 100 (30 × 39⅜) Centre Georges Pompidou, Paris (AM 4289 P.o). Don de la Société des Amis du Musée national d'art moderne, 1965

20 Max Pechstein, *Zwei Frauenackte im Zimmer*, 1909. 49.5 × 65.5 (19½ × 25⅞). Museum Ludwig, Cologne. Photo akg-images. © Pechstein Hamburg/Tökendorf/DACS 2024

21 Ernst Ludwig Kirchner, *Frauenbildnis (Portrait of a Woman)*, 1911. Oil on canvas, 117.79 × 87.95 (46⅜ × 34⅝). Collection Buffalo AKG

Art Museum. General Purchase Funds, 1957 (1957:3R). Photo Brenda Bieger, Buffalo AKG Art Museum.
22 Edvard Munch, *Dance of Life*, 1899–1900. Oil on canvas, 191 × 125 (75¼ × 49¼). National Museum, Oslo (NG.M.00941)
23 Emil Nolde, *Prophet*, 1912. Woodcut on paper, 32.3 × 22 (12¾ × 8¾). British Museum, London (1980,1011.45). © Nolde Stiftung Seebüll
24 Marianne Werefkin, *Wäsherinnen (Washerwomen)*, *c.* 1909. 50.5 × 64.6 (20 × 25½). Städtische Galerie im Lenbachhaus und Kunstbau, Munich, Gabriele Münter Stiftung 1957 (GMS 711)
25 Erma Bossi, *Interior with Lamp*, 1909. Oil on paper, 23.5 × 32.6 (9⅜ × 12⅞). Städtische Galerie im Lenbachhaus und Kunstbau, Munich, Gabriele Münter Stiftung 1957 (GMS 673)
26 Natalia Goncharova, *Bûcherons* (Lumberjacks), 1911. Gouache on paper, 25.5 × 26.5 (10⅛ × 10½) Centre Pompidou, Paris, Legs de Nina Kandinsky, 1981 © The artist's estate
27 Wassily Kandinsky, *Improvisation 26 (Rudern)*, 1911. Oil on canvas, 97 × 107.5 (38 × 42⅜). Städtische Galerie im Lenbachhaus und Kunstbau, Munich, Gabriele Münter Stiftung 1957 (GMS 66)
28 Wassily Kandinsky, *Fragment 2 for Composition VII*, 1913. Oil on canvas, 87.63 × 99.69 (34½ × 39¼). Photo Buffalo AKG Art Museum/Art Resource, NY/Scala, Florence
29 Gabriele Münter, *Studie mit weißen Flecken Program (Study with White Spots)*, *1912*. Oil on paper, 38.7 × 25.7 × 0.4 (15¼ × 10⅛ × ¼). Städtische Galerie im Lenbachhaus und Kunstbau, Munich, Gabriele Münter Stiftung 1957. © DACS 2024
30 August Macke, *Rokoko*, 1912. Oil on canvas, 89 × 89 (35⅛ × 35⅛) National Museum, Oslo, Loan from Sparebankstiftelsen DNB 2010 (NMK. DEP.2010.0002). Photo Anne Hnasteen Jarre
31 Franz Marc, *Kühe, rot, grün, gelb* (Cows, red, green, yellow), 1911. Oil on canvas, 62 × 87.5 (24½ × 34½). Städtische Galerie im Lenbachhaus und Kunstbau, Munich (G 13140)
32 Franz Marc, *Reh im Klostergarten (Deer in the Monastery)*, 1912. Oil on canvas, 75.7 × 101 (29⅞ × 39⅞). Städtische Galerie im Lenbachhaus und Kunstbau, Munich G13323
33 George Grosz, *The Funeral (Dedication to Oskar Panizza)*, 1918. Oil on canvas, 140 × 110 (55⅛ × 43⅜). Stuttgart, Staatsgalerie (Inv 2338). © Estate of George Grosz, Princeton, N.J./DACS 2024
34 Lou Albert-Lasard, *Boîte de nuit (Nightclub)*. Oil on canvas, 81 × 70 (32 × 27⅝). Musées de la ville de Strasbourg, M. Bertola
35 Käthe Kollwitz, *In Memoriam Karl Liebknecht (Gedenkblatt fur Karl Liebknecht)*, 1920. Woodcut, printed in black ink on thick Japan paper, 35 × 50 (13⅞ × 19¾). Dr Richard A. Simms collection of prints and drawings by Käthe Kollwitz and other artists, 1770s-2007, undated, The Getty Research Institute, Los Angeles (2016.PR.34)
36 Conrad Felixmüller, *Soldier in a Madhouse*, 1918. Lithograph printed in red and blue-violet on laid paper. Image: 38.42 × 30.96 (15⅛ × 12¼) irregular, Sheet: 46.04 × 36.99 (18⅛ × 14⅝). Los Angeles County Museum of Art, The Robert Gore Rifkind Center for German Expressionist Studies (M.82.287.16). Digital Image Museum Associates/ LACMA/Art Resource NY/Scala, Florence. © DACS 2024
37 Conrad Felixmüller, *Death of the Poet Walter Rheiner*, 1925. Oil on canvas, 185.4 × 129.5 9 (73 × 51). Private Collection. Photo SuperStock/ Christie's Images Ltd. © DACS 2024
38 Erich Heckel, *Badende an der Förde (Bathers at the Fjord)*, 1913. Oil on canvas, 97 × 113 (38½ × 44½). Museum Bochum, Germany. Photo akg-images. © DACS 2024
39 Paula Modersohn-Becker, *Kneeling Woman with Child at her Breast*, 1907. Oil and tempera on canvas, 113 × 74 (44½ × 29¼). Staatliche Museen zu Berlin, Nationalgalerie, 1985 Purchase by Dr. Ludwig Roselius, Hamburg, from special funds of the Prussian Cultural Heritage Foundation
40 David Bomberg, *The Gorge, Ronda, Spain*, 1935. Oil, 75 × 58 (29⅝ × 22⅞). Middlesborough Institute of Modern Art. © The Estate of David Bomberg. All Rights Reserved, DACS 2024
41 Henri Matisse, *Marguerite au chat noire*, 1910. Oil on canvas, 94 × 64 × 2.3 (37⅛ × 25¼ × 1). Centre Pompidou, Paris, MNAM-CCI (AM 2013-544)
42 Paul Klee, *Botanical Theatre*, 1934. Oil, watercolour, pen on paper on cardboard, 50 × 67 (19¾ × 26½). Städtische Galerie im Lenbachhaus und Kunstbau, Munich, Dauerleihgabe der Gabriele Münter- und Johannes Eichner-Stiftung, München (G 15632/AK 24)
43 Pablo Picasso, *Trois figures sous un arbre (Three Figures Under a Tree)*, 1908. Oil on canvas, 99 × 99 (39 × 39). Musée National Picasso-Paris. GrandPalaisRmn/Mathieu Rabea. © Succession Picasso/DACS, London 2024
44 Ernst Ludwig Kirchner, *Ins Meer Schreitende (Striding into the Sea)*, 1912. Oil on canvas, 146.40 × 200 (57¾ × 78¾). Staatsgalerie Stuttgart (2729)
45 Chaïm Soutine, *Landscape at Céret*, *c.* 1920–21. Oil on canvas, support: 55.9 × 83.8 (22⅛ × 33) frame: 91.1 × 112.1 × 10.9 (35⅞ × 44¼ × 4⅜). Tate, London, purchased 1964

46 André Derain, *Forest at Martigues*, 1908. Oil on canvas, 81.3 × 100.3 (32 × 39½). The Art Institute of Chicago, Arthur Jerome Eddy Memorial Collection
47 Mikhail Larionov, *Promenade. Vénus de boulevard*, 1912–13. Oil on canvas, 117 × 87 (46⅛ × 34⅜). Centre Pompidou, Paris, MNAM-CCI (Inv. AM 1982-436) © The artist's estate
48 Egon Schiele, *Lyricist*, 1911. Oil on canvas, 80.5 × 80 (31¾ × 31½). Leopold Museum, Vienna (Inv. 450). Photo akg-images
49 Henrik Sørensen, *Gudrun at the Door*, 1917. Oil on canvas, 106 × 84.3 (41¾ × 33¼). National Museum, Oslo (NG.M.01174). © DACS 2024
50 Sigrid Hjertén, *Den röda rullgardinen (The Red Blind)*, 1916. Oil on canvas, 115 × 89 (45⅜ × 35⅛). Moderna Museet, Stockholm. Donation 1987 från Iván, Rebecca och Rakel Grünewald
51 Siri Derkert, *Självporträtt (Self-Portrait)*, 1915. Oil on canvas, 76 × 56 (30 × 22⅛). Moderna Museet, Stockholm (NM 5024).
52 Edvard Munch, *Moonlight*, 1895. Oil on canvas, 93 × 110 (36⅝ × 43⅜). National Museum, Oslo (NG.M.02815). Photo Børre Høstland/Høstland, Børre
53 Edvard Munch, *Puberty*, 1894. Oil on canvas, 151.5 × 110 × 2.6 (59¾ × 43⅜ × 1⅛) National Museum, Oslo (NG.M. 00807). Photo Børre Høstland/Lathion, Jacques
54 Gustave de Smet, *De Veiei Aarde (The Fertile Ground)*, 1917. 113.5 × 134 (44¾ × 52⅞). Collection Stedelijk Museum, Amsterdam
55 Jan Wiegers, *Landschap met rode bomen (Landscape with Red Trees)*, 1922. Oil on canvas, 71.8 × 72.2 × 3.1 (28⅜ × 28½ × 1¼). Collection Stedelijk Museum, Amsterdam
56 Jan Altink, *Koopvrouw op landweg* (Merchant Woman on Country Road), 1925. Oil on canvas, 70.5 × 58.8 (27⅞ × 23¼). Collection Groninger Museum, acquired with support from the Kamminga Fund. Photo Marten de Leeuw
57 Albert Müller, *Mütter mit Kindern (Mother with Children)*, 1925. Oil on canvas, 100 × 110 (39⅜ × 43⅜). Kunstmuseum Basel (Inv. G1966.2)
58 Hermann Scherer, *Atelierfest* (Party in the Studio), 1925. Oil on canvas, 145.5 × 150.5 (57⅜ × 59⅜). Kunstmuseum Basel (Inv. G 1977.11)
59 Mary Swanzy, *Abstract*, undated. Oil on board, 40 × 60 (15¾ × 23⅝). Irish Museum of Modern Art, IMMA Collection: Donation, Maire and Maurice Foley, 2000. © Artist's Estate
60 Guan Zilan, *Portrait of Miss L*, 1929. Oil on canvas, 90 × 75 (35½ × 29⅝). National Art Museum of China, Beijing
61 Tarsila do Amaral, *The Moon*, 1928. Oil on canvas, 110 × 110 (43⅜ × 43⅜). The Museum of Modern Art, New York, Gift of Joan H. Tisch (by exchange). © Tarsila do Amaral
62 Irma Stern, *Girl in a Print Dress*, 1939. Oil, 69 × 66.5 (27¼ × 26¼). Courtesy of the Trustees of the Irma Stern Collection, Cape Town. © The Irma Stern Trust, DACS 2024
63 Maggie Laubser, *Vrou met twee kinders (Woman with Two Children)*, 1928. Stellenbosch University, South Africa. © The Estate of Maggie Laubser/DALRO/DACS 2024
64 Carl-Henning Pedersen, *Fantasy II*, *c.* 1943. Oil on canvas, 96.7 × 96.7 (38⅛ × 38⅛). Kunsten Museum of Modern Art Aalborg. Photographer Niels Fabaek. © DACS 2024
65 Egill Jacobsen, *Accumulation*, 1938. Oil on canvas, 80 × 65.6 (31½ × 25⅞). SMK, Copenhagen (KMS 4972). © DACS 2024
66 Fritz Winter, *Komposition über erste Blüten im Walde*, 1940. Oil on canvas, 90 × 115 (35½ × 45⅜). Kunstmuseum Stuttgart, Konrad Knöpfel-Stiftung. Photo bpk/Frank Kleinbach. © DACS 2024
67 Asger Jorn, *Untitled*, 1943–44. Oil on canvas, 125 × 99.7 (49¼ × 39¼). Louisiana Museum of Modern Art. Donation: New Carlsberg Foundation. Photo Poul Buchard/Brøndum. © Donation Jorn, Silkeborg/billedkunst.dk/DACS 2024
68 Paul Klee, *Der Vollmond (The Full Moon)*, 1919. Oil on cardboard paper, 49.8 × 38 (19⅝ × 15). Bayerische Staatsgemäldesammlungen - Sammlung Moderne Kunst in der Pinakothek der Moderne München (Inv. 15249)
69 Eijler Bille, *Figure*, 1942. Oil on canvas 111.8 × 81.2 (44⅛ × 32). Kunsten Museum of Art Aalborg. Photo Niels Fabaek Inv. NK 382
70 Egill Jacobsen, *Orange Object II*, 1943. 143.5 × 107 × 5.5 (56⅛ × 42¼ × 2¼). Collection Stedelijk Museum Amsterdam. © DACS 2024
71 Marsden Hartley, *The Aero*, 1914. Oil on canvas, 100.3 × 81.2 (39½ × 31⅛). National Gallery of Art, Washington, Andrew W. Mellon Fund (1970.31.1)
72 Marsden Hartley, *The Old Bars, Dogtown*, 1936. Oil on composition board, 45.7 × 61.1 (18 × 24⅛). Whitney Museum of American Art, New York (37.26)
73 Arshile Gorky, *Diary of a Seducer*, 1945. Oil on canvas, 126.7 × 157.5 (50 × 62). Museum of Modern Art, New York, Gift of Mr and Mrs William A. Burden, 1985 (340.1985)
74 Willem de Kooning, *Woman I*, 1950–52. Oil and metallic paint on canvas, 192.7 × 147.3 (75⅝ × 58).

Museum of Modern Art, New York. © The Willem de Kooning Foundation/Artists Rights Society (ARS), New York and DACS, London 2024

75 Grace Hartigan, *Summer Street*, 1956. Oil on canvas, 204.47 × 147.96 (80½ × 58¼). National Gallery of Art, Washington. Corcoran Collection (Gift of Dorothy C. Miller) (2014.136.132). © Estate of Grace Hartigan

76 Norman Lewis, *Multitudes*, 1946. Oil on canvas, 100 × 67.3 (39⅜ × 26½). The Art Institute of Chicago, Kate S. Buckingham Endowment Fund; Director's Discretionary Acquisition Fund; Eloise W. Martin Legacy Endowment Fund. © Estate of Norman Lewis; Courtesy of Michael Rosenfeld Gallery LLC, New York, NY

77 Willi Baumeister, *Steingarten II*, 1939. Oil on canvas, 65.3 × 54.3 (28 × 62¼) Kunstmuseum, Stuttgart. Photo akg-images. © DACS 2024

78 Jackson Pollock, *Full Fathom Five*, 1946. Oil on canvas with nails, tacks, buttons, key, coins, cigarettes, matches etc., 129.2 × 76.5 (50⅞ × 30⅛). Museum of Modern Art, New York, Gift of Peggy Guggenheim (Inv. 186.1952). © The Pollock-Krasner Foundation ARS, NY and DACS, London 2024

79 Adolph Gottlieb, *Vigil*, 1948. Oil on canvas, 91.8 × 121.9 (36⅛ × 48in.) Whitney Museum of American Art, New York (49.2). © Adolph and Esther Gottlieb Foundation/VAGA at ARS, NY and DACS, London 2024

80 Mark Rothko, *Entombment, I*, 1946. Opaque watercolour and ink on paper, 52.4 × 66 (20⅝ × 26). Whitney Museum of American Art, New York (47.10). © 2024 Kate Rothko Prizel & Christopher Rothko ARS, NY and DACS, London

81 Mark Rothko, *1957 # 20*, 1957. Oil on canvas, 233 × 193 (91¾ × 76). National Gallery of Australia, Canberra, Purchased 1981. © 2024 Kate Rothko Prizel & Christopher Rothko ARS, NY and DACS, London

82 Janet Sobel, *Untitled*, *c.* 1946–48. Enamel and sand on board, 43.9 × 35.6 (17⅜ × 14). The Menil Collection, Houston, Gift of Leonard Sobel and Family. Photo James Craven. © Estate of Janet Sobel

83 Jackson Pollock, *Number 1, 1950* (Lavender Mist), 1950. 221 × 299.7 (87 × 118). National Gallery of Art, Washington, Ailsa Mellon Bruce Fund (1976.37.1). © The Pollock-Krasner Foundation ARS, NY and DACS, London 2024

84 Lee Krasner, *Combat*, 1965. Oil on canvas, 179 × 410.4 (70½ × 161⅝). National Gallery of Victoria, Melbourne Felton Bequest 1992. © The Pollock-Krasner Foundation ARS, NY and DACS, London 2024

85 Lee Krasner, *Three in Two*, 1956. Oil on canvas, 190.5 × 147.3 (75 × 58). Private Collection, San Francisco. © The Pollock-Krasner Foundation ARS, NY and DACS, London 2024

86 Jackson Pollock, *Guardians of the Secret*, 1943. Oil on canvas, 122.89 × 191.47 (48⅜ × 75⅜). San Francisco Museum of Modern Art/Bridgeman Images. © The Pollock-Krasner Foundation ARS, NY and DACS, London 2024

87 Lee Krasner, *Bald Eagle*, 1955. Oil, paper and canvas collage on linen, 195.6 × 130.8 (77 × 51½). Collection of Audrey Irmas, Los Angeles. © The Willem de Kooning Foundation/Artists Rights Society (ARS), New York and DACS, London 2024

88 Philip Guston, *Processional*, 1957. Oil on canvas, 121.92 × 107 (48 × 42⅛). The Doris and Donald Fisher Collection at the San Francisco Museum of Modern Art. Courtesy Hauser and Wirth. © The Estate of Philip Guston

89 Hans Hofmann, *Pompeii*, 1959. Oil on canvas, 214 × 132.7. Tate, London, Purchased 1981. © ARS, NY and DACS, London 2024

90 Helen Frankenthaler, *Round Trip*, 1957. Oil on canvas, 178.4 × 178.4 (70¼ × 70¼). Buffalo AKG Art Museum/Art Resource, NY/Scala, Florence. © Helen Frankenthaler Foundation, Inc./ARS, NY and DACS, London 2024

91 Jean Fautrier, *Femme douce*, 1946. Spanish white coating, blanc de Meudon, charcoal, pigments, pastel and oil on paper mounted on canvas, 97 × 145.5 (38¼ × 57⅜). Pompidou Centre, Paris, MNAM-CCI (AM 1982-12). © ADAGP, Paris and DACS, London 2024

92 Henri Michaux, *Peintre à l'encre de Chine*, 1961–62. Chinese ink on paper, 81 × 141.5 (32 × 55¾). Centre Pompidou, Paris, MNAM-CCI. © ADAGP, Paris and DACS, London 2024

93 Alan Davie, *Image of the fish god No. 2*, 1956. Oil on board, 152.4 × 121.9 (60 × 48). © The Estate of Alan Davie. All rights reserved. DACS 2024

94 Eugène Brands, *Sign in Orion*, 1948. Wood, paint, linen, paper, metal 93 × 83 × 7 (36⅝ × 32¾ × 2⅞). CollectionStedelijk Museum, Amsterdam. Image courtesy Sitchting Eugène Brands. © Eugène Brands

95 Else Alfelt, *Jorden-Vandet og Bjergene*, 1952. Oil on canvas, 122.1 × 183 (48⅛ × 39⅞). Kunsten Museum of Art Aalborg (NK 9). © DACS 2024

96 Pierre Alechinsky, *Le bleu de Methylène*, 1974, Acrylic on paper on canvas, 114.5 × 154 (45⅛ × 60¾). National Museum, Oslo, gift from the Friends of the National Gallery 1975. Photo Andreas Harvik. © ADAGP, Paris and DACS, London 2024

97 Constant, *Homo Ludens*, 1964. Oil on linen, 161.5 × 187 × 4 (63⅝ × 73⅝ × 1⅝). Collection Stedelijk Museum, Amsterdam (A 39078). © DACS 2024
98 Asger Jorn, *Instructive Extruction of a Konstructif Destruction* (sic), 1966. Oil on canvas, 89 × 116 × 2.8 (35⅛ × 45¾ × 1⅛) Louisiana Museum of Modern Art, Donation The Merla Art Foundation. © Donation Jorn, Silkeborg/ billedkunst.dk/DACS 2024
99 Carl-Henning Pedersen, *Mennesker og den gule stjerne*, 1950. Oil on canvas, 118.5 × 101 (46¾ × 39⅞). Kunsten Museum of Art Aalborg. Photographer Niels Fabaek. © DACS 2024
100 Karel Appel, *Archaic Life*, 1961. Oil on canvas, 230 × 300 (90⅝ × 118⅛). Collection Stedelijk Museum Amsterdam (A 21604). © Karel Appel Foundation /DACS 2024
101 Asger Jorn (with Constant, Karel Appel, Erik Nyholm and Corneille) *Cobra-Modification (on a painting by Richard Mortensen)*, 1949. Oil on canvas, 42.5 × 62.2 (16¾ × 24½). Image courtesy Jorn Museum, Silkeborg. © Donation Jorn, Silkeborg/billedkunst.dk/DACS 2024
102 Karel Appel, *Questioning Children*, 1949. Gouache on wood, 87.3 × 59.8 × 15.8 (34⅜ × 23⅝ × 6¼). Tate, London, Presented by the artist 1986. © Karel Appel Foundation/DACS 2024
103 Lotti van der Gaag, *Bird of Prey*, 1952, Bronze. Collection Museum Boijmans Van Beuningen, Rotterdam. Photo Studio Tromp. © DACS 2024
104 Jacqueline de Jong, *Rencontre Accidentel (Accidental Painting)*, 1964. Oil on canvas, 128.2 × 194.1 × 4.1 (50½ × 76½ × 1⅝). Collection Stedelijk Museum Amsterdam. Image courtesy Pippy Houldsworth Gallery, London. Photo Gert Jan van Rooj. © Jacqueline de Jong 2024
105 Francis Bacon, *Figures in a Landscape*, 1956–57. Oil on canvas, 152.5 × 118 (60 × 46½). Birmingham City Museum and Art Gallery, presented by the Contemporary Art Society, 1959. Photo Prudence Cuming Associates Ltd. © The Estate of Francis Bacon. All rights reserved, DACS/Artimage.
106 Jean Dubuffet, *Corps de dame, Jardin fleuri*, 1950. Oil on canvas, 116 × 89.1 (45¾ × 35⅛). The Philadelphia Museum of Art/Art Resource/Scala, Florence. © ADAGP, Paris and DACS, London 2024
107 Magda Cordell, *Figure 59*, *c.* 1958. Oil and acrylic on masonite, 243.8 × 152.4 (96 × 60). Buffalo AKG Art Museum/Art Resource, NY/Scala, Florence. © Magda Cordell McHale.
108 Kazuo Shiraga, *Golden Wings Brushing the Clouds Incarnated from Earthly Wide Star (Chikatsusei Maunkinshi)*, 1960. Oil on canvas, 130 × 195 (51⅛ × 76¾). The Art Institute of Chicago/Art Resource, NY/Scala, Florence. © The Estate of Kazuo Shiraga.
109 Sam Middleton, *Come Sunday*, 1962. Mixed media on board, 94 × 124.5 × 3.5 (37⅛ × 49⅛ × 1½). Stedelijk Museum Amsterdam (A21625). Photo Tolo Balaguer/Alamy Stock Courtesy Spanierman Modern. © Estate of Sam Middleton
110 Ian Fairweather, *The Pool*, 1959. Synthetic polymer paint on cardboard on hardboard, 96.5 × 117.8 (38 × 46½). Image courtesy Art Gallery of New South Wales, Sydney. Purchased with funds provided by the Cézanne Dinner Fund 1999. © Estate of Ian Fairweather. All rights reserved, DACS 2024
111 John Olsen, *Dylan's Country*, 1957. Oil on canvas, 92.0 × 72.5 (36¼ × 28⅝). Art Gallery of New South Wales, Sydney, purchased 1958. © Art Gallery of New South Wales
112 Wook-Kyung Choi, *Untitled*, *c.* 1960s. Acrylic on canvas, 64 × 93 (25.2 × 36.6). Image Courtesy Tina Kim Gallery. Photo by Hyunjung Rhee. © Artist's estate
113 Pablo Picasso, *Femme nue au collier (Nude Woman with Necklace)*, 1968. Oil on canvas, 113.5 × 161.7 (44¾ × 63¾). Tate, London, purchased 1983. © Succession Picasso/DACS, London 2024
114 Franz Hitzler, *Untitled*, 1978. Tempera, oil, chalk on paper 30.4 × 21.6 (12 × 8⅝). Städtische Galerie im Lenbachhaus und Kunstbau, Munich (G15884). © DACS 2024
115 Maria Lassnig, *Die Last des Fleisches (The Burden of the Flesh)*, 1973. Oil on canvas, 184 × 250 (72½ × 98½). The ALBERTINA Museum, Vienna (GE 166). © Maria Lassnig Foundation
116 Arnulf Rainer, *Schranken (Barrier)*, 1974/75. Mixed media and photograph, 87 × 122 . The ALBERTINA Museum, Vienna (Inv. 46650). © Arnulf Rainer
117 Arnulf Rainer, Cross, 1986. Oil on cardboard and wood, 200.7 × 79.9 (79⅛ × 31½). The ALBERTINA Museum, Vienna - The ESSL Collection (Inv. EDLSB1695). © Arnulf Rainer
118 Ursula Schultze-Bluhm, *Meine Berlin-Träume in Mittenwalde*, 1977. Oil on canvas, 185 × 230 (72⅞ × 90⅝). Von der Heydt Museum Wuppertal, Dauer- leihgabe der Bundesrepublik Deutschland - Sammlung Zeitgenössische Kunst (Inv. Nr. D 0191). © Museum Ludwig, Cologne
119 Ursula Schultze-Bluhm, *Une nuit dans le parc Monceau à 23.00/Eines Nachts, im Park Monceau um 23 Uhr*, 1961. Oil on canvas 97 × 146 (38¼ × 57½). Courtesy Galerie Christophe Gaillard Paris/ Brussels/Le Tremblay. © Photo Rebecca Fanuele. © Museum Ludwig, Cologne

120 Georg Baselitz, *Untitled*, 1982–83. Limewood. Tate, London, Acquired by purchase and gift from Hartmut and Silvia Ackermeier, Berlin 1993. © Georg Baselitz 2024
121 Georg Baselitz, *The Brücke Choir (Der Brückechor)*, 1983. Oil on canvas, 280 × 450 (110¼ × 98½). Private Collection. Photo Christie's Images/Bridgeman Images © Georg Baselitz 2024
122 Helmut Middendorf, *Grossstadteingeborene (Natives of the Big City)*, 1982. Dispersion on canvas, 230 × 190 (90⅝ × 74⅞). Private Collection. © Helmut Middendorf
123 Markus Oehlen, *Untitled*, 1984. Acrylic and wax on canvas, 200 × 299.7 (78¾ × 118). Saint Louis Art Museum, Partial and promised gift of Betsy Millard, the Earl and Betsy Millard Collection (81:2003a,b). © Markus Oehlen
124 Rainer Fetting, *Drummer and Guitarist*, 1979. Distemper on canvas, 200 × 290 (78¾ × 114¼). Berlinische Galerie Museum für Moderne Kunst, Purchased with funds from the artist support of the Senator for Cultural Affairs, Berlin, 1979. Photo akg-images. © Rainer Fetting
125 Elvira Bach, *Schwarz und Bleich*, 1985, Oil on canvas, 230 × 380 (90⅝ × 149⅝). Galerie Kaess-Weiss, Stuttgart. Photo akg-images. © DACS 2024
126 Bernard Schultze, *rifrost*, 1958. Oil on canvas, three-dimensional elements, 120 × 100 × 32 (47¼ × 39⅜). Museum Ludwig, Cologne. Photo Rheinisches Bildarchiv Köln (rba_d035689). © DACS 2024
127 Anselm Kiefer, *Ways of World Wisdom: The Battle of Hermann*, 1978. Mixed media painting, 290 × 200 (114¼ × 78¾). Art Gallery of New South Wales, Sydney, Gift of Vicki Olsson & Geoff Ainsworth AM 2013, in appreciation of Tony Bond OAM, Head Curator of International art, 1984 to 2013. Donated through the Australian Government's Cultural Gifts Program. Courtesy Gagosian, London. © Anselm Kiefer.
128 Anselm Kiefer, *Ausgießung (Emanation)*, 1982–86. Oil on canvas with affixed lead object and straw, 330 × 555 × 55 (129⅞ × 218½ × 21⅝). Louisiana Museum of Modern Art. Donation: The New Carlsberg Foundation. Courtesy Gagosian, London. © Anselm Kiefer.
129 Jean-Michel Basquiat, *Notary*, 1983. Acrylic, oil paintstick and paper collage on canvas with wood supports, 180.3 × 401.3 (71 × 158). Princeton University Art Museum/Art Resource NY/Scala, Florence. © Estate of Jean-Michel Basquiat. Licensed by Artestar, New York
130 Jean-Michel Basquiat, *Kings of Egypt II*, 1982. Oil on canvas, 183.5 × 183.5 × 4 (72¼ × 72¼ × 1⅝). Collection Museum Boijmans Van Beuningen, Rotterdam. Loan Stichting Museum Boijmans Van Beuningen, gift Hans Sonnenberg. Photo Studio Tromp. © Estate of Jean-Michel Basquiat. Licensed by Artestar, New York
131 Purvis Young, *Carrying the Angel to the People*, 1994. Paint and wood, 203.2 × 124.5 (80 × 49). Souls Grown Deep Foundation. © 2024 Purvis Young/Artists Rights Society (ARS), New York
132 Bessie Harvey, *Seven Faces of Eve*, 1987. Baltimore Museum of Art, Gift of the Souls Grown Deep Foundation; and purchase with exchange funds from the Pearlstone Family Fund and partial gift of The Andy Warhol Foundation for the Visual Arts, Inc. © ARS, NY and DACS, London 2024
133 Thornton Dial, *Shadows of the Field*, 2008. String, twine, synthetic cotton batting, wood, burlap, sheet metal, cloth rags, nails, staples, and enamel on canvas on wood, 200.7 × 266.7 × 12.7 (79 × 105 × 5). Metropolitan Museum of Art, New York, Gift of the Souls Grown Deep Foundation. Photo Stephen Pitkin/Pitkin Studio, courtesy Souls Grown Deep. © Estate of Thornton Dial
134 Thornton Dial, *Graveyard Traveller/Selma Bridge*, 1992. Rope, carpet, burlap, tin, wood, plastic bagging, paint-can lids, pinecones, carpet, plastic hose, wire screen, rope, metal, oil, enamel, and Splash Zone compound on canvas on wood, 217.2 × 370.8 × 15.2 (85.5 × 146 × 6). Souls Grown Deep Foundation. Photo Gamma One Conversions. © Estate of Thornton Dial
135 Ronald Lockett, *Once Something Has Lived it Can Never Really Die*, 1996. Wood, enamel, graphite, tin, found materials, industrial sealing compound, on wood, 144.8 × 128.3 × 10.2 (57 × 50.5 × 4). Collection of the High Museum of Art, museum purchase and gift of the Souls Grown Deep Foundation. Photo Stephen Pitkin/Pitkin Studio. © ARS, NY and DACS, London 2024
136 Soeki Irodikromo, *Untitled*, 1971. Oil on canvas, 174 × 104 (65⅝ × 41). Collection Stedelijk Museum Amsterdam. © Estate of Soeki Irodikromo
137 Erwin de Vries, *Mexican Woman in Profile*, 1989. Acrylic on canvas, 100 × 120 (39⅜ × 47¼). Collection Stedlijk Museum Amsterdam, acquired with support from the Mondriaan Fund, 1996. © Estate of Erwin de Vries
138 Iris Kensmil, *Mellow Dance*, 2007. Ink, charcoal, pastel, spray-paint on papier, 122 × 125 (48⅛ × 49¼). Collection Stedelijk Museum Amsterdam. © Iris Kensmil
139 Michael Tedja, *Narrow Escape*, 2002. Mixed media on linen, 270.5 × 580.5 (106½ × 228⅝).

Collection Stedlijk Museum Amsterdam. © Michael Tedja

140 Cecily Brown, *Trouble in Paradise*, 1999. Oil on canvas, 191.2 × 229.3 × 5.1 (75⅜ × 90⅜ × 2⅛). Tate, London, purchased 2000. Courtesy the artist and Thomas Dane Gallery. © Cecily Brown

141 Eddie Martinez, *Outer Worlder*, 2021. Oil, acrylic and spray paint on canvas in artist's frame, 182.9 × 274.3 (72 × 108). Photo JSP Art Photography. © Eddie Martinez

142 Arnaldo Roche Rabell, *The Subconscious Knows How to Kill His Son*, 1993. Oil on canvas, 189 × 135 (74½ × 53¼). Image courtesy George Adams Gallery. © Roche-Rabell Estate

143 Tu Hongtao, *Wind through the Valley*, 2018–19. Oil on canvas, 130 × 100 (51¼ × 39⅜). Image courtesy of Tu Hongtao Studio and Lévy Gorvy Dayan

144 John Walker, *Clock and Shell*, 2022. Oil on canvas, 182 × 172 (71¾ × 67¾). Messums, London. © John Walker

145 Zhang Zipiao, *Brain 04*, 2023. Oil on canvas, 160 × 200 (63 × 78¾). © Zhang Zipiao

Index

References in *italics* indicate illustration number

World of Art

"This kind of book at this kind of price is what art publishing should be about"
—*New York Times Book Review*

"An extraordinarily rich and varied series"
—Linda Nochlin

The World of Art series is a comprehensive, accessible, indispensable companion to the history of art and its latest developments, covering themes, artists and movements that span centuries and the gamut of visual culture around the globe.

You may also like:

Abstract Art
Anna Moszynska

Abstract Expressionism
David Anfam

Cézanne
Richard Verdi

Color in Art
John Gage
Foreword by Kelly Grovier

Dada
Art and Anti-Art
Hans Richter

Digital Art
Christiane Paul

Fauvism
Sarah Whitfield

Outsider Art
Colin Rhodes

For more information about Thames & Hudson, and the World of Art series, visit **thamesandhudsonusa.com**